SO-AXM-668

Lecture Notes in Economics and Mathematical Systems

547

Founding Editors:

M. Beckmann
H. P. Künzi

Managing Editors:

Prof. Dr. G. Fandel
Fachbereich Wirtschaftswissenschaften
Fernuniversität Hagen
Feithstr. 140/AVZ II, 58084 Hagen, Germany

Prof. Dr. W. Trockel
Institut für Mathematische Wirtschaftsforschung (IMW)
Universität Bielefeld
Universitätsstr. 25, 33615 Bielefeld, Germany

Editorial Board:

A. Basile, A. Drexl, H. Dawid, K. Inderfurth, W. Kürsten, U. Schittko

Marc Wildi

Signal Extraction

Efficient Estimation, 'Unit Root'-Tests and Early Detection of Turning Points

With 80 Figures and 15 Tables

 Springer

Author

PD Dr. Marc Wildi
Institute for Data Analysis and Processdesign (IDP)
Technopark / Jägerstrasse 2
Postfach 805
8401 Winterthur, Switzerland

Library of Congress Control Number: 2004111007

ISSN 0075-8442
ISBN 3-540-22935-3 Springer Berlin Heidelberg New York

This work is subject to copyright. All rights are reserved, whether the whole or part
of the material is concerned, specifically the rights of translation, reprinting, re-use of
illustrations, recitation, broadcasting, reproduction on microfilms or in any other way,
and storage in data banks. Duplication of this publication or parts thereof is permitted
only under the provisions of the German Copyright Law of September 9, 1965, in its
current version, and permission for use must always be obtained from Springer-Verlag.
Violations are liable for prosecution under the German Copyright Law.

Springer is a part of Springer Science+Business Media

springeronline.com

© Springer-Verlag Berlin Heidelberg 2005
Printed in Germany

The use of general descriptive names, registered names, trademarks, etc. in this
publication does not imply, even in the absence of a specific statement, that such
names are exempt from the relevant protective laws and regulations and therefore
free for general use.

Typesetting: Camera ready by author
Cover design: *Erich Kirchner*, Heidelberg

Printed on acid-free paper   42/3130Di   5 4 3 2 1 0

Herzlichen Dank Herr Stier und liebe Grüsse an 2*A+B+V Wildi

Foreword

The material contained in this book originated in interrogations about modern practice in time series analysis.

- Why do we use models optimized with respect to one-step ahead forecasting performances for applications involving multi-step ahead forecasts?
- Why do we infer 'long-term' properties (unit-roots) of an unknown process from statistics essentially based on short-term one-step ahead forecasting performances of particular time series models?
- Are we able to detect turning-points of trend components earlier than with traditional signal extraction procedures?

The link between 'signal extraction' and the first two questions above is not immediate at first sight. Signal extraction problems are often solved by suitably designed symmetric filters. Towards the boundaries ($t = 1$ or $t = N$) of a time series a particular symmetric filter must be approximated by asymmetric filters. The time series literature proposes an intuitively straightforward solution for solving this problem:

- Stretch the observed time series by forecasts generated by a model.
- Apply the symmetric filter to the extended time series.

This approach is called '*model-based*'. Obviously, the forecast-horizon grows with the length of the symmetric filter. Model-identification and estimation of unknown parameters are then related to the above first two questions. .

One may further ask, if this approximation problem and the way it is solved by model-based approaches are important topics for practical purposes? Consider some 'prominent' estimation problems:

- The determination of the seasonally adjusted actual unemployment rate.
- An assessment of the 'trend' of the actual GDP movement.
- Inferences about the 'global heating' in recently observed climatologic changes.

These problems all suggest that there is some kind of 'signal' which is overlapped by undesirable perturbations which mask the actual state of an interesting phenomenon. Formally, *actuality* of the estimates translates into *boundary* signal estimation. Signals often have a prospective component towards the boundary $t = N$: the detection of a turning-point of a trend component is informative about the future of the time series. So the corresponding estimation problem is highly relevant for many applications. Furthermore, Since model-based approaches like TRAMO/SEATS or Census X-12-ARIMA[1] are widely

---

[1]Although X-12-ARIMA is not a 'pure' model-based approach, see chapter 2, the procedure nevertheless relies on forecasts for computing boundary estimates.

used for 'signal extraction' one may then ask if the resulting method is *efficient*[2]?

The empirical results obtained in chapter 7 and more recently in Wildi, Schips[99][3] demonstrate that 'traditional' model-based boundary signal estimates are far from being efficient. The examples demonstrate that the relative mean-square error (between outputs of symmetric and asymmetric filters) can be reduced substantially (more than 30% in the mean over all time series considered) when using the efficient estimation method presented in this book. Moreover, the new method outperforms model-based approaches for *all* 41 time series in Wildi/Schips[99]. Optimal filter designs and properties of important statistics involved in the estimation problem are presented in chapters 3 and 4. The consistency, the efficiency and the asymptotic distribution of the resulting filter parameter estimates are derived in chapter 5 for a wide class of input signals (processes). An extension of this method which enables a *faster detection of turning points* for 'smooth' trend components is also presented in chapter 5. Chapter 6 presents finite sample issues and empirical examples are to be found in chapters 7 and 8.

As shown in chapter 7 as well as in Wildi/Schips[99] the observed inefficiency of model-based approaches is partly due to wrongly inferred unit-roots. The business survey data analyzed in Wildi/Schips[99] cannot be integrated because the time series are bounded. However, traditional unit-root tests such as (augmented) Dickey-Fuller or Phillips-Perron are often unable to reject the null hypothesis (integration) for such time series.
It is in fact strange that 'long-term' dynamics (unit-roots) are often inferred from statistics based on 'short term' one-step ahead forecasting performances of particular time series models. Experience suggests that short term forecasting performances generally do not allow for sufficiently strong rejection of the null hypothesis : *'Traditional' ADF- or PP-test-statistics may be well-suited for short-term (one-step ahead) forecasting but they are often misleading for problems requiring good multi-step ahead forecasting performances.*
In the general context of 'signal extraction', unit-roots are important because they are related to particular restrictions of the asymmetric filters, see chapter 5. Therefore, great attention has been devoted to 'unit-roots' in this particular context and new solutions - which 'fit' specifically the signal extraction problem - are presented in chapter 5.

---

[2]It is known that one- and multi-step-ahead forecasting performances may be conflicting, see chapter 1. Therefore it is surprising that few attention has been deserved to efficiency issues in signal extraction problems.

[3]The authors analyze the performance of trend boundary estimates for a representative sample of 41 business survey indicators

Contents

Part I

Theory

1

Introduction

1.1 Overview

For many applications a well known problem is to 'extract' or equivalently to estimate some predefined 'signal' or component from a time series contaminated by 'noise' (which is not necessarily a white noise process). Consider

$$X_t = Y_t + \nu_t \qquad (1.1)$$

where X_t is observed, Y_t is the interesting signal and ν_t overlaps and 'contaminates' the signal. Let $t \in \mathbb{Z}$ (discrete time) and assume $X_1, X_2, ..., X_N$ have been observed. The problem is to 'compute' values for the unknown $Y_1, Y_2, ..., Y_N$. The following figures illustrate some practically relevant signals for monthly economic time series.

- In fig.1.1, a particular time series (described in chapter 7) and a 'trend' defined by the canonical decomposition (see section 2.3) can be seen.
- In fig.1.2, the same time series and the 'seasonally adjusted' component (signal) defined by the canonical decomposition (see section 2.3) can be seen.
- Finally, both signals are compared in fig.1.3.

These examples are treated in detail in chapters 7 and 8. The signals are documented in chapter 2.

A general approach for estimating Y_t given X_t in 1.1 relies on stochastic processes. The observable process X_t is then called the *input process* or the *input signal* and Y_t is called the *output signal* (this is because Y_t can often be estimated by the output of a particular filter, see section 1.2 below). It is intuitively reasonable to allow a signal estimation method to depend on the particular stochastic 'properties' of the input process X_t in 1.1. As an example, assume

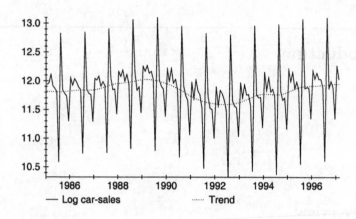

Fig. 1.1. Original series and trend

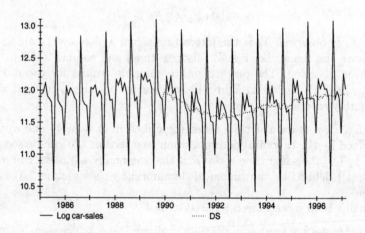

Fig. 1.2. Original and seasonally adjusted series

$$X_{1t} := Y_t + A_1 \cos(t\omega_1 + \Phi_1)$$
$$X_{2t} := Y_t + A_1 \cos(t\omega_1 + \Phi_1) + A_2 \cos(t\omega_2 + \Phi_2)$$

where $\omega_1 \neq \omega_2$ and Φ_1 and Φ_2 are independent random variables uniformly distributed in $[-\pi, \pi]$. Suppose the interesting signal is given by $Y_t = \cos(t\omega + \Phi)$, where Φ is uniformly distributed in the interval $[-\pi, \pi]$. X_{it}, $i = 1, 2$ and Y_t

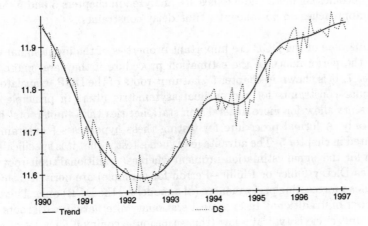

Fig. 1.3. Trend and seasonally adjusted series

are particular harmonic processes. The latter (Y_t) can be extracted from X_{2t} by eliminating $A_1 \cos(t\omega_1 + \Phi_1)$ and $A_2 \cos(t\omega_2 + \Phi_2)$. This may be achieved by a suitable 'filter' (see chapter 3). If the input process is X_{1t} instead, then the same filter could be used for extracting Y_t in principle. However, it is readily seen that the resulting estimation method would be unnecessarily complicated. In fact, a simpler filter eliminating $A_1 \cos(t\omega_1 + \Phi_1)$ 'only' could be used. For processes which are not deterministic (as the harmonic processes above) too complicated devices are generally inefficient: eliminating additional components involves a 'cost' which is quantified in chapter 5. Therefore, knowledge of particular stochastic properties of the DGP (Data Generating Process) of X_t is necessary for computing *efficient* signal estimates. If the relevant properties of X_t are unknown, then they must be inferred from the sample $X_1, ..., X_N$. Model-based approaches (MBA) are widely used for solving signal extraction problems because they *try* to infer the DGP of X_t from a finite sample $X_1, ..., X_N$. Resulting signal estimates can account for stochastic properties of the input signal X_t but *the efficiency cannot be asserted in general* (see section 1.2).

A new method, called *direct filter approach* (DFA) is presented here for solving the signal estimation problem. The main advantages of this approach are *efficiency* and *flexibility*. Filters can be optimized with respect to the traditional mean square error criterion or with respect to another practically important objective, namely the *'fast detection of turning-points'*. Often, signal estimates are subject to significant time delays towards the end point $t = N$ of a finite sample. Therefore, 'turning-points' of the signal cannot be detected 'in time'. The DFA enables to constrain filters such that the time delay becomes smaller. These issues are analyzed in chapters 3 and 5. Model-based approaches do not allow for time delay constraints.

Unit-roots of the DGP are important properties of the input signal which affect the performance of the estimation procedure if they are ignored, see chapter 7. It is shown in chapter 5 that unit-roots of the DGP 'translate' into particular constraints for the optimal asymmetric filter. In principle these constraints allow for more general non-stationarities than 'unit-roots' of the DGP only. A formal procedure for testing these hypotheses (constraints) is presented in chapter 5. The advantage of such a test is that it is specifically designed for the signal estimation problem whereas 'traditional' unit-root tests (such as Dickey-Fuller or Phillips-Perron for example) are derived from one-step ahead forecasting performances (of a model for the DGP) only. Therefore, the power of 'traditional' tests against stationary alternatives with roots close to the unit-circle is typically low (this situation is common for a lot of applications including many economic time series) because a 'long-term' property (a unit-root at frequency zero) is inferred from a statistic based on 'short-term' performances. Cochrane [18], p.914, argues "These models (ARIMA) ... draw inferences about the long-run dynamics from a model fit to the short-run dynamics ... However, if the long-run dynamics cannot be captured in the model used to study the short-run, these identification procedures bias conclusions about long-run behavior". The new test implicitly accounts for one- *and* multi-step ahead forecasting performances and it is explicitly designed for the signal estimation problem.

For the proposed DFA, particular attention is accorded to *finite sample issues* (overfitting problem, see chapter 6). 'Parsimony' in the sense of 'cautiously' parameterized models (see Box and Jenkins [9]) is a relevant concept. Feldstein [31], p.829, argues: "A useful model is not one that is 'true' or 'realistic' but one that is parsimonious, plausible and informative". The proposed direct filter approach is based on a new filter class, so called *Zero-Pole-Combination* (ZPC-) filters. ZPC-filters are obtained by a parsimonious parameterization of ARMA-filters for which each parameter (degree of freedom) becomes straightforwardly interpretable, see chapter 3.
Although the principle of parsimony may help in alleviating the overfitting problem, it is not a 'panacea'. Therefore, new solutions are proposed for the DFA in order to avoid specific overfitting problems, see chapter 6. Empirical evidences listed in chapters 7 and 8 confirm the effectiveness of the proposed method. Simulated and 'real-world' time series are analyzed and the performances of the DFA and the MBA are compared both 'in' and 'out of sample'.

A signal estimation method which relies on an explicit model for the DGP of X_t is called a MBA. Different methods have been proposed which are characterized by various assumptions and/or model structures. Chapter 2 provides an (necessarily limited) overview on the topic. Model-based approaches are often referenced as 'the MBA' here and in the following chapters (despite methodological differences of various approaches) by opposition to 'the DFA' which does not rely on an explicit model for the DGP of X_t. A brief description of the MBA is proposed in the following section. It is suggested that the optimization criterion underlying the MBA does not 'match' the signal estimation problem for misspecified models (which is the rule in practice). Therefore, model-based estimates may be inefficient. Empirical results in chapter 7 as well as in Wildi/Schips[99] confirm this statement.

1.2 A General Model-Based-Approach

For 'general' (stationary or non-stationary integrated) linear stochastic processes, the signal estimation problem is solved by *linear filters*. A (linear) filter is a sequence γ_k, $k \in \mathbb{Z}$ of square summable (in our context real) numbers: $\sum_{k=-\infty}^{\infty} |\gamma_k|^2 < \infty$. MA-, AR- and ARMA-filters are characterized by particular finite sets of parameters generating γ_k. If the sequences $\hat{Y}_t$ and X_t are related by

$$\hat{Y}_t = \sum_{k=-\infty}^{\infty} \gamma_k X_{t-k} \tag{1.2}$$

then $\hat{Y}_t, X_t$ are called the *output* and the *input signals* of the filter γ_k respectively. If $X_t = Y_t + \nu_t$ where X_t, Y_t and ν_t are linear stochastic processes, then it has been shown that the best estimate $\hat{Y}_t$ (in the mean square sense) of Y_t is the output of a particular linear filter if some 'mild' assumptions are satisfied (see Whittle [95] for stationary X_t and Bell [4] for non-stationary integrated X_t; results for non-linear processes are presented in Gihman and Skorohod [39], p.273-274).

For a realization of infinite length $(..., X_{-2}, X_{-1}, X_0, X_1, X_2, ...)$ (infinite sample), the best extraction filter is generally *symmetric* ($\gamma_k = \gamma_{-k}, k > 0$) and of *infinite order* (i.e. there does not exist a n_0 such that $\gamma_k = 0$ for all $k > n_0$). The symmetry ensures that the phase or equivalently the time shift of the filter vanishes, see chapter 3. The following example illustrates these properties for a particular signal estimation problem: X_t is given by 1.1, where ν_t is a white noise process and Y_t is a random walk (so called Muth-model, see for example Mills [67] p.69 ff.):

$$X_t = Y_t + \nu_t$$
$$Y_t = Y_{t-1} + \epsilon_t$$

where ϵ_t, ν_t are independent iid sequences. The best mean square estimate of the signal (the random-walk) is then given by :

$$\hat{Y}_t = \frac{(1-\theta)^2}{1-\theta^2} \sum_{k=-\infty}^{\infty} \theta^{|k|} X_{t-k}$$

where θ depends on the signal to noise ratio (the ratio of the variances of ν_t and ϵ_t). The optimal filter coefficients $\frac{(1-\theta)^2}{1-\theta^2}\theta^{|k|}$ are symmetric and decay exponentially fast but they never vanish if $\theta \neq 0$.

Clearly, filters of infinite order cannot be used if the available input sample $X_1, ..., X_N$ is finite. But the symmetry property leads to problems even for filters of finite orders. Difficulties arise if t is 'close' to the boundaries $t = 1$ or $t = N$ of the sample. Therefore, the filter output $\hat{Y}_t$ of the symmetric filter (which solves the so called *signal extraction problem*) must be estimated too, say by $\hat{\hat{Y}}_t$. The latter is called a solution of the *finite sample signal estimation problem*. Model-based approaches provide solutions for both $\hat{Y}_t$ and $\hat{\hat{Y}}_t$. The latter problem is solved as follows (see Stier and Wildi [87] and Wildi [98]) :

- replace unknown X_i ($i < 1$ or $i > N$) in 1.2 by fore- and/or backcasts $\hat{X}_i$ generated from a model of the DGP (for example an ARIMA or a RegARIMA-model, see Findley et al.[32] or EUROSTAT [30])
- apply the symmetric filter $(\gamma_k)_{k \in \mathbb{Z}}$ to the 'extended' sample $X_t^e :=$
$$\begin{cases} \hat{X}_t & t \notin \{1, ..., N\} \\ X_t & \text{else} \end{cases}$$

One obtains :

$$\hat{Y}_t = \sum_{k=-\infty}^{\infty} \gamma_k X_{t-k}^e \tag{1.3}$$

$$= \sum_{k=t-N}^{t-1} \gamma_k X_{t-k} + \sum_{k=-\infty}^{t-N-1} \gamma_k \hat{X}_{t-k} + \sum_{k=t}^{\infty} \gamma_k \hat{X}_{t-k}$$

$$= \sum_{k=t-N}^{t-1} \gamma_k X_{t-k} + \sum_{k=-\infty}^{t-N-1} \gamma_k \sum_{j=1}^{N} a_{t-k,j} X_j + \sum_{k=t}^{\infty} \gamma_k \sum_{j=1}^{N} a_{t-k,j} X_j$$

$$= \sum_{j=1}^{N} \gamma_{t-j} X_j + \sum_{j=1}^{N} \left(\sum_{k=-\infty}^{t-N-1} \gamma_k a_{t-k,j} \right) X_j + \sum_{j=1}^{N} \left(\sum_{k=t}^{\infty} \gamma_k a_{t-k,j} \right) X_j$$

$$= \sum_{j=1}^{N} \hat{\gamma}_{t-j} X_j \tag{1.4}$$

where $a_{t-k,j}$ are the coefficients of X_j, $j = 1, ..., N$, in the (linear) forecasting function of $\hat{X}_{t-k}$ if $t - k \notin \{1, ..., N\}$ and

$$\hat{\gamma}_{t-j} := \begin{cases} \gamma_{t-j} + \sum_{k=-\infty}^{t-N-1} \gamma_k a_{t-k,j} + \sum_{k=t}^{\infty} \gamma_k a_{t-k,j} & j = 1, ..., N \\ 0 & \text{else} \end{cases} \tag{1.5}$$

Note that $(\hat{\gamma}_{t-j})_{j=1,...,N}$ depends on t and that it is an *asymmetric* filter in general.

If the DGP of X_t is known, then the above estimate $\hat{\hat{Y}}_t$ satisfies a mean square optimality criterion (see for example Cleveland [15], Bell [3], Bell [4], Huot and all [55] and Bobbitt and Otto [7]). The 'true model' (DGP) can be used for

1. linearizing the sample (identify 'outliers' or 'shifts' and remove them from the original series)
2. supplying missing values
3. defining components and corresponding symmetric signal extraction filters for realizations of infinite length (see chapter 2)
4. supplying fore- and backcasts in order to compute signal estimates for finite samples.

In the following, the last point i.e. the determination of an efficient signal estimate for finite samples is analyzed. This is an important problem for many applications (an example is given in section 1.5) because in practice only finitely many observations of an input process X_t are available. It is now suggested that the MBA does not efficiently solve this problem if the DGP is unknown.

If the DGP is unknown, then a 'suitable' model must first be identified. In this case, 'misspecification' is the rule for most applications, see for example Box [8]. Therefore, it is generally impossible to assert optimality properties for the proposed MBA. Also, in case of misspecification the minimization of the one-step ahead mean-square forecasting error does not necessarily 'match' the signal estimation problem (for finite samples) because 1.3 involves one- *and multi-step-ahead* forecasts. Clements and Hendry [14], p.244, argue : "as it is not possible to prove that 1-step estimation is optimal when models are misspecified, dynamic estimation could improve multi-period forecast accuracy" (dynamic estimation means that parameters of forecasting functions are estimated separately for each forecasting step, by minimizing directly the corresponding forecasting error) and p.282 "Indeed the 'best' model on 1-step forecasts need not dominate at longer horizons". However, dynamic estimation is cumbersome and it is not a 'panacea', as shown by the same authors. With regards to the model selection procedure, Clements and Hendry p.281. claim "we find that the usual criteria based on t- and F-tests are not applicable when models are to be chosen on the basis of their ability to multi-step forecast". As a result, inferences based on 'traditional' tests do not straightforwardly extend to estimation problems involving multi-step ahead forecasts (such as the signal estimation problem). But even if the right model has been selected (for example in an artificial simulation context), Clements and Hendry are warning against careless use p.292 "... a poor forecast could result from the estimated DGP relative to the false autoregressive model" (in their study, the 'false' model is a pure random-walk model whereas the true DGP is a stationary process with an AR-root close to one). The authors show that the relative performances of 'true' and 'false' models generally depend on the chosen forecast horizon.

Consequently, *the model-based optimization procedure does not 'match' the signal estimation problem for finite samples if the DGP is unknown because one-step and multi-step ahead forecasting performances are generally conflicting in the presence of misspecification.* In fact $E[(\hat{Y}_t - \hat{\hat{Y}}_t)^2]$ should be minimized instead of the mean square error of the residuum in the model equation for X_t. More generally, *optimizing with respect to 'short term' performances (one-step ahead forecasts) may be misleading when estimating 'long term' components (like a trend for example).*

The approximation of $\hat{Y}_t$ by $\hat{\hat{Y}}_t$ can be stated in terms of a filter approximation problem. For that purpose, a suitable 'distance' measure is needed. The DFA bases on the minimization of such a measure. It is shown in chapter 5 that the solution of the corresponding optimization criterion minimizes $E[(Y_t - \hat{Y}_t)^2]$ up to an error term which is smallest among a general class of estimators. Also, the asymptotic distribution of the estimated filter parameters can be derived, see chapter 5. Therefore, inferences for the DFA are not based on one-step ahead performances only (as for the MBA) but implicitly account for one- and multi-step ahead performances simultaneously. This is particularly important when testing for unit-roots for example, see chapters 5 and 7, since unit-roots determine the 'long-term' dynamics of a process.

Before introducing the DFA, a well known identification problem is stated in the following section.

1.3 An Identification Problem

Let

$$X_t = T_t + C_t + S_t + I_t \tag{1.6}$$

Then there are $4N$ unknowns or unobservable variables for N equations only. Without additional (strong) assumptions the components on the right hand side are unidentified. To simplify, suppose one is interested in estimating the trend T_t given $X_1, ..., X_N$. If it is assumed that the trend evolves according to a predefined deterministic time pattern (for example a polynomial in t) then 'ad hoc' filters can be used (for example a Spencer filter, see Brockwell and Davis [10] and Kendall and Stuart [57] or a Henderson filter, see Gray and Thomson [41]). However, components such as the trend are often assumed to be stochastic. In this case various identifying assumptions exist like for example:

- impose perfect dependence of the components so that knowledge of a particular one determines the others (see Beveridge and Nelson [6] and section 2.2 below);
- impose independence of the components and regularity or smoothness of trend and seasonal components (see the canonical decomposition in Hillmer and Tiao [52], Burman [11] and section 2.3 below).
- specify the individual component-models a priori (see the structural models approach in Grether and al. [70], Harvey [47] and section 2.4 below);

The above methods rely on explicit components (see section 2): the components are then estimated by the output of a particular 'extraction' filter. Alternatively, components could be defined implicitly by the output of a filter satisfying a particular criterion. As an example, the output T_t of a Hodrick-Prescott filter minimizes

$$\sum_{t=1}^{N}(X_t - T_t)^2 + \lambda \sum_{t=2}^{N-1}((T_{t+1} - T_t) - (T_t - T_{t-1}))^2 \qquad (1.7)$$

where λ is given a priori. Larger λ lead to increased 'smoothness' of the filter output, see Hodrick and Prescott [54]. The first term penalizes deviations of T_t from the original time series and the second one penalizes 'roughness' (as defined by the mean of the squared second order differences). A similar approach underlies the Henderson filter, see Henderson [51] and section 2.5 below. Many of these methods were introduced by Whittaker [93] and [94]. At first sight, the identification problem seems to be 'circumvented' by implicit component definitions. However, criteria such as 1.7 are often difficult to interpret. For the Henderson filter, Wallis [92] p.164 argues: "... nor any later author has asked whether the symmetric Henderson filter produces a good estimate of the trend, however: for this purpose the trend is simply defined as the Henderson output". Moreover, the identification problem is often shifted towards the more or less arbitrary choice of a particular parameter of the filter (for example λ in 1.7).
The following fig.1.4 plots the Hodrick-Prescott 'growth component' T_t (solid line, $\lambda := 1600$ is a 'default' setting for many applications) and the canonical trend from TRAMO/SEATS (dotted line, see section 2.3) for a particular time series (UK-car-sales series, see chapter 7).

To summarize, the signal *identification* problem can be stated as follows

- different particular signal definitions generally lead to different components, see for example figs.1.4 and 2.11;
- a priori knowledge is always necessary for a unique identification of the components in 1.6, due to the 'large' number of unobservable variables (which define the so called 'structural form' of the process X_t). Therefore, a 'universal' definition of unobservable components of a time series is impossible. At last, implicit subjective convictions based on individual experience seem to motivate particular definitions.

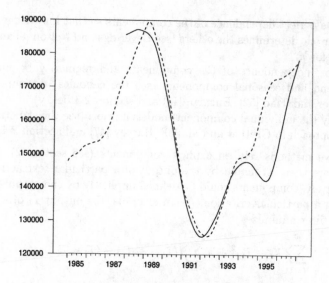

Fig. 1.4. HP- and Tramo/SEATS-Trend

Bell [5] p. 176 argues that "in seasonal adjustment the components are really artificial constructs presumed useful to estimate; there is no objective 'truth'". In agreement with this comment, neither a new component definition nor a corresponding symmetric extraction filter are proposed here. Instead, *the signal estimation problem for finite samples* $(\hat{\hat{Y}}_t)$ *is stressed: given* $t \in \{1, ..., N\}$ *and* $\hat{Y}_t$ *the output of a symmetric signal extraction (or 'smoothing') filter of possibly infinite order, find* $\hat{\hat{Y}}_t$ *which approximates* $\hat{Y}_t$ *given* $X_1, ..., X_N$.

In the next section, the DFA is briefly introduced. This is a new signal estimation method for finite samples. The presentation is informal. 'Technical' issues are postponed to following chapters.

1.4 The Direct Filter Approach

The following section relies on Wildi [98]. Suppose (the output of) some symmetric filter with transfer function $\Gamma(\omega)$, $-\pi \leq \omega \leq \pi$ must be approximated by (the output of) an asymmetric filter with transfer function $\hat{\Gamma}(\omega)$. As seen in the preceding section, the asymmetry results from the 'truncation' of realizations of infinite length. For notational convenience one 'hat' of the estimates $\hat{Y}_t$ and $\hat{\hat{Y}}_t$ in section 1.2 is eliminated. Therefore, $\hat{Y}_t$ becomes Y_t (the output of the symmetric filter) and $\hat{\hat{Y}}_t$ becomes $\hat{Y}_t$ (the output of the asymmetric filter). Assume $\Omega_N := \{\omega_k | \omega_k = k2\pi/N, |k| = 0, ..., [N/2]\}$ where $[N/2]$ is the greatest integer smaller or equal to $N/2$ and N is the sample size. Assume for simplicity of exposition that X_t is stationary (generalizations for non-stationary integrated processes are provided in chapter 5) and let

$$I_{NX}(\omega_k) := \frac{1}{2\pi N} \left| \sum_{t=1}^{N} X_t \exp(-i\omega_k t) \right|^2 \qquad (1.8)$$

denote the *periodogram* of the input process computed for $\omega_k \in \Omega_N$, see chapter 4. Then, under suitable regularity assumptions (see chapter 5) the solution $\hat{\Gamma}_0(\cdot)$ of

$$\min_{\hat{\Gamma}} \frac{2\pi}{N} \sum_{k=-[N/2]}^{[N/2]} |\Gamma(\omega_k) - \hat{\Gamma}(\omega_k)|^2 I_{NX}(\omega_k) \qquad (1.9)$$

generates an output $\hat{Y}_{t0}$ which minimizes $E[(Y_t - \hat{Y}_t)^2]$ up to an asymptotically negligible error term which is smallest possible (for a given class of estimators, see below). This result was first stated in Wildi [96]. The solution of 1.9 is attained within a general class of filters described in chapter 3. An intuitive explanation of the preceding statement can be given by considering the following approximation:

$$\frac{2\pi}{N} \sum_{k=-[N/2]}^{[N/2]} |\Gamma(\omega_k) - \hat{\Gamma}(\omega_k)|^2 I_{NX}(\omega_k) \simeq \frac{2\pi}{N} \sum_{k=-[N/2]}^{[N/2]} I_{N\Delta Y}(\omega_k) \quad (1.10)$$

$$= \frac{1}{N} \sum_{t=1}^{N} (Y_t - \hat{Y}_t)^2 \qquad (1.11)$$

where $\Delta Y_t := Y_t - \hat{Y}_t$. The approximation 1.10 corresponds to a *finite sample convolution* and 1.11 corresponds to *a finite sample spectral decomposition* of the mean square filter approximation error (see chapter 5). Under suitable regularity assumptions, 1.11 is a *best linear unbiased estimate* (BLUE) of the theoretical mean square error $E[(Y_t - \hat{Y}_t)^2]$, see chapter 5. Efficiency of the DFA then depends on the error term in the approximation 1.10: it is shown that the expression on the left hand side is a *superconsistent estimate* of 1.11, see chapter 5. Therefore, the DFA 'inherits' the efficiency property (BLUE) of 1.11, i.e. $\hat{Y}_{t0}$ minimizes $E[(Y_t - \hat{Y}_t)^2]$ up to an error term which is smallest possible among the class of linear estimators (of $E[(Y_t - \hat{Y}_t)^2]$). Note that in general Y_t and therefore 1.11 and $E[(Y_t - \hat{Y}_t)^2]$ are unknown for finite samples whereas the left hand side of 1.10 can be computed.

In order to derive the consistency and the efficiency as well as the distribution of the estimated filter parameters for a large class of input signals (including non-stationary integrated processes) technical results involving the periodogram 1.8 are needed. These are reported in chapter 4 and in the appendix. It is shown in chapter 5 that 1.9 can be generalized so that the time delay of the resulting filter is 'smaller'. It is then possible to detect 'turning-points' of a particular component earlier, see chapter 8.

The proposed signal estimation method for finite samples is called a *direct* filter approach because the coefficients $\hat{\gamma}_k$ of the resulting asymmetric filter are computed 'directly' from the minimization of (an efficient estimate of) the mean square error $E[(Y_t - \hat{Y}_t)^2]$. In comparison, the filter coefficients of model-based approaches are derived indirectly from the equivalence between 1.3 and 1.4. They rely on the minimization of the mean square *one*-step ahead forecasting error of the model (whereas the signal estimation problem requires good one- and multi-step ahead forecasting performances). Moreover, time constraints (for the resulting asymmetric filter) cannot be 'build' into 1.3 for the MBA so that turning-points of trend components cannot be detected 'earlier'.

In the following section, a typical application for an efficient finite sample signal estimation method is provided. Also, the content of the following chapters is briefly summarized.

1.5 Summary

For economic time series, interesting signals are often seasonally adjusted components or trends, see chapter 2 (recall that component definitions depend on strong a priori assumptions, see section 1.3). An efficient and general signal estimation method is needed for these important applications because economic time series are characterized by randomness (the DGP is not deterministic) and complex dynamics. Moreover, 'typical' users are often interested in signal estimates for time points near the upper boundary $t = N^1$. Consequently, filters are heavily asymmetric so that efficient estimation methods are required.

A new method, the DFA, is presented here. The book is organized as follows:

- In chapter 2, model-based approaches are presented. The aim is not to provide an exhaustive list of existent methods but to describe established procedures which are implemented in 'widely used' software packages. The objective is to compare the DFA to established MBA.
- The main concepts needed for the description of filters in the frequency domain (such as transfer functions, amplitude functions or phase functions) are proposed in chapter 3. A new filter class (ZPC-filters) is derived whose characteristics 'match' the signal estimation problem.
- For the DFA, an eminent role is awarded to the periodogram (or to statistics directly related to the periodogram). It 'collects' and transforms the

---

[1]For assessing the actual state of the 'business cycle' for example

information of the sample $X_1, ..., X_N$ into a form suitable for the signal estimation problem. Therefore, properties of the periodogram and technical details related to the DFA are analyzed in chapter 4. In particular, the statistic is analyzed for integrated processes. Stochastic properties of *squared* periodogram ordinates are analyzed in the appendix. Both kind of results are omitted in the 'traditional' time series literature and are needed here for proving theoretical results in chapter 5. An explorative instrument for assessing possible 'unit-root misspecification' of the filter design for the DFA is proposed also.

• The main theoretical results for the DFA are reported in chapter 5: the consistency, the efficiency, the generalization to non-stationary integrated input processes, the generalized conditional optimization (resulting in asymmetric filters with smaller time delays) and the asymptotic distribution of the estimated filter parameters (which enables hypothesis testing). In particular, a generalized unit-root test is proposed which is designed for the signal estimation problem.

• In order to prove the results in chapter 5, regularity assumptions are needed. One of these assumptions is directly related to finite sample issues (overfitting problem). Therefore, the overfitting problem is analyzed in chapter 6. Overparameterization and overfitting are distinguished and new procedures are proposed for 'tackling' their various aspects. An estimation of the order of the asymmetric filter is presented (which avoids more specifically overparameterization), founding on the asymptotic distribution of the parameter estimates. The proposed method does not rely on 'traditional' information criteria, because the DGP of X_t is not of immediate concern. However, it is shown in the appendix that 'traditional' information criteria (like AIC for example) may be considered as special cases of the proposed method. Also, new procedures ensuring regularity of the DFA solution are proposed which solve specific overfitting problems. The key idea behind these new methods is to modify the original optimization criterion such that overfitting becomes 'measurable'. It is felt that these ideas may be useful also when modelling the DGP for the MBA.

• Empirical results which are based on the simulation of artificial processes ($I(2)$, $I(1)$ and stationary processes) and on a 'real-world' time series are presented in chapter 7. The DFA is compared with the MBA with respect to mean square performances. It is shown that the DFA performs as well as maximum likelihood estimates for artificial times series. If the DGP is unknown, as is the case for the 'real-world' time series, the DFA outperforms two established MBA, namely TRAMO/SEATS and CENSUS X-12-ARIMA (see chapter 2 for a definition). The increased performance is achieved with respect to various signal definitions (two different trend signals and a particular seasonal adjustment) both 'in' and 'out of sample'. It is also suggested that statistics relying on the one-step ahead forecasts, like 'traditional' unit-root tests (augmented Dickey-Fuller and Phillips-Perron tests) or diagnostic tests (like for example Ljung-Box tests) may

be misleading for the signal estimation problem if the true DGP is unknown. Instead, specific instruments derived in chapters 4, 5 and 6 are
used for determining the optimal filter design for the DFA. These instruments, which are based on estimated filter errors (rather than one-step
ahead forecasting errors of the model), indicate smaller integration orders
for the analyzed time series (I(1)- instead of I(2)-processes as 'proposed'
by the majority of the unit-root tests). A possible explanation for these
differences may be seen in the fact that filter errors implicitly account
for one- *and* multi-step ahead forecasts simultaneously. A further analysis of the revision errors (filter approximation errors) suggests that the
I(2)-hypothesis should be rejected indeed.

- Finally, an empirical comparison of the DFA and the MBA with respect
to their ability of detecting 'turning-points' (of two different trend components) is conducted in chapter 8. The MBA is compared with the 'original'
DFA and with the result of a generalized constrained optimization (whose
filter solution has a smaller time delay). As in the preceding chapter, the
DFA generally outperforms the MBA with respect to the proposed criterion.

In the following chapter 2, well established model-based approaches are presented. Two of them are used as 'benchmarks' in chapters 7 and 8.

2

Model-Based Approaches

2.1 Introduction

Model-based approaches attempt to identify the DGP of the input process and to estimate its parameters. They provide

1. Definitions of the theoretical components Y_{tj} (identification), where $j = 1, ..., n$ and n is the number of components.
2. Estimates $\hat{Y}_{tj}$ of the components for realizations of infinite length.
3. Estimates $\hat{\hat{Y}}_{tj}$ of the components for finite samples.

The general identification problem analyzed in section 1.3 led us to examine the last estimation problem only. Therefore, we here use the terminology 'model-based approach' whenever a method relies on back- or forecasts generated by a model for approximating $\hat{Y}_{tj}$ by $\hat{\hat{Y}}_{tj}$. From this perspective, the well-known X-11-ARIMA and X-12-ARIMA procedures can be considered as 'model-based' although the definitions of the signals at the first stage are 'implicit' (not model-based), see for example Dagum [22], Findley et al. [32] and section 2.5 below.

Most of the approaches to be presented here are based on the following two decompositions of X_t

$$X_t = T_t + C_t + S_t + I_t \tag{2.1}$$
$$X_t = T_t C_t S_t I_t \tag{2.2}$$

where T_t, C_t, S_t and I_t are the 'trend', the 'cyclical', the 'seasonal' and the 'irregular' components respectively (see Nerlove, Grether and Carvalho [70] for an interpretation of these components). The number of four components is not to be seen as a limitation. More (or less) components may be considered too. The multiplicative decomposition (2.2) can be justified by the observation that seasonal or irregular variations often grow with the 'level' T_t of a series.

Methods based on the multiplicative decomposition can be defined explicitly (see section 2.5) or they can be derived from the additive representation (2.1) by using a preliminary log-transform of X_t. Besides the additive and the multiplicative decompositions, some methods allow for additional representations of X_t, see for example section 2.5.

Additive or multiplicative component *models* are defined by supplying specific stochastic assumptions. Model-based approaches generally differ with respect to these assumptions. For the MBA in the following section, components are assumed to be *dependent*.

2.2 The Beveridge-Nelson Decomposition

The Beveridge-Nelson decomposition is a so called 'ARIMA'-model-based-approach. Let

$$X_t = T_t + C_t$$

where it is assumed that

$$X_t = X_{t-1} + \mu + \Xi(B)\epsilon_t \tag{2.3}$$

where $\Xi(B) := \sum_{k=0}^{\infty} \xi_k B^k = \frac{\sum_{k=0}^{p} \alpha_k B^k}{\sum_{j=0}^{q} \beta_j B^j}$ is a stable ARMA operator ($\alpha_0 = \beta_0 = 1$), see Beveridge and Nelson [6]. Consider a forecast $\hat{X}_{t+k}|X_t, X_{t-1}, \ldots$ of X_{t+k} for k 'large':

$$
\begin{aligned}
\hat{X}_{t+k} &= k\mu + X_t + \left(\sum_{j=1}^{k} \xi_j\right)\epsilon_t + \left(\sum_{j=2}^{k+1} \xi_j\right)\epsilon_{t-1} + \ldots \\
&\simeq k\mu + X_t + \left(\sum_{j=1}^{\infty} \xi_j\right)\epsilon_t + \left(\sum_{j=2}^{\infty} \xi_j\right)\epsilon_{t-1} + \ldots \\
&=: k\mu + T_t
\end{aligned}
$$

where $\left|\sum_{j=1}^{\infty} \xi_k\right| \leq \sum_{j=1}^{\infty} |\xi_k| < \infty$ because of the ARMA-structure (which induces an exponential decay of the coefficients). The slope of the forecast is given by μ and its 'level' is defined by T_t which is a stochastic process. In fact

$$T_t - T_{t-1} = \mu + \left(\sum_{j=0}^{\infty} \xi_j\right)\epsilon_t \tag{2.4}$$

so that T_t is a random walk with drift μ. Beveridge and Nelson call T_t the *permanent component*: "the value the original series would have if it were on the long-run path (as defined by the long run forecast) in the current time period. The permanent component is then the long-run forecast of the series adjusted for its mean rate of change...", see [6], p.156.

Remarks

- The permanent component can be interpreted as a 'trend'. From (2.4) the successive trend increments increase by $\mu + \left(\sum_{k=0}^{\infty} \xi_k\right) \epsilon_t$. If $\left|\sum_{k=0}^{\infty} \xi_k\right| > 1$ then the trend is more 'erratic' than the original series. Figure 2.1 illustrates the latter point : the solid line corresponds to a seasonally adjusted series (UK-car-sales series, see chapter 7) whereas the dotted line corresponds to the Beveridge-Nelson 'trend'. The permanent component T_t is estimated using the software-package 'RATS' (see below). AR- and MA-model orders were set to $p = 0$ and $q = 1$ so that $X_t - X_{t-1}$ is a MA(1) process. The estimated positive lag coefficient θ then implies $\sum_{j=0}^{\infty} \xi_j = 1 + \theta > 1$ in (2.4). Note that this phenomenon ('erratic' trend) has lead to criticism, see for example Metz [66] p.290. In fact, for many applications 'smooth' components are of interest (because it is felt that 'short term' variations should be 'smoothed out').
- As shown in equation 10 in Beveridge and Nelson [6] the 'cyclical' component $C_t := X_t - T_t$ is stationary and its innovation process is given by ϵ_t. Therefore, trend and cyclical components are *dependent* since they share the same innovation ϵ_t : the 'shocks' which generate the business cycle are the same as those which generate the growth process. Beveridge and Nelson interpret C_t as "a stationary process which represents the forecastable momentum present at each time period but which is expected to be dissipated as the series tends to its permanent level", see [6], p.158.
- Finite sample signal extraction problems do not exist here because T_t can be computed without knowledge of 'future' observations $X_{N+1}, X_{N+2}, ...$ as can be seen from (2.4).

An algorithm for computing the Beveridge-Nelson-decomposition has been proposed in Newbold [71]. This algorithm has been implemented in RATS. The corresponding procedure is called 'bndecomp.src'. The text-file can be downloaded from www.estima.com. The time series in figure 2.1 has been computed accordingly. Note that (2.3) does not allow for a seasonal component. Therefore, the input series has been previously seasonally adjusted. The corresponding seasonal adjustment procedure is presented in the following section.

2.3 The Canonical Decomposition

The following model-based approach is based on ARIMA-models too. However, the identifying assumptions for the components are 'at the opposite' of those in the preceding section (recall section 1.3). Indeed, it is assumed that T_t,

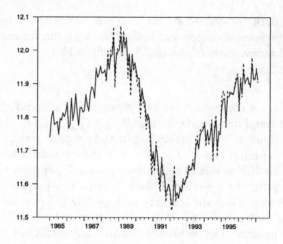

Fig. 2.1. UK-car sales (solid) and Permanent Component (dotted)

S_t and I_t are independent processes and that T_t and S_t are 'smooth'. Hillmer and Tiao [53] argue "To perform seasonal adjustment of the data, an *arbitrary* choice must be made. Considering that the seasonal and trend components should be *slowly* evolving, it seems reasonable to extract as much white noise as possible from the seasonal and trend components... Thus we seek to maximize the innovation variance of the noise component". The "slowly evolving" (smooth) trend and seasonal components or, more precisely, the maximization of the variance of the noise component characterizes the canonical decomposition.

Once an ARIMA-model for the DGP of X_t has been selected and (parameters) estimated, models for the individual DGP's of the components must be defined such that

- the resulting model is *admissible* i.e. the components sum up to X_t and are independent and
- the components may be interpreted as 'trend', 'seasonal' or 'irregular'.

Together with the above 'smoothness' property (see Box, Hillmer and Tiao [37] and Pierce [21]) these assumptions uniquely define the components. A good 'initiation' to the method is given in Maravall and Pierce [65] who consider a very simple ARIMA-process generating trend, seasonal and irregular variations. This is described in the following section.

2.3.1 An Illustrative Example

Let

$$(1 - B^2)X_t = (1 - B)(1 + B)X_t = \epsilon_t \tag{2.5}$$

which may be suitable for modelling semiannual data for example, see Maravall and Pierce [65]. The latter authors call the above difference equation a "prototypical seasonal adjustment model". Consider the following (fractial) decomposition of the 'z-transform' of the above model

$$\frac{\sigma_\epsilon^2}{1-z^2} = \frac{\sigma_\epsilon^2}{(1-z)(1+z)} = \sigma_T^2 \frac{1-\beta z}{(1-z)} + \sigma_S^2 \frac{1-\gamma z}{(1+z)} + \sigma_I^2$$

where the denominators $1-z$ and $1+z$ determine the trend (unit-root at frequency 0) and the seasonal (unit-root at frequency π) components respectively and $\sigma_T, \sigma_S, \sigma_I$ are the standard deviations of the corresponding component innovations. Maravall and Pierce [65] p.362 argue "in order to avoid model multiplicity, we assume $|\beta| \leq 1$, $|\gamma| \leq 1$". One can show by straightforward calculations that for orthogonal (independent) components

$$\sigma_T^2 = \frac{\sigma_X^2}{4(1-\beta)^2}$$

$$\sigma_S^2 = \frac{\sigma_X^2}{4(1+\gamma)^2}$$

$$\sigma_I^2 = \left(\frac{-\beta}{4(1-\beta)^2} + \frac{\gamma}{4(1+\gamma)^2} \right) \sigma_X^2$$

see equations 3.6 and 3.7 in Maravall/Pierce [65]. Thus, in order that $\sigma_I^2 > 0$ one must have

$$-\beta(1+\gamma)^2 + \gamma(1-\beta)^2 \geq 0 \tag{2.6}$$

It is easily seen that this condition does not uniquely identify the parameters. The inequality (2.6) determines the set of *admissible solutions*. According to the above definition, the canonical decomposition determines the unique one for which the variance of the irregular component is maximized or, equivalently, for which the variances of the trend innovations and the seasonal innovations are *minimized*, resulting in $\beta = -1, \gamma = 1$ (recall that $|\beta| \leq 1$, $|\gamma| \leq 1$).

Definition 2.1 (Components of the Canonical Decomposition). *Under the above assumptions (additive orthogonal model, $\sigma_I^2 \to$ max) the components for model (2.5) are defined by*

$$T_t := \frac{1+B}{1-B} \epsilon_t^T$$

$$S_t := \frac{1-B}{1+B} \epsilon_t^S$$

$$I_t := \epsilon_t^I$$

Orthogonality here means that $\epsilon_t^T, \epsilon_{t+i}^S, \epsilon_{t+k}^I$ are pairwise orthogonal (independent) for any t, i, k. It is easily seen that the canonical condition determines uniquely the parameters β, γ and thus the components. Inserting in (2.1) leads to

$$X_t = \frac{1+B}{1-B}\epsilon_t^T + \frac{1-B}{1+B}\epsilon_t^S + \epsilon_t^I$$

The pseudo spectral density of T_t is $h_T(\omega) = \frac{\sigma_T^2}{2\pi}\frac{|1+\exp(-i\omega)|^2}{|1-\exp(-i\omega)|^2}$. For $\omega \neq 0$ it is a decreasing function which vanishes in $\omega = \pi$ ('smoothness'). Therefore, the canonical decomposition 'partitions' the noise in such a way that the trend becomes as smooth as possible. The following comment can be found in EUROSTAT [30] "Is this assumption ($\sigma_I^2 \rightarrow$ max) reasonable? We *believe* it is. Even if this assumption is *arbitrary*, it seems *reasonable*, since seasonal component and trend are as stable as possible, *meeting the economic requirements*".

After the components have been defined, they must be estimated. For realizations of infinite length, estimation is traditionally achieved by Wiener-Kolmogorov filtering (which has been generalized to non-stationary integrated processes in Pierce [74] and Bell [4]). The procedure is illustrated for the trend. The estimate $\tilde{T}_t$ of T_t given $..., X_{-2}, X_{-1}, X_0, X_1, X_2, ...$ is

$$\tilde{T}_t = \frac{\sigma_T^2}{\sigma_X^2}\frac{\Psi_T(B)\Psi_T(F)}{\Psi_X(B)\Psi_X(F)}X_t \tag{2.7}$$

where $\Psi_X(B), \Psi_T(B)$ are the transfer functions of X_t and T_t, B and F are the backward and forward operators and σ_T^2 and σ_X^2 are the variances of the innovations of the trend and of X_t respectively. This procedure is intuitively very appealing. Indeed, the inverted operator $\Psi_X(B)$ (denominator) transforms X_t into ϵ_t. The operator in the numerator then transforms a suitable 'portion' of the innovation ϵ_t (of X_t), namely $\frac{\sigma_T^2}{\sigma_X^2}$, into the estimated trend $\tilde{T}_t$. Although optimal (in a mean square sense) this procedure has two undesirable consequences.

- The same innovation process ϵ_t 'generates' all estimated components. Therefore, *the estimated components must be dependent*.
- The (pseudo) spectra of the estimated components are 'distorted'. The filter in (2.7) produces 'dips'. The pseudo spectral density of $\tilde{T}_t$ vanishes at seasonal frequencies (whereas the pseudo spectral density of T_t does not vanish there), see Burman [11] and EUROSTAT [30], p.45. This is true for the estimated seasonally adjusted and irregular components too. So for example, the spectral density of the estimated irregular component is not constant (as it should be for a white noise component). The reason for these undesirable properties of the estimated components is again the dependence of the estimates: $\tilde{T}_t$, $\tilde{S}_t$ and $\tilde{I}_t$ are based on (the same) ϵ_t whereas T_t, S_t and I_t are based on independent processes ϵ_t^T, ϵ_t^S and ϵ_t^I.

Therefore, the filter 'erroneously' removes spectral power belonging to (the unobservable and indistinguishable) ϵ_t^T, ϵ_t^S and ϵ_t^I respectively.

The above problem is 'well known' in the econometric literature. The 'structural form' on the right hand side of (2.1) cannot be recovered from the 'reduced form' on the left hand side (econometric constraints enabling a recovery of the corresponding signals are not given).

For model (2.5) the filter equation (2.7) becomes

$$\tilde{T}_t = \frac{\sigma_T^2}{\sigma_X^2}(1+B)^2(1+F)^2 X_t \qquad (2.8)$$

For finite samples problems exist near the boundaries $t = 1, 2$ and $t = N-1, N$ because X_{-1}, X_0 and X_{N+1}, X_{N+2} in (2.8) are not observed. Consider the problem for general processes X_t. If the DGP (of X_t) is known, then, as argued in section 1.2, optimal estimates of a particular component, say estimates $\tilde{T}_t$ of $\tilde{T}_t$, are obtained by replacing X_t, for $t \notin \{1, ..., N\}$ by back- and forecasts:

$$\check{T}_t := \sum_{j=-\infty}^{0} \gamma_{t-j} \hat{X}_j + \sum_{j=1}^{N} \gamma_{t-j} X_j + \sum_{j=N+1}^{\infty} \gamma_{t-j} \hat{X}_j \qquad (2.9)$$

where $\hat{X}_j$ is the optimal fore- or backcast of X_j. In particular, if $t = N$ then

$$\check{T}_N = \sum_{j=-\infty}^{0} \gamma_{N-j} \hat{X}_j + \sum_{j=1}^{N} \gamma_{N-j} X_j + \sum_{j=N+1}^{\infty} \gamma_{N-j} \hat{X}_j$$

$$\sim \sum_{j=1}^{N} \gamma_{N-j} X_j + \sum_{j=N+1}^{\infty} \gamma_{N-j} \hat{X}_j \qquad (2.10)$$

The approximation (2.10) is valid for 'large' N because the filter coefficients γ_j (induced by ARMA-models) converge exponentially fast to 0. Therefore, backcasts can often be neglected when estimating a signal towards the end point $t = N$.

For finite samples, a further consequence of the canonical decomposition (chosen as an identifying device) is commented in Maravall and Pierce [65], p.375: "the revision variances are maximized at the canonical decomposition values ... The occurrence of larger revisions may indicate a price paid for choosing the canonical decomposition (i.e. a trade-off between size of the revision and cleanness of signal)". The term 'revision variances' corresponds to $E[(\tilde{T} - \check{T}_t)^2]$ (or more generally to $E[(\tilde{Y} - \check{Y}_t)^2]$, where $\tilde{Y}_t$ is the output of the symmetric signal extraction filter and $\check{Y}_t$ is the output of the asymmetric finite sample filter, see section 2.3.4).
It is true that the revision error variances for the trend and for the season are

maximized for the canonical decomposition. Therefore, the inverse is true for the seasonally adjusted component: its revision error is minimized. In fact, by definition, the 'canonical season' has less power than any other admissible seasonal component. Thus, the 'canonical' seasonal adjustment filter removes a minimal amount of spectral power so that the resulting revision errors are indeed minimized. Combining this property with the fact that statistical agencies aim at 'stable' estimates (i.e. none or 'small' revisions or updates of past estimates) may explain why model-based procedures relying on the canonical decomposition (such as TRAMO/SEATS for example) are called *seasonal adjustment procedures'* instead of 'trend extraction-' or 'signal extraction procedures' for example. It should be stressed however that *the smaller revision errors for the seasonally adjusted time series (of the canonical decomposition) are not due to improved statistical performances but to an arbitrary definition of the signal.* As a result, the seasonally adjusted signal corresponding to the canonical decomposition is generally 'rough' which is not necessarily an advantage (when assessing the presence of turning-points for example).

From a methodological point of view the listed 'deficiencies' of the proposed component estimates such as

- large revision errors (except for the seasonally adjusted signal),
- dependent estimates (whereas 'true' components are independent)
- and 'distorted' pseudo spectral densities

are unsatisfactory. However, the underlying problems (causing these deficiencies) cannot be solved more efficiently by other statistical methods. If the proposed model and its assumptions are felt 'reasonable' and if the DGP is known, then the proposed estimation method is efficient for realizations of infinite length as well as for finite samples . If the DGP (of X_t) is unknown, then 'signals' are generally misspecified and corresponding estimates are inefficient, recall section 1.2.

In the next section a practically more relevant process is analyzed. The corresponding 'airline'-model is often selected by TRAMO or CENSUS-X12-ARIMA for modelling particular time series.

2.3.2 The Airline-Model

The so called 'airline'-model

$$(1 - B)(1 - B^{12})X_t = (1 - \theta_1 B)(1 - \theta_{12} B^{12})\epsilon_t \qquad (2.11)$$

(see Box and Jenkins [9]) is often used for modelling monthly time series. A report of EUROSTAT [30], p.19 states that "as extended evidences have shown, the airline model can be used very often to describe a great number of series". The model depends on three parameters only which are easily interpretable : θ_1 and θ_{12} measure the 'stability' of the trend and of the seasonal components and σ_ϵ^2 measures the variance of the innovation of X_t. Despite its advantages, the airline model is to be criticized:

- Season and trend are not properly separated. The parameter θ_{12} 'acts' simultaneously on the trend and on the season (see also section 2.4 for a method which 'solves' this problem).
- X_t is an I(2)-process with a double unit-root at frequency zero and simple unit-roots at the frequencies $k\pi/6$, $k = 1, ..., 6$. Differencing a time series twice often leads to non-invertible moving-average terms. Maravall [32], p.156 argues that "moderate overdifferencing causes, in practice, little damage". However, it is not clear what the terms 'moderate' and 'little damage' mean. It is well known that non-invertibility can lead to forecasting problems (because a convergent AR-representation does not exist). More generally, it is shown in chapter 5 that *imposing too large integration orders results in asymmetric filters satisfying constraints which are unnecessarily severe and which impair the fit* (i.e. which induce larger revision errors). Empirical evidences based on simulation results are reported in chapter 7.
- Seasonal unit-roots are often difficult to interpret because seasons are allowed to 'permute' for such a model. If for example it is known that summer levels always exceed winter levels, then seasonal unit roots are misspecified, see also the concluding remarks in section 2.3.5.
- The unique parameter θ_{12} cannot account for different seasonal patterns (for example a large unstable fundamental $\pi/6$ and smaller stable harmonics $k\pi/6$, $k = 2, ..., 6$). However, such patterns can be observed for time series for which the airline-model 'feigns' reasonably good fits, see for example chapter 7.

Nevertheless, 'airline-models' are often selected by software packages like TRAMO or CENSUS-X-12-ARIMA (in particular for monthly economic time series). They are often 'preferred' by information criteria (like AIC) and they often 'pass' diagnostic tests (like Ljung-Box for example). In the following, a slightly more general process is analyzed. Canonical components and extraction filters are derived for

$$(1 - B)(1 - B^s)X_t = (1 - \theta_1 B)(1 - \theta_s B^s)\epsilon_t$$

which admits a 'periodicity' of arbitrary length s. In the remaining of the section, canonical components and rules for computing the extraction filters for the airline model are derived.

Despite its simplicity, the airline-model leads to algebraically cumbersome derivations. Therefore, results already obtained in the literature are extensively used in the following. The canonical components are used (among other possible signal definitions) for the examples in the last two chapters so that a brief overview is given here. Readers which are not interested in these particular results may skip the remaining of the section which is not needed for understanding the DFA or for interpreting the empirical results in the last two chapters.

It is assumed that $\sigma_\epsilon^2 = 1$ mainly for notational simplicity. One can then verify by partial fractions that

$$
\frac{(1 - \theta_1 B)(1 - \theta_s B^s)(1 - \theta_1 F)(1 - \theta_s F^s)}{(1 - B)(1 - B^s)(1 - F)(1 - F^s)} =
$$

$$
\frac{Q_T(B)}{(1 - B)^2(1 - F)^2} + \frac{Q_s(B)}{U(B)U(F)} + \theta_1\theta_s \tag{2.12}
$$

where

$$
Q_T(B) := \frac{(1 - \theta_1)^2(1 - \theta_s)^2}{s^2} \left[1 + \left(\frac{\theta_s s^2}{(1 - \theta_s)^2} + \frac{s^2 - 4}{12} + \frac{(1 + \theta_1)^2}{4(1 - \theta_1)^2} \right) \right.
$$

$$
\left. (1 - B)(1 - F) \right] \tag{2.13}
$$

and

$$
(1 - B)^2(1 - F)^2 Q_S(B) := (1 - \theta_s)^2(1 - \theta_1)^2 \left(1 - \frac{1}{s^2} U(B)U(F) \right)
$$

$$
+\theta_1(1 - B)(1 - F) - \left(\frac{s^2 - 4}{12s^2}(1 - \theta_1)^2 + \frac{(1 + \theta_1)^2}{4s^2} \right) \tag{2.14}
$$

$$
(1 - B^s)(1 - F^s)
$$

where $U(B) := \sum_{k=0}^{s-1} B^k$ so that $1 - B^s = (1 - B)U(B)$. These equations are for example derived in Hillmer and Tiao [53] p.331 (note that the coefficient $(1 - \theta_s)^2$ erroneously stands on the left hand side of (2.14) in the cited literature). The first term in (2.12) can be interpreted as trend (the pseudo spectral density exhibits an infinite peak at frequency 0), the second one is a seasonal component (infinite spectral peaks at seasonal frequencies) and the last one corresponds to the irregular component. The above authors then show that the condition

$$
\theta_s \geq 0 \tag{2.15}
$$

ensures admissibility of the model (i.e. a decomposition into additive orthogonal components). More precisely, Hillmer and Tiao [53] p.331 define

$$
Q_S^*(B) := Q_S(B) + U(B)U(F) \left(C - \frac{\theta_s(1 - \theta_1)^2}{4} \right) \tag{2.16}
$$

$$
Q_T^*(B) := Q_T(B) - C(1 - B)^2(1 - F)^2 \tag{2.17}
$$

where $C := \dfrac{Q_T(-1)}{16}$, assuming that the constant -1 in $Q_T(-1)$ replaces back- and forwardshift operators B and $F = B^{-1}$ in the expression (2.13) for Q_T. A simple algebraic manipulation shows that (2.12) becomes

$$\frac{Q_T^*(B)}{(1-B)^2(1-F)^2} + \frac{Q_s^*(B)}{U(B)U(F)} + \theta_s \frac{(1+\theta_1)^2}{4} \tag{2.18}$$

Therefore, if $\theta_s > 0$, then the last (constant) term in the above expression corresponds to the (constant) spectral density of the irregular component (which must be positive) whereas the first two terms correspond to the (pseudo) spectral densities of the trend and the seasonal components respectively (in order to obtain the pseudo spectral densities, B and F must be replaced by $\exp(-i\omega)$ and $\exp(i\omega)$ and the terms must be suitably normalized). From a practical point of view, airline-models are interesting because admissibility - i.e. the existence of an orthogonal additive component decomposition - is easily verified.

The expression (2.18) is an admissible (but not necessarily the canonical) decomposition. In order to obtain the canonical decomposition, the variance of the irregular component must be maximized. In this case, spectral power could not be 'transferred' anymore from the trend or the seasonal components to the irregular component in (2.18). Note that any transferred spectral mass (of trend or seasonal components) must correspond to white noise i.e. it should be a constant. It is readily seen that (2.17) and the definition of C imply that the pseudo spectral density of the trend (2.17) vanishes at π. Therefore, a positive constant cannot be removed from the pseudo spectral density of the trend (2.17). Since the canonical decomposition is unique, the trend (2.17) must already be the canonical trend.

For the seasonal component, the expression $Q_S^*(\exp(-i\omega))$, where $\exp(-i\omega)$ replaces the operator B and $\exp(i\omega)$ replaces the operator F in (2.16), does generally not vanish as a function of ω. This can be seen as follows. If θ_s is sufficiently small then

$$\frac{Q_T(-1)}{16} := \frac{(1-\theta_1)^2(1-\theta_s)^2}{16s^2}\left[1 + \left(\frac{\theta_s s^2}{(1-\theta_s)^2} + \frac{s^2-4}{12} + \frac{(1+\theta_1)^2}{4(1-\theta_1)^2}\right)\right.$$

$$\left.(1-(-1))(1-(-1))\right]$$

$$\approx \frac{(1-\theta_1)^2}{16s^2}\left[1 + O(\theta_s) + \frac{s^2-4}{3} + \frac{(1+\theta_1)^2}{(1-\theta_1)^2}\right]$$

$$= O(1)$$

Therefore $C - \dfrac{\theta_s(1-\theta_1)^2}{4} > 0$ in (2.16) as soon as θ_s is sufficiently small. It follows that

$$Q_S^*(\exp(-i\omega)) := Q_S(\exp(-i\omega))$$

$$+U(\exp(-i\omega))U(\exp(i\omega))\left(C - \frac{\theta_s(1-\theta_1)^2}{4}\right)$$
$$> 0$$

for all ω. In fact, the second term on the right of the equality vanishes only for $\omega := k\pi/s$, $k = 1, ..., s$ but the first term does generally not vanish there since it corresponds to a seasonal component.

Since $Q_S^*(\exp(-i\omega))$ does not vanish, it is possible to 'transfer' a white noise component from S_t to I_t. The canonical seasonal component may be computed by the following device: find ω_0 so that $Q_S^*(\exp(-i\omega_0))$ is minimal and define

$$Q_S^{**}(B) := Q_S^*(B) - U(B)U(F)C_2 \tag{2.19}$$

where $C_2 := \dfrac{Q_S^*(\exp(-i\omega_0))}{U(\exp(-i\omega_0))U(\exp(i\omega_0))}$. The canonical decomposition for the airline model is then obtained from:

$$\frac{Q_T^*(B)}{(1-B)^2(1-F)^2} + \frac{Q_s^{**}(B)}{U(B)U(F)} + \theta_s \frac{(1+\theta_1)^2}{4} + C_2 \tag{2.20}$$

where $C_2 > 0$. Once the canonical components have been defined it remains to derive the coefficients of the optimal signal extraction filters, see (2.7). Besides the convolution rule the following is useful for deriving corresponding expressions :

$$\sum_{k=0}^{\infty}\gamma_k B^k \sum_{k=0}^{\infty}\gamma_k F^k = \sum_{j=0}^{\infty}\left(\sum_{k=j}^{\infty}\gamma_k\gamma_{k-j}\right)(B^j + F^j)$$

By suitably combining both rules the coefficients may be computed from (2.7), setting in the expression on the left hand side of (2.12) (for the denominator) and (2.17) (for the numerator $Q_T^*(B)$ of the trend) or (2.19) (for the numerator $Q_S^{**}(B)$ of the seasonal component).

Analytical derivations of the transfer functions of the symmetric extraction filters are 'cumbersome'. Instead, the following figures illustrate transfer functions for a particular example (a model used in chapter 7). In figure 2.2 the transfer function of the canonical trend extraction filter can be seen for the model

$$(1-B)(1-B^{12})X_t = (1-0.60B)(1-0.27B^{12})\epsilon_t \tag{2.21}$$

In figure 2.3 the transfer functions of the seasonal adjustment filters for an admissible component (solid line) and for the canonical component (dotted line) can be seen for the above model (2.21). The 'peaks' of the canonical seasonal adjustment filter are larger than those of the other extraction filter. In fact, the canonical season has less power than any other admissible seasonal component. Therefore, the corresponding seasonal adjustment filter has to remove less spectral power (smaller revision errors, recall the previous section).

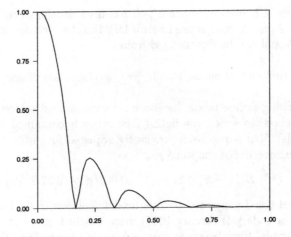

Fig. 2.2. Extraction filter : canonical trend

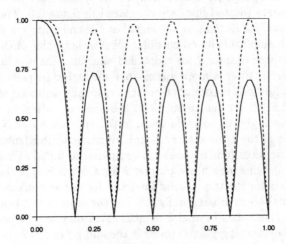

Fig. 2.3. Extraction filter SA: canonical (dotted) and an admissible (solid)

2.3.3 An Example

The following results illustrate the boundary signal estimation problem towards the end point $t = N$ of a sample, where symmetric filters must be replaced by asymmetric designs. A formal description of the example is postponed to chapter 7 after the theoretical 'background' has been provided. It is therefore not necessary to understand precisely the way the results are obtained here.

The proposed MBA has been implemented in TRAMO/SEATS which can be downloaded from www.bde.es. The method is also available in DEMETRA, a user friendly Windows interface which has been developed by EUROSTAT (version 2.0, April 22 2002 is used here). DEMETRA includes also CENSUS-X12-ARIMA and can be downloaded from

http://forum.europa.eu.int/Public/irc/ dsis/eurosam/library.

The following airline-model has been selected and estimated by TRAMO for the UK-car-sales series, see fig.2.4 (the series is contained in the sample files of DEMETRA: it has been previously adjusted for outliers by TRAMO and log-transformed, see chapter 7) :

$$(1 - B)(1 - B^{12})X_t = (1 - 0.60B)(1 - 0.27B^{12})\epsilon_t \qquad (2.22)$$

The canonical trend generated by this model is shown in fig.2.4. As t moves towards the boundary (February 1997) more weight is given to forecasts and the (finite sample) filter becomes more and more asymmetric. The amplitude functions (see chapter 3 for a definition) of the symmetric (solid line) and the asymmetric filters (dotted line) are compared in figure 2.5. The asymmetric filter can be used for estimating the signal at the end point $t = N$. It is easily seen that both amplitude functions differ substantially: this difference leads to revision errors, see chapter 7 for a detailed analysis. The amplitude function of the asymmetric filter is more 'permeable' for higher frequencies.

The trend (solid line) is compared to the seasonally adjusted signal (dotted line) in fig. 2.6. As for the trend filter, the seasonal adjustment (SA) filter becomes increasingly asymmetric towards the end point $t = N$. The amplitude functions of the symmetric seasonal adjustment filter (solid line) and of the asymmetric filter (dotted line) are compared in fig.2.7. Finally, the time delays (one unit=one month, see chapter 3 for a definition) of the asymmetric boundary filters for the trend (solid line) and for the seasonal adjustment filter (dotted line) are compared in fig.2.8. For the asymmetric trend extraction filter the delay increases beyond 3 months. This may lead to problems when the detection of 'turning points' towards the end point $t = N$ is an issue.

The importance of asymmetric boundary filters for practical applications was stressed in section 1.5. Ideally, the time delay of the asymmetric filter should vanish and its selectivity properties (amplitude function) should be as good as those of the symmetric filter. Unfortunately, both requirements cannot be met simultaneously, see chapter 3. If the time delay of the asymmetric filter is 'too large' or if its amplitude function is not selective enough, then its output signal is a poor estimate. It is therefore quite surprising that the properties of the asymmetric boundary filters (of TRAMO or X-12-ARIMA) have not been analyzed or that the corresponding software packages do not provide this information (if it exists). Instead, transfer functions of *symmetric* filters only are available for SEATS (or the corresponding version of SEATS in DEMETRA). This 'lack of interest' may perhaps be explained by the 'faith' modelers put into the forecasting-ability of their models. Indeed, if the DGP

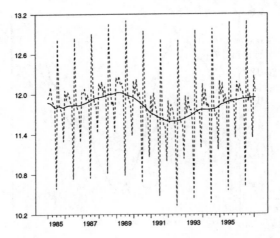

Fig. 2.4. Original series (dotted) and canonical trend (solid)

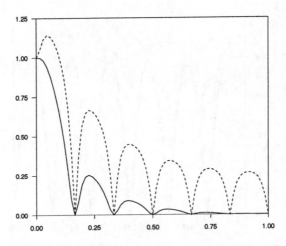

Fig. 2.5. Amplitude of symmetric (solid) and asymmetric (dotted) trend filters

were known, then the resulting asymmetric boundary filters (2.24) would 'automatically' generate optimal estimates in the mean square sense. Therefore, a further analysis of the characteristics of the asymmetric boundary filters would be unnecessary. Findley et al [32] p.176 argue: "Maravall seems to place a heavy reliance on quantities calculated from ARIMA models *under the assumption that the models are correct*, a reliance that goes beyond mere use of a MBA to try to achieve good seasonal adjustments".
If the DGP is unknown and must be inferred from the data then

- models are generally misspecified and

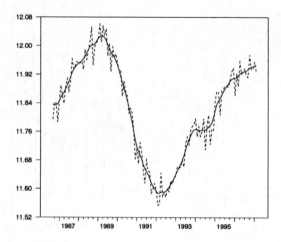

Fig. 2.6. Trend (solid) and seasonally adjusted signals (dotted)

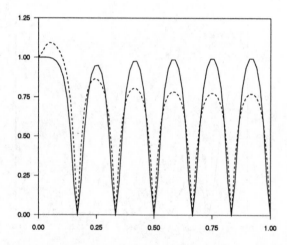

Fig. 2.7. Amplitude symmetric (solid) and asymmetric (dotted) SA-filters

- the optimization criterion for the MBA (the minimization of the one-step ahead mean square forecasting error) does not 'match' the signal estimation problem, see section 1.2.

Therefore, the asymmetric filters of the MBA are generally suboptimal and characteristics such as selectivity and time delay may be informative. Moreover, if one is interested in detecting turning points then time delays (of the asymmetric filter) are important even if the DGP is known.

It is shown in section 5.4 that the revision error variance (i.e. the variance of the filter error) can be decomposed into selectivity and time delay

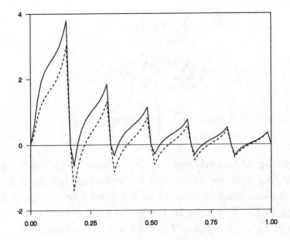

Fig. 2.8. Time delays trend (solid) and SA (dotted)

'components'. Therefore, an analysis of the characteristics of the asymmetric filters (as given by amplitude and time delay functions) can reveal 'deficiencies' which are not detected by traditional diagnostic tools (relying on the one-step ahead forecasting error). More generally, assume that the output Y_t of a symmetric filter is to be estimated for a particular time point, say $t = N$. Then instruments are needed

- for the selection of the 'best' asymmetric filter design (instead of the 'best' model)
- for the estimation of corresponding filter parameters (instead of model parameters)
- for a diagnostic of the performances of the filter (instead of a 'check' of model assumptions)

Corresponding instruments which 'match' specifically the particular structure of the signal estimation problem are proposed in the following chapters. A detailed empirical analysis of these issues is provided in chapters 7 and 8. *For the signal estimation problem, inferring the DGP from a sample of observations is not of prime importance. Instead, an optimal asymmetric filter minimizing the revision error variance is sought. For that purpose the way the information is being processed differs from optimal one-step ahead forecasting.* The revision error variance for the MBA is analyzed in the following section.

2.3.4 The Revision Error Variance

Let $\tilde{Y}_t$ be the output of a symmetric filter (for example the estimate of a signal Y_t as defined by the canonical decomposition). Then

$$\tilde{Y}_t = \sum_{k=-\infty}^{\infty} \gamma_k X_{t-k}$$

$$= \sum_{k=-\infty}^{\infty} \gamma_k \sum_{j=0}^{\infty} b_j \epsilon_{t-k-j}$$

$$= \sum_{k=-\infty}^{\infty} \left(\sum_{j=0}^{\infty} b_j \gamma_{k-j} \right) \epsilon_{t-k} \tag{2.23}$$

where b_k are the MA-coefficients of X_t. These need not to be absolutely summable i.e. X_t may be integrated for example, but in this case it is assumed that X_t has been initialized in the past (for example $X_0 = 0$). The coefficients γ_k in (2.23) belong to the symmetric extraction filter. Therefore, the estimate of Y_{N-r}, $r = 0, ..., N-1$ for the finite sample is

$$\check{Y}_{N-r} = \sum_{k=-r}^{N-r-1} \left(\sum_{j=0}^{\infty} b_j \gamma_{k-j} \right) \epsilon_{N-r-k}$$

because back- and/or forecasts of ϵ_t vanish for $t < 1$ or $t > N$. Note that if $N - r$ is 'large', then the estimate for finite samples can be approximated by

$$\check{Y}_{N-r} \simeq \sum_{k=-r}^{\infty} \left(\sum_{j=0}^{\infty} b_j \gamma_{k-j} \right) \epsilon_{N-r-k} \tag{2.24}$$

because the 'weights' $\sum_{j=0}^{\infty} b_j \gamma_{k-j}$ often converge rapidly to zero (as k increases). Therefore, the revision error variance towards the upper boundary is

$$E[(\tilde{Y}_{N-r} - \check{Y}_{N-r})^2] = \sigma^2 \left\{ \sum_{k=-\infty}^{-r-1} \left(\sum_{j=0}^{\infty} b_j \gamma_{k-j} \right)^2 \right. \tag{2.25}$$

$$\left. + \sum_{k=N-r}^{\infty} \left(\sum_{j=0}^{\infty} b_j \gamma_{k-j} \right)^2 \right\}$$

$$\approx \sigma^2 \sum_{k=-\infty}^{-r-1} \left(\sum_{j=0}^{\infty} b_j \gamma_{k-j} \right)^2 \tag{2.26}$$

where σ^2 is the innovation variance. The right hand side of (2.25) corresponds to the accumulated variance of those ϵ_t which do not appear in the expression on the left hand side of (2.24). The approximation (2.26) is valid if $N - r$ is 'large' because the approximation (2.24) (right hand side) can be used.

The following remarks conclude the presentation of the MBA based on the canonical decomposition.

2.3.5 Concluding Remarks

1. If the DGP is unknown, then the definition of the signals is implicitly dependent on N since it depends on the selected model and on estimated parameters. These issues are discussed in Dosse and Planas [26], p.7. One solution for solving the problem is to 'freeze' models and parameters.

2. Some authors (see for example Hylleberg [56] or Grether and Nerlove and Carvalho [70]) argue that the orthogonality assumption needed for the identification of the components may be a source of misspecification for the model. Indeed, these authors present convincing evidences against the orthogonality assumption of trend and season for particular economic time series.

3. Unaccounted changes in seasonal patterns may lead to spurious seasonal unit-roots, see for example Ghysels [38] or Franses [33]. Often the seasonal unit-root model is "a convenient misspecification" ([38] p. 166). Hylleberg [56] p. 168 argues "that unit-roots only exist at some of the seasonal frequencies". Therefore, the $1 - B^{12}$ operator may be misspecified.

4. Signals are completely defined by the input series X_t and the particular DGP identification and estimation method. Therefore, signals are 're-vealed' (identified) only a posteriori (after a suitable model has been esti-mated). In particular, signals do not depend on the 'research' interest of particular users (see for example Canova [13]). For the analysis of business-cycles Garcia-Ferrer and Bujosa-Brun [35] argue : "... the other methods (the canonical decomposition as implemented in TRAMO/SEATS and the structural models as implemented in STAMP 5.0) provide less smooth variations, and their associated trend derivatives are too volatile and ir-regular to be useful for dating turning-points in monthly data". Analysis and criticism of the canonical components are provided in Stier [83] and [84].

5. An admissible decomposition of an ARIMA-model into orthogonal compo-nents is generally related to parameter restrictions. For the airline model this amounts to a simple restriction for θ_s ($\theta_s > 0$) which is generally achieved because the I(2)-assumption often induces a 'convenient' overdif-ferencing of real-world time series. Therefore 'admissibility' is generally not an issue when using an airline model.

6. The results in section 2.3.2 demonstrate that the (canonical) decomposi-tion into orthogonal components can be involving: analytical expressions are often complicated non-linear functions of the parameters even for the relatively simple airline model. The resulting 'complexity' (of the canoni-

cal decomposition) implicitly restricts the set of possible ARIMA-models for a time series X_t.

The model-based approaches relying on the earlier Beveridge-Nelson decomposition and on the canonical decomposition are based on ARIMA-models for X_t. In the following section another method is presented which is based on models for the *components* of X_t.

2.4 Structural Components Model

Without strong arbitrary a priori hypotheses the components T_t, C_t, S_t and I_t in (2.1) are not uniquely defined for the preceding two approaches. 'Models' for the components (the transfer functions on the right hand side of (2.20)) are unknown a priori since they are derived (by partial fractions) from the ARIMA-model for X_t which is unknown too (a priori). Therefore, it is generally impossible to account for 'a priori knowledge' about the components. Moreover, the components may be uninterpretable a posteriori. Grether, Nerlove and Carvalho [70] and Harvey [47] circumvent the identification and interpretation problems by specifying 'plausible' models (DGP's) *for the components* a priori.

The MBA in the preceding two sections corresponded to a 'top-down' identification strategy for which the DGP of X_t is decomposed into uniquely defined components. The present approach is a 'bottom-up' modelling strategy which derives the DGP of X_t from the prespecified DGP's of its components. Harvey and Todd [49], p.341-358 motivate the structural components model by the following arguments :

- ARIMA-models are often difficult to identify ('traditional' methods like correlogram and partial autocorrelation analysis do not always provide accurate estimates of the model orders p, q for small samples)
- the relation of the DGP of X_t to its components is often 'obscure' (transfer functions of the components are 'cumbersome' non-linear functions of the parameters of the DGP, see section 2.3.2). Therefore, an interpretation of the resulting components is difficult or impossible to achieve.

Harvey [48] p.194 argues that "The problem with ARIMA class is that there are many models and parameter values which have no sensible interpretation and give forecast functions which may have undesirable properties". Harvey and Todd [49] suggest that "an alternative way of proceeding is to formulate models directly in terms of trend, seasonal and irregular components. This necessarily limits the choice to those models that have forecast functions satisfying any prior considerations. Such models will be termed structural models".

Definition 2.2. *Their so called basic structural model (BSM) is defined by*

$$X_t = T_t + S_t + \epsilon_t$$
$$T_t = T_{t-1} + \beta_{t-1} + \nu_t$$
$$\beta_t = \beta_{t-1} + \xi_t$$
$$S_t = -\sum_{k=1}^{s-1} S_{t-k} + \eta_t$$

where the noise terms are (mutually independent) iid gaussian random variables. T_t can be interpreted as a 'locally' linear trend with varying (adaptive) level and slope:

- for $\sigma_\xi^2 > 0$ the 'slope' β_t is a random walk process,
- for $\sigma_\xi^2 = 0$ the trend T_t is a random walk with drift $\beta_t \equiv \beta_0$
- for $\sigma_\nu^2 = \sigma_\xi^2 = 0$ the trend T_t is a linear function of t with slope β_0

As for the trend, the parameter σ_η^2 'controls' the stability of the seasonal component. The only parameters in the above model are the variances of the white noise processes. The authors argue that "although the model is relatively simple, it contains the main ingredients necessary for a time series forecasting procedure in that it projects a local linear trend and a local seasonal pattern into the future". Further advantages of the model are:

- no identification problem and no admissibility constraints
- the DGP of X_t is given by

$$X_t = \frac{\rho_t}{(1-B)^2} + \frac{\eta_t}{U(B)} + \epsilon_t$$

where ρ_t is an MA(1) process (see for example Harvey and Todd [49], p.346 for a derivation). Since one can show that distinct parameters act separately on trend and season, a confusion is excluded here (recall that θ_{12} influences both the season and the trend for the airline-model).

As shown in Harvey [47], model parameters and components can be efficiently estimated by a so called 'state space approach', using the well known Kalman-filter (and smoother) for deriving the likelihood function (if the assumptions of the model are satisfied). A state space representation of the BSM is given by

$$
\begin{pmatrix} T_t \\ \beta_t \\ S_t \\ S_{t-1} \\ \cdots \\ S_{t-(s-2)} \end{pmatrix}
=
\begin{pmatrix}
1 & 1 & 0 & \cdots & 0 & 0 \\
0 & 1 & 0 & \cdots & 0 & 0 \\
0 & 0 & -1 & \cdots & -1 & -1 \\
0 & 0 & 1 & \cdots & 0 & 0 \\
\cdots & \cdots & \cdots & \cdots & \cdots & 0 \\
0 & 0 & 0 & \cdots & 1 & 0
\end{pmatrix}
\begin{pmatrix} T_{t-1} \\ \beta_{t-1} \\ S_{t-1} \\ S_{t-2} \\ \cdots \\ S_{t-(s-1)} \end{pmatrix}
+
\begin{pmatrix} \nu_t \\ \xi_t \\ \eta_t \\ 0 \\ \cdots \\ 0 \end{pmatrix}
$$

$$X_t = (\,1\ 0\ 1\ 0\ \cdots\ 0\,) \begin{pmatrix} T_t \\ \beta_t \\ S_t \\ S_{t-1} \\ \cdots \\ S_{t-s} \end{pmatrix} + \epsilon_t$$

see Harvey [47]. Evidently, more complex components models (than those implied by the BSM) can be considered. The trend can for example be defined by a 'local' polynomial of arbitrary order, see Harrison and Stevens [46]. A recent survey of possible seasonal models (DGP's) is given in Proietti [76]. The latter author also compares various models with respect to their forecasting performances.

The structural components model provides an alternative approach for defining signals and deriving an expression for the DGP of X_t ('bottom-up' modelling strategy). However, despite obvious differences to the MBA in the previous two sections, the structural components model-based approach does not solve the finite sample signal estimation problem (namely to approximate symmetric filters by asymmetric designs) differently. In fact, state space models and the Kalman filter provide a 'convenient' method for deriving the likelihood function of the DGP of X_t (if the components are not misspecified). Since the model assumes gaussian white noise sequences, the optimization criterion bases on the minimization of the *one*-step ahead mean-square forecasting error (as for the previous two MBA). The main difference to the preceding ARIMA-MBA lies in the 'coding' of the information i.e. in the structure of the model for the DGP of X_t.

If the DGP is unknown, then models are generally misspecified. Inferences about the integration order of the process based on hypotheses of the type $\sigma_\nu^2 = 0$ or $\sigma_\xi^2 = 0$ are often difficult to assess and decisions based on one-step ahead forecasting performances may be misleading for multi-step ahead usage. Therefore, the signal estimates - especially boundary estimates - are generally inefficient because the signal estimation problem involves one- and multi-step ahead forecasts. Ultimately, advocates of the structural components model argue that the 'amount of misspecification' may be smaller or at least that misspecification is better 'under control' for the particular 'coding' (of the information) proposed by this approach. However, it is not clear why this claim should be pertinent in the context of the boundary estimation problem of signal extraction. In order to overcome the discrepancy between the one-step ahead forecasting performance (on which the method relies) and the accuracy of the resulting asymmetric filter (which is of interest) too parsimonious models are generally selected which cannot fully account for the 'salient' features of practical time series (the more or less complex low-frequency and seasonal components). An alternative 'coding' of the information is proposed in chapter 3 where a new filter class is presented - so called ZPC-filters - which are specifically designed for the boundary signal estimation problem.

The following arguments should also be taken into account.

- There are known limitations for the Kalman-filter approach, see for example Maddala and Kim [44] p. 475-478.
- Arbitrary identifying assumptions of the ARIMA-MBA in the preceding two sections are replaced by arbitrary a priori definitions of the DGP's of the components for the structural components model.

The structural components model approach has been implemented in STAMP (Structural Time series Analyzer, Modeler and Predictor). See http://stamp-software.com for more information about the topic.

2.5 CENSUS X-12-ARIMA

X-12-ARIMA is the latest version of the seasonal adjustment procedure of the Census Bureau (Washington). It is described in Findley et al [32] (see also the reference manual [72]). Both documents as well as the software package can be downloaded from the ftp-server ftp.census.gov. Readers interested in technical details are referred to these sources. In this section, the presentation of X-12-ARIMA is informal.

X-12-ARIMA combines so called 'regARIMA'-models and the well known X-11 procedure. The latter has become "something of a standard that was used by statistical agencies around the world", see Findley et al [32] p.127. Basically, the 'novelty' of X-12-ARIMA is to provide model-based 'information' to X-11 in order to enhance boundary estimates (finite sample estimation problem). Therefore, one can distinguish the 'new' model-based part and the 'old' X-11 part (note that more filter specifications and new decompositions are now available in X-11 which has been 'refreshed' too).

In X-11 various decompositions such as an additive, a multiplicative, a log-additive or a pseudo-additive decomposition are provided, see section 1.1 in Findley et al.[32]. Descriptions of the X-11 'default' procedures for various decomposition are also provided in this article, p.149. The following three stages can be distinguished:

1. Compute preliminary estimates of the trend and the season based on 'simple' filters (for example a centered 12-term moving average for the trend). A first seasonal adjustment is performed.
2. More 'sophisticated' trend filters, so called Henderson-filters, are used to estimate the trend based on the previously adjusted series. Final seasonal factors are computed for the detrended series. The final seasonal adjustment is performed.

3. Compute the final trend using a Henderson filter (whose order can be made 'data dependent') for the previously seasonally adjusted series. The final irregular component is obtained as $I_t := X_t - T_t - S_t$ for the additive decomposition (and similarly for the other decompositions).

The transfer function of the resulting trend filter is shown in Findley et al. [32], fig.3 p.131 (symmetric filter). Edel and Stier [27], p.207-222 use an ingenious device for computing the transfer function of the trend and the seasonal adjustment filter of X-11 empirically, see figs. 1-4 and 9-12 in the cited document. Analytic expressions for these functions are generally not available because different filters 'interact' in a complex way in the three-stage procedure briefly described above. Therefore, empirical evaluations are important for assessing the properties of X-11.

The central trend filter of X-11 is the Henderson filter (which 'interacts' with various filters in the three stage procedure). The symmetric Henderson filter has been originally designed for satisfying a 'smoothness' criterion subject to the restriction that a cubic polynomial (in t) can pass the filter without being altered, see Henderson [50], [51]. More recently, Gray and Thomson [41] have shown that some requirements are unnecessarily severe. To see this, let

$$X_{t+j} := a + b(t+j) + c(t+j)^2 \ , \ j = -(n+3), -(n+2), ..., n \quad (2.27)$$

The authors show that the coefficients h_j of a Henderson filter of order n are determined by requiring

$$\sum_{j=-n}^{n} h_j X_{t+j} = X_t$$

and

$$E\left[\left\{\Delta^3 \left(\sum_{j=-n}^{n} h_j(X_{t+j} + \epsilon_{t+j})\right)\right\}^2\right] = E\left[\{\Delta^3(\sum_{j=-n}^{n} h_j \epsilon_{t+j})\}^2\right] \rightarrow \min$$

where Δ^3 is the third difference operator and ϵ_t is a gaussian white noise sequence (the equality follows from $\Delta^3 X_{t+j} = 0$). The above expectation may be interpreted as a measure of smoothness so that the Henderson filter satisfies a smoothness optimality criterion. It can be shown that $h_j = h_{-j}$ so that the symmetry is a consequence of the above weaker requirements. Since the coefficients h_j correspond to a Henderson filter, cubic polynomials pass the filter also without being altered.

The output of the Henderson filter of order n must become 'smoother' for increasing n because quadratic (or cubic) polynomials have at most one (or two) turning point(s) in $-(n+3), -(n+2), ..., n$. Evidently, large n imply heavily asymmetric boundary filters: improved smoothness induces larger revision errors towards the end point $t = N$. This statement is not specific to Henderson filters but merely results from a fundamental uncertainty principle, which is for example described in Grenander [42] and Priestley [75] chap. 7. The 13-term ($n = 13$) Henderson filter is often used for monthly data. However, the trend cannot be very smooth because a cubic polynomial can exhibit two extremes in the corresponding interval (of length 13). Therefore, the trend is not free of 'subannual' variations, see for example figure 2.10 below and Schips and Stier [81] and Findley et al.[32],p.130 and fig.3 p.131. Attempts for weakening the problem have been proposed in Dagum [23] and Dagum et al. [24]. Findley et al [32] p.134 argue that "X-11's relatively short-term trends cannot fully capture long-term correlation in the data if it exists". The relatively small order $n = 13$ is often preferred because it is associated with revision errors of 'acceptable' size towards the end point $t = N$. For the newer X-12-ARIMA procedure, the order of the Henderson filter can be made data dependent through the so called 'variable trend cycle routine', see Findley et al.[32] p 150,151.

Towards the boundaries of the sample, the symmetric filters of X-11 are originally replaced by asymmetric filters, so called 'Musgrave Surrogates', see Findley et al.[32], p.150. The latter minimize the error variance of the estimates if the input process is a linear trend overlapped by gaussian white noise, see Musgrave [69] and Laniel [60]. Wallis [92] argues that X-11 is an inconsistent procedure because the symmetric Henderson filter assumes a local cubic trend, whereas the asymmetric filter assumes a local linear trend (see also the reply of Findley et al. [32] p.173, which argue that pure MBA are inconsistent too). This concludes the brief informal overview of the 'old' X-11-part.

X-12-ARIMA uses so called regARIMA-models. The 'regression part' accounts for deterministic effects (such as for example 'calendar effects'), for singular effects (for example outliers or level shifts) or even for missing data, see for example [32] p.129. Once these effects have been removed, the 'ARIMA-part' provides forecasts of the 'adjusted' or 'linearized' series. Note that both aspects cannot be strictly separated in practice: regression- and ARIMA-part interact until a 'convenient' regARIMA-model is identified. As a result, symmetric filters of X-11 can be used for the series extended by back- and forecasts (the original asymmetric filters of X-11 are no more of prime importance). Therefore, X-12-ARIMA solves the finite sample signal estimation problem as described in section 1.2.

Wallis [92] p. 165 argues "In any event X-12-ARIMA is not a model-based approach". Findley et al. [32] p. 172 confirm this statement "no stochastic model can produce an adjustment filter, through conventional signal extraction, that contains just the U(B)(1+F) unit-roots (as given in X-11)" and on p. 173 "no stochastic model leads to any of the symmetric Henderson filters because the latter's transfer functions are negative for some frequencies, something that cannot result from Wiener-Kolmogorov signal extraction". In fact the filters of the 'old' X-11 (and thus of X-12) are not explicitly designed for estimating a properly defined stochastic component (attempts have been made to approximate the additive decomposition of X-11 by linear signal extraction filters, see for example Wallis [91] and Cleveland and Tiao [17]). Wallis [92] p.164 argues : "neither Musgrave nor any later author has asked whether the symmetric Henderson filter produces a good estimate of the trend, however: for this purpose the trend is simply defined as the Henderson output". In our view, this is not completely correct, since the trend is defined as the output of the Henderson filter in *the last stage* of the above procedure: the corresponding filter is something like a 'Henderson with seasonal dips'.

Henderson filters satisfy a particular smoothness criterion whose relation to 'signal extraction' is not immediately obvious. For X-11 (and X-12) a 'component' like the trend has no other interpretation than being the output of the corresponding filter. Schaeffer [80], p.35 classifies X-11 into the family of so called 'implicit' seasonal adjustment procedures (implicitly defined components). With respect to 'detrending' Wallis [92] p.164 argues:"thus Henderson detrending reduces an I(4) series to I(0) and overdifferences an I(d) series if $d < 4$. Overdifferencing implies noninvertibility of the output series and hence the absence of a convergent autoregressive representation". This may be important if the detrended series is to be forecasted.

The above objections address the definition of the components for the 'old' X-11-part. However, the signal estimation problem for finite samples is solved by the 'new' ARIMA-MBA. Therefore, X-12-ARIMA is considered as a MBA in the particular perspective of this book.

Implicit component definitions are a drawback because interpretations are not possible. However, it is not clear if model-based approaches propose a 'better' solution (see for example section 2.3.5). Cleveland [16] p. 154 argues: "It can be difficult to model time series, and X-12 appears to deal with awkward series better than many signal-extraction procedures would, or at least do it with less work" and, as stated already, Findley et al. [32] p.176 argue "Maravall seems to place a heavy reliance on quantities calculated from ARIMA models *under the assumption that the models are correct*, a reliance that goes beyond mere use of a MBA to try to achieve good seasonal adjustments". Note that the last argument addresses X-12-ARIMA too, so for example Morry and Chhab [68] p. 161 "not all series lend themselves readily to regARIMA modelling" and the same authors p.163 : "it does not necessarily follow, however, that the method with the lower forecast errors yields better seasonally adjusted estimates". The last statement confirms forecasting issues briefly mentioned in section 1.2 and analyzed in Clements and Hendry [14]. This concludes our informal overview on X-12-ARIMA. A short example is now provided.

X-11 has become "something like a standard" and as such it is available in various statistical software packages like for example SAS, RATS, SPSS or Eviews. The 'new' X-12-ARIMA has not yet supplanted X-11 in all these packages (probably because they provide own identification and estimation procedures for the DGP of X_t). X-12-ARIMA can be downloaded from ftp.census.gov. Comfortable versions with graphical facilities and easy access to diagnostic tools have been implemented in Eviews 4 and in DEMETRA, see section 2.3.3. The latter is used here.

The X-12-ARIMA trend for the UK car-sales series is shown in fig. 2.9 (the series has been linearized and log-transformed, see chapter 7). X-12-ARIMA

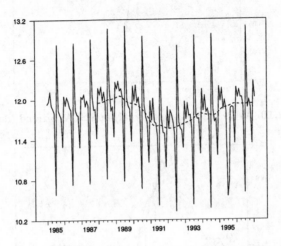

Fig. 2.9. Input series (solid) and X-12-ARIMA trend (dotted)

trend (solid line) and SEATS trend (dotted line) are compared in figure 2.10. As can be seen, the order of the (automatically) selected 13-term Henderson filter may be too low (there are unnecessarily many turning-points). Finally, the permanent component of the Beveridge-Nelson decomposition ('rough' series) is compared to the trends of X-12-ARIMA and SEATS in figure 2.11. As can be seen, *different identifying (a priori) assumptions may lead to dramatic differences between outputs of the symmetric filters for the theoretical components (here : trends).*

This concludes the (necessarily restrictive) presentation of important 'established' MBA. In the next chapter the main concepts for characterizing filters in the frequency domain are proposed. A well-known general class of asymmetric filters is then derived for the boundary signal estimation problem. In order to improve 'out of sample' results and to control for overfitting a new filter class is proposed and analyzed. It is characterized by improved 'parsimony' (few parameters to estimate) and a straightforward interpretation of the remaining degrees of freedom. This filter class is used for the examples in chapters 7 and 8.

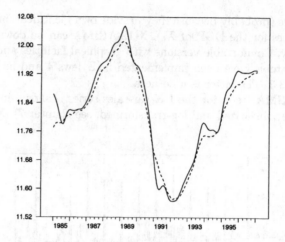

Fig. 2.10. X-12-ARIMA trend (solid) and SEATS trend (dotted)

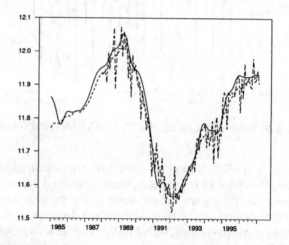

Fig. 2.11. Census-, Tramo- and Beveridge-Nelson-trends

3

QMP-ZPC Filters

The objective is to approximate (outputs of) symmetric filters by (outputs of) asymmetric filters towards the boundaries of a sample. A general filter class is needed here because input signals and symmetric filters are of a general form too, recall section 1.5 and chapter 2. Some care is needed however, since it was suggested in section 1.1 that 'excessive' generality may lead to overfitting problems : good 'in sample' performances may be contradicted by poor 'out of sample' performances. Therefore, a *general* and *parsimonious* filter class is proposed in this chapter.

In Section 3.1 concepts relevant to the frequency domain are presented: an informal introduction to the theoretical material presented in chapter 5 is provided. In section 3.2 parsimonious filter designs (ARMA, minimum phase and quasi minimum phase (QMP) filters) are introduced. Finally, a new filter class, the so called zero-pole combination (ZPC) filter, is presented in section 3.3. The latter filter design is characterized by a constraint which stresses further parsimony and which enables a straightforward interpretation of the remaining degrees of freedom.

3.1 Filters : Definitions and Concepts

Definition 3.1. *A sequence γ_k of square summable numbers ($\sum_{k=-\infty}^{\infty} |\gamma_k|^2 < \infty$) is called a filter. The complex function $\Gamma(\cdot) : [-\pi, \pi] \to \overline{\mathbb{C}}$ defined by :*

$$\Gamma(\omega) := \sum_{k=-\infty}^{\infty} \gamma_k \exp(-ik\omega)$$

is called the transfer function of the filter γ_k. If the sequences Y_t and X_t are related by

$$Y_t = \sum_{k=-\infty}^{\infty} \gamma_k X_{t-k}$$

then Y_t, X_t are called the output and the input signals of the filter γ_k respectively.

In the following, the concepts of 'filter' and 'transfer function' are merged. Therefore, $\Gamma(\cdot)$ is called a filter. Conditions under which this identification is allowed formally are well known, see for example Gasquet and Witomsky [36] or standard textbooks in functional or Fourier analysis. A sufficient condition for this 'merging' is the continuity of $\Gamma(\cdot)$ on $[-\pi, \pi]$ which is assumed in the following. A filter $\Gamma(\cdot)$ is called *real* if $\gamma_k \in \mathbb{R}$ for all k (in this case $\Gamma(0) \in \mathbb{R}$) and it is called *symmetric* if $\gamma_k = \gamma_{-k}$ for all k. If $\Gamma(\cdot)$ is symmetric and real then $\Gamma(\omega) \in \mathbb{R}$ for all ω.

Let $X_1, ..., X_N$ be a finite sample and consider the signal

$$Y_t = \sum_{k=-\infty}^{\infty} \gamma_k X_{t-k}$$

where $\Gamma(\cdot)$ is some real filter : if there exist t_0, k_0 such that $1 \leq t_0 \leq N$ and $t_0 - k_0 < 1$ or $t_0 - k_0 > N$ and $\gamma_{k_0} \neq 0$ then Y_{t_0} cannot be computed directly from $X_1, ..., X_N$. Instead, Y_{t_0} has to be estimated. For that purpose, define the following general distance measure between two filters $\Gamma(\cdot)$ and $\hat{\Gamma}(\cdot)$:

$$\sum_{k=-[N/2]}^{[N/2]} |\Gamma(\omega_k) - \hat{\Gamma}(\omega_k)|^2 G(\omega_k) \qquad (3.1)$$

where $\omega_k \in [-\pi, \pi]$ for all k and where it is assumed that $G(\cdot) \geq 0$ and the coefficients of $\hat{\Gamma}(\cdot)$ satisfy:

$$\hat{\gamma}_k = 0 , \ k \notin \{t_0 - 1, ..., t_0 - N\} \qquad (3.2)$$

The latter condition ensures that the output

$$\hat{Y}_{t_0} = \sum_{k=t_0-N}^{t_0-1} \hat{\gamma}_k X_{t_0-k} \qquad (3.3)$$

can be computed using the finite sample $X_1, ..., X_N$. Thus an estimate $\hat{Y}_{t_0}$ of the unknown Y_{t_0} may be defined by the output of the filter $\hat{\Gamma}(\cdot)$ minimizing (3.1). For particular ω_k and particular 'weights' $G(\omega_k)$ it is shown in chapter 5 that the resulting $\hat{Y}_{t_0}$ satisfies an optimality criterion for a general class of input signals X_t. However, the necessary theoretical background must be put up first.

A direct optimization of the filter coefficients $\hat{\gamma}_k$ in (3.3) involves too many unknown parameters. Therefore, an attempt should be made to 'parameterize' the $\hat{\gamma}_k$ using 'few' parameters. For that purpose, the classical ARMA-approximation method is proposed here (see for example Box and Jenkins [9] and Stier and Wildi [86]). Consider the following input-output relation:

$$Y_t = \sum_{k=1}^{Q} a_k Y_{t-k} + \sum_{k=-r}^{q} b_k X_{t-k} \tag{3.4}$$

where $r := N - t_0$, $Q + q + r << N$ and where it is assumed that the roots of the characteristic polynomial $1 - \sum_{k=1}^{Q} a_k z^k$ lie outside the unit circle. The resulting filter is called a *stable ARMA filter*. It is then well known that the input-output relation (3.4) can be expressed by

$$Y_t = \sum_{k=-r}^{\infty} c_k X_{t-k} \tag{3.5}$$

where the coefficients c_k decay towards 0 in a suitable manner, e.g. exponentially fast. Expression (3.5) is called the equivalent $MA(\infty)$ representation of the ARMA filter. The sequence c_k is now determined by $Q + q + r + 1 (<< N)$ parameters only. One difficulty remains, since the coefficients in (3.5) do not satisfy (3.2). This problem may be solved for example by

- truncating the equivalent $MA(\infty)$-representation of the ARMA-filter at $k = t_0 - 1$ or
- by a suitable *initialization* of the filter (corresponding solutions are presented in the appendix).

Note however an important difference between ARMA-*processes* and (3.4): for the former, the input signal is a white noise sequence whereas for the latter the input signal X_t is a general - not necessarily stationary - process.

From definition 3.1 the transfer function of the ARMA-filter (3.4) is given by

$$
\begin{aligned}
\hat{\Gamma}^p(\omega) &= \frac{\sum_{k=-r}^{q} b_k \exp(-ik\omega)}{1 - \sum_{k=1}^{Q} a_k \exp(-ik\omega)} \\
&= C \exp(ir\omega) \frac{\prod_{j=1}^{n}(Z_{2j-1} - \exp(-i\omega))(Z_{2j} - \exp(-i\omega))}{\prod_{k=1}^{n'}(P_{2k-1} - \exp(-i\omega))(P_{2k} - \exp(-i\omega))} \\
&\quad \times \frac{\prod_{j=2n+1}^{q+r}(Z_j - \exp(-i\omega))}{\prod_{k=2n'+1}^{Q}(P_k - \exp(-i\omega))}
\end{aligned}
\tag{3.6}
$$

where $Z_{2j} := \bar{Z}_{2j-1}$, $j = 1, ..., n$ and $P_{2k} := \bar{P}_{2k-1}$ (i.e. (Z_{2j-1}, Z_{2j}), $j = 1, ..., n$ are complex conjugate *zeroes* and (P_{2k-1}, P_{2k}), $k = 1, ..., n'$ are complex conjugate *poles*) and $Z_j, j = 2n + 1, ..., q + r$ are real zeroes, $P_k, k = 2n' + 1, ..., Q$ are real poles and C is a real constant (normalization). The equivalent representation (3.6) follows from a factorization of the numerator and denominator polynomials in the 'variable' $\exp(-i\omega)$. The index 'p' denotes the number of parameters i.e. $q + r + Q + 1 = p$. For notational simplicity the index 'p' is dropped (if it is not explicitly required) so that $\hat{\Gamma}^p(\omega)$

is written $\hat{\Gamma}(\omega)$. *Stability* (or equivalently the existence of a convergent MA representation of the ARMA filter) requires $|P_k| > 1, k = 1, ..., Q$ and *invertibility* requires $|Z_k| > 1, k = 1, ..., q + r$ (invertibility means that the filter possesses a convergent AR representation). The importance of these properties of the ARMA filter is stressed in section 3.2. Here and in the following, ARMA-filters are denoted with a 'hat' because they are used for solving the signal estimation problem for finite samples.

Consider the following identity

$$\Gamma(\omega) \equiv |\Gamma(\omega)| \exp(i \arg(\Gamma(\omega)) \tag{3.7}$$

where $\Gamma(\cdot)$ is a general transfer function (not necessarily symmetric or of 'ARMA-form') and note that $\Gamma(\cdot)$ determines $\arg(\cdot)$ up to multiples of 2π if the transfer function does not vanish.

Definition 3.2. *Let γ_k be a real filter whose transfer function $\Gamma(\cdot)$ is continuous, vanishes nowhere and satisfies $\Gamma(0) > 0$. The amplitude and the phase functions of $\Gamma(\omega)$ are then defined by*

$$A(\omega) := |\Gamma(\omega)|$$
$$\Phi(\omega) := -\arg(\Gamma(\omega))$$

where $\arg(\cdot)$ is defined as a continuous and odd function of ω.

Remarks

- $\Gamma(0) = \sum_{k=-\infty}^{\infty} \gamma_k \in \mathbb{R}$ by assumption. Therefore, the requirement $\Gamma(0) > 0$ in the previous definition is well defined. It constrains the 'sign' of the filter.
- Since the phase is odd and continuous it must satisfy $\Phi(0) = 0$.
- The 'traditional' $\arctan(\cdot)$ function (as it is implemented in most software packages) does generally not fulfill the above requirements for $\arg(\cdot)$. In particular, it is generally discontinuous.
- The phase function of a real and symmetric filter vanishes identically.

If $\Gamma(\cdot)$ does not vanish and is analytic in a region including the unit circle, then the phase function is infinitely often differentiable : from (3.7) the solution is given by

$$\Phi(\omega) := i\Big(\ln(\Gamma(\omega)) - \ln(A(\omega)) \Big) \tag{3.8}$$

where $\ln(\cdot)$ is defined as the principal branch of the complex logarithm, see for example Ahlfors [1], chap.8. Requiring $\arg(\cdot)$ to be continuous and odd uniquely determines the phase function of stable invertible ARMA-filters :

Proposition 3.3. *The phase function $\hat{\Phi}(\cdot)$ of a stable invertible ARMA filter exists and is uniquely defined.*

Proof. Stability requires $|P_k| > 1, k = 1, ..., Q$ so that the transfer function is analytic in an annulus containing the unit circle. Invertibility requires $|Z_k| > 1, k = 1, ..., q + r$ and thus there exists an open set including the unit circle for which the (analytic) transfer function does not vanish. From (3.8) a continuous and odd phase function then exists. Assume $\hat{\Phi}(\cdot)$ and $\hat{\Phi}'(\cdot)$ are two continuous and odd functions satisfying

$$\hat{\Gamma}(\omega) = \hat{A}(\omega) \exp(-i\hat{\Phi}(\omega)) \tag{3.9}$$

Then $1 = \exp\left(-i\left(\hat{\Phi}(\omega) - \hat{\Phi}'(\omega)\right)\right)$ for all ω because the transfer function does not vanish on the unit circle. Thus $\hat{\Phi}(\omega) = \hat{\Phi}'(\omega) + k(\omega)2\pi$ where $k(\omega) \in \mathbb{Z}$. The mean value theorem then implies $k(\omega) \equiv k_0$. Since both functions are odd and continuous, they satisfy $\hat{\Phi}(0) = \hat{\Phi}'(0) = 0$, so that $k_0 = 0$ which proves the proposition. $\square$

If

$$\hat{\Gamma}(\cdot) := \prod_{k=1}^{m} \hat{\Gamma}_k(\cdot)$$

is a stable invertible ARMA filter then $\sum_{k=1}^{m} \hat{\Phi}_{\Gamma_k}(\cdot)$ is a continuous and odd function satisfying (3.7). Thus the uniqueness property implies

$$\hat{\Phi}_{\hat{\Gamma}_1 \cdots \hat{\Gamma}_m}(\cdot) = \sum_{k=1}^{m} \hat{\Phi}_{\hat{\Gamma}_k}(\cdot) \tag{3.10}$$

so that the phase function is a homomorphism.

The following description of the properties of the phase function as well as its interpretation are informal. It provides a first introduction in concepts treated in chapter 5. Let the (complex) input signal of a stable and invertible ARMA filter satisfying $\hat{\Gamma}(0) > 0$ be given by $X_t := \exp(i\omega t)$, $t \in \mathbb{Z}$. From

$$\sum_{k=-r}^{\infty} \hat{\gamma}_k \exp(i\omega(t-k)) = \exp(i\omega t) \sum_{k=-r}^{\infty} \hat{\gamma}_k \exp(-i\omega k) = \exp(i\omega t)\hat{\Gamma}(\omega) \tag{3.11}$$

one deduces that $X_t, t \in \mathbb{Z}$ is a periodic *eigensignal* of the filter with eigenvalue $\hat{\Gamma}(\omega)$. Denote $\hat{\Gamma}(X_t) := \sum_{k=-r}^{\infty} \hat{\gamma}_k X_{t-k}$. The linearity of the filter then implies:

$$\hat{\Gamma}(\text{Re}(X_t)) + i\hat{\Gamma}(\text{Im}(X_t)) = \hat{\Gamma}(X_t) = \text{Re}(\hat{\Gamma}(X_t)) + i\,\text{Im}(\hat{\Gamma}(X_t))$$

This together with (3.11) implies that $\cos(\omega t)$ and $\sin(\omega t)$ are eigenfunctions too. Moreover, input and output signals are related by

$$\cos(t\omega) \rightarrow A(\omega)\left[\cos(t\omega)\cos(-\hat{\Phi}(\omega)) - \sin(t\omega)\sin(-\hat{\Phi}(\omega))\right]$$

$$= A(\omega)\cos(t\omega - \hat{\Phi}(\omega)) \qquad (3.12)$$

$$\sin(t\omega) \to A(\omega)\left[\cos(t\omega)\sin(-\hat{\Phi}(\omega)) + \sin(t\omega)\cos(-\hat{\Phi}(\omega))\right]$$

$$= A(\omega)\sin(t\omega - \hat{\Phi}(\omega)) \qquad (3.13)$$

where $A(\cdot) := |\Gamma(\cdot)|$, so that

$$\cos(t\omega) \to A(\omega)\cos(\omega(t - \hat{\Phi}(\omega)/\omega))$$
$$\sin(t\omega) \to A(\omega)\sin(\omega(t - \hat{\Phi}(\omega)/\omega))$$

Thus $\hat{\phi}(\omega) := \hat{\Phi}(\omega)/\omega$ may be interpreted as a *time shift function* of the ARMA filter at frequency ω. Equation (3.10) then shows that time shifts of serially connected filters add (homomorphism). Moreover,

$$\lim_{\omega \to 0} \hat{\phi}(\omega) = \lim_{\omega \to 0} \hat{\Phi}(\omega)/\omega = \left.\frac{d\hat{\Phi}}{d\omega}\right|_{\omega=0}$$

exists because $\hat{\Phi}(\omega)$ was defined as a continuous (infinitely often differentiable for stable and invertible ARMA-filters, see above) and odd function. The existence follows from $\hat{\Phi}(0) = 0$ and from a Taylor series approximation at the origin. The time shift $\hat{\phi}(0)$ of the filter at frequency zero plays an important role for integrated input processes, see section 5.3.

The condition $\hat{\Gamma}(0) > 0$ required in definition 3.2 is necessary because the identity $-\cos(t\omega) = \cos(t\omega+\pi)$ implies that the phase function of a filter satisfying $\hat{\Gamma}(0) < 0$ cannot be both continuous and odd (because $\Phi(0) = \pi$). Also, the time shift of such a filter cannot be bounded if $\omega \to 0$ (i.e. $\pi/\omega \to \infty$ as ω approaches zero). The time shift is an important characteristic of an asymmetric filter because 'good' filters (generating 'good' signal estimates) are characterized by 'small' time shifts and 'good' selectivity properties, see for example chapters 5, 7 and 8. The time shift is defined for most relevant signal extraction filters (such as seasonal adjustment or trend filters for example) because they often satisfy $\hat{\Gamma}(0) = 1 > 0$, i.e. the assumption $\hat{\Gamma}(0) > 0$ is satisfied.

Definition 3.2 can be extended to non-invertible ARMA filters with zeroes on the unit circle. The phase then becomes a piecewise continuous and odd function (formal aspects are ignored here).

The amplitude function $A(\omega)$ may be interpreted as the weight (damping if $A(\omega) < 1$, amplification if $A(\omega) > 1$) given by the filter to a sinusoidal input signal of frequency ω. It characterizes the *selectivity* properties of a filter.

In (3.1), the signal estimation problem is reduced to the minimization of a particular measure of the 'distance' between transfer functions. This problem can now be stated in terms of amplitude and phase functions, i.e. in terms of selectivity and time shift 'fitting'. Suppose $\hat{\Gamma}(\cdot)$ is used for approximating $\Gamma(\cdot)$. Then

- $\hat{A}(\omega)$ should 'mimic' $A(\omega)$ and
- $\hat{\Phi}(\cdot)$ should 'mimic' $\Phi(\cdot)$ (the latter vanishes identically for symmetric filters).

Both the selectivity properties (as given by the amplitude functions) and the time shifts should match as closely as possible. Section 3.2 and chapter 5 show that these requirements are conflicting so that *efficient boundary signal estimation is the result of an optimal compromise between both requirements.*

The aim of decomposing the transfer function into amplitude and phase functions is *to separate selectivity and time shift properties of a filter.* This gives access to more flexible optimization procedures, including for example the 'faster' detection of turning points (of a particular trend component) by computing filters with 'best' possible selectivity characteristics subject to a time shift (phase) constraint, see section 5.4. *Model-based approaches do not allow for such flexibility* because the transfer function of the boundary filter (1.4) is obtained implicitly. Therefore, a decomposition into phase and amplitude matchings is impossible.

In the next section a first restriction of the ARMA-filter class is proposed. This is based on time-shift properties of the filters.

3.2 A Restricted ARMA Filter Class : QMP-filters

Moving-average or more generally ARMA-filters are well known filter classes. A comparison of both classes is given in Stier [85], section 17.5 together with a presentation of particular filter designs. In this section, a restricted class of ARMA filters is derived whose (desirable) properties 'match' the signal estimation problem for finite samples.

Definition 3.4. *A stable ARMA filter is called minimum phase if and only if all its zeroes Z_k lie outside the unit circle (invertibility) and $r = 0$ in (3.6) (causality).*

Invertibility and stability imply that the ARMA representation of the filter is equivalent to convergent $AR(\infty)$ or $MA(\infty)$ representations: X_t may be recovered from $Y_{t-r}, Y_{t-r-1}, \ldots$ and analogously Y_t may be recovered from $X_{t+r}, X_{t+r-1}, \ldots$. Causality requires $r = 0$. Therefore, minimum phase filters can be used for estimating a signal at the end point $t = N$ of a sample. Before generalizing this filter class, an optimality property of minimum phase filters is presented here.

Proposition 3.5. *Every stable, causal and non-invertible ARMA filter $\hat{\Gamma}'(\cdot)$ without zeroes on the unit circle can be uniquely decomposed into a minimum phase filter $\hat{\Gamma}(\cdot)$ and an allpass filter (a filter whose amplitude function is identically equal to one), i.e.:*

$$\hat{\Gamma}'(\omega) = \hat{\Gamma}(\omega) H_{ap}(\omega) \tag{3.14}$$

where $|H_{ap}(\cdot)| \equiv 1$ and where the time shift of the allpass filter is positive.

A proof is provided in Oppenheim and Schafer [73], p.352. The above proposition and the identity (3.10) imply that *minimum phase ARMA filters are characterized by small(est) time shifts* (for a given amplitude function). Since the time shift is generally positive in the passband of the filter (for trend extraction or for seasonal adjustment filters for example) it follows that minimum phase filters are 'optimal' designs.

Definition 3.6. *A stable ARMA filter $\hat{\Gamma}(\cdot)$ as given by (3.6) is called quasi minimum phase (QMP) if it factorizes into*

$$\hat{\Gamma}(\omega) := \exp(ir\omega) \prod_{k=1}^{n} \left(Z_k' - \exp(-i\omega) \right) \tilde{\Gamma}(\omega) \tag{3.15}$$

where $\tilde{\Gamma}(\omega)$ is minimum phase, $0 \leq r \leq N-1$ and $Z_k' := \exp(i\lambda_k), k = 1, ..., n$.

The identity (3.10) implies that the QMP filter $\hat{\Gamma}(\cdot)$ in (3.15) inherits the property of small(est) time shift from the minimum phase filter $\tilde{\Gamma}(\omega)$. Moreover, the proposed QMP filter class enables

- optimal signal estimation at arbitrary time points $N-r$ (the term $\exp(ir\omega)$ in (3.15) indicates that the full sample $X_1, ..., X_N$ can be used for estimating Y_{N-r}, see for example the correspondence of (3.4) and (3.6))
- 'handling' of non-stationary integrated input processes by including a 'unit-root' operator $\prod_{k=1}^{n} \left(Z_k' - \exp(-i\omega t) \right)$ (a formal treatment is given in section 5.3).

QMP filters are a general parsimonious filter class satisfying an optimality property (smallest time shift) which make them 'natural' candidates for boundary filter approximation problems. Section 3.3 presents a further and final restriction strengthening and improving the parsimony concept.

An intuitive explanation of the minimum time shift property of minimum phase filters can be given in the time domain. Oppenheim and Schafer [73] chap.7 prove the inequality

$$\sum_{j=0}^{n} \hat{\gamma}_j^2 \geq \sum_{j=0}^{n} (\hat{\gamma}_j')^2 \tag{3.16}$$

for all n, where the coefficients $\hat{\gamma}_j$ and $\hat{\gamma}'_j$ belong to $\hat{\Gamma}(\cdot)$ and $\hat{\Gamma}'(\cdot)$ in (3.14). Using the Parseval relation (A.11) (see the appendix):

$$\sum_{j=0}^{\infty}(\hat{\gamma}'_j)^2 = \int_{-\pi}^{\pi} \hat{A}'(\omega)^2 d\omega = \int_{-\pi}^{\pi} \hat{A}(\omega)^2 d\omega = \sum_{j=0}^{\infty} \hat{\gamma}_j^2$$

Therefore, (3.16) implies that the minimum phase filter gives less weight to past observations which reflects the smaller time shift.

Ideally, the time shift of an asymmetric filter should vanish and the latter should be as selective as the symmetric filter. It is shown in the following theorem that both requirements cannot be met simultaneously because phase and amplitude functions are related.

Theorem 3.7. *Amplitude and phase functions of a minimum phase filter satisfy*

$$\ln(\hat{A}(\omega)) = c + \frac{1}{2\pi}PV \int_{-\pi}^{\pi} \hat{\Phi}(\theta) \cot\left(\frac{\theta - \omega}{2}\right) d\theta$$
$$\hat{\Phi}(\omega) = -\frac{1}{2\pi}PV \int_{-\pi}^{\pi} \ln(\hat{A}(\theta)) \cot\left(\frac{\theta - \omega}{2}\right) d\theta$$

(3.17)

where c is a constant and PV means the principal value of the integral.

Note that the function $\cot(\theta)$ has a singularity at $\theta = 0$. This fact motivates the use of a special class of integrals denoted by 'principal value'. It is defined by considering the 'symmetric' limit: $\lim_{\delta \to 0} \left(\int_{-\pi}^{\omega-\delta} + \int_{\omega+\delta}^{\pi}\right)$. The expressions (3.17) then exist because $\cot(\cdot)$ is an odd function and because the integrated functions are regular (infinitely often differentiable).

Remarks

- The proof makes use of $\hat{\tilde{\Gamma}}(\omega) := \ln(\hat{\Gamma}(\omega)) = \ln(\hat{A}(\omega)) - i\hat{\Phi}(\omega)$ which is analytic in an open region containing the unit circle if $\hat{\Gamma}(\omega)$ is minimum phase. Hence, it relates real and imaginary parts of an analytic function, see for example Oppenheim and Schafer [73] chap.7 (note that the phase has an opposite sign in the cited document).
- Since $\cot(\cdot)$ is periodic and odd, equation (3.17) implies that $\hat{\Phi}(\omega) = 0$ for all ω whenever $\hat{A}(\omega)$ is constant. Both conditions together imply $\hat{\Gamma}(\omega) = K \in \mathbb{R}$, i.e. the filter is not selective at all.
- A straightforward consequence of the above theorem is that the best asymmetric filter (which minimizes the revision error variance) must result from a 'compromise' between an amplitude matching (i.e. 'small' $|A(\omega) - \hat{A}(\omega)|$) and a time shift (phase) matching (i.e. 'small' $|\Phi(\omega) - \hat{\Phi}(\omega)|$) where $A(\cdot)$ and $\Phi(\cdot)(\equiv 0)$ are the amplitude and the phase functions of the symmetric filter. These and related issues are analyzed in chapter 5.

In the last section of this chapter a final restriction of the QMP filter class is proposed which stresses on the *parsimony* concept. It is shown that the parameters of the proposed filter class are straightforwardly interpretable. Empirical results confirming improved 'out of sample' performances of this filter design are presented in chapter 7.

3.3 ZPC-Filters

Definition 3.8. *An ARMA filter $\hat{\Gamma}(\cdot)$ is called a pure zero-pole-combination (or simply a ZPC-) filter if and only if*

- *the number of poles is equal to the number of zeroes, i.e. $Q = q + r$, and*
- *all poles $P_k, k = 1, ..., Q$ and zeroes $Z_j, j = 1, ..., Q$ may be grouped into pairs $(Z_k, P_k), k = 1, ..., Q$, called zero-pole pairs, for which $\arg(P_k) = \arg(Z_k)$.*

An ARMA filter (3.6) consisting of one zero-pole pair is called an elementary ZPC-filter. An ARMA filter with zero-pole pairs and 'single' zeroes and/or poles is called a mixed ZPC-filter.

It is readily seen that the elementary ZPC-filter $C(Z - \exp(-i\omega))/(P - \exp(-i\omega))$ with $\arg(Z) = \arg(P)$ is more general than a single zero or a single pole: simply let $|Z| \to \infty$ or $|P| \to \infty$ and set $C := 1/Z$ or $C = P$ in order to obtain a single pole or a single zero. Each zero-pole pair $(P_k, Z_k), k = 1, ..., p$ has three degrees of freedom which may be given for example by $\lambda_k, |Z_k|$ and $|P_k|$. However, it is shown below that the set of 'parameters'

- λ_k,
- $|Z_k|$,
- $(|Z_k| - 1)/(|P_k| - 1)$, where $|P_k| > 1$ (stability)

is more appealing.

An analysis of the properties of ZPC-filters is necessary in order to motivate the constraint $\arg(Z_k) = \arg(P_k)$. For that purpose assume

$$\hat{\Gamma}(\omega) = C \frac{Z - \exp(-i\omega)}{P - \exp(-i\omega)} \tag{3.18}$$

is an elementary ZPC-filter with $\lambda := -\arg(P) = -\arg(Z)$. An important property of elementary ZPC-filters, namely the monotonicity of the amplitude function on both sides of λ, is derived in the following proposition. The 'non-monotonicity' of the amplitude function of particular filter designs may result in 'overshooting' (see for example Stier [85], section 17.5, fig.17.24 and 17.25) which results in inefficient seasonal adjustment or trend extraction. The monotonicity property of ZPC-filters is needed in the proof of proposition 3.11 below.

Proposition 3.9. *For* $Z = (1 + x)\exp(-i\lambda)$, $P = (1 + y)\exp(-i\lambda)$ *and* $0 \leq x < y$ *the amplitude function* $\hat{A}(\omega) := |\hat{\Gamma}(\omega)|$ *has a unique minimum in* λ. *More precisely*

$$\frac{\partial \hat{A}(\omega)}{\partial \omega} < 0 \; if \; \omega < \lambda$$

$$\frac{\partial \hat{A}(\omega)}{\partial(\omega)} = 0 \; if \; \omega = \lambda \; and \; x > 0$$

$$\frac{\partial \hat{A}(\omega)}{\partial(\omega)} > 0 \; if \; \omega > \lambda$$

If $0 < y < x$ *then the amplitude function has a unique maximum in* λ.

Proof. Assume first $x > 0$ and let

$$\ln\left|\frac{Z - \exp(-i\omega)}{P - \exp(-i\omega)}\right| = \ln(\hat{A}(\omega)) - \ln(|C|)$$

Thus

$$\frac{d}{d\omega}\ln(\hat{A}(\omega)) = \frac{d}{d\omega}\ln(|Z - \exp(-i\omega)|) - \frac{d}{d\omega}\ln(|P - \exp(-i\omega)|) \qquad (3.19)$$

Analyzing the first term on the right of this equality :

$$\frac{d}{d\omega}\ln(|Z - \exp(-i\omega)|)$$

$$= \frac{1}{|Z - \exp(-i\omega)|}\frac{d}{d\omega}|Z - \exp(-i\omega)|$$

$$= \frac{1}{|Z - \exp(-i\omega)|^2}\Big\{\mathrm{Re}(Z - \exp(-i\omega))\mathrm{Re}(i\exp(-i\omega))$$

$$+ \mathrm{Im}(Z - \exp(-i\omega))\mathrm{Im}(i\exp(-i\omega))\Big\}$$

$$= \frac{1}{|Z - \exp(-i\omega)|^2}\Big\{ -\mathrm{Re}(Z - \exp(-i\omega))\mathrm{Re}(i\exp(i\omega))$$

$$+ \mathrm{Im}(Z - \exp(-i\omega))\mathrm{Im}(i\exp(i\omega))\Big\}$$

$$= -\frac{\mathrm{Re}\Big[(Z - \exp(-i\omega))i\exp(i\omega)\Big]}{|Z - \exp(-i\omega)|^2}$$

$$= -\frac{\mathrm{Re}\Big[iZ\exp(i\omega)\Big]}{|Z - \exp(-i\omega)|^2}$$

$$= \frac{\mathrm{Im}\Big[Z\exp(i\omega)\Big]}{|Z - \exp(-i\omega)|^2} \qquad (3.20)$$

$$=: M_Z(\omega)$$

Thus (3.19) becomes

$$\frac{d}{d\omega}\ln(\hat{A}(\omega)) = M_Z(\omega) - M_P(\omega) \tag{3.21}$$

where P simply replaces Z in the expression for $M_P(\omega)$ corresponding to (3.20). It is easily verified, that $M_Z(\lambda) = M_P(\lambda) = 0$ because $Z\exp(i\lambda)$ is real in (3.20). From (3.21) and from

$$\frac{d}{d\omega}\ln(\hat{A}(\cdot)) = \frac{d\hat{A}(\cdot)}{d\omega}\frac{1}{\hat{A}(\cdot)} \tag{3.22}$$

it then follows that the derivative of the amplitude function must vanish in λ if $x > 0$ (because $\hat{A}(\lambda) > 0$). Moreover, it is easily verified that the derivative of the amplitude function vanishes whenever $\omega - \lambda = k\pi$, $k \in \mathbb{Z}$ since then $Z\exp(i\omega) \in \mathbb{R}$ in (3.20), so that M_Z vanishes in (3.21) (and analogously for M_P). Let $\omega - \lambda \neq k\pi$ and $x \geq 0$. Then:

$$
\begin{aligned}
\frac{1}{M_Z(\omega)} &= \frac{|Z - \exp(-i\omega)|^2}{\operatorname{Im}\left[Z\exp(i\omega)\right]} \\
&= \frac{(1+x)^2 + 1 - 2(1+x)\cos(\lambda - \omega)}{(1+x)\sin(\omega - \lambda)} \\
&= \left((1+x) + \frac{1}{1+x}\right)\frac{1}{\sin(\omega - \lambda)} + 2\cot(\lambda - \omega) \\
&= \left((1+x) + \frac{1}{1+x}\right)f(\omega) + g(\omega)
\end{aligned}
$$

and equivalently

$$\frac{1}{M_P(\omega)} = \left((1+y) + \frac{1}{1+y}\right)f(\omega) + g(\omega)$$

with $f(\omega - \lambda)$ being an odd function 'centered' in λ. The assumption $x < y$ then implies $1/M_Z(\cdot) < 1/M_P(\cdot)$ for $\omega > \lambda$ and $1/M_Z(\cdot) > 1/M_P(\cdot)$ for $\omega < \lambda$. This result together with (3.21), (3.22) and the positivity of the amplitude function proves that

$$\frac{d\hat{A}(\omega)}{d\omega}\begin{cases} < 0 \text{ if } \omega < \lambda \\ > 0 \text{ if } \omega > \lambda \end{cases} \tag{3.23}$$

A similar reasoning applies if $x > y$ which completes the proof of the proposition. $\quad\square$

The monotonicity of the amplitude function (on both sides of λ) of two particular ZPC-filters can be seen in fig.3.2. In the following theorem another important property of ZPC-filters is analyzed. It is shown that the filter effect (damping or amplification) can be concentrated in an open interval of arbitrary width containing λ (the common argument of the zero and the pole). Therefore 'components' with frequencies outside this interval remain almost unaffected by the filter. This property is important for seasonal adjustment since only the seasonal spikes are to be removed. The other components should 'pass' the filter without being affected.

Theorem 3.10. *Let* $\hat{\Gamma}(\cdot)$ *be defined by (3.18) where it is assumed for simplicity that* $C := 1$ *and let* $\lambda \in [-\pi, \pi]$. *Let also* $\epsilon, \delta > 0$ *and* $0 < r \neq 1$ *be arbitrary real numbers (r may even be infinite). Define* $Z = (1+x)\exp(-i\lambda)$, $P = (1+y)\exp(-i\lambda)$ *in (3.18). Then there exist* $x \geq 0, y > 0$ *(where y does not depend on r) so that*

- $\hat{A}(\lambda) = 1/r$ *and*
- $|\hat{A}(\omega) - 1| < \delta, \ |\hat{\Phi}(\omega)| < \delta$ *and* $|\hat{\Gamma}(\omega) - 1| < \delta$ *whenever* $|\omega - \lambda| > \epsilon$

where $\hat{A}(\cdot)$ *and* $\hat{\Phi}(\cdot)$ *are the amplitude and phase functions of* $\hat{\Gamma}(\cdot)$.

Remark

- For $r = 1$ the pole and the zero cancel so that parameters are not uniquely defined. Therefore, $r = 1$ has been excluded in the above assumptions.
- For $r > 1$ the filter 'damps' components whereas for $r < 1$ components are amplified. However, the effect (amplification or damping) can be concentrated in an open interval of arbitrarily small width containing λ.

Proof of the theorem. For the proof it is assumed that $r > 1$ so that $\hat{A}(\lambda) < 1$ i.e. the filter damps input signals. Consider first the following fig.3.1 where P and Z are the pole and the zero of the ZPC-filter and $\Delta\omega$ is a small

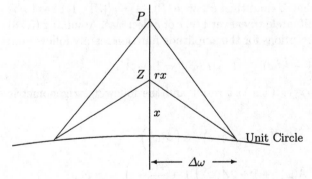

Fig. 3.1. Elementary ZPC-filter in the plane

arc on the complex unit circle (so that it may be approximated by a small line segment). From $x := |Z| - 1$ and $\hat{A}(\lambda) = 1/r$ it follows that $y = |P| - 1 = rx$:

the damping factor r thus determines the relative locations of the zero and the pole. It remains to determine either x or y so that the theorem is true. The complex transfer function is analyzed first.

For that purpose, x $(= |Z| - 1)$ is sought so that

$$
\delta > |1 - \hat{\Gamma}(\omega)| = \left| \frac{P - \exp(-i\omega) - (Z - \exp(-i\omega))}{P - \exp(-i\omega)} \right|
$$

$$
= \frac{(r-1)x}{|P - \exp(-i\omega)|}
$$

$$
= \frac{(r-1)x}{|1 + rx - \exp(-i\nu)|} \tag{3.24}
$$

for all $\{\omega \,|\, |\omega - \lambda| \geq \epsilon\}$ where $\nu := \Delta\omega = \omega - \lambda$ in (3.24). Since the denominator is monotonic in ν this condition reduces to a condition on the boundary $\nu = \pm\epsilon$:

$$
\delta > \left| \frac{(r-1)x}{1 + rx - \exp(-i\epsilon)} \right| \sim \left| \frac{(r-1)x}{rx + i\epsilon} \right| \tag{3.25}
$$

Note that if ϵ is small, then the boundary condition justifies the approximation of the arc $\Delta\omega$ by a straight line in fig. 3.1. From $|rx \pm i\epsilon|^2 = (rx)^2 + \epsilon^2$ the approximation (3.25) becomes

$$
\delta^2 \epsilon^2 > [(r-1)^2 - \delta^2 r^2] x^2
$$

If $r < 1/(1-\delta)$ the above inequality is satisfied for all $x = |Z| - 1 > 0$ (because the filter almost degenerates to the identity). Otherwise x must satisfy

$$
x < \frac{\delta\epsilon}{\sqrt{(r-1)^2 - \delta^2 r^2}} \tag{3.26}
$$

The inequality shows that Z (and thus P, since $|P| - 1 = r(|Z| - 1)$) has to be located closer to the unit circle whenever $1/r$, ϵ or δ decrease. Assuming (3.26) to be satisfied, the assumptions for the amplitude function readily follow from

$$
\delta > |1 - \hat{\Gamma}(\omega)| \geq |1 - |\hat{\Gamma}(\omega)|| = |1 - \hat{A}(\omega)|
$$

for all ω with $|\omega - \lambda| > \epsilon$. This last result and the following trigonometric identity

$$
|\hat{\Gamma}(\omega) - 1|^2 = \hat{A}(\omega)^2 + 1 - 2\hat{A}(\omega) \cos\left(\hat{\Phi}(\omega)\right)
$$

$$
= \hat{A}(\omega)^2 + 1 - 2\hat{A}(\omega)\left(1 - \frac{\hat{\Phi}(\omega)^2}{2}\right) + O(\hat{\Phi}(\omega)^4)
$$

$$
\sim (\hat{A}(\omega) - 1)^2 + \hat{A}(\omega)\hat{\Phi}(\omega)^2 \tag{3.27}
$$

then show that $\delta^2 > |1 - \hat{\Gamma}(\omega)|^2 \geq \hat{A}(\omega)\hat{\Phi}(\omega)^2$, so that $|\hat{\Phi}(\omega)| < \delta/\sqrt{1-\delta} \simeq \delta$. Define $x := x(r)$ by

$$x := \frac{\delta\epsilon}{r} \tag{3.28}$$

Then (3.26) is satisfied:

$$x = \frac{\delta\epsilon}{r} < \frac{\delta\epsilon}{r\sqrt{1-\delta^2}} < \frac{\delta\epsilon}{\sqrt{(r-1)^2 - \delta^2 r^2}}$$

Since $|P-1| = y = rx = \delta\epsilon > 0$ does not depend on r the proof is completed. A similar proof applies to the case $0 < r < 1$ (in this case the ZPC-filter amplifies sinusoidal input signals of frequency λ). $\square$

Note that the filter remains stable even if $r \to \infty$ because $|P| > 0$ does not depend on r. The next result shows that weaker conditions (than (3.26)) lead to $|\hat{A}(\omega) - 1| < \delta$. An interpretation of this result is that in a given sense the fit of the amplitude function is easier than the fit of the phase function.

Proposition 3.11. *Let the assumptions of the preceding theorem be fulfilled and assume $\hat{A}(\lambda) = 1/r < 1$. Then $|\hat{A}(\omega) - 1| < \delta$ for all $|\omega - \lambda| > \epsilon$ whenever*

$$x < \frac{\sqrt{2\delta}\,\epsilon}{\sqrt{r^2(1-2\delta) - 1}}$$

where $x := |Z| - 1$.

Proof. First an $x > 0$ is sought so that $\hat{A}(\lambda) = 1/r$ and

$$|1 - \hat{A}^2(\omega)| < 2\delta \tag{3.29}$$

for $|\omega - \lambda| > \epsilon$. Proposition 3.9 implies that $\hat{A}(\omega)$ is strictly monotonic on each side of λ so that (3.29) reduces to a condition on the boundary $\lambda \pm \epsilon$:

$$2\delta > |1 - \hat{A}^2(\lambda \pm \epsilon)| \simeq \left| 1 - \frac{x^2 + \epsilon^2}{(rx)^2 + \epsilon^2} \right|$$

where the pythagorean identity was used (approximate the small arc $\Delta\omega$ by a straight line of length ϵ in figure 3.1). This implies

$$x^2 \left(r^2(1-2\delta) - 1 \right) < 2\delta\epsilon^2$$

If $r < 1/\sqrt{1-2\delta}$ then the last inequality is satisfied for all $x = |Z| - 1 > 0$ (because the filter almost degenerates to an allpass). Otherwise x must satisfy

$$x < \frac{\sqrt{2\delta\epsilon}}{\sqrt{r^2(1-2\delta) - 1}} \tag{3.30}$$

Since

$$2\delta > |1 - \hat{A}^2(\omega)| = |1 - \hat{A}(\omega)||1 + \hat{A}(\omega)| \qquad (3.31)$$

it follows immediately that $|1-\hat{A}(\omega)| < 2\delta$ and thus $2-2\delta < |1+\hat{A}(\omega)| < 2+2\delta$ so that (3.31) implies

$$|1 - \hat{A}(\omega)| < \frac{2\delta}{|1 + \hat{A}(\omega)|} = \delta + O(\delta^2) \simeq \delta$$

if δ is small, which proves the proposition. $\square$

Note that (3.30) is weaker than (3.26) since δ is replaced by $\sqrt{\delta}$ in the former condition. The degrees of freedom (parameters) p_1, p_2, p_3 of an elementary ZPC-filter (3.18) can be interpreted as follows:

1. The common argument $p_1 := \lambda$ of the zero and the pole determines the frequency for which the amplitude of the filter has an extremum (damping or amplification).
2. Assume the filter is 'normalized' : for example $|\hat{\Gamma}(0)| = 1$ so that $|C| = \left|\frac{P-1}{Z-1}\right|$ in (3.18). Define the 'parameter'

$$p_2 := \frac{|P - 1|}{|Z - 1|} \frac{(|Z| - 1)}{(|P| - 1)} \qquad (3.32)$$

   Then p_2 determines the relative damping (amplification) of a sinusoidal input signal of frequency λ (when compared to components with frequencies close to zero). If $|\lambda| >> \max(|Z| - 1, |P| - 1)$, then p_2 can be approximated by $(|Z| - 1)/(|P| - 1)$.
3. Let λ be given and suppose $|Z|$ and $|P|$ are varied such that $\hat{A}(\lambda)$ remains constant. Then the third parameter $p_3 := |Z|$ determines the *width* ϵ (of the interval where the filter damps or amplifies) for a given approximation δ (see theorem 3.10). Figures 3.2 (amplitude functions) and 3.3 (phase functions) illustrate this effect for a damping effect (by a factor two) in $\lambda = \pi/2$ and for the alternative parameter values $p_3 := |Z_1| = 1.1$ (dotted lines) and $p_3 := |Z_1| = 1.01$ (solid lines). A comparison of both figures confirms that the amplitude function seems easier to approximate than the phase function: for $|Z| = 1.01$ the amplitude function converges rapidly (to a constant $|Z - 1|/|P - 1|$) whereas the decay of the phase function (in absolute value) is slower on both sides of $\lambda := \pi/2$: this fact is established in proposition 3.11 in which it is shown that weaker conditions are necessary for ensuring the convergence of the amplitude function towards the identity. Note also that $\hat{\Phi}(0) \neq 0$ here because the filters are complex.

ZPC filters strengthen the parsimony concept and their degrees of freedom (parameters) are straightforwardly interpretable. The plots in the above figures suggest that ZPC-designs can be advantageously used for seasonal adjustment (because non-seasonal components remain 'almost unaffected').

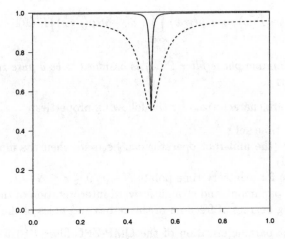

Fig. 3.2. Amplitude for $|Z| = 1.1$ (dotted) and $|Z_1| = 1.01$ (solid)

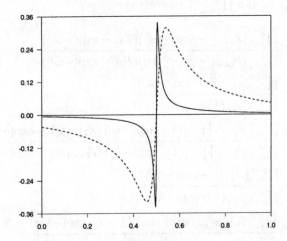

Fig. 3.3. Phase for $|Z| = 1.1$ (dotted) and $|Z_1| = 1.01$ (solid)

Empirical results (see chapter 7) confirm this conjecture.

Recall the definition 3.6 for a QMP filter :

$$\hat{\Gamma}(\omega) := \exp(ir\omega) \prod_{k=1}^{n} \left(Z'_k - \exp(-i\omega) \right) \tilde{\Gamma}(\omega)$$

where Z'_k are zeroes on the unit circle.

Definition 3.12. *The class of QMP-ZPC filters is defined by*

$$\hat{\Gamma}(\omega) := \exp(ir\omega) \prod_{k=1}^{n} \left(Z'_k - \exp(-i\omega) \right) \tilde{\Gamma}'(\omega)$$

where the minimum phase filter $\tilde{\Gamma}'(\omega)$ is assumed to be a pure zero-pole combination filter.

These filters are characterized by the following properties:

- minimum time shift,
- generality (the unit-root operator can be used when the input process is integrated)
- estimation for arbitrary time points $N - r$, $0 \leq r \leq N - 1$,
- enhanced parsimony and straightforward interpretation of the parameters (remaining degrees of freedom of the zeroes and poles of the filter).

An equivalent parameterization of the QMP-ZPC-filter $\hat{\Gamma}(\cdot)$ is given by dividing numerator and denominator polynomials of the minimum phase filter $\tilde{\Gamma}'(\cdot)$ by $\prod_{j=1}^{q+r} Z_j$ and $\prod_{j=1}^{Q} P_j$ respectively:

$$
\begin{aligned}
\tilde{\Gamma}'(\omega) &= C \frac{\prod_{j=1}^{n''}(Z_{2j-1} - \exp(-i\omega))(Z_{2j} - \exp(-i\omega))}{\prod_{k=1}^{n'}(P_{2k-1} - \exp(-i\omega))(P_{2k} - \exp(-i\omega))} \\
&\quad \times \frac{\prod_{j=2n''+1}^{q+r}(Z_j - \exp(-i\omega))}{\prod_{k=2n'+1}^{Q}(P_k - \exp(-i\omega))} \\
&= C \frac{\prod_{j=1}^{q+r} Z_j}{\prod_{j=1}^{Q} P_j} \times \frac{\prod_{j=1}^{n''}(1 - \exp(-i\omega)/Z_{2j-1})(1 - \exp(-i\omega)/Z_{2j})}{\prod_{k=1}^{n'}(1 - \exp(-i\omega)/P_{2k-1})(1 - \exp(-i\omega)/P_{2k})} \\
&\quad \times \frac{\prod_{j=2n''+1}^{q+r}(1 - \exp(-i\omega)/Z_j)}{\prod_{k=2n'+1}^{Q}(1 - \exp(-i\omega)/P_k)} \\
&= D \frac{\prod_{j=1}^{n''}(1 - z_{2j-1}\exp(-i\omega))(1 - z_{2j}\exp(-i\omega))}{\prod_{k=1}^{n'}(1 - p_{2k-1}\exp(-i\omega))(1 - p_{2k}\exp(-i\omega))} \\
&\quad \times \frac{\prod_{j=2n''+1}^{q+r}(1 - z_j\exp(-i\omega))}{\prod_{k=2n'+1}^{Q}(1 - p_k\exp(-i\omega))}
\end{aligned}
\tag{3.33}
$$

where $D := C \dfrac{\prod_{j=1}^{q+r} Z_j}{\prod_{j=1}^{Q} P_j}$ and $z_j = 1/Z_j$ and $p_k = 1/P_k$. The parameters z_j and p_k of the minimum phase filter are now *within* the unit disk. Moreover, the ZPC constraint (common argument) straightforwardly extends to the new set of parameters. This new set is often preferred to the previous one, because vanishing MA- or AR-coefficients (in (3.4)) are associated with vanishing zeroes z_j or poles p_k (whereas $Z_j \rightarrow \infty$ or $P_k \rightarrow \infty$ which leads to inconsistency of estimates and undesirable properties of their variance-covariance matrix for overparameterized designs).

It was argued at the beginning of this chapter, that suitable choices of ω_k and $G(\omega_k)$ in (3.1) can lead to a criterion for which the (asymmetric) filter solution has 'desirable properties'. In chapter 5 it is shown that the optimal weighting function $G(\cdot)$ is closely related to the periodogram. Therefore, some well known and also some new results are presented for the periodogram in the following chapter 4. These are necessary for deriving asymptotic as well as finite sample results for the DFA.

4

The Periodogram

Within the methodological framework of the new signal estimation procedure (DFA), an eminent role is attributed to the periodogram or to statistics directly related to the periodogram: it 'collects' and transforms the information of the sample $X_1, ..., X_N$. Therefore, properties of the periodogram (used in (1.9)) are presented in this chapter. Some results are well known (so references to the literature are given only), others are generalizations of known results or are new. In the latter two cases, extensive proofs are given.

In sections 4.1 and 4.2 spectral decomposition and convolution theorems are presented based on the periodogram. The obtained results are generalized to non-stationary integrated processes in section 4.3. Explorative instruments for deciding between different optimization procedures or filter designs are derived.
The results of these sections are the 'main core'. Sporadic uses of particular stochastic properties of the periodogram make it necessary to develop other aspects further. These are reported in chapter B in the appendix.

4.1 Spectral Decomposition

Define $\bar{X} := 1/N \sum_{t=1}^{N} X_t$ (sample mean) and $\Omega_N := \{\omega_k | \omega_k = k\pi/[N/2], |k| = 0, ..., [N/2]\}$ where $[N/2]$ is the greatest integer smaller or equal to $N/2$ and N is the sample size.

Definition 4.1. *Define the discrete Fourier transform of* $X_1, ..., X_N$ *by :*

$$\Xi_{NX}(\omega_k) := \frac{1}{\sqrt{2\pi N}} \sum_{t=1}^{N} X_t \exp(-it\omega_k) \qquad (4.1)$$

Note that the discrete Fourier transform defined for $\omega_k \in \Omega_N$ may be extended to the real interval $[-\pi, \pi]$, see below. Define the weights

$$w_k := \begin{cases} 1, & -[N/2] \le k \le [N/2] \text{ if } N \text{ is odd} \\ \begin{cases} 1, & |k| < N/2 \\ 1/2, & |k| = N/2 \end{cases} & \text{if } N \text{ is even} \end{cases} \tag{4.2}$$

The following discrete orthogonality relations are useful in the sequel:

$$\sum_{j=1}^{N} \exp(-ij\omega_k) = \exp(-i\omega_k)\frac{1 - \exp(-iN\omega_k)}{1 - \exp(-i\omega_k)} = \begin{cases} 0, & k \ne 0 \\ N, & k = 0 \end{cases} \tag{4.3}$$

An *orthogonal spectral decomposition* of $X_1, ..., X_N$ may be obtained from the following proposition:

Proposition 4.2. *Let X_t be a finite sequence of length N and let $\Xi_{NX}(\omega_k)$ be the discrete Fourier transform of X_t. Then*

$$X_t = \frac{\sqrt{2\pi}}{\sqrt{N}} \sum_{k=-[N/2]}^{[N/2]} \exp(it\omega_k)w_k\Xi_{NX}(\omega_k) \tag{4.4}$$

Proof. A complete proof is provided here, because in the literature mostly the case of an odd integer N is found only. If N is even, then $[N/2] = N/2$. Thus

$$\frac{\sqrt{2\pi}}{\sqrt{N}} \sum_{k=-N/2}^{N/2} w_k \exp(it\omega_k)\Xi_{NX}(\omega_k)$$

$$= \frac{1}{N} \sum_{k=-N/2}^{N/2} w_k \exp(it\omega_k) \sum_{j=1}^{N} X_j \exp(-ij\omega_k)$$

$$= \frac{1}{N} \sum_{j=1}^{N} X_j \sum_{k=-N/2}^{N/2} w_k \exp(-i(j-t)\omega_k) \tag{4.5}$$

$$= \frac{1}{N} \sum_{j=1}^{N} X_j \exp(-i(j-t)\omega_{-N/2}) \sum_{k=0}^{N} w_k \exp(-i(j-t)\omega_k)$$

$$= \frac{1}{N} \sum_{j=1}^{N} X_j \exp(-i(j-t)\omega_{-N/2}) \sum_{k=1}^{N} \exp(-i(j-t)\omega_k)$$

$$= X_t$$

where the last equality follows from the orthogonality relations (4.3). If N is odd then $w_k = 1$ for all k and (4.5) becomes :

$$\frac{1}{N} \sum_{j=1}^{N} X_j \sum_{k=-[N/2]}^{[N/2]} \exp(-i(j-t)\omega_k)$$

$$= \frac{1}{N} \sum_{j=1}^{N} X_j \exp(-i(j-t)\omega_{-[N/2]-1}) \sum_{k=1}^{N} \exp(-i(j-t)\omega_k)$$

$$= X_t$$

which completes the proof of the proposition. $\square$

By analogy to (A.1) (see the appendix) (4.4) is called an orthogonal spectral decomposition of the sequence X_t. Note however that stationarity is not required here. The expression $\dfrac{\sqrt{2\pi}}{\sqrt{N}}w_k \Xi_{NX}(\omega_k)$ corresponds to the orthogonal incremental process $dZ(\omega)$ in (A.1).

Definition 4.3. *The periodogram of a sequence X_t, $t = 1, ..., N$ is defined by*

$$I_{NX}(\omega_k) := |\Xi_{NX}(\omega_k)|^2 \ , \quad k = -[N/2], ..., [N/2] \tag{4.6}$$

Up to now the sequence $X_1, ... X_N$ is completely arbitrary. If X_t is a stochastic process (which is assumed in the following) then the statistic $I_{NX}(\omega_k)$ is a random variable. Its distribution is analyzed in chapter B in the appendix. Note that the above definition slightly differs from the original one in Schuster [82] by a normalizing constant.

Equation (4.3) implies

$$I_{NX}(\omega_k) = \frac{1}{2\pi N}\left|\sum_{t=1}^{N}(X_t - C)\exp(-it\omega_k)\right|^2 \tag{4.7}$$

for any constant C if $\omega_k \neq 0$. In particular

$$I_{NX}(\omega_k) = \frac{1}{2\pi N}\left|\sum_{t=1}^{N}(X_t - \bar{X})\exp(-it\omega_k)\right|^2 \tag{4.8}$$

so that the periodogram is 'immunized' against the parameter $\mu := E[X_t]$ if $\omega_k \neq 0$. For $\omega_0(= 0)$ however

$$I_{NX}(0) = \frac{1}{2\pi N}\left(\sum_{t=1}^{N}X_t\right)^2 = \frac{N}{2\pi}\bar{X}^2 \tag{4.9}$$

The following proposition shows that the periodogram can be interpreted as an estimate of the spectral density $h(\omega_k)$ (see also (A.6) in the appendix):

Proposition 4.4. *The periodogram of a sequence $X_1, ..., X_N$ satisfies*

$$I_{NX}(\omega_k) = \begin{cases} \dfrac{1}{2\pi}\displaystyle\sum_{j=-(N-1)}^{N-1}\hat{R}(j)\exp(-ij\omega_k) \ , & |k| = 1, ..., [N/2] \\[2mm] \dfrac{N}{2\pi}\bar{X}^2 & k = 0 \end{cases} \tag{4.10}$$

where

$$\hat{R}(j) := \frac{1}{N}\sum_{t=1}^{N-|j|}X_t X_{t+|j|} \tag{4.11}$$

A proof showing the equivalence of (4.6) and (4.10) is given in Priestley [75] lemma 6.1.1. If X_t is a stationary process and $E[X_t] = \mu \neq 0$, then X_t may be replaced by the 'centered' variables $X'_t := X_t - \bar{X}$. The statistics $\hat{R}(j)$ corresponding to X'_t are then the usual estimators of the autocovariance function. From (4.8) and (4.10) one deduces

$$I_{NX'}(\omega_k) = \begin{cases} I_{NX}(\omega_k) & k \neq 0 \\ \dfrac{N}{2\pi}\bar{X}'^2 = 0 & \text{else} \end{cases} \tag{4.12}$$

The following proposition presents a spectral decomposition of the autocovariance estimates (see also its analogue (A.5) in the appendix).

Proposition 4.5. *Let X_t be a finite sequence.*

- *$\hat{R}(j)$ defined in (4.11) can be decomposed into*

$$\hat{R}(j) = \frac{2\pi}{N} \sum_{k=-[N/2]}^{[N/2]} w_k \exp(-ij\omega_k) I_{NX}(\omega_k) \tag{4.13}$$

  where the weights w_k are given by (4.2).
- *The sample variance of X_t can be decomposed into*

$$\frac{1}{N} \sum_{t=1}^{N} (X_t - \bar{X})^2 = \frac{2\pi}{N} \sum_{k=-[N/2]}^{[N/2]} w_k I_{NX}(\omega_k) - \bar{X}^2 \tag{4.14}$$

Proof. A proof of the first assertion follows exactly the same line as the proof of proposition 4.2, using (4.10) and the orthogonality relations (4.3). The second assertion follows from (4.13) and

$$\frac{1}{N} \sum_{t=1}^{N} (X_t - \bar{X})^2 = \hat{R}(0) - \bar{X}^2$$

which completes the proof of the proposition. $\square$

There exist different extensions of the periodogram from the discrete set $\omega_k, |k| = 0, ..., [N/2]$ to the continuous set $\omega \in [-\pi, \pi]$. Fuller [34] defines a piecewise constant function:

$$I_{NX}(\omega) := I_{NX}(\omega_k) \tag{4.15}$$

if $\omega_k - \pi/N < \omega \leq \omega_k + \pi/N$. A motivation for this particular extension is given in theorem B.2 in the appendix. It is also possible to extend the definition of the periodogram 'directly' by allowing $\omega \in [-\pi, \pi]$ in (4.6) or (4.10) :

$$I_{NX}(\omega) = \frac{1}{2\pi N} \left| \sum_{t=1}^{N} X_t \exp(-it\omega) \right|^2 \tag{4.16}$$

The proof of lemma 6.1.1 in Priestley [75] shows that (4.6) and (4.10) are identical for the latter extension. If $X_t' := X_t - \bar{X}$ and if the extension (4.16) is used, then in general $I_{NX'}(\omega) \neq I_{NX}(\omega)$ if $\omega \notin \Omega_N$. Also, the stochastic properties of the resulting random function will become more complex (see for example the last assertion of Theorem B.4 in the appendix). Extension (4.16) is useful for defining the periodogram of integrated processes, see 4.35.

4.2 Convolution Theorem

Let ϵ_t be a weakly stationary white noise process : $E[\epsilon_t] = 0$, $E[\epsilon_t^2] = \sigma^2 < \infty$ and $E[\epsilon_t \epsilon_{t+i}] = 0$ for all $i \neq 0$ and let

$$X_t = \mu_x + \sum_{k=-\infty}^{\infty} b_k \epsilon_{t-k} \tag{4.17}$$

be a two-sided stationary MA(∞)-process. The following definition proposes an important *regularity* condition.

Definition 4.6. *A filter $\Gamma(\cdot)$ is said to belong to the class C_f^u, $u \in \mathbb{R}$, if*

$$\sum_{k=-\infty}^{\infty} |\gamma_k||k|^u < \infty$$

By analogy, the MA-process X_t in (4.17) is said to belong to the class C_f^u if

$$\sum_{k=-\infty}^{\infty} |b_k||k|^u < \infty$$

The above definition does not make a distinction between processes and filters. Instead, the rate of decay of the MA-parameters (of the filter or of the MA-process) is of interest. Immediate consequences of the above definition are:

1. $C_f^u \supset C_f^v$ if $v > u$.
2. A stationary ARMA-process X_t is in C_f^u for all $u > 0$ (denoted by $X_t \in C_f^\infty$).
3. $X_t \in C_f^u$ implies

$$\sum_{j=-\infty}^{\infty} |R(j)||j|^u < \infty \tag{4.18}$$

A proof of the second assertion follows from proposition 2.2 in Hamilton [45] and the last assertion follows from $R(j) = \sigma^2 \sum_{k=-\infty}^{\infty} b_k b_{k+j}$ and the following proposition:

Proposition 4.7. *If a_j, b_k are sequences satisfying $\sum_{j=-\infty}^{\infty} |a_j| |j|^u < \infty$, $\sum_{k=-\infty}^{\infty} |b_k| |k|^v < \infty$ where $u, v \geq 0$, then*

$$\sum_{j=-\infty}^{\infty} \left| \sum_{k=-\infty}^{\infty} a_k b_{j\pm k} \right| |j|^{\min(u,v)} < \infty$$

Proof. Let $w := \min(u, v) \geq 0$. Then

$$\sum_{j=-\infty}^{\infty} \left| \sum_{k=-\infty}^{\infty} a_k b_{j\pm k} \right| |j|^w \leq \sum_{j=-\infty}^{\infty} \sum_{k=-\infty}^{\infty} |a_k b_{j\pm k}| |j|^w$$

$$\leq \sum_{-\infty}^{\infty} \sum_{-\infty}^{\infty} |a_k b_{j\pm k}| \max(1, 2^{w-1})(|j \pm k|^w + |k|^w)$$

$$= \max(1, 2^{w-1})$$

$$\left(\sum_{-\infty}^{\infty} |a_k| \sum_{-\infty}^{\infty} |b_j| |j|^w + \sum_{-\infty}^{\infty} |a_k| |k|^w \sum_{-\infty}^{\infty} |b_j| \right)$$

$$< \infty$$

which completes the proof of the proposition. □

The following convolution theorem corresponds to theorem A.3 in the appendix. The first two assertions of the theorem are 'classical' results if X_t is a white noise process. A generalization to MA(∞) input processes is proposed here. The last assertion is a generalization of a result in Brockwell and Davis [10] (proposition 10.8.5). It is used for deriving the efficiency of the DFA.

Theorem 4.8. *Assume X_t is given by (4.17), let $Y_t = \sum_{k=-\infty}^{\infty} \gamma_k X_{t-k}$ be the output of the filter $\Gamma(\cdot)$ with coefficients γ_k and assume $\omega_k \in \Omega_N$.*

1. If $X_t, \Gamma(\cdot) \in C_f^0$ and $\mu_x = 0$ then

$$I_{NY}(\omega_k) = |\Gamma(\omega_k)|^2 I_{NX}(\omega_k) + R_{NYX}(\omega_k)$$

where $\lim_{N\to\infty} \sup_{\omega_k \in \Omega_N} E[|R_{NYX}(\omega_k)|] = 0$.

2. If $X_t \in C_f^0$, $\Gamma(\cdot) \in C_f^{1/2}$ and $\mu_x = 0$ then

$$\Xi_{NY}(\omega_k) = \Gamma(\omega_k) \, \Xi_{NX}(\omega_k) + R'_{NYX}(\omega_k)$$
$$E[|R'_{NYX}(\omega_k)|^2] = O(1/N) \tag{4.19}$$

where $\Xi_{NY}(\cdot)$ was defined in (4.1) and the approximation is uniform in ω_k. Moreover,

$$I_{NY}(\omega_k) = |\Gamma(\omega_k)|^2 \, I_{NX}(\omega_k) + R_{NYX}(\omega_k) \tag{4.20}$$

where $E[|R_{NYX}(\omega_k)|] = O(1/\sqrt{N})$ uniformly in ω_k.

3. *Assume $\Gamma(\cdot)$ is real. If $\mu_x \neq 0$ then the above results are valid for $\omega_k \neq 0$. For $\omega_0 = 0$ one obtains the approximation :*

$$I_{NY}(0) = |\Gamma(0)|^2 I_{NX}(0)$$

$$+ R_{NY'X'}(0) + 2\frac{\sqrt{N}}{\sqrt{2\pi}}\Gamma(0)\mu_x R'_{NY'X'}(0) \qquad (4.21)$$

where $Y'_t = Y_t - E[Y_t]$, $X'_t = X_t - E[X_t]$ so that the error terms $R_{NY'X'}(0)$, $R'_{NY'X'}(0)$ meet the respective assertions of the theorem for the case $\mu_x = 0$.

4. *If $X_t \in C^0_f$ and $\Gamma(\cdot) \in C^{1/2}_f$ then*

$$\frac{2\pi}{N} \sum_{j=-[N/2]}^{[N/2]} w_j I_{NY}(\omega_j)$$

$$= \frac{2\pi}{N} \sum_{j=-[N/2]}^{[N/2]} w_j |\Gamma(\omega_j)|^2 I_{NX}(\omega_j) + r_N \qquad (4.22)$$

where $E[|r_N|] = o(1/\sqrt{N})$.

Proof. Assume first $E[X_t] = 0$. A proof if X_t is an iid sequence with finite fourth order moments is given in Brockwell and Davis [10], theorem 10.3.1. These results are extended here to more general input processes. From

$$\Xi_{NY}(\omega) = \frac{\sqrt{2\pi}}{\sqrt{N}} \sum_{t=1}^{N} Y_t \exp(-it\omega)$$

$$= \frac{\sqrt{2\pi}}{\sqrt{N}} \sum_{t=1}^{N} \left(\sum_{k=-\infty}^{\infty} \gamma_k X_{t-k} \right) \exp(-it\omega)$$

$$= \sum_{k=-\infty}^{\infty} \gamma_k \exp(-ik\omega) \frac{\sqrt{2\pi}}{\sqrt{N}} \sum_{t=1}^{N} X_{t-k} \exp(-i(t-k)\omega)$$

$$= \sum_{k=-\infty}^{\infty} \gamma_k \exp(-ik\omega) \frac{\sqrt{2\pi}}{\sqrt{N}} \sum_{t=1-k}^{N-k} X_t \exp(-it\omega) \qquad (4.23)$$

it follows that

$$R'_{NYX}(\omega) = \sum_{k=-\infty}^{\infty} \gamma_k \exp(-ik\omega)$$

$$\frac{\sqrt{2\pi}}{\sqrt{N}} \left(\sum_{t=1-k}^{N-k} X_t \exp(-it\omega) - \sum_{t=1}^{N} X_t \exp(-it\omega) \right) \qquad (4.24)$$

Thus

$$E[|R'_{NYX}(\omega)|^2] = E\Bigg[\Bigg| \sum_{j=-\infty}^{\infty} \sum_{k=-\infty}^{\infty} \gamma_j \gamma_k \exp(-ij\omega) \exp(ik\omega)$$

$$\frac{\sqrt{2\pi}}{\sqrt{N}} \left(\sum_{t=1-j}^{N-j} X_t \exp(-it\omega) - \sum_{t=1}^{N} X_t \exp(-it\omega) \right)$$

$$\frac{\sqrt{2\pi}}{\sqrt{N}} \left(\sum_{t=1-k}^{N-k} X_t \exp(it\omega) - \sum_{t=1}^{N} X_t \exp(it\omega) \right) \Bigg| \Bigg]$$

$$\leq \frac{2\pi}{N} \sum_{j=-\infty}^{\infty} \sum_{k=-\infty}^{\infty} |\gamma_j||\gamma_k| 2 \min(|j|, |k|, N)$$

$$\times \sum_{l=-\infty}^{\infty} |R(l)| \tag{4.25}$$

$$\leq 2 \frac{2\pi \sum_{l=-\infty}^{\infty} |R(l)|}{N} \sum_{j=-\infty}^{\infty} \sum_{k=-\infty}^{\infty} |\gamma_j| \min(|j|^{1/2}, N^{1/2})$$

$$\times |\gamma_k| \min(|k|^{1/2}, N^{1/2}) \tag{4.26}$$

$$= \begin{cases} o(1) & \text{first assertion} \\ O(1/N) & \text{second assertion} \end{cases} \tag{4.27}$$

where the inequality (4.25) follows by noting that the differences of the two sums on the left involve $\min(2j, 2N)$ and $\min(2k, 2N)$ summands only. The last equality (4.27) follows from (4.18) and the required assumptions, in particular the autocovariance function is absolutely summable by (4.18). Finally, the approximation (4.20) then follows from:

$$I_{NY}(\omega) = |\Gamma(\omega)|^2 I_{NX}(\omega)$$
$$+ 2\text{Re}\big(R'_{NYX}(-\omega)\Gamma(\omega)\Xi_{NX}(\omega) \big) + |R'_{NYX}(\omega)|^2 \tag{4.28}$$

and the preceding result (using the Cauchy-Schwartz inequality for the middle term on the right hand side of 4.28). If $\mu_x \neq 0$ then the preceding results are true for $\omega_k \neq 0$ (by orthogonality of the exponential family for $\omega_k \in \Omega_N$). Define $X'_t := X_t - \mu_x$, $\bar{X} := 1/N \sum_{t=1}^{N} X_t$, $\mu_y := E[Y_t]$, $\bar{Y}' := \bar{Y} - \mu_y$, and $\bar{Y} := 1/N \sum_{t=1}^{N} Y_t$. A proof of the third assertion then follows from

$$|\Gamma(0)|^2 I_{NX}(0) = |\Gamma(0)|^2 \frac{N}{2\pi} \bar{X}^2$$

$$= |\Gamma(0)|^2 \frac{N}{2\pi} (\bar{X}' + \mu_x)^2$$

$$= |\Gamma(0)|^2 I_{NX'}(0) + 2\Gamma(0) \frac{\sqrt{N}}{\sqrt{2\pi}} \Xi_{NX'}(0)\Gamma(0)\mu_x + \frac{N}{2\pi}|\Gamma(0)|^2\mu_x^2$$

$$= I_{NY'}(0) + 2\frac{\sqrt{N}}{\sqrt{2\pi}} \Xi_{NY'}(0)\Gamma(0)\mu_x + \frac{N}{2\pi}|\Gamma(0)|^2\mu_x^2$$

$$-R_{NY'X'}(0) - 2\frac{\sqrt{N}}{\sqrt{2\pi}}\Gamma(0)\mu_x R'_{NY'X'}(0)$$

$$= \frac{N}{2\pi}\left(\bar{Y}'^2 + 2\bar{Y}'\mu_y + \mu_y^2\right) - R_{NY'X'}(0)$$

$$-2\frac{\sqrt{N}}{\sqrt{2\pi}}\Gamma(0)\mu_x R'_{NY'X'}(0)$$

$$= I_{NY}(0) - R_{NY'X'}(0) - 2\frac{\sqrt{N}}{\sqrt{2\pi}}\Gamma(0)\mu_x R'_{NY'X'}(0)$$

which completes the proof of the third assertion. A proof of the last assertion may be based on proposition 10.8.5. in Brockwell and Davis [10]. However, the latter result is shown only for $\Gamma(\cdot)$ being a one-sided stable ARMA filter (which is more restrictive than $\Gamma(\cdot) \in C_f^{1/2}$) and $X_t = \epsilon_t$ being a white noise process. Therefore, a generalization is needed here. For that purpose consider

$$R'_{NYX}(\omega_j) = \sum_{k=-\infty}^{\infty} \gamma_k \exp(-ik\omega_j)$$

$$\frac{\sqrt{2\pi}}{\sqrt{N}}\left(\sum_{t=1-k}^{N-k} X_t \exp(-it\omega_j) - \sum_{t=1}^{N} X_t \exp(-it\omega_j)\right)$$

$$= \sum_{k=-\infty}^{\infty} \gamma_k \exp(-ik\omega_j)\frac{\sqrt{2\pi}}{\sqrt{N}}$$

$$\left[\sum_{t=1}^{\min(k,N)} \left(X_{t-k}\exp(-i(t-k)\omega_j) - X_{N+t-k}\exp(-i(N+t-k)\omega_j)\right)\right.$$

$$+ \sum_{t=1}^{\min(-k,N)} \left(X_{N+1-t-k}\exp(-i(N+1-t-k)\omega_j)\right.$$

$$\left.\left. -X_{1-t-k}\exp(-i(1-t-k)\omega_j)\right)\right]$$

$$= \sum_{k=-\infty}^{\infty} \gamma_k \exp(-ik\omega_j)\frac{\sqrt{2\pi}}{\sqrt{N}}$$

$$\left[\sum_{t=1}^{\min(k,N)} \left(X_{t-k} - X_{N+t-k}\right)\exp(-i(t-k)\omega_j)\right.$$

$$\left. + \sum_{t=1}^{\min(-k,N)} \left(X_{N+1-t-k} - X_{1-t-k}\right)\exp(-i(1-t-k)\omega_j)\right]$$

where the last equality follows from $\omega_j \in \Omega_N$. From (4.28) the error term r_N in (4.22) can be decomposed according to

$$r_N = \frac{2\pi}{N} \sum_{j=-[N/2]}^{[N/2]} w_j 2\text{Re}\big(R'_{NYX}(-\omega_j)\Gamma(\omega_j)\Xi_{NX}(\omega_j)\big)$$

$$+ \frac{2\pi}{N} \sum_{j=-[N/2]}^{[N/2]} w_j |R'_{NYX}(\omega_j)|^2$$

From (4.27) the second term is negligible. Consider therefore

$$\frac{2\pi}{N} \sum_{j=-[N/2]}^{[N/2]} w_j R'_{NYX}(-\omega_j)\Gamma(\omega_j)\Xi_{NX}(\omega_j)$$

$$= \left(\frac{2\pi}{N}\right)^2 \sum_{j=-[N/2]}^{[N/2]} \sum_{k=-\infty}^{\infty} \sum_{l=-\infty}^{\infty} I_{\{l>0\}}$$

$$\times \sum_{r=1}^{\min(l,N)} \sum_{t=1}^{N} \gamma_k \gamma_l X_t \Big(X_{r-l} - X_{N+r-l}\Big) w_j \exp(-i(k-r+t)\omega_j)$$

$$+ \left(\frac{2\pi}{N}\right)^2 \sum_{j=-[N/2]}^{[N/2]} \sum_{k=-\infty}^{\infty} \sum_{l=-\infty}^{\infty} I_{\{l<0\}}$$

$$\times \sum_{r=1}^{\min(-l,N)} \sum_{t=1}^{N} \gamma_k \gamma_l X_t \Big(X_{N+1-r-l} - X_{1-r-l}\Big)$$

$$w_j \exp(-i(k-1+r+t)\omega_j)$$

where $I_{\{l>0\}}$ and $I_{\{l<0\}}$ are indicator functions. For k,l,r fixed let $s = r - k \mod(N)$ so that

$$\frac{1}{N} \sum_{j=-[N/2]}^{[N/2]} w_j \exp(-i(k-r+t)\omega_j) = \begin{cases} 0 & t \neq s \\ 1 & \text{else} \end{cases}$$

Thus

$$E\left[\left|\frac{1}{N} \sum_{t=1}^{N} \gamma_k \gamma_l X_t \Big(X_{r-l} - X_{N+r-l}\Big) \sum_{j=-[N/2]}^{[N/2]} w_j \exp(-i(k-r+t)\omega_j)\right|\right]$$

$$\leq 2|\gamma_k \gamma_l| E[X_t^2]$$

and analogously

$$E\left[\left|\frac{1}{N} \sum_{t=1}^{N} \gamma_k \gamma_l X_t \Big(X_{N+1-r-l} - X_{1-r-l}\Big)\right.\right.$$

$$\left.\left.\sum_{j=-[N/2]}^{[N/2]} w_j \exp(-i(k-1+r+t)\omega_j)\right|\right]$$

$$\leq 2|\gamma_k \gamma_l| E[X_t^2]$$

Therefore

$$E[|r_N|] \approx E\left[\left\|\frac{2\pi}{N} \sum_{j=-[N/2]}^{[N/2]} w_j \mathrm{Re}\left(R'_{NYX}(-\omega_j)\Gamma(\omega_j)\Xi_{NX}(\omega_j)\right)\right\|\right]$$

$$\leq E\left[\left\|\frac{2\pi}{N} \sum_{j=-[N/2]}^{[N/2]} w_j R'_{NYX}(-\omega_j)\Gamma(\omega_j)\Xi_{NX}(\omega_j)\right\|\right]$$

$$\leq \frac{4\pi^2}{N} \sum_{k=-\infty}^{\infty} \sum_{l=-\infty}^{\infty} 2|\gamma_k \gamma_l|\, |\min(|l|,N)|\, E[X_t^2]$$

$$= o(1/\sqrt{N})$$

where the last equality follows from

$$\frac{1}{N}\sum_{k=-\infty}^{\infty}\sum_{l=-\infty}^{\infty}|\gamma_k\gamma_l|\,|\min(|l|,N)| \leq \frac{1}{\sqrt{N}}\sum_{k=-\infty}^{\infty}|\gamma_k|\sum_{l=-\infty}^{\infty}|\gamma_l||\sqrt{l}|\frac{\sqrt{\min(|l|,N)}}{\sqrt{N}}$$

$$= o(1/\sqrt{N})$$

since $\Gamma(\cdot) \in C_f^{1/2}$ and $\displaystyle\lim_{N\to\infty}\frac{\sqrt{\min(|l|,N)}}{\sqrt{N}} = 0$ for each l. This completes the proof of the theorem. $\Box$

Remarks

- A stronger result than that in the second assertion of the above theorem is presented in theorem 6.2.2 in Priestley [75], namely

$$I_{NY}(\omega) = |\Gamma(\omega)|^2 I_{NX}(\omega) + R_{NYX}(\omega)$$

where

$$E[|R_{NYX}(\omega)|^2] = O(1/N^{2\alpha}) \tag{4.29}$$

for $\Gamma \in C_f^\alpha$ and X_t a white noise sequence. Unfortunately, this result is false for arbitrary α as can be seen by the following argument:

$$E[I_{NY}(\omega)] = \frac{1}{2\pi}\sum_{k=N-1}^{N-1}\left(1 - \frac{|k|}{N}\right)R_Y(k)\exp(-ik\omega)$$

see (4.10). Thus the bias of the periodogram of Y_t is of order $1/N$ if Y_t is not white noise. On the other hand, the periodogram of the white noise sequence X_t is unbiased (see for example Brockwell and Davis [10], p.344). This contradicts (4.29) if $\alpha > 1/2$ (private note of H.R. Kuensch). Theorem

6.2.2 in Priestley [75],p.424, relies on a result in Walker [90]: in that article, α was not explicitly constrained to be less than $1/2$ although a look at the proofs on p.111, 113, 115 reveals that the approximations (inequalities) are valid for $\alpha \leq 1/2$ only (Walker uses δ instead of α).

- It is shown in equation (4.10) that $I_{NY}(0) = \frac{N}{2\pi}\bar{Y}^2 = O(N)$ if $\mu_y \neq 0$. Therefore, the error term $R_{NY'X'}(0) + 2\frac{\sqrt{N}}{\sqrt{2\pi}}\Gamma(0)\mu R'_{NY'X'}(0) = O(1)$ in (4.21) is negligible.

In the next section properties of the periodogram of non-stationary integrated processes are analyzed. It is shown that explorative instruments useful for selecting particular filter designs (constraints) for the DFA can be derived from these results.

4.3 The Periodogram for Integrated Processes

In this section important properties of the periodogram of integrated input processes are presented which are not discussed in the literature. Also, a set of explorative instruments (specific to the signal estimation problem) are derived from these results. The proposed instruments can be used for choosing optimal filter designs.

Assume the process X_t satisfies

$$\prod_{k=1}^{p}(1 - Z_k B)^{d_k} X_t = \beta(B)\epsilon_t$$

where $Z_k = \exp(i\lambda_k)$ (and B is the backshift operator) and d_k, $k = 1,...,p$ are positive integers. Let $\tilde{X}_t := \beta(B)\epsilon_t = \sum_{k=-\infty}^{\infty} b_k\epsilon_{t-k} \in C_f^0$ and assume also that the spectral density of $\tilde{X}_t$ satisfies $\tilde{h}(\lambda_k) > 0$ (so that X_t is indeed integrated). Recall that the spectral density of $\tilde{X}_t$ must exist because its coefficients were assumed to be absolutely summable, see (4.18). Define the order of integration d of X_t as $d := \max_k(d_k)$. Then X_t is called an $I(d)$-process with $\sum d_k$ unit-roots.

4.3.1 Integrated Processes of Order One

Let $Z = \exp(i\lambda)$ and assume that the process X_t satisfies the difference equation

$$\tilde{X}_t = X_t - ZX_{t-1} = \beta(B)\epsilon_t \tag{4.30}$$

where $\tilde{X}_t \in C_f^0$, $E[\tilde{X}_t] = 0$. If

$$\tilde{h}(\lambda) > 0 \tag{4.31}$$

then X_t has a simple unit-root located at frequency λ.

Definition 4.9. *The pseudo spectral density $h(\omega)$ of X_t is defined by*

$$h(\omega) := \begin{cases} \dfrac{\tilde{h}(\omega)}{|1 - Z\exp(-i\omega)|^2} & \omega \neq \lambda \\ \infty & \omega = \lambda \end{cases}$$

Assume for sake of simplicity that the process is initialized in $t = -1$ i.e. $X_{-1} = 0$. Therefore, $X_t = \sum_{j=0}^{t} Z^j \tilde{X}_{t-j}$. The following theorem summarizes results from theorem B.10 in the appendix.

Theorem 4.10. *Let X_t and $\tilde{X}_t$ be defined by (4.30) i.e. $\tilde{X}_t \in C_f^0$, $E[\tilde{X}_t] = 0$, $Z = \exp(i\lambda)$, $\tilde{h}(\lambda) > 0$, $X_{-1} = 0$ and let*

$$\Omega_{N+1} := \{\omega_k \,|\, \omega_k = k2\pi/(N+1), \; |k| = 0, ..., [(N+1)/2]\}$$

For $\omega \notin \Omega_{N+1}$ define the periodogram $I_{N+1X}(\omega)$ by (4.16) and use a similar extension for the discrete Fourier transform $\Xi_{N+1X}(\omega)$.

- *If $\omega_k \neq \lambda$ then*

$$I_{N+1X}(\omega_k) = \frac{\left|\Xi_{N+1\tilde{X}}(\omega_k) - \nu\right|^2}{|1 - Z\exp(-i\omega_k)|^2} \tag{4.32}$$

  where the random variable $\nu := Z^{N+1}\Xi_{N+1\tilde{X}}(\lambda)$ is independent of ω_k.
- *If $X_t \in C_f^0$ and $\lambda \in \Omega_{N+1}$ then*

$$I_{N+1X}(\lambda) = (N+1)^2 \zeta_\lambda \quad where \quad \lim_{N\to\infty} E[\zeta_\lambda] = \tilde{h}(\lambda)/3 \tag{4.33}$$

Proof. Only the first assertion is proved here (see theorem B.10 in the appendix for a complete proof). Consider:

$$I_{N+1X}(\omega) = \frac{1}{2\pi(N+1)} \left| \sum_{t=0}^{N} X_t \exp(-it\omega) \right|^2$$

$$= \frac{1}{2\pi(N+1)} \left| \sum_{t=0}^{N} \left(\sum_{j=0}^{t} Z^j \tilde{X}_{t-j} \right) \exp(-it\omega) \right|^2$$

$$= \frac{1}{2\pi(N+1)} \left| \sum_{t=0}^{N} \tilde{X}_t \left(\sum_{j=0}^{N-t} Z^j \exp(-i(j+t)\omega) \right) \right|^2$$

$$= \frac{1}{2\pi(N+1)} \left| \sum_{t=0}^{N} \tilde{X}_t \exp(-it\omega) \left(\sum_{j=0}^{N-t} Z^j \exp(-ij\omega) \right) \right|^2 \tag{4.34}$$

$$= \frac{1}{2\pi(N+1)} \left| \sum_{t=0}^{N} \tilde{X}_t \exp(-it\omega) \frac{1 - Z^{N-t+1}\exp(-i(N-t+1)\omega)}{1 - Z\exp(-i\omega)} \right|^2$$

$$= \frac{1}{|1 - Z\exp(-i\omega)|^2} \frac{1}{2\pi(N+1)}$$

$$\left| \sum_{t=0}^{N} \tilde{X}_t \exp(-it\omega) - Z^{N+1}\exp(-i(N+1)\omega) \sum_{t=0}^{N} \tilde{X}_t Z^{-t} \right|^2$$

$$= \frac{|\Xi_{N+1\tilde{X}}(\omega) - Z^{N+1}\exp(-i(N+1)\omega)\Xi_{N+1\tilde{X}}(\lambda)|^2}{|1 - Z\exp(-i\omega)|^2} \qquad (4.35)$$

If $\omega \in \Omega_{N+1}$, then $\exp(-i(N+1)\omega) \equiv 1$ which proves the first assertion of the theorem (see the appendix for a proof of the second assertion). □

Remark

- Theorem 4.8 (convolution theorem) does not apply here, since the filter co-efficients of $1/|1 - Z\exp(-i\omega_k)|^2$ do not converge to zero (or, equivalently, the MA-coefficients of X_t do not converge to zero). Theorem B.10 in the appendix shows that the periodogram is biased even asymptotically (as an estimate of the pseudo spectral density) and that $I_{NX}(\omega_k)$ and $I_{NX}(\omega_l)$ are correlated even asymptotically for $k \neq l$. The 'infinite memory' induced by the integration operator is responsible for these undesirable properties.

The important special case $Z = 1$ (i.e. $X_t = X_{t-1} + \tilde{X}_t$) is treated in the following corollary.

Corollary 4.11. *Assume $X_t - X_{t-1} = \tilde{X}_t$ with $\tilde{X}_t \in C_f^0$ and $\tilde{h}(0) > 0$ (so that X_t is indeed integrated). Assume also $X_{-1} = 0$ and the sample is given by $X_0, ..., X_N$. Define an adjusted time series by $X'_t := X_t - tX_N/(N+1)$. Then*

$$I_{N+1X'}(\omega_k) = \begin{cases} 0 & \omega_k = 0 \\ \dfrac{I_{N+1\tilde{X}}(\omega_k)}{|1 - \exp(-i\omega_k)|^2} & else \end{cases} \qquad (4.36)$$

where $I_{N+1X'}(\cdot)$ is the periodogram of the adjusted series.

Proof.

$$\tilde{X}_t = \Delta X_t = X_t - X_{t-1} = X'_t - X'_{t-1} + C = \Delta X'_t + C$$

where $C := X_N/(N+1)$. Equation (4.7) then implies

$$I_{N+1\tilde{X}}(\omega_k) = I_{N+1\Delta X'}(\omega_k) \qquad (4.37)$$

for all $\omega_k(\in \Omega_{N+1}) \neq 0$. Note also that $\overline{\Delta X} := \sum_{t=0}^{N} \Delta X_t/(N+1) = X_N/(N+1)$ (because $X_{-1} = 0$). Therefore $\overline{\Delta X'} = \overline{\Delta X} - \overline{\Delta X} = 0$. It follows that

$$I_{N+1X'}(\omega_k) = \frac{|\Xi_{N+1\Delta X'}(\omega_k) - \nu|^2}{|1 - \exp(-i\omega_k)|^2} \tag{4.38}$$

$$= \frac{I_{N+1\Delta X'}(\omega_k)}{|1 - \exp(-i\omega_k)|^2}$$

$$= \frac{I_{N+1\tilde{x}}(\omega_k)}{|1 - \exp(-i\omega_k)|^2}$$

for all $\omega_k(\in \Omega_{N+1}) \neq 0$. The first equality follows from the first assertion of theorem 4.10. The second one uses $\overline{\Delta X'} = 0$ and (4.12) which imply $\Xi_{N+1\Delta X'}(0) = \overline{\Delta X'}\sqrt{(N+1)/2\pi} = 0$ and therefore the random variable ν vanishes in (4.32) or equivalently in (4.38). The last equality follows from (4.37) which completes the proof of the corollary. □

It is shown in the corollary that the periodogram of (the adjusted series) X_t' may be considered as an estimate of the pseudo spectral density of the integrated process, at least for $\omega_k \neq 0$. Unfortunately this estimate is very poor for $\omega_0 = 0$ (since it equals zero whereas the pseudo spectral density is infinite). If it is known that X_t is integrated, then $I_{N+1X'}(0) := \infty$ is the right choice. Otherwise, $I_{N+1X'}(0)$ can be replaced by $I_{N+1X}(0) = \frac{N+1}{2\pi}\overline{X}^2$. This is a more 'flexible' estimate because

- for stationary input signals proposition 7.5 in Hamilton [45] proves that

$$Var(\overline{X}) = E[\overline{X}^2] \simeq \frac{2\pi}{N+1}h(0)$$

  i.e. $E[I_{N+1X}(0)] \simeq \tilde{h}(0)$ (if $E[X_t] = 0$)
- and for integrated processes it is shown in theorem 4.10 (second assertion) that

$$E[I_{N+1X}(0)] \simeq 2\pi\frac{(N+1)^2}{3}\tilde{h}(0)$$

  which grows quadratically in N and linearly in $\tilde{h}(0)$.

Therefore, $\frac{N+1}{2\pi}\overline{X}^2$ adapts for stationary as well as $I(1)$-processes (these issues may play a role in signal extraction, especially for 'misspecified' designs, see sections 5.3 and 7.2).

In the following section, results for the periodogram of $I(2)$-processes are presented. A generalization of the above corollary 4.11 is proposed. It is shown that these results can be used for deriving explorative instruments for choosing among different possible filter designs for the DFA.

4.3.2 The Periodogram for $I(2)$-Processes

Let $(1 - ZB)^2Y_t = \beta(B)\epsilon_t$ with $Z = \exp(i\lambda)$ and define $X_t := (1 - ZB)Y_t$. Assume also $\tilde{h}(\lambda) > 0$ where $\tilde{h}(\cdot)$ is the spectral density of $\tilde{X}_t := (1 - ZB)X_t$

(so that X_t is an $I(1)$-process and Y_t is $I(2)$). Define the pseudo spectral density of Y_t by

$$h_Y(\omega) := \begin{cases} \dfrac{\tilde{h}(\omega)}{|1 - Z\exp(-i\omega t)|^4} & \omega \neq \lambda \\ \infty & \omega = \lambda \end{cases} \tag{4.39}$$

Equation (4.32) implies

$$I_{N+1Y}(\omega_k) = \frac{1}{2\pi(N+1)} \left| \frac{\sum_{t=0}^{N} X_t \exp(-it\omega_k)}{1 - Z\exp(-i\omega_k)} - \frac{M}{1 - Z\exp(-i\omega_k)} \right|^2 \tag{4.40}$$

where $M := Z^{N+1} \sum_{t=0}^{N} X_t Z^{-t}$ is independent of ω_k. Furthermore, (4.33) implies that

$$\frac{1}{2\pi(N+1)} |M|^2 = \frac{1}{2\pi(N+1)} \left| \sum_{t=0}^{N} X_t \exp(-i\lambda t) \right|^2$$

$$= I_{N+1X}(\lambda) = O(N^2) \tag{4.41}$$

Applying theorem 4.10 twice (for $I_{NY}(\lambda)$ and then for $I_{NX}(\lambda)$) implies that

$$I_{N+1Y}(\lambda) = O(N^4) \tag{4.42}$$

Remark

- Assume $|\omega_k - \lambda| > \delta$ where δ is fixed (independent of N) and satisfies $\pi - \lambda > \delta > 0$. Equations (4.40) and (4.41) imply that the bias of the periodogram (as an estimate of the pseudo spectral density) at ω_k is of order $O(N^2)$ which shows that this statistic is not to be recommended for processes whose integration order is equal to or greater than two. Section 7.2 exemplifies the consequences of this 'misspecification' using a simulated example.

Important special cases for the location of the unit-roots are treated in the following generalization of corollary 4.11.

Corollary 4.12. *1. Assume $(1 - B)^2 Y_t = \tilde{X}_t$ with $\tilde{X}_t \in C_f^0$ and $\tilde{h}(0) > 0$ (so that $d = 2$) and let Y_t be initialized in the past (for example $Y_{-1} = 0$). Assume $Y_0, Y_1, ..., Y_N$ are observed and define*

$$Y_t' := Y_t - t\left(\overline{\Delta Y} - \frac{N-1}{2}\overline{\Delta^2 Y}\right) - \frac{t^2}{2}\left(\overline{\Delta^2 Y}\right) \tag{4.43}$$

where $\overline{\Delta Y}$ and $\overline{\Delta^2 Y}$ are the arithmetic means of $\Delta Y_t := Y_t - Y_{t-1}$ and $\Delta^2 Y_t := Y_t - 2Y_{t-1} + Y_{t-2}$. Then

$$I_{N+1Y'}(\omega_k) = \begin{cases} 0 & \omega_k = 0 \\ \dfrac{I_{N+1\tilde{X}}(\omega_k)}{|1 - \exp(-i\omega_k)|^4} & else \end{cases} \tag{4.44}$$

2. If $(1 - B)(1 - B^{12})Y_t = \tilde{X}_t$ with $\tilde{X}_t \in C_f^0$ and $\tilde{h}(k\pi/6) > 0$, $k = 0, 1, ..., 6$ (so that $d = 2$), then define

$$Y_t'' := Y_t - \frac{t}{12}\left(\overline{\Delta_{12}Y} - \frac{N-1}{2}\overline{\Delta_{12}\Delta Y}\right)$$

$$-\left(\frac{t^2}{24} + \frac{t}{2}\right)(\overline{\Delta_{12}\Delta Y}) \qquad (4.45)$$

where $\overline{\Delta_{12}Y}$ and $\overline{\Delta_{12}\Delta Y}$ are the sample means of $Y_t - Y_{t-12}$ and $Y_t - Y_{t-1} - Y_{t-12} + Y_{t-13}$. It then follows that

$$I_{N+1Y''}(\omega_k) =$$
$$\begin{cases} 0 & \omega_k = 0 \\ \dfrac{I_{N+1\tilde{X}}(\omega_k)}{|1 - \exp(-i\omega_k)|^2|1 - \exp(-i12\omega_k)|^2} & if \begin{array}{l} \omega_k \neq j\pi/6, \\ j = 0, ..., 6 \end{array} \end{cases} \qquad (4.46)$$

It is here assumed that all sample means are computed from $t = 0$ to $t = N$, otherwise the above expressions must be slightly modified.

Proof. A proof of the corollary is established for (4.44) only (a similar proof applies to (4.46)). From

$$\Delta Y_t' = \Delta Y_t - \left(\overline{\Delta Y} - \frac{N-1}{2}\overline{\Delta^2 Y}\right) - (t - 1/2)(\overline{\Delta^2 Y})$$

$$= \Delta Y_t - \overline{\Delta Y} - (\overline{\Delta^2 Y})\left((t - 1/2) - \overline{(t - 1/2)}\right)$$

$\left(\text{where } \overline{(t - 1/2)} = (N - 1)/2 \text{ is the arithmetic mean of } t - 1/2\right)$ and from

$$\Delta^2 Y_t' = \Delta^2 Y_t - \overline{\Delta^2 Y} = \tilde{X}_t - \overline{\tilde{X}} \qquad (4.47)$$

one deduces

$$\overline{\Delta Y'} = \overline{\Delta^2 Y'} = 0 \qquad (4.48)$$

Moreover, (4.47) together with (4.7) imply

$$I_{N+1\Delta^2 Y'}(\omega_k) = I_{N+1\tilde{X}}(\omega_k) \qquad (4.49)$$

for $\omega_k(\in \Omega_{N+1}) \neq 0$. It follows that

$$I_{N+1Y'}(\omega_k) = \frac{|\Xi_{N+1\Delta Y'}(\omega_k) - \nu_1|^2}{|1 - \exp(-i\omega_k)|^2} \qquad (4.50)$$

$$= \frac{I_{N+1\Delta Y'}(\omega_k)}{|1 - \exp(-i\omega_k)|^2}$$

$$= \frac{|\Xi_{N+1\Delta^2 Y'}(\omega_k) - \nu_2|^2}{|1 - \exp(-i\omega_k)|^4} \qquad (4.51)$$

$$= \frac{I_{N+1\Delta^2 Y'}(\omega_k)}{|1 - \exp(-i\omega_k)|^4}$$

$$= \frac{I_{N+1\tilde{X}}(\omega_k)}{|1 - \exp(-i\omega_k)|^4}$$

for $\omega_k(\in \Omega_{N+1}) \neq 0$. The first equality follows from the first assertion of theorem 4.10. The second one uses (4.48) and (4.12) which imply $\Xi_{N+1\Delta Y'}(0) = \overline{\Delta Y'}\sqrt{(N+1)/2\pi} = 0$ and therefore the random variable ν_1 vanishes in (4.32) or equivalently in (4.50). The third equation again follows from the first assertion of theorem 4.10 (applied to $I_{N+1\Delta Y'}(\omega_k)$). As before, the fourth equality follows from (4.48) and (4.12) (implying $\Xi_{N+1\Delta^2 Y'}(0) = \overline{\Delta^2 Y'}\sqrt{(N+1)/2\pi} = 0$). Finally, the last equality follows from (4.49), which completes the proof of the corollary. $\square$

Defining an adjusted series Y_t' or Y_t'' as done in the above corollary may seem unnecessarily complicated if the only issue is to replace the poor estimate $I_{NY}(\omega_k)$ by (4.44) or (4.46). However, the adjusted series Y_t' or Y_t'' are interesting *per se* since they may be used advantageously for selecting particular filter designs. More precisely, they can give indications as to whether the DGP is integrated or not. This is shown in the following examples.

Assume Y_t is integrated of order two with roots $Z_1 = Z_2 = 1$ and $Y_{-1} = Y_{-2} = 0$. A straightforward calculation (see for example the development preceding (4.35)) shows that

$$(1 - \exp(-i\omega_k))\Xi_{N+1Y}(\omega_k) = \Xi_{N+1\Delta Y}(\omega_k) - \Xi_{N+1\Delta Y}(0) \quad (4.52)$$

Since ΔY_t is I(1) with a unit-root at frequency zero, it is shown in theorem 4.10 that the second term on the right of this equality is of order $\Xi_{N+1\Delta Y}(0) = O(N)$ so that it dominates $\Xi_{N+1\Delta Y}(\omega_k)$ if $|\omega_k| > \delta$, where δ is held fixed (independent of N). Therefore

$$\begin{aligned}
I_{N+1Y}(\omega_k) &= \frac{|\Xi_{N+1\Delta Y}(\omega_k) - \Xi_{N+1\Delta Y}(0)|^2}{|1 - \exp(-i\omega_k)|^2} \\
&\simeq \frac{|\Xi_{N+1\Delta Y}(0)|^2}{|1 - \exp(-i\omega_k)|^2} \\
&> \frac{|\Xi_{N+1\Delta Y}(\omega_k)|^2}{|1 - \exp(-i\omega_k)|^2} \\
&= \frac{I_{N+1\Delta Y}(\omega_k)}{|1 - \exp(-i\omega_k)|^2} \\
&= \frac{|\Xi_{N+1\tilde{X}}(\omega_k) - \Xi_{N+1\tilde{X}}(0)|^2}{|1 - \exp(-i\omega_k)|^4}
\end{aligned}$$

Taking expectations implies that

$$\begin{aligned}
E[I_{N+1Y}(\omega_k)] &> E\left[\frac{|\Xi_{N+1\tilde{X}}(\omega_k) - \Xi_{N+1\tilde{X}}(0)|^2}{|1 - \exp(-i\omega_k)|^4}\right] \\
&\approx E\left[\frac{|\Xi_{N+1\tilde{X}}(\omega_k)|^2}{|1 - \exp(-i\omega_k)|^4}\right] + E\left[\frac{|\Xi_{N+1\tilde{X}}(0)|^2}{|1 - \exp(-i\omega_k)|^4}\right]
\end{aligned}$$

$$> E\left[\frac{I_{N+1\tilde{X}}(\omega_k)}{|1 - \exp(-i\omega_k)|^4}\right]$$

$$= E[I_{N+1Y'}(\omega_k)]$$

where the orthogonality of $\Xi_{N+1\tilde{X}}(\omega_k)$ and $\Xi_{N+1\tilde{X}}(0)$ is used in deriving the approximation and where $I_{N+1Y'}(\omega_k)$ is the periodogram of the adjusted series. Thus, $I_{N+1Y}(\omega_k)$ asymptotically dominates $I_{N+1Y'}(\omega_k)$ (in the mean). Let for example

$$(1 - B)(1 - B^{12})Y_t = (1 - 0.6B)(1 - 0.5B)\epsilon_t$$

A particular realization (dotted line) and the result of an adjustment of order two Y_t'' (4.45) (solid line) of this process are shown in figure 4.1. To see the

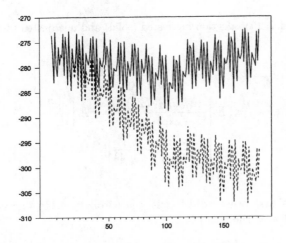

Fig. 4.1. Adjustment for an I(2)-process (adjusted : solid line)

effect of the adjustment compare the periodograms of Y_t and Y_t'' in figure 4.2 (the smallest frequency corresponds to ω_1) : spectral power which 'contaminates' the periodogram of Y_t has been removed in the adjusted series Y_t'' (this power corresponds to ν in (4.32)).

Assume now Y_t is integrated of order one with the root $Z = 1$ and let $Y_{-1} = 0$. It is shown in (4.52) (or (4.35)) that

$$I_{N+1Y}(\omega_k) = \frac{|\Xi_{N+1\Delta Y}(\omega_k) - \Xi_{N+1\Delta Y}(0)|^2}{|1 - \exp(-i\omega_k)|^2}$$

Since ΔY_t is stationary, equation (B.10) (see theorem B.4 in the appendix) shows that $\Xi_{N+1\Delta Y}(\omega_k)$ and $\Xi_{N+1\Delta Y}(0)$ are asymptotically uncorrelated random variables if $\omega_k \neq 0$. Therefore

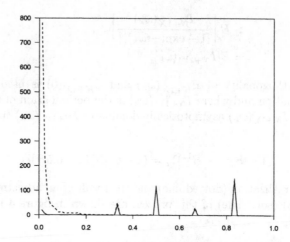

Fig. 4.2. Periodogram : adjusted (solid) and unadjusted (dotted)

$$
\begin{aligned}
E\left[I_{N+1Y}(\omega_k)\right] &= E\left[\frac{|\Xi_{N+1\Delta Y}(\omega_k) - \Xi_{N+1\Delta Y}(0)|^2}{|1 - \exp(-i\omega_k)|^2}\right] \\
&\simeq E\left[\frac{|\Xi_{N+1\Delta Y}(\omega_k)|^2}{|1 - \exp(-i\omega_k)|^2}\right] + E\left[\frac{|\Xi_{N+1\Delta Y}(0)|^2}{|1 - \exp(-i\omega_k)|^2}\right] \\
&> E\left[\frac{|\Xi_{N+1\Delta Y}(\omega_k)|^2}{|1 - \exp(-i\omega_k)|^2}\right] \\
&= E\left[I_{N+1Y'}(\omega_k)\right]
\end{aligned}
$$

where Y_t' is a first order adjustment, see corollary 4.11. The two examples above suggest that the condition

$$
\sum_{\substack{k \neq 0}}^{N/2} I_{N+1Y}(\omega_k) > \sum_{\substack{k \neq 0}}^{N/2} I_{N+1Y'}(\omega_k) \tag{4.53}
$$

or equivalently

$$
\frac{1}{N+1}\sum_{t=0}^{N}(Y_t - \overline{Y})^2 > \frac{1}{N+1}\sum_{t=0}^{N}(Y_t' - \overline{Y'})^2 = \frac{1}{N+1}\sum_{t=0}^{N}(Y_t')^2 \tag{4.54}
$$

are indicative for a unit-root of the process Y_t (at frequency zero). Note that the latter inequality (4.54) follows from (4.53) and the discrete spectral decomposition (4.14). Note also that (4.54) affords less computational efforts than (4.53) (which justifies use of adjusted series here).

As an example consider

$$
(1 - B)Y_t = (1 - 0.6B)(1 - 0.5B)\epsilon_t
$$

A particular realization (dotted line) and a (first order) adjustment (solid line) of this process are shown in figure 4.3. The sample variances are

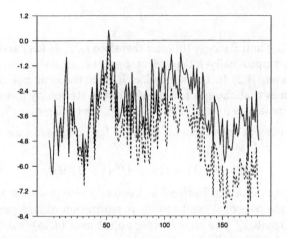

Fig. 4.3. Adjusted (solid) and original (dotted) time series

$$2.62 = \frac{1}{N+1}\sum_{t=0}^{N}(Y_t - \overline{Y})^2 > \frac{1}{N+1}\sum_{t=0}^{N}(Y_t' - \overline{Y'})^2 = 1.99$$

The above examples illustrate the 'underadjustment' effect which is due to the asymptotic dominance of the periodogram of the unadjusted (integrated) series, as seen in (4.53). Consider now examples of 'overadjustment'. Assume $Y_t \in C_f^0$ (so that adjustment is unnecessary). From (4.52) and using $\omega_1 = \pi/[N/2]$ one obtains

$$\Xi_{N+1\Delta Y}(\omega_1) = (1 - \exp(-i\omega_1))\Xi_{N+1Y}(\omega_1) + \Xi_{N+1\Delta Y}(0)$$

$$= (1 - \exp(-i\omega_1))\Xi_{N+1Y}(\omega_1) + \frac{\sqrt{N+1}}{\sqrt{2\pi}}\overline{\Delta Y}$$

$$= (1 - \exp(-i\omega_1))\Xi_{N+1Y}(\omega_1) + \frac{1}{\sqrt{2\pi(N+1)}}(Y_N - Y_{-1})$$

$$= O(1/N) + O(1/\sqrt{N})$$

(recall that $\omega_1 = \pi/[N/2]$ which explains the $O(1/N)$ term in the last equality).Therefore, the periodogram of the (over)adjusted series satisfies

$$I_{N+1Y'}(\omega_1) = \frac{|\Xi_{N+1\Delta Y}(\omega_1)|^2}{|1 - \exp(-i\omega_1)|^2}$$

$$= \frac{O(1/N)}{O(1/N^2)}$$

$$= O(N)$$

Since the periodogram of the original series is $I_{N+1Y}(\omega_1) = O(1)$, 'overadjustment' produces spurious spectral power (towards ω_1).

Remark

- $\Xi_{N+1\Delta Y}(\omega_1)$ and $\Xi_{N+1\Delta Y}(0)$ (and therefore $I_{N+1\Delta Y}(\omega_1)$ and $I_{N+1\Delta Y}(0)$) are not asymptotically independent here, as suggested by theorem B.4 (and theorem B.2) in the appendix. In fact theorem B.4 (and theorem B.2) assumes that the spectral density of the stationary process is strictly positive whereas here $h_{\Delta Y}(0) = 0$ (due to 'overdifferencing').

The 'overadjustment' effect can be observed for integrated processes too. Let for example

$$(1 - B^{12})Y_t = (1 - 0.4B)(1 - 0.5B)\epsilon_t \tag{4.55}$$

Attention is focused on the unit-root at frequency zero (a similar analysis could be made for the 'seasonal' unit-roots). A realization of this process (dotted line) and the result Y_t'' of a second order adjustment (4.45) (solid line) can be seen in figure 4.4. The adjustment of order two is 'misspecified' here since the process is I(1). As can be seen in fig.4.5, the adjustment does not significantly

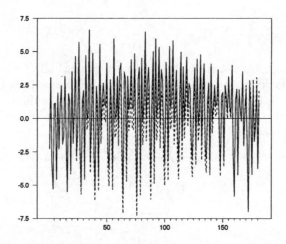

Fig. 4.4. Overadjustment for an I(1)-process (solid line)

affect 'high frequencies' (both periodograms are almost indistinguishable). However, for $\omega_1 = \pi/[N/2]$ one obtains

$$\frac{I_{N\Delta_{12}Y}(\omega_1)}{|1 - \exp(-i12\omega_1)|^2} = 0.073$$

$$I_{NY}(\omega_1) = 0.52$$

$$I_{NY''}(\omega_1) = 4.8$$

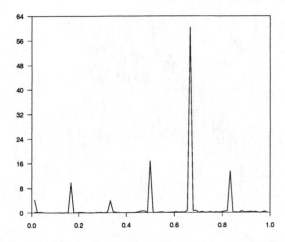

Fig. 4.5. Periodogram : (over)adjusted (solid) and unadjusted (dotted)

where $I_{N\Delta_{12}Y}(\cdot)$ is the periodogram of the stationary MA(2)-process on the right of (4.55). The first estimate is the 'natural' (unbiased) estimate of the pseudo spectral density. As expected, the adjustment of order two (for an I(1)-process) has induced spurious spectral power towards ω_1: $I_{NY''}(\omega_1)$ is significantly larger than the other two statistics. Also, the periodogram of the integrated process $I_{NY}(\omega_1)$ dominates the 'natural' estimate as expected by the previous 'underadjustment' effect. Note that the unit root at frequency zero is not easy to detect here because it is 'masked' by the $1 + B + ... + B^{11}$ operator in $1 - B^{12} = (1 - B)(1 + B + ... + B^{11})$ and by the negative MA-coefficients in (4.55).

In the last example, 'overadjustment' of order two is analyzed. Consider the (stationary) ARMA-process

$$(1 - 0.7B)Y_t = (1 - 0.4B)(1 - 0.5B)\epsilon_t$$

A realization (dotted line) and the result Y_t'' of an adjustment of order two (4.45) (solid line) are shown in figure 4.6. As can be seen by comparing the periodograms in fig.4.7, the unnecessary adjustment induces 'large' spurious spectral power towards $\omega_1 = \pi/[N/2]$.

To summarize : ignoring a unit-root implies that the periodogram of the integrated time series asymptotically dominates the periodogram of the adjusted series ('underadjustment'). On the contrary, 'overdifferencing' ('overadjustment') implies that the periodogram of the already stationary series is asymptotically dominated by the periodogram of the erroneously adjusted series. More generally, the unbiased estimate of the (pseudo) spectral density of the input signal is asymptotically dominated by the misspecified (biased)

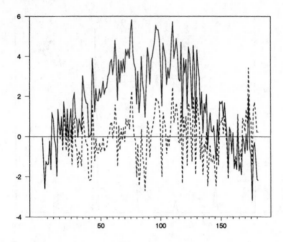

Fig. 4.6. Overadjustment for an I(0)-process (solid line)

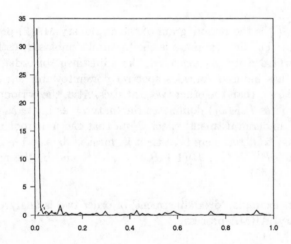

Fig. 4.7. Periodogram : adjusted (solid) and unadjusted (dotted)

'under' or 'overadjusted' spectral estimates. Therefore, adjusted series (Y_t' or Y_t''), periodograms of adjusted and of unadjusted (original) series and conditions like (4.53) or equivalently (4.54) can be used for an explorative analysis of unit-roots as shown above. However, these instruments are not an alternative to 'traditional' unit-root tests (for example Dickey-Fuller or Phillips-Perron tests). This point is now briefly discussed.

It is shown in chapter 5 that the best choice for the weighting function $G(\cdot)$ in (3.1) is the unbiased estimate of the (pseudo) spectral density of the input signal X_t. Therefore, 'local' differences

$$I_{N+1Y}(\omega_k) > I_{N+1Y'}(\omega_k)$$

or

$$I_{N+1Y}(\omega_k) < I_{N+1Y'}(\omega_k)$$

(where Y_t' is the adjusted series) towards 'potential' unit-root frequencies (for example frequency zero) or 'global' difference measures

$$\sum_{k\neq 0}^{N/2} I_{N+1Y}(\omega_k) > \sum_{k\neq 0}^{N/2} I_{N+1Y'}(\omega_k)$$

or

$$\sum_{k\neq 0}^{N/2} I_{N+1Y}(\omega_k) < \sum_{k\neq 0}^{N/2} I_{N+1Y'}(\omega_k)$$

give indications for the choice of the optimal weighting function $G(\cdot)$. The direction '>' indicates a possible 'underadjustment' (ignored unit-root) whereas the direction '<' suggests unnecessary 'overadjustment' (overdifferencing).

The choice of the best weighting function $G(\cdot)$ improves the performances of the resulting optimal asymmetric filter. Therefore, the proposed explorative instruments emphasize the boundary signal estimation problem (instead of the determination of the DGP). It is shown in section 5.3 that unit-roots of integrated processes induce particular constraints for the optimal asymmetric filters. Therefore, 'unit-roots' for the MBA are transposed into 'constraints' for the DFA. However, such constraints (i.e. particular designs of the asymmetric filters) may enhance the finite sample performances of the filters whether or not the input process is integrated. The proposed explorative instruments indicate which filter design (constraint) possibly performs better. Therefore, these instruments cannot replace traditional unit-root tests because they 'measure' a different aspect of the problem. As shown in chapter 7, a unit-root identified by a MBA for a particular series does not necessarily lead to a corresponding identification of a filter constraint for the asymmetric filter by the newly developped statistics for the DFA and conversely: both sets of statistical instruments measure different aspects of the same problem which are suited for their respective application fields. If a unit-root assumption enhances the one-step ahead forecasting performance of a particular model (for the DGP of X_t), then it does not necessarily follow that the corresponding constraint for the asymmetric filter improves the signal estimation performance (and conversely). Both problems are different for finite samples and an efficient solution for one does not necessarily lead to an efficient solution for the other. Adjusted series and periodograms of adjusted series are used as explorative instruments for inferring the best filter design in chapter 7, where the performances of various methods are compared empirically. Formal instruments (tests and filter selection criteria specifically derived for the signal estimation problem) for choosing among different filter designs are obtained from the distribution of the filter parameters in sections 5.7 and 6.2.

Remarks

- The adjusted time series satisfies $Y_0' = Y_N'$ (first order adjustment) and $\Delta Y_0' = \Delta Y_N'$ (second order adjustment), i.e. the 'levels' and the 'slopes' for $t = 0$ and $t = N$ are identical. This is achieved by subtracting linear (first order) or quadratic (second order) time trends whose coefficients are estimates of the means of the first and second order differences, see corollary 4.12. If $Y_t \in C_f^0$, then these estimates are of order $O(1/\sqrt{N})$ (see for example Brockwell and Davis [10] theorem 7.1.2 p.219). For integrated processes however these estimates do not vanish asymptotically (they do not even converge). The resulting 'spurious' linear or quadratic time trends induce the bias of the periodogram of the unadjusted integrated time series. By eliminating the 'spurious' trend through a suitable adjustment the periodogram of the resulting time series becomes an unbiased estimate of the (pseudo) spectral density for $\omega_k \neq 0$.

- 'Over' or 'underadjustment' can be detected by the fact that the unbiased estimate of the (pseudo) spectral density is dominated by the misspecified (under- or overadjusted) biased spectral estimates. If an adjusted time series is not 'overadjusted', then the transformation 'flattens' the original series which results in smaller unbiased estimates for the (pseudo) spectral density. However, in the presence of overadjustment the original series is 'inflated' which produces spurious spectral power (bias).

- Generalizations to arbitrary integration orders d are not difficult. The adjustment then removes a polynomial of order d in t. However, for most applications $d = 2$ is sufficient.

- A comparison of (4.44) and (4.39) reveals that the periodogram of the adjusted series Y_t' can be interpreted as estimate of the pseudo spectral density of the integrated process Y_t, at least for $\omega_k \neq 0$ (a similar conclusion would hold for (4.46)). But it is again a very poor estimate for $\omega_0 = 0$. As in the preceding section, the poor estimate $I_{N+1Y'}(0) = 0(= I_{N+1Y''}(0))$ can be replaced by $I_{N+1Y}(0) = \frac{N+1}{2\pi}\overline{Y}^2$ for frequency $\omega_0 = 0$. This choice is more sensible since the resulting estimate is able to adapt for unit-roots asymptotically.

In this chapter, properties of the periodogram were analyzed for stationary and integrated processes. Moreover, explorative instruments (specific to the signal estimation problem) for deciding between possible filter designs were derived from these results. The properties analyzed so far are useful for establishing theoretical results for the DFA in the following chapter 5.

5

Direct Filter Approach (DFA)

The new DFA briefly presented in section 1.4 is analyzed formally in this chapter. It is shown that the obtained signal estimates are consistent and efficient for a large class of input signals. For the DFA, the filter coefficients are obtained 'explicitly' by minimizing an efficient estimate of the revision error variance whereas for the MBA the filter coefficients are obtained 'implicitly' by minimizing the one-step ahead mean square forecasting error of a suitable time series model. Therefore, the DFA is efficient and 'more flexible'. So for example the 'fit' of the transfer functions (of symmetric and asymmetric filters) can be decomposed into the 'fit' of the amplitude functions and the 'fit' of the time shift (phase) functions. The separation of 'selectivity' and 'time shift' properties of the asymmetric filter can be used for optimizing filters subject to a time shift constraint. Therefore, it is possible to detect 'turning points' (for example of a trend signal) earlier than for traditional model-based methods.

An informal introduction is provided in section 5.1 where the main concepts are presented. In Sections 5.2 and 5.3 the *consistency* of the DFA is derived for stationary and non-stationary (integrated) input signals. In section 5.4 a generalized conditional optimization procedure is presented. The result is a filter with optimal selectivity properties subject to a time shift constraint. The efficiency of the direct filter approach is assessed in section 5.5. Two alternatives are analyzed: a 'linearized' approach and a solution based on a 'non-linear convolution'. The common asymptotic distribution of the estimated filter parameters is derived in section 5.6 under a generalized stationarity requirement. Thus, parameter hypotheses can be tested in the DFA and a criterion for inferring the optimal number of parameters of the asymmetric filter can be derived. Also, a 'unit-root' test specific to the signal estimation problem is proposed in section 5.7. Finally, a link between the DFA and the MBA is presented in section 5.8.

5.1 Overview

The transfer function of an ARMA filter is given by (recall (3.6)):

$$
\hat{\Gamma}_r^{Qq}(\omega) = C \exp(ir\omega) \frac{\prod_{j=1}^{n}(Z_{2j-1} - \exp(-i\omega))(Z_{2j} - \exp(-i\omega))}{\prod_{k=1}^{n'}(P_{2k-1} - \exp(-i\omega))(P_{2k} - \exp(-i\omega))}
\tag{5.1}
$$

$$
\times \frac{\prod_{j=2n+1}^{q+r}(Z_j - \exp(-i\omega))}{\prod_{k=2n'+1}^{Q}(P_k - \exp(-i\omega))}
$$

$$
= \sum_{k=-r}^{\infty} \hat{\gamma}_k \exp(-ik\omega)
$$

where (Z_{2j-1}, Z_{2j}), $j = 1, ..., n$ and (P_{2k-1}, P_{2k}), $k = 1, ..., n'$ are pairs of complex conjugate numbers (zeroes and poles) and Z_j, $j = 2n + 1, ..., q + r$, P_k, $k = 2n' + 1, ..., Q$ are real numbers (zeroes and poles). The superscript 'Qq' and the subscript r determine the AR- and the MA-orders of the filter (which are Q and $q + r$ respectively). Moreover, r indicates estimation for the time point $t = N - r$ in the sample, see definition 3.6. If the number of parameters $p = Q + q + r + 1$ is relevant (but not the AR- or MA-orders), then the filter is also denoted by $\hat{\Gamma}_r^p(\cdot)$. Note that an ARMA-filter assumes knowledge of a semi-infinite sample $..., X_{N-2}, X_{N-1}, X_N$. For simplicity of exposition, this problem is ignored here but solutions are proposed in section D.1 in the appendix.

Estimation for the time point $t = N - r$ implies that $N - r$ sample values $X_1, ..., X_{N-r}$ can be used 'on the left' of the filter and r sample values $X_{N-r+1}, ..., X_N$ 'on the right'. If $r \neq N/2$, then the filter $\hat{\Gamma}_r^p(\cdot)$ is generally asymmetric. Therefore, the estimation problem becomes more difficult for 'small' r. In principle, the filter (5.1) could be used for estimating $Y_{N-r'}$, where $r' > r$. However, such a choice would generally be inefficient because additional information as given by $X_{N-(r'-r)+1}, X_{N-(r'-r)+2}, ..., X_N$ can be used for estimating $Y_{N-r'}$.

Define $\Delta Y_{tr}^{Qq} := Y_t - \hat{Y}_{tr}^{Qq}$ where Y_t is the (unknown) output of a symmetric filter $\Gamma(\cdot)$ and $\hat{Y}_{tr}^{Qq}$ is the output of the (generally) asymmetric filter $\hat{\Gamma}_r^{Qq}(\cdot)$. Then a solution of

$$
\min_{\hat{\Gamma}_r^{Qq}} E[(\Delta Y_{tr}^{Qq})^2]
\tag{5.2}
$$

solves the signal estimation problem for the time point $t = N - r$ in the class of ARMA$(Q, q + r)$-filters. This is not necessarily the 'best' filter when considering a larger class of admissible solutions. However, in finite samples 'good' solutions can often be achieved for suitable choices of Q and q (this problem is discussed in section 6.2). Therefore, estimation of the parameters of ARMA$(Q, q + r)$-filters is of interest in this chapter. For notational convenience, 'Qq' and 'r' are often dropped from the notations $\hat{\Gamma}_r^{Qq}(\omega)$ or $\hat{Y}_{tr}^{Qq}$ if not explicitly required. But *beware of misinterpretation*:

$$\frac{1}{N}\sum_{t=1}^{N}(\Delta Y_t)^2 := \frac{1}{N}\sum_{t=1}^{N}(Y_t - \hat{Y}_{tr}^{Qq})^2 \neq \frac{1}{N}\sum_{t=1}^{N}(Y_t - \hat{Y}_{t,N-t}^{Qq})^2$$

The expression on the left hand side of the inequality is the sample estimate of (5.2) (which is of interest), whereas the expression on the right hand side is not meaningful: $\hat{Y}_{t,N-t}^{Qq}$ and $\hat{Y}_{t',N-t'}^{Qq}$ are outputs of *different* filters if $t \neq t'$. Also, the expression

$$\min_{\hat{\Gamma}} E[(\Delta Y_t)^2]$$

implicitly assumes an optimization for some fixed Q, q if not explicitly stated otherwise.

Note that the distinction between ZPC- (zero-pole-combination) and general ARMA-filters is not relevant in this chapter, because *asymptotic* results are analyzed only. The ZPC-constraint, namely the common argument of the zero-pole pair, intends to weaken overfitting which is a problem in finite samples (see chapters 6 and 7 for corresponding issues).

For most applications neither Y_t nor the data generating process of X_t (and thus of $\Delta Y_t := Y_t - \hat{Y}_t$) are known. Therefore, an approximation of the expectation in (5.2) is needed. Assume the input signal is a stationary MA process:

$$X_t = \mu + \sum_{k=-\infty}^{\infty} b_k \epsilon_{t-k} \qquad (5.3)$$

where ϵ_t is white noise. Consider the following expression :

$$\frac{2\pi}{N}\sum_{k=-[N/2]}^{[N/2]} w_k |\Delta\Gamma(\omega_k)|^2 I_{NX}(\omega_k)$$

where $\Delta\Gamma(\cdot) := \Gamma(\cdot) - \hat{\Gamma}(\cdot)$ and $\omega_k \in \Omega_N$. The weights w_k are defined in (4.2) and $I_{NX}(\cdot)$ is the periodogram of the input signal X_t, see section 4.1. The convolution theorem 4.8 shows that $|\Delta\Gamma(\omega_k)|^2 I_{NX}(\omega_k)$ can be interpreted as $I_{N\Delta Y}(\omega_k)$, i.e. as the periodogram of the output of the filter $\Delta\Gamma(\cdot)$. Thus

$$\frac{2\pi}{N}\sum_{k=-[N/2]}^{[N/2]} w_k |\Delta\Gamma(\omega_k)|^2 I_{NX}(\omega_k) \simeq \frac{2\pi}{N}\sum_{k=-[N/2]}^{[N/2]} w_k I_{N\Delta Y}(\omega_k) \qquad (5.4)$$

Note also that the left hand side can be computed from $X_1, ..., X_N$ whereas the right hand side cannot in general (since Y_t is unknown). Summing up

$I_{N\Delta Y}(\omega_k)$ in (5.4) corresponds to a (discrete) spectral decomposition of the natural estimate of the final revision error variance:

$$\frac{2\pi}{N} \sum_{k=-[N/2]}^{[N/2]} w_k I_{N\Delta Y}(\omega_k) = \frac{1}{N} \sum_{t=1}^{N} (\Delta Y_t)^2 \qquad (5.5)$$

The idea of the direct filter approach is the following : *find a filter $\hat{\Gamma}(\cdot)$ which minimizes the left hand side of (5.4). The corresponding filter output then minimizes (5.5) (up to a negligible error term), the latter expression being a natural (and efficient) estimate of (5.2).*
A formal development is provided in the following sections.

5.2 Consistency (Stationary MA-Processes)

The DFA is analyzed for stationary MA(∞) input processes. Wold's theorem (see section A.1.2 in the appendix) shows that a general stationary process can be decomposed into the sum of a MA(∞)-process and a linear deterministic harmonic process. Harmonic processes are ignored here, basically because most empirical time series seem not to be 'overlapped' by strictly sinusoidal components. Therefore, the class of MA-processes can be considered as a general class of stationary input signals.

Assume the symmetric (extraction) filter satisfies $\Gamma(\cdot) \in C_f^0$, so that the function $\Gamma(\cdot)$ is continuous and bounded. Therefore, it may seem 'natural' to require $\hat{\Gamma}(\cdot)$ to be bounded uniformly in N (i.e. independently of N). Assume also $X_t \in C_f^0$ so that the spectral density $h(\cdot)$ of the input process is continuous and bounded, see proposition B.1 in the appendix. Imposing continuity (in some sense uniformly) of the approximating ARMA filter seems another 'natural' and more restrictive requirement (examples of bounded and discontinuous (in the limit) filters are provided in chapter 6). These issues are now motivated more formally.

Assume that the input process X_t is regular (i.e. it is not linear deterministic, see section A.1.2 in the appendix). Then X_t admits a one-sided MA-representation $X_t = \sum_{k=0}^{\infty} b_k \epsilon_{t-k}$ (of possibly infinite order, see section A.1.2 in the appendix). Assume also that this one-sided representation is invertible, i.e. that X_t admits a (absolutely) convergent AR representation $X_t = \sum_{k=1}^{\infty} a_k X_{t-k} + \epsilon_t$ with $\sum_{k=1}^{\infty} |a_k| < \infty$ (this is for example useful when computing forecasts for the MBA). Finally, assume $X_t \in C_f^0$ so that its spectral density function exists (recall that the spectral density is the Fourier transform of the autocovariance function and use (4.18)). Invertibility implies that $h(\omega) = \sigma^2 \left| \sum_{k=0}^{\infty} b_k \exp(-ik\omega) \right|^2 > 0$ for all ω (otherwise a λ would exist such that $1 - \sum_{k=1}^{\infty} a_k \exp(-ik\lambda) = 1/\sum_{k=0}^{\infty} b_k \exp(-ik\lambda) = \infty$ which contradicts the absolute summability of the sequence a_k). Using the fact that

$1/\sum_{k=0}^{\infty} b_k B^k$ transforms X_t into ϵ_t, (2.24) then implies that the transfer function of the filter minimizing (5.2) is given by

$$\hat{\Gamma}_r^{\infty}(\omega) := \frac{\sum_{k=-r}^{\infty}\left(\sum_{j=0}^{\infty} b_j \gamma_{k-j}\right)\exp(-ik\omega)}{\sum_{j=0}^{\infty} b_j \exp(-ij\omega)} \tag{5.6}$$

The subscript r of $\hat{\Gamma}_r^{\infty}(\omega)$ indicates estimation for the time point $t = N - r$ (the filter (5.6) assumes knowledge of $X_{t+r}, X_{t+r-1}, \ldots$) and the superscript ∞ indicates that the filter may involve infinitely many parameters. It is easily seen from equation (5.6) that the optimal filter $\hat{\Gamma}_r^{\infty}$ is continuous and bounded (use $|\sum_{j=0}^{\infty} b_j \exp(-ij\omega)|^2 = h(\omega) > 0$, and proposition 4.7 for the numerator polynomial), which confirms the regularity requirements stated above.

Since the coefficients b_j are generally unknown, $\hat{\Gamma}_r^{\infty}(\cdot)$ is unknown too and must be estimated. Therefore, solutions generally depend on N, the length of the sample. From the preceding discussion it is then natural to require *uniform* continuity (stability of the ARMA-filters) of the estimated solutions:

Definition 5.1. *A sequence of ARMA filters* $\hat{\Gamma}_N(\cdot)$ *is called uniformly stable or uniformly continuous if* $\sum_{k=-r}^{\infty} |\hat{\gamma}_{Nk}| < M$ *for some* $M > 0$, *where* M *does not depend on* N.

If the number of parameters p is fixed (independent of N), then definition 5.1 implies that for stable ARMA filters

$$\sum_{k=-r}^{\infty} |\hat{\gamma}_{Nk}||k|^{\alpha} < M_{\alpha}$$

for all α (where $M_{\alpha} > 0$ does not depend on N but on α). Section 6.4 extends definition 5.1 to ARMA filters for which the number of parameters $p = p(N)$ may increase unboundedly as a function of N.
It is now assumed that a sequence of estimates $\hat{\Gamma}_{0N}(\cdot)$ *of (5.6) is uniformly stable. This can be achieved by techniques presented in chapter 6.*

In the following proposition it is shown that the left hand side of (5.4) is a (super)consistent estimate of the right hand side expression for fixed stable ARMA filters.

Proposition 5.2. *Let* $X_t \in C_f^0$ *be the stationary MA-process (5.3)*

$$X_t = \mu_x + \sum_{k=-\infty}^{\infty} b_k \epsilon_{t-k}$$

and let

$$\frac{2\pi}{N} \sum_{k=-[N/2]}^{[N/2]} w_k |\Delta\Gamma(\omega_k)|^2 I_{NX}(\omega_k) = \frac{1}{N}\sum_{t=1}^{N}(\Delta Y_t)^2 + r_N \tag{5.7}$$

where $\Delta\Gamma(\cdot) := \Gamma(\cdot) - \hat{\Gamma}(\cdot)$ *and* $\Delta Y_t := Y_t - \hat{Y}_t$. *Assume further that* $\hat{\Gamma}(\cdot)$ *is a fixed and stable ARMA-filter.*

- *If* $\Gamma(\cdot) \in C_f^0$ *then* $\lim_{N\to\infty} E[|r_N|] = 0$.
- *If* $\Gamma(\cdot) \in C_f^{1/2}$ *then* $E[|r_N|] = o(1/\sqrt{N})$.

Proof. If $\Gamma(\cdot) \in C_f^{\alpha}$ then the stability of $\hat{\Gamma}(\cdot)$ and the triangular inequality $|\gamma_k - \hat{\gamma}_k| \le |\gamma_k| + |\hat{\gamma}_k|$ imply that $\Delta\Gamma(\cdot) \in C_f^{\alpha}$. Define $\overline{\Delta Y} := \frac{1}{N}\sum_{t=1}^{N} \Delta Y_t$ and consider

$$\frac{1}{N}\sum_{t=1}^{N}(\Delta Y_t)^2 = \frac{2\pi}{N}\sum_{k=-[N/2]}^{[N/2]} w_k I_{N\Delta Y}(\omega_k)$$

$$= \frac{2\pi}{N}\sum_{k=-[N/2]}^{[N/2]} w_k |\Delta\Gamma(\omega_k)|^2 I_{NX}(\omega_k) + r_N$$

where the second equality follows from the spectral decomposition of the sample variance, see proposition 4.5. Theorem 4.8 then implies

$$E[|r_N|] \le \frac{2\pi}{N}\sum_{k=-[N/2]}^{[N/2]} w_k E\left[|R_{N\Delta YX}(\omega_k)|\right] \tag{5.8}$$

$$= \begin{cases} o(1) & \text{first assertion} \\ O(N^{-1/2}) & \text{second assertion} \end{cases}$$

However, a stronger result is needed for the second assertion. This is given by (4.22) in the last assertion of theorem 4.8. □

The error r_N is called 'convolution error' because it is determined by $R_{N\Delta YX}(\omega_k)$ in theorem 4.8. The left hand side of (5.7) can be computed (using $X_1, ..., X_N$ only). It is shown in the above proposition that this expression is a superconsistent estimate (i.e. the error is of smaller order than $1/\sqrt{N}$) of the unknown 'sample variance' $\frac{1}{N}\sum_{t=1}^{N}(\Delta Y_t)^2$. The following theorem shows that the left hand side of (5.7) is also a consistent estimate of the revision error variance $E[(\Delta Y_t)^2]$. The 'decomposition' of the resulting approximation error into the above convolution error r_N and an additional error term is useful when analyzing the efficiency of the DFA, see section 5.5. More importantly, the theorem shows that the approximation remains valid for the sequence of stochastic filters minimizing the left hand side of (5.7), provided the latter define a uniformly stable sequence.

Theorem 5.3. *1. Let* $\hat{\Gamma}(\cdot)$ *be a fixed stable ARMA-filter, let* X_t *be given by (5.3) and assume* ϵ_t *is iid and* $E[\epsilon_t^4] < \infty$. *Furthermore let*

$$\frac{2\pi}{N}\sum_{k=-[N/2]}^{[N/2]} w_k |\Delta\Gamma(\omega_k)|^2 I_{NX}(\omega_k) = E[(\Delta Y_t)^2] + R_N \tag{5.9}$$

where $\omega_k \in \Omega_N$ and $\Delta\Gamma(\cdot) := \Gamma(\cdot) - \hat{\Gamma}(\cdot)$.

- *If $X_t, \Gamma \in C_f^0$ then $\lim_{N \to \infty} E[\|R_N\|] = 0$.*

- *If $X_t \in C_f^0$, $\Gamma \in C_f^\alpha$ and $\alpha \geq 1/2$ then $E[\|R_N\|] = O\left(\frac{1}{\sqrt{N}}\right)$.*

2. If the sequence of solutions $\hat{\Gamma}_{0N}(\cdot)$ of

$$\min_{\hat{\Gamma}} \frac{2\pi}{N} \sum_{k=-[N/2]}^{[N/2]} w_k |\Delta\Gamma(\omega_k)|^2 I_{NX}(\omega_k) \tag{5.10}$$

is uniformly stable, then the results obtained in the preceding assertion remain valid for the stochastic filters $\hat{\Gamma}_{0N}(\cdot)$.

Proof. For the first assertion the required assumptions together with the triangular inequality $|\gamma_k - \hat{\gamma}_k| \leq |\gamma_k| + |\hat{\gamma}_k|$ imply $\Delta\Gamma(\cdot) \in C_f^\alpha$ whenever $\Gamma(\cdot) \in C_f^\alpha$ (since $\hat{\Gamma}(\cdot) \in C_f^\infty$ by the stability assumption). This together with $X_t \in C_f^0$ and proposition 4.7 implies $\Delta Y_t \in C_f^0$. Therefore

$$E[(\Delta Y_t)^2] = Var(\Delta Y_t) + E[\Delta Y_t]^2$$

$$= \frac{1}{N} \sum_{t=1}^{N} (\Delta Y_t - \overline{\Delta Y})^2 + r_{N1} + \left(\overline{\Delta Y}\right)^2 + r_{N2} \tag{5.11}$$

$$= \frac{2\pi}{N} \sum_{k=-[N/2], k \neq 0}^{[N/2]} w_k |\Delta\Gamma(\omega_k)|^2 I_{NX}(\omega_k)$$

$$+ \frac{2\pi}{N} |\Delta\Gamma(0)|^2 I_{NX}(0) + r_{N1} + r_{N2} + r_{N3} \tag{5.12}$$

where $E[r_{Ni}^2] = O(1/N), i = 1, 2$ (see for example Brockwell and Davis [10] remark 1 p.230 and theorem 7.1.2 p.219) and $E[\|r_{N3}\|] = o(1)$ or $E[\|r_{N3}\|] = O(1/\sqrt{N})$ depending on the above assumptions (see proposition 5.2).

Since the above proof only requires stability of the ARMA-filter it remains valid if the constant (fixed) filter $\hat{\Gamma}(\cdot)$ is replaced by the stochastic filter $\hat{\Gamma}_{0N}(\cdot)$ provided the sequence $\hat{\Gamma}_{0N}(\cdot)$ is uniformly stable. To see this, note first that r_{N1} and r_{N2} in (5.12) remain bounded as asserted by the theorem because $\Gamma(\cdot) - \hat{\Gamma}_{0N}(\cdot) \in C_f^\alpha$ uniformly in N:

$$\sum_{k=-\infty}^{\infty} |\gamma_k - \hat{\gamma}_{k0N}||k|^\alpha < \sum_{k=-\infty}^{\infty} (|\gamma_k| + |\hat{\gamma}_{k0N}|)|k|^\alpha < M_\alpha$$

(where M_α can be chosen independently of N) whenever $\Gamma(\cdot) \in C_f^\alpha$. Therefore, the assumption $X_t \in C_f^0$ and proposition 4.7 imply $Y_t - \hat{Y}_{t0N} \in C_f^0$ uniformly in N, i.e. $\sum_{k=-\infty}^{\infty} |c_{k0N}| < M'$ where c_{k0N} are the MA-coefficients of $Y_t - \hat{Y}_{t0N}$ and M' can be chosen independently of N. Brockwell and Davis [10] (remark 1 p.230 and theorem 7.1.2 p.219) then show that r_{N1} and r_{N2}

converge as required.

The remaining 'error' r_{N3} in (5.12) has been analyzed in the preceding proposition or, more precisely, in theorem 4.8. It can be verified directly by analyzing the corresponding proof, that the uniform stability assumption implies $r_{N3} = o(1/\sqrt{N})$ as claimed. This completes the proof of the theorem. $\square$

The consistency of the DFA is proved in the following corollary. It is assumed that the unknown solution $\tilde{\Gamma}(\cdot)$ of

$$\min_{\hat{\Gamma}} E[(Y_t - \hat{Y}_t)^2]$$

is selected in the class of ARMA$(Q, q+r)$-filters, where Q and q are fixed, and that it is stable (the latter requirement has been motivated at the beginning of section 5). Denote by $\tilde{\gamma}_k$ and $\tilde{Y}_t$ the MA-coefficients and the output of $\tilde{\Gamma}(\cdot)$.

Corollary 5.4. *Let the assumptions of theorem 5.3 be satisfied and assume also that the sequence of ARMA$(Q, q + r)$-filters $\hat{\Gamma}_{0N}(\cdot)$ solving*

$$\min_{\hat{\Gamma}} \frac{2\pi}{N} \sum_{k=-[N/2]}^{[N/2]} w_k |\Delta\Gamma(\omega_k)|^2 I_{NX}(\omega_k) \qquad (5.13)$$

is uniformly stable. Then the output $\hat{Y}_{t0N}$ of $\hat{\Gamma}_{0N}(\cdot)$ satisfies

$$E[(Y_t - \hat{Y}_{t0N})^2] = E[(Y_t - \tilde{Y}_t)^2] + R_N \qquad (5.14)$$

where $R_N = o(1)$ or $R_N = O(1/\sqrt{N})$ depending on $\Gamma \in C_f^0$ or $\Gamma \in C_f^{1/2}$.

Proof. The corollary is proved for $\Gamma \in C_f^{1/2}$, i.e. $R_N = O(1/\sqrt{N})$ (a similar proof would apply if $\Gamma \in C_f^0$). Let

$$E[(Y_t - \hat{Y}_{t0N})^2] = \min_{\hat{\Gamma}} E[(Y_t - \hat{Y}_t)^2] + R_N$$

and suppose

$$\frac{1/\sqrt{N}}{R_N} = o(1) \qquad (5.15)$$

It is shown that this hypothesis leads to a contradiction:

$$\min_{\hat{\Gamma}} \frac{2\pi}{N} \sum_{k=-[N/2]}^{[N/2]} w_k |\Delta\Gamma(\omega_k)|^2 I_{NX}(\omega_k)$$

$$= \frac{2\pi}{N} \sum_{k=-[N/2]}^{[N/2]} w_k |\Gamma(\omega_k) - \hat{\Gamma}_{0N}(\omega_k)|^2 I_{NX}(\omega_k)$$

$$= E[(Y_t - \hat{Y}_{t0N})^2 + O(1/\sqrt{N})$$
$$= \min_{\hat{\Gamma}} E[(Y_t - \hat{Y}_t)^2] + O(R_N)$$

$$= \min_{\hat{\Gamma}} \left(\frac{2\pi}{N} \sum_{k=-[N/2]}^{[N/2]} w_k |\Delta\Gamma(\omega_k)|^2 I_{NX}(\omega_k) + R'_N \right) + O(R_N)$$

$$= \min_{\hat{\Gamma}} \left(\frac{2\pi}{N} \sum_{k=-[N/2]}^{[N/2]} w_k |\Delta\Gamma(\omega_k)|^2 I_{NX}(\omega_k) \right) + O(R_N)$$

The second equality follows from theorem 5.3, second assertion. The third equality is a consequence of (5.15). The last equality follows from the first assertion of theorem 5.3, using the stability of the solution of $\min_{\hat{\Gamma}} E[(Y_t - \hat{Y}_t)^2]$ which implies that $R'_N = O(1/\sqrt{N})$ so that R_N asymptotically dominates R'_N (by assumption (5.15)). Since $R_N \neq 0$ by assumption, the above development contradicts (5.15) which completes the proof of the corollary. □

The resulting signal estimation procedure is called a *direct filter approach* because the ARMA-filter $\hat{\Gamma}_{0N}(\cdot)$ 'directly' minimizes (a consistent estimate of) the revision error variance.

Remarks

1. The uniform stability requirement is necessary for establishing the preceding result. One can implement uniform stability in the form of a constrained optimization. Often $\sup_\omega |\Gamma(\omega)|$ is known a priori (symmetric trend estimation and seasonal adjustment filters for example often satisfy $\sup_\omega |\Gamma(\omega)| = 1$). Boundedness of the functions $\hat{\Gamma}_{0N}(\cdot)$ may be achieved by imposing $\sup_\omega |\hat{\Gamma}_{0N}(\omega)| < M_1$ where M_1 is an a priori bound (for example $M_1 := 1$). Alternatively, a constraint of the type $\sup_\omega |\partial\hat{\Gamma}_{0N}(\omega)/\partial d\omega| < M_2$ could be used. However, such restrictions are often not easily interpretable. So for example the amplitude function of the best *asymmetric* trend extraction filter often exceeds 1, see for example fig.2.5. Therefore, an a priori choice of the bounds M_1 or M_2 is not obvious in general. An alternative method is to restrict the poles, i.e. to require $|P_k| > 1 + \epsilon$ for $k = 1, ..., Q$, where $\epsilon > 0$ is fixed. However, the (a priori) choice of ϵ is still arbitrary. Chapter 6 presents more refined devices which let the data choose the 'degree of smoothness' required for the asymmetric filter $\hat{\Gamma}_{0N}(\cdot)$.

2. The interpretation of (5.9) is intuitively appealing : the signal estimation problem for finite samples and stationary input signals corresponds to a weighted sum of transfer function errors (sampled at $\omega_k \in \Omega_N$). The (non-parametric) weighting function is the periodogram of the input signal. The periodogram is a measure of the 'power' of the signal in the intervals $[\omega_{k-1}, \omega_k]$. Therefore, the strength of the corresponding compo-

nents of X_t 'modulates' the fit of the asymmetric transfer function. The approach is essentially based on discrete spectral decomposition (of the sample revision error variance) and on discrete convolution results.

3. The filter $\Delta\Gamma(\cdot) \in C_f^\alpha$ is a continuous function. Therefore $|\Delta\Gamma(\cdot)|^2$ 'smooths' the periodogram in (5.9). Using non-parametric consistent estimates of the spectral density of X_t ('smoothed' periodogram) is unnecessary here.

4. An alternative proof of theorem 5.3 could be based on

$$\frac{2\pi}{N} \sum_{k=-[N/2]}^{[N/2]} w_k |\Delta\Gamma(\omega_k)|^2 I_{NX}(\omega_k) \simeq \frac{2\pi}{N} \sum_{k=-[N/2]}^{[N/2]} w_k |\Delta\Gamma(\omega_k)|^2 h(\omega_k)$$

$$\simeq \int_{-\pi}^{\pi} |\Delta\Gamma(\omega)|^2 h(\omega) d\omega \qquad (5.16)$$

$$= E[(Y_t - \hat{Y}_t)^2]$$

where suitable regularity assumptions are needed for ensuring a good approximation. A justification for the approach followed in proposition 5.2 and theorem 5.3 is the better understanding of efficiency problems (see section 5.5). On the other hand, the above approximation steps (based on the integration of the spectral density) reveal uniform stability problems better (see chapter 6).

5. The approach taken in (5.14) implicitly accounts for one- *and* multi-step ahead forecasts (as opposed to the MBA whose parameters are optimized with respect to one-step ahead performances only). Note also that forecasting problems resulting from non- or 'nearly' non-invertible input processes are avoided (using the DFA).

6. It is easily seen from (4.10) and (5.12) that the difference between $\hat{\Gamma}(\cdot)$ and $\Gamma(\cdot)$ at frequency $\omega_0 = 0$ induces a *bias* (of the estimate $\hat{Y}_t$) and that the differences of the transfer functions at $\omega_k \neq 0$ determine the *variance* of the estimate. Consider an estimate of the bias:

$$\left(\overline{\Delta Y}\right)^2 = \frac{2\pi}{N} I_{N\Delta Y}(0)$$

$$= \frac{2\pi}{N} \left(|\Delta\Gamma(0)|^2 I_{NX}(0) + R_{N\Delta YX}(0) \right) \qquad (5.17)$$

where the first equality follows from definition 4.4 and where the error term is

$$R_{N\Delta YX}(0) = R_{N\Delta Y'X'}(0) + 2\frac{\sqrt{N}}{\sqrt{2\pi}} \Delta\Gamma(0)\mu_X R'_{N\Delta Y'X'}(0) \qquad (5.18)$$

see (4.21). The bias problem can be 'tackled' as follows:

• Constrain the optimization by requiring $\hat{\Gamma}(0) = \Gamma(0)$ (see for example section 5.3). As a consequence $|\Delta\Gamma(0)|^2 = 0$ which implies that the bias vanishes asymptotically, see (5.17) and (5.18) (note that $R_{N\Delta Y'X'}(0) = o(1)$, see theorem 4.8). Unfortunately, the constraint $\hat{\Gamma}(0) = \Gamma(0)$ is unnecessarily severe for stationary input processes.

- A better method is proposed here. Transform X_t to $X'_t := X_t - \bar{X}$ so that $I_{NX'}(0) = 0$. If X'_t is used instead of X_t, then the bias vanishes asymptotically ($R_{N\Delta Y'X'}(0) = o(1)$ in (5.17), see theorem 4.8). In the next step the optimal filter $\hat{\Gamma}_{0N}(\cdot)$ is computed using the periodogram of X'_t. The transformed signal X'_t is then mapped to the corresponding filter output $\hat{Y}'_t$. In order to 'recover' the optimal estimate $\hat{Y}_t$ define

$$\hat{Y}_t := \hat{Y}'_t + \hat{\Gamma}_{0N}(0)\bar{X}$$

which can be motivated by invoking the linearity of the filter. Unfortunately, $I_{NX'}(0) = 0$ so that $\hat{\Gamma}_{0N}(0)$ is generally suboptimal. The following definition is recommended instead

$$\hat{Y}_t := \hat{Y}'_t + \Gamma(0)\bar{X}$$

It can be shown that the proposed 'level correction' $\Gamma(0)\bar{X}$ is an asymptotically best linear unbiased estimate of the level μ_y of Y_t, see for example Brockwell and Davis [10] p.220. Therefore, the filter $\hat{\Gamma}_{0N}(\cdot)$ can be optimized for minimizing specifically the variance, neglecting thereby the bias problem. Moreover, a (generally unnecessarily severe) restriction of the form $\hat{\Gamma}(0) \equiv \Gamma(0)$ can be avoided.

In the following, the index N of the solution $\hat{\Gamma}_{0N}(\cdot)$ (minimizing (5.9)) is dropped if not explicitly required. Denote the result obtained in corollary 5.4 by

$$\min_{\hat{\Gamma}} \frac{2\pi}{N} \sum_{k=-[N/2]}^{[N/2]} w_k |\Delta\Gamma(\omega_k)|^2 I_{NX}(\omega_k) \leftrightarrow$$

$$\min_{\hat{\Gamma}} E[(Y_t - \hat{Y}_t)^2] + O\left(\frac{1}{\sqrt{N}}\right) \tag{5.19}$$

where the left-right-arrow '$\leftrightarrow$' indicates that both expressions are equal and that the solution $\hat{\Gamma}_0(\cdot)$ of the left hand side is also a solution of the right hand side (and vice versa).

In this section, sufficient conditions ensuring (5.19) in the case of *linear* input processes were presented. Chapter E in the appendix analyzes an extension of the DFA to non-linear input processes. The following section proposes a generalization of the DFA (as given by (5.19)) to non-stationary integrated processes.

5.3 Consistency (Integrated Processes)

It is assumed that the input process X_t is integrated and that the unit-roots are known. One can then show that the basic idea of the DFA, namely to estimate the revision error variance by a consistent functional of the asymmetric filter (see (5.9)), can be generalized. The key requirements for this generalization are additional regularity assumptions and a set of constraints. If they are satisfied, the revision error variance is finite (although the variance of the input process is infinite). Therefore, if the signal Y_t is integrated, then Y_t and $\hat{Y}_t$ must be *cointegrated*.

The existence of unit-roots and the a priori knowledge of their location(s) on the unit circle are 'academic' assumptions useful for establishing formal proofs. Nevertheless 'potential' unit-roots and their location are often known a priori (for economic time series for example, possible 'candidates' are $\exp(-i\lambda_k)$, where $\lambda_0 = 0$ and λ_k $k > 1$ correspond to 'seasonal' fundamental or harmonics). Unit-root tests (for example Dickey-Fuller- or Phillips-Perron- or HEGY-tests, see for example Hamilton [45], chap.17) offer formal approaches for testing such hypotheses. Tests specific to the signal estimation problem (as solved by the DFA) are presented in section 5.7. The importance of unit-roots, i.e. consequences of unit-root misspecification(s), are illustrated empirically in section 7.2. In the present section, attention is restricted to asymptotic results under the assumption that the unit-roots are known. Thus a particular aspect of the signal estimation problem is highlighted formally.

Let

$$\tilde{X}_t := \mu + \prod_{j=1}^{n} \left(\exp(-i\lambda_j) - B \right)^{d_j} X_t \tag{5.20}$$

where $d_j \in \mathbb{N}$ are integers, B is the backshift operator, X_t is a real process and $\tilde{X}_t$ is a stationary real MA-process. It is assumed that X_t has been suitably initialized in the 'past' (for example $X_0 = X_{-1} = ... = X_{-\max(d_j)} = 0$). It is also assumed that $\tilde{X}_t \in C_f^0$ (so that its spectral density $\tilde{h}(\cdot)$ exists) and that $\tilde{h}(\lambda_j) > 0$ for $j = 1, ..., n$. Therefore, X_t is integrated. Assume $\Gamma(\cdot)$ is sufficiently regular (see below for a formal requirement) and define

$$\Delta\tilde{\Gamma}(\omega) := \begin{cases} \dfrac{\Delta\Gamma(\omega)}{\prod_{j=1}^{n} \left(\exp(-i\lambda_j) - \exp(-i\omega) \right)^{d_j}} & \omega \neq \lambda_j, \forall j \\[3ex] \dfrac{(-1)^{d_l} \sum_{k=-\infty}^{\infty} \Delta\gamma_k k^{d_l} \exp(-ik\lambda_l)}{d_l! \exp(-id_l\lambda_l) \prod_{j \neq l} \left(\exp(-i\lambda_j) - \exp(-i\lambda_l) \right)^{d_j}} & \omega = \lambda_l \end{cases} \tag{5.21}$$

where $\Delta\Gamma(\omega) := \Gamma(\omega) - \hat{\Gamma}(\omega)$ and $\Delta\gamma_k$ are the corresponding MA-coefficients. The limiting expression for $\omega = \lambda_l$ is derived from Taylor series developments of numerator and denominator polynomials : it exists if certain assumptions are satisfied (see below) and then the revision error variance is finite. Define also $\Delta\Gamma^i(\omega)$ as the i-th. derivative of $\Gamma(\omega) - \hat{\Gamma}(\omega)$ with respect to ω, where $\Delta\Gamma^0(\omega) := \Gamma(\omega) - \hat{\Gamma}(\omega)$ for $i = 0$.

The following theorem is needed for generalizing the preceding results for stationary input signals to non-stationary integrated input signals.

Theorem 5.5. *Let X_t defined in (5.20) be the input signal of $\Gamma(\cdot)$ and assume X_t has been initialized in the past (for example $X_0 = 0$). Assume*

- *the regularity requirements:*
  - *$\Gamma(\cdot) \in C_f^{d+\delta+\alpha}$ where $d := \max(d_j)_{j=1,...,n}$, $\delta > 0$ and $\alpha \geq 0$.*
  - *$\hat{\Gamma}(\cdot)$ is a stable ARMA-filter and*
  - *$\tilde{X}_t \in C_f^0$ and $\tilde{h}(\lambda_j) > 0$ for $j = 1, ..., n$.*
- *the constraints :*

$$\Delta\Gamma^{(i)}(\lambda_j) = 0, \ i = 0, ..., d_j - 1 \ and \ j = 1, ..., n \qquad (5.22)$$

where $\Delta\Gamma^{(i)}(\cdot)$ has been defined above.

Then the following assertions are true :

- *$\Delta Y_t := Y_t - \hat{Y}_t \in C_f^0$ and thus ΔY_t is a stationary process. Moreover condition (5.22) is necessary for ensuring the finiteness of the revision error variance.*
- *$\Delta\tilde{\Gamma}(\cdot) \in C_f^\alpha$ where $\Delta\tilde{\Gamma}(\cdot)$ has been defined above.*

Proof. The theorem is proved for two unit-roots λ_1 and λ_2, i.e. for integration orders $d = 1, 2$ only. Similar arguments apply to larger integration orders. Define

$$\Delta\Gamma^1(\omega) := \frac{\Delta\Gamma(\omega)}{\big(\exp(-i\lambda_1) - \exp(-i\omega)\big)}$$

so that:

$$\sum_{k=-\infty}^{\infty} \Delta\gamma_k \exp(-ik\omega) = \big(\exp(-i\lambda_1) - \exp(-i\omega)\big) \sum_{k=-\infty}^{\infty} \Delta\gamma_k^1 \exp(-ik\omega)$$

Thus

$$\Delta\gamma_k^1 = \sum_{j=0}^{\infty} \Delta\gamma_{k+j} \exp(i(j+1)\lambda_1) \qquad (5.23)$$

Introducing the second unit-root and using (5.23) for

$$\Delta\tilde{\Gamma}(\omega) = \frac{\Delta\Gamma^1(\omega)}{\big(\exp(-i\lambda_2) - \exp(-i\omega)\big)}$$

leads to:

$$\Delta\tilde{\gamma}_k = \sum_{j=0}^{\infty} \Delta\gamma_{k+j}^1 \exp(i(j+1)\lambda_2)$$

$$= \exp(i(\lambda_1 + \lambda_2)) \sum_{j=0}^{\infty} \left(\exp(ij\lambda_2) \sum_{l=0}^{\infty} \Delta\gamma_{k+j+l} \exp(il\lambda_1) \right)$$

$$= \exp(i(\lambda_1 + \lambda_2)) \sum_{j=0}^{\infty} \left(\Delta\gamma_{k+j} \sum_{l=0}^{j} \exp(il\lambda_2) \exp(i(j-l)\lambda_1) \right)$$

$$= \exp(i(\lambda_1 + \lambda_2)) \sum_{j=0}^{\infty} \left(\Delta\gamma_{k+j} \exp(ij\lambda_1) \sum_{l=0}^{j} \exp(il(\lambda_2 - \lambda_1)) \right)$$

$$= \exp(i(\lambda_1 + \lambda_2)) \sum_{j=0}^{\infty} \Delta\gamma_{k+j} \exp(ij\lambda_1) \frac{\exp(i(j+1)(\lambda_2 - \lambda_1)) - 1}{\exp(i(\lambda_2 - \lambda_1)) - 1}$$

$$=: \sum_{j=0}^{\infty} \Delta\gamma_{k+j} \exp(ij\lambda_1) f(j, \lambda_1, \lambda_2) \qquad (5.24)$$

where $\Delta\tilde{\gamma}_k$ are the coefficients of (5.21) and the definition of $f(\cdot)$ is straight-forward. Assume first $d = 1$ i.e. $\lambda_1 \neq \lambda_2$.

- By assumption $\Delta\Gamma(\lambda_1) = \Delta\Gamma(\lambda_2) = 0$. Thus

$$\sum_{j=-\infty}^{\infty} \Delta\gamma_{k+j} \exp(ij\lambda_1) f(j, \lambda_1, \lambda_2) = C_1 \Delta\Gamma(\lambda_1) + C_2 \Delta\Gamma(\lambda_2) = 0$$

where C_1 and C_2 are constants (the first equality can be verified straight-forwardly by inserting the definition of $f(\cdot)$ and simplifying). Therefore, $\Delta\tilde{\gamma}_k$ can be written as:

$$\Delta\tilde{\gamma}_k = \begin{cases} \sum_{j=0}^{\infty} \Delta\gamma_{k+j} \exp(ij\lambda_1) f(j, \lambda_1, \lambda_2) & k \geq 0 \\ -\sum_{j=-\infty}^{-1} \Delta\gamma_{k+j} \exp(ij\lambda_1) f(j, \lambda_1, \lambda_2) & k < 0 \end{cases} \qquad (5.25)$$

- Assuming $k \geq 0$, one obtains

$$|\Delta\tilde{\gamma}_k| = \left| \sum_{j=0}^{\infty} \Delta\gamma_{k+j} \exp(ij\lambda_1) f(j, \lambda_1, \lambda_2) \right|$$

$$\leq M \sum_{j=0}^{\infty} |\Delta\gamma_{k+j}|$$

$$\leq M \frac{1}{k^{\alpha+\delta+d}} \sum_{j=-\infty}^{\infty} |\Delta\gamma_{k+j}| |k+j|^{\alpha+\delta+d}$$

$$= O(k^{-\alpha-\delta-d}) \qquad (5.26)$$

where $M = \sup_j |f(j, \lambda_1, \lambda_2)| < 2/|\exp(i(\lambda_2 - \lambda_1)) - 1|$. A similar result is obtained for $k < 0$, using (5.25). For $d = 1$ and $\delta > 0$ the last result implies $\Delta\tilde{\Gamma}(\cdot) \in C_f^\alpha$ as was to be proved.

Assume now $\lambda_1 = \lambda_2 = \lambda$ so that $d = 2$ and thus $f(j, \lambda_1, \lambda_2) = \exp(i2\lambda)(j+1)$ (use de l'Hopital's rule for example). Therefore, (5.24) implies

$$\Delta\tilde{\gamma}_k = \exp(i2\lambda) \sum_{j=0}^{\infty} \Delta\gamma_{k+j} \exp(ij\lambda)(j+1)$$

The identity

$$\Delta\tilde{\gamma}_k = \begin{cases} \exp(i2\lambda) \sum_{j=0}^{\infty} \Delta\gamma_{k+j} \exp(ij\lambda)(j+1) & k \geq 0 \\ -\exp(i2\lambda) \sum_{j=-\infty}^{-1} \Delta\gamma_{k+j} \exp(ij\lambda)(j+1) & k < 0 \end{cases} \tag{5.27}$$

follows (for $k < 0$) from:

$$\sum_{j=-\infty}^{\infty} \Delta\gamma_{j+k} \exp(-ij\lambda)(-i(j+1)) = \exp(i\lambda) \frac{d}{d\omega} \left(\exp(i(k-1)\omega)\Delta\Gamma(\omega)\right)\Big|_{\omega=\lambda}$$

$$= 0$$

where (5.22) is used, i.e. $\Delta\Gamma(\lambda) = 0 = \frac{d}{d\omega}\Delta\Gamma(\omega)\big|_{\omega=\lambda}$. It is now shown that $\Delta\tilde{\Gamma}(\cdot) \in C_f^\alpha$. Assume first $k \geq 0$ so that

$$|\Delta\tilde{\gamma}_k| = \left| \sum_{j=0}^{\infty} \Delta\gamma_{k+j} \exp(ij\lambda)(j+1) \right|$$

$$\leq \sum_{j=0}^{\infty} |\Delta\gamma_{k+j}|(j+1)$$

$$\leq \frac{1}{k^{\alpha+\delta+d-1}} \sum_{j=-\infty}^{\infty} |\Delta\gamma_{k+j}||k+j|^{\alpha+\delta+d-1}|j+1|$$

$$= O(k^{-\alpha-\delta-d+1}) \tag{5.28}$$

and similarly for $k < 0$, using the identity (5.27). Therefore $\Delta\tilde{\Gamma}(\cdot) \in C_f^\alpha$, since $d = 2$. This proves the second assertion of the theorem. A proof of the first assertion follows from

$$\Delta Y_t = \sum_{k=-\infty}^{\infty} \Delta\tilde{\gamma}_k \tilde{X}_{t-k}$$

$$= \sum_{k=-\infty}^{\infty} \left(\sum_{j=-\infty}^{\infty} \Delta\tilde{\gamma}_j b_{k-j} \right) \epsilon_{t-k}$$

(where b_j are the MA-coefficients of $\tilde{X}_t$). Since $\Delta\tilde{\Gamma}(\cdot) \in C_f^0$ and $\tilde{X}_t \in C_f^0$, proposition 4.7 implies that $\Delta Y_t \in C_f^0$ as required. The 'necessity' part of the assertion follows from the spectral decomposition of the variance of the stationary process ΔY_t:

$$Var(\Delta Y_t) = \frac{1}{2\pi} \int_{-\pi}^{\pi} |\Delta\tilde{\Gamma}(\omega)|^2 \tilde{h}(\omega) d\omega$$

where $\tilde{h}(\cdot)$ is the spectral density of the stationary process $\tilde{X}_t$ and $\Delta\tilde{\Gamma}(\cdot)$ is defined in (5.21). Since the continuous spectral density $\tilde{h}(\cdot)$ satisfies $\tilde{h}(\lambda_j) > 0$ for all unit-root frequencies (by assumption) the integral remains bounded if and only if the expression in (5.21) exists. Therefore, the constraints (5.22) are necessary. This completes the proof of the theorem. $\square$

The necessity part in the second assertion of the theorem implies that the condition (5.22) (together with regularity assumptions) is important because otherwise the variance of the filter error would be infinite (asymptotically). A practical implementation of this condition is therefore proposed now.

The condition (5.22) can be realized by a conditional optimization of the zeroes and poles of $\hat{\Gamma}(\cdot)$ on the left hand side of (5.9). In particular, if $n = 1, d_1 = 1, \lambda_1 = 0$ (random walk $X_t = X_{t-1} + \tilde{X}_t$) and $\Gamma(\cdot)$ is a real symmetric extraction filter satisfying $\Gamma(0) \neq 0$ then

$$\hat{\Gamma}_C(\omega) := C_{\hat{\Gamma}}\hat{\Gamma}(\omega)$$
$$C_{\hat{\Gamma}} := \Gamma(0)/\hat{\Gamma}(0) \qquad (5.29)$$

provides a simple parameterization of the 'conditional' ARMA filter $\hat{\Gamma}_C(\cdot)$ (since $\hat{\Gamma}_C(0) = \Gamma(0)$ or equivalently (5.22) is satisfied). For the simple random-walk hypothesis, the condition (5.22) or equivalently $\hat{\Gamma}_C(0) = \Gamma(0)$ therefore implies equivalence of the 'levels' of the outputs Y_t and $\hat{Y}_t$. This is quite reasonable, since random-walks grow unboundedly (in absolute value).

If $\Gamma(0) = 0$ then define $\hat{\Gamma}_C(\omega) := (1 - \exp(-i\omega))\hat{\Gamma}(\omega)$. The last definition straightforwardly extends to more general processes with unit-roots $Z_j = \exp(i\lambda_j), j = 1, ..., s$, where $\lambda_j \neq \lambda_k$ for $j \neq k$. If $\Gamma(\lambda_j) = 0, j = 1, ..., s$ as for example in seasonal adjustment filters, then :

$$\hat{\Gamma}_C(\omega) := \left[\prod_{j=1}^{s} (\exp(-i\lambda_j) - \exp(-i\omega))(\exp(i\lambda_j) - \exp(-i\omega)) \right] \hat{\Gamma}(\omega)$$

satisfies the conditions (5.22). The above *first order conditions* for processes with integration order one therefore amount to a *perfect matching of the transfer functions of $\Gamma(\cdot)$ and $\hat{\Gamma}(\cdot)$ at the unit-root frequencies.*

This requirement can often be weakened. Note first that (5.29) does not depend on the phase function of the ARMA-filter (because the filters are real). If $\Gamma(\lambda_j) = 0$ for all unit-root frequencies $\lambda_j \neq 0$ (seasonal adjustment or trend extraction filters generally satisfy this assumption), then $\hat{\Gamma}_C(\lambda_j) = \Gamma(\lambda_j) = 0$, $j = 1, ..., s$ do not depend on the phase function of the ARMA-filter. Therefore, in this particular situation (which is often given in practice), the first order conditions can be alternatively stated as *perfect matching of the amplitude functions at the unit-root frequencies*. Note however that this 'weak form' of (5.22) assumes $\Gamma(\lambda_j) = 0$ for $\lambda_j \neq 0$. Otherwise it is generally false (i.e. the phase must be accounted for).

In chapter 7 so called 'airline'-models are used. These models assume the existence of a process of integration order two (double unit-root at frequency zero). Therefore, additional second order conditions must be considered in (5.22). Assume first $\Gamma(0) \neq 0$ (for example a trend extraction or a seasonal adjustment filter). A simple parameterization of a corresponding 'conditional' ARMA-filter, denoted by $\hat{\Gamma}_{CC}(\omega)$, is given by

$$\hat{\Gamma}_{CC}(\omega) := \hat{\Gamma}_C(\omega)\left(2 - \frac{\hat{\Gamma}_C(\omega)}{\Gamma(0)}\right) \tag{5.30}$$

where $\hat{\Gamma}_C(\omega)$ is defined in (5.29). In fact one easily verifies that $\Delta\Gamma^{(0)}(0) := \Gamma(0) - \hat{\Gamma}_{CC}(0) = 0$ and $d\hat{\Gamma}_{CC}(\omega)/d\omega\big|_{\omega=0} = 0$. The last result shows that

$$\Delta\Gamma^{(1)}(0) := d(\Gamma(\omega) - \hat{\Gamma}_{CC}(\omega))/d\omega\big|_{\omega=0} = 0$$

in (5.22) (use the symmetry of the extraction filter $\Gamma(\cdot)$ which implies $d\Gamma(\omega)/d\omega\big|_{\omega=0} = 0$). A disadvantage of (5.30) is to be seen in the convolution of $\hat{\Gamma}_C(\omega)$ with itself which may worsen the initialization problem of the ARMA-filter (see sections 3.1 and D.1 in the appendix). Therefore an alternative solution is proposed here. Consider

$$\hat{\Gamma}_{CC}(\omega) = \hat{A}_{CC}(\omega)\exp(-i\hat{\Phi}_{CC}(\omega))$$

so that

$$\frac{d\hat{\Gamma}_{CC}(\omega)}{d\omega} = \frac{d\hat{A}_{CC}(\omega)}{d\omega}\exp(-i\hat{\Phi}_{CC}(\omega)) - i\hat{A}_{CC}(\omega)\exp(-i\hat{\Phi}_{CC}(\omega))\frac{d\hat{\Phi}_{CC}(\omega)}{d\omega}$$

$$= -i\hat{A}_{CC}(\omega)\exp(-i\hat{\Phi}_{CC}(\omega))\frac{d\hat{\Phi}_{CC}(\omega)}{d\omega} \tag{5.31}$$

where for the moment it is assumed that $\hat{\Gamma}_{CC}(0) = \Gamma(0)$ (first order condition only) so that $A(0) = \hat{A}_{CC}(0)$. Note that $d\hat{A}_{CC}(\omega)/d\omega\big|_{\omega=0} = 0$ because the ARMA-filter is assumed to be real (and thus the amplitude function is an even function with an extremum at frequency zero). Since $\hat{A}_{CC}(0) = A(0) = |\Gamma(0)| > 0$ by assumption, the derivative in (5.31) vanishes at $\omega = 0$ (which implies $\Delta\Gamma^{(1)}(0) = 0$, i.e. (5.22), see above) if and only if

$$\frac{d\hat{\Phi}_{CC}(\omega)}{d\omega} = \lim_{h \to 0}\frac{\hat{\Phi}_{CC}(h) - \hat{\Phi}_{CC}(0)}{h} = \hat{\phi}_{CC}(0) = 0 \tag{5.32}$$

where the definition of the time shift function has been used (together with the fact that the phase function vanishes at $\omega = 0$, recall definition 3.2). Therefore, the *second order condition* for processes with a double unit-root at frequency zero is equivalent with a *vanishing time shift* of the ARMA-filter $\hat{\Gamma}_{CC}(\cdot)$ (at frequency zero) which may be satisfied by a simple constrained optimization. The following device is used for the examples in chapter 7: let

$$\hat{\Gamma}_{CC}(\omega) := \frac{Z - \exp(-i\omega)}{P - \exp(-i\omega)} \hat{\Gamma}'_{CC}(\omega)$$

and assume that (Z, P) is a real stable and invertible zero-pole-pair i.e. $Z \in \mathbb{R}$ and $Z > 1$ and analogously for P. It is now shown how to choose Z and P so that the second order condition is satisfied (the first order condition is achieved by a simple normalization which does not affect the time shift-condition).

$$0 = \left.\frac{d\hat{\Gamma}_{CC}(\omega)}{d\omega}\right|_{\omega=0} = i\frac{P - Z}{(P - 1)^2}\hat{\Gamma}'_{CC}(0) - \frac{Z - 1}{P - 1}\left.\frac{d\hat{\Gamma}'_{CC}(\omega)}{d\omega}\right|_{\omega=0}$$

Solving for P results in:

$$P = \frac{Z\hat{\Gamma}'_{CC}(0) + i(Z - 1)\left.\dfrac{d\hat{\Gamma}'_{CC}(\omega)}{d\omega}\right|_{\omega=0}}{\hat{\Gamma}'_{CC}(0) + i(Z - 1)\left.\dfrac{d\hat{\Gamma}'_{CC}(\omega)}{d\omega}\right|_{\omega=0}} \tag{5.33}$$

which can be solved for any $Z > 1$ under the constraint $P > 1$ (stability). Note that $\hat{\Gamma}'_{CC}(0)$ and $i\left.\frac{d\hat{\Gamma}'_{CC}(\omega)}{d\omega}\right|_{\omega=0} = -(i^2)\hat{A}'_{CC}(0)\hat{\phi}'_{CC}(0)$ (see (5.31)) are real numbers, so that P is indeed real. Moreover, if $Z > 1$, then $P > 1$ is 'automatically' satisfied if $\hat{\Gamma}'_{CC}(0) > 0$ and $\hat{\phi}'_{CC}(0) > 0$ (the latter ensures that $i(Z - 1)\left.\frac{d\hat{\Gamma}'_{CC}(\omega)}{d\omega}\right|_{\omega=0} > 0$ in (5.33)). These conditions are satisfied for asymmetric ARMA-approximations of many important signal extraction filters (for example general trend extraction or seasonal adjustment filters). Equivalently, solving for Z would result in

$$Z = \frac{iP\hat{\Gamma}'_{CC}(0) + (P - 1)\left.\dfrac{d\hat{\Gamma}'_{CC}(\omega)}{d\omega}\right|_{\omega=0}}{i\hat{\Gamma}'_{CC}(0) + (P - 1)\left.\dfrac{d\hat{\Gamma}'_{CC}(\omega)}{d\omega}\right|_{\omega=0}} \tag{5.34}$$

Until now, the (most important) case $\Gamma(0) \neq 0$ was analyzed for an I(2)-process. If $\Gamma(0) = 0$, then using the symmetry of the extraction filter (which implies $d\Gamma(\omega)/d\omega|_{\omega=0} = 0$) implies that $\hat{\Gamma}_{CC}(\omega) := (1 - \exp(-i\omega))^2 \hat{\Gamma}(\omega)$ satisfies $\Delta\Gamma^{(0)}(0) = \Delta\Gamma^{(1)}(0) = 0$ as required by (5.22).

An intuitive explanation for the second order condition $\hat{\phi}_{CC}(0) = 0$ (for the case $\Gamma(0) \neq 0$) can be given as follows. The 'slope' (first difference) of a realization of an I(2)-process (with a double unit-root at frequency zero) is a random-walk. Thus the slope grows unboundedly in absolute value as time passes. Therefore, the paths are 'strongly' trending so that filters with non-vanishing time shifts are penalized.

Proposition 3.11 already suggested that 'amplitude matching' is a simpler task than 'phase (or time shift) matching'. It is therefore not surprising that the 'weak form' of the first order conditions relate to the amplitude function (provided $\Gamma(\lambda_j) = 0$ for $\lambda_j \neq 0$) and that second order conditions relate to the time shift (phase) function.

These remarks conclude the practical implementation of the important condition (5.22) (for most practically relevant cases). An extension of the DFA to integrated input processes is proposed in the following corollary. Assume $\tilde{X}_t \in C_f^0$, so that the spectral density $\tilde{h}(\cdot)$ exists and is continuous (recall (4.18)). Moreover, it is assumed that $\tilde{h}(\lambda_j) \neq 0$ for $j = 1, ..., n$. This condition ensures that the 'local' integration order of X_t at λ_j is indeed d_j, for $j = 1, ..., n$ (i.e. assumption (5.22) is not unnecessarily severe).

Corollary 5.6. *Let X_t and $\tilde{X}_t$ be defined by (5.20) and let the assumptions of theorem 5.5 be satisfied.*

1. *If the assumptions of proposition 5.2 or theorem 5.3 are satisfied for the stationary input signal $\tilde{X}_t$ then the corresponding assertions remain true if the expression on the left hand side of (5.9) is replaced by*

$$\frac{2\pi}{N} \sum_{k=-[N/2]}^{[N/2]} w_k |\Delta \tilde{\Gamma}(\omega_k)|^2 I_{N\tilde{X}}(\omega_k) \tag{5.35}$$

i.e. if one replaces X_t by $\tilde{X}_t$ and $\Delta\Gamma(\cdot)$ by $\Delta\tilde{\Gamma}(\cdot)$ (as defined in (5.21)) in (5.7) and (5.9).
2. *If the assumptions of corollary 5.4 are satisfied, then*

$$\min_{\hat{\Gamma}_C} \frac{2\pi}{N} \sum_{k=-[N/2]}^{[N/2]} w_k |\Delta \tilde{\Gamma}(\omega_k)|^2 I_{N\tilde{X}}(\omega_k) \leftrightarrow$$

$$\min_{\hat{\Gamma}} E[(Y_t - \hat{Y}_t)^2] + O\left(\frac{1}{\sqrt{N}}\right) \tag{5.36}$$

where $\hat{\Gamma}_C(\cdot)$ satisfies (5.22) and the error term is of order $O(1/\sqrt{N})$ in absolute mean.

Recall that the symbol '$\leftrightarrow$' indicates that the expressions on both sides are equal and that a solution of the left hand side (which is constrained by

(5.22)) also is a solution of the right hand side (which is not constrained a priori) and vice versa.

Proof of the corollary. If the sequence of constrained (ARMA) filters $\hat{\Gamma}_{CON}(\cdot)$ minimizing (5.35) is uniformly stable (as assumed by theorem 5.3), then the approximations (5.26) and (5.28) in the proof of theorem 5.5 can be made independent of N. Therefore, the assertions of theorem 5.5 remain true for the sequence $\hat{\Gamma}_{CON}(\cdot)$ (independently of N). In particular, the second assertion shows that the (set of) conditions (5.22) are necessary. Therefore, the filter minimizing the right hand side of (5.36) must satisfy the conditions (5.22). Furthermore, the first assertion of theorem 5.5 ensures that $\Delta\tilde{\Gamma}(\cdot) \in C_f^\alpha$, i.e. the regularity assumptions required by proposition 5.2 or theorem 5.3 are satisfied. Therefore, the latter results can be applied to the stationary input signal $\tilde{X}_t \in C_f^0$, replacing $\Delta\Gamma(\cdot)$ by $\Delta\tilde{\Gamma}(\cdot)$ in (5.7) and (5.9) as claimed. As a consequence, corollary 5.4 can be applied, implying (5.36) (by analogy to (5.19)). This completes the proof of the corollary. $\square$

The following remarks complete the analysis for integrated processes. Assume for the sake of simplicity that $n = 1$ and $\lambda_1 = 0$ in (5.20). Thus, X_t is a non-stationary process of integration order one with a single unit-root at frequency zero. The (conditional) filter $\hat{\Gamma}_C(\cdot)$ defined in (5.29) then satisfies the condition (5.22). Denote the Fourier coefficients of $\hat{\Gamma}_C(\cdot)$ by $\hat{\gamma}_{Ck}$.

Remarks:

- The expression on the left hand-side of (5.36) may be formally rewritten as

$$\min_{\hat{\Gamma}_C} \frac{2\pi}{N} \sum_{k=-[N/2]}^{[N/2]} |\Delta\Gamma(\omega_k)|^2 \frac{I_{N\tilde{X}}(\omega_k)}{\prod_{j=1}^{n} \left(\exp(-i\lambda_j) - \exp(-i\omega) \right)^{d_j}} \qquad (5.37)$$

where the singularities are replaced by the limiting values obtained in theorem 5.5. Theorem 4.10 shows that $E\left[\left| I_{NX}(\omega_k) - \dfrac{I_{N\tilde{X}}(\omega_k)}{|1 - \exp(-i\omega_k)|^2} \right| \right] = O(1)$ for all $\omega_k \neq 0$, so that solutions minimizing (5.37) and solutions minimizing the left hand side of (5.9) (which is based on the periodogram of the integrated process) generally differ. Which solution is the better? The results above imply that the periodogram of the *differenced* (stationary) process $\tilde{X}_t$ must be used in order to derive the optimal approximation to $\Gamma(\cdot)$. The main reason for this is that the coefficients of the filter $\dfrac{1}{1 - \exp(-i\omega_k)}$ never decay, thus the convolution theorem 4.8 cannot be applied anymore (i.e. $I_{NX}(\omega_k) \neq \dfrac{1}{|1 - \exp(-i\omega_k)|^2} I_{N\tilde{X}}(\omega_k) + o(1)$, see theorem 4.10).

- Adjusted series (see corollaries 4.11 and 4.12) are interesting, because their periodograms are identical with the weighting function in (5.37) (except for $\omega_0 = 0$). Applications are given in chapter 7.
- The filter $\Delta\tilde{\Gamma}(\cdot)$ and the process $\hat{X}_t$ are mathematical 'constructs' used for estimating the parameters of $\hat{\Gamma}(\cdot)$. They are not of interest per se.
- Assume that the assumptions of theorem 5.5 and of corollary 5.6 are satisfied so that $\tilde{X}_t \in C_f^0$. If $E[\tilde{X}_t] = 0$, then $I_{N\tilde{X}}(0) = \dfrac{N}{2\pi}\left(\overline{\tilde{X}}\right)^2 = O(1)$,

where $\overline{\tilde{X}}$ is the sample mean of the differenced stationary process (see for example Brockwell and Davis [10] theorem 7.1.2, p.219, and use $\tilde{X}_t \in C_f^0$). It is also shown in theorem 5.5 that $\Delta\tilde{\Gamma}(\cdot)$ as defined in (5.21) is bounded. Therefore $\dfrac{2\pi}{N}|\Delta\tilde{\Gamma}(0)|^2 I_{N\tilde{X}}(0) = O(1/N)$ can be neglected in (5.36): *if* $\mu = 0$, *then the bias problem can be neglected asymptotically* (recall remark 6, p.100).

Suppose now that $\mu \neq 0$ in (5.20) so that X_t has a linear drift. Then it follows that $I_{N\tilde{X}}(0) = \dfrac{N}{2\pi}\left(\overline{\tilde{X}}\right)^2 = O(N)$. As a consequence, the frequency $\omega_0 = 0$ cannot be neglected in (5.36): *if* $\mu \neq 0$, *then the bias problem does not vanish even asymptotically*. The interpretation of the difference between both cases (no drift vs. drift) is straightforward : while a pure random walk is asymptotically almost surely bounded by $\pm\sigma\sqrt{2N\ln(\ln(N))}$ (the so called *law of the iterated logarithm*, see for example theorem 2.1.13 in Embrechts et al. [28]) the corresponding bound for a random walk with drift increases linearly. In the latter case, the accuracy of the approximation of the level of Y_t must be enhanced. This is accomplished by 'strengthening' the order of the constraint $\hat{\Gamma}_C(0) = \Gamma(0)$. In fact, consider

$$\lim_{\omega \to 0}\left|\frac{\partial \Delta\Gamma_C(\omega)}{\partial \omega}\right| = \left|\sum_{k=-\infty}^{\infty}(\gamma_k - \hat{\gamma}_{Ck})k\right| = |\Delta\tilde{\Gamma}(0)| \qquad (5.38)$$

where the second equality follows from (5.21). A look at the left hand side of (5.36) shows that if $I_{N\tilde{X}}(0) = \dfrac{N}{2\pi}\left(\overline{\tilde{X}}\right)^2$ increases (quadratically) as a function of μ, then $|\Delta\tilde{\Gamma}(0)|^2$ (and thus the derivative in (5.38)) must decrease, since $|\Delta\tilde{\Gamma}(0)|^2$ is weighted by $I_{N\tilde{X}}(0)$. As a consequence, $\Delta\Gamma_C(\cdot)$ or, more precisely, the phase of $\Delta\Gamma_C(\cdot)$ becomes more 'flat' in $\omega_0 = 0$ (because the derivative must decrease in (5.38)). *The first order approximation now tends towards a higher order approximation* located between orders one and two. The random walk with drift therefore corresponds to an intermediate case between I(1)-processes without drift and I(2)-processes whose 'slope' is asymptotically infinite in absolute value (for the latter the derivative in (5.38) must vanish, recall (5.32)).

The remarks above conclude the extension of the direct filter approach to non-stationary integrated processes. As many practical examples demonstrate, a solution $\hat{\Gamma}_0(\cdot)$ of (5.19) or a solution $\hat{\Gamma}_{C0}(\cdot)$ of (5.36) (depending on X_t being stationary or integrated) often implies substantial time shifts (delays) of the output signal, see for example fig.2.8. This may be problematic if the detection of a 'turning point' (of the signal) towards the boundary $t = N$ of the sample is a key issue. Therefore, the next section presents a generalized conditional optimization procedure. Its solution is a filter with optimal selectivity properties under a time shift constraint.

5.4 Conditional Optimization

Often the detection of a 'turning point' (of the signal) towards the boundary $t = N$ of a sample is an issue in applications. Without further hypotheses, the concept of a 'turning point' is somewhat diffuse (recall by analogy the identification problem of a 'component' of a time series in section 1.3). However, it is not possible to review here identifying assumptions for 'turning points' discussed in the literature. Instead, a simple definition is provided: a turning point is a local extremum of a trend signal. Evidently, this definition depends on the (a priori) choice of the trend signal (see for example Proietti [76] for more 'sophisticated' definitions). Identifying turning points as extremes of trend signals permits illustrating the effects of the proposed method more clearly. Examples are provided in chapter 8.

For simplicity it is assumed that X_t is a stationary MA process (the presented results are straightforwardly extended to integrated processes). The task of detecting turning points 'earlier' involves the dimension of time. As seen in section 5.1, the time shift function of an asymmetric ARMA-filter $\hat{\Gamma}(\cdot)$ is $\hat{\phi}(\omega) := \hat{\Phi}(\omega)/\omega$ where $\hat{\Phi}(\omega)$ is the phase function of the filter. If $\Gamma(\cdot)$ is a real symmetric positive (≥ 0) filter (which is true for a large class of problems) then $\Phi(\omega) \equiv 0$. For convenience it is therefore assumed that $\Phi(\omega) = 0 = \phi(\omega)$. In this case, obvious time shift conditions for the asymmetric filter are for example $|\hat{\phi}(\omega_k)| < \delta_k$ where δ_k are some small prespecified numbers. However, this seems to be a too simplistic approach:

1. According to (3.17) phase and amplitude functions are 'intimately' related. Therefore, the numbers δ_k should be carefully selected because otherwise the amplitude function (or equivalently the selectivity properties of the asymmetric ARMA-filter) could be severely damaged.
2. The set of conditions $|\hat{\phi}(\omega_k)| < \delta_k$, for $k = 1, ..., n$ may be large. This can affect the algorithmic performance (speed of convergence).
3. There does not exist any 'reasonable' a priori criterion for choosing δ_k. Moreover:
   - Time-shifts essentially affect components in the pass band of the filters (since the remaining components are damped or eliminated). It is therefore intuitively reasonable to 'weight' time shift constraints (for

example with the amplitude functions of symmetric and asymmetric filters).

- Time shift constraints at frequency ω_k should account for the presence or absence of corresponding components in the input signal X_t. This can be achieved by periodogram 'weights'.

The above intuitive requirements can be formalized. To see this, decompose $|\Delta\Gamma(\omega)|^2 = |\Gamma(\omega) - \hat{\Gamma}(\omega)|^2$ into

$$
\begin{aligned}
|\Gamma(\omega) - \hat{\Gamma}(\omega)|^2 &= A(\omega)^2 + \hat{A}(\omega)^2 - 2A(\omega)\hat{A}(\omega)\cos\left(\hat{\Phi}(\omega) - \Phi(\omega)\right) \\
&= (A(\omega) - \hat{A}(\omega))^2 \\
&\quad + 2A(\omega)\hat{A}(\omega)\left[1 - \cos\left(\hat{\Phi}(\omega) - \Phi(\omega)\right)\right]
\end{aligned}
\tag{5.39}
$$

It is now assumed that $\Phi(\omega) \equiv 0$ (symmetric extraction filter). Inserting (5.39) into the left hand side of (5.9) gives

$$
\frac{2\pi}{N} \sum_{k=-[N/2]}^{[N/2]} (A(\omega_k) - \hat{A}(\omega_k))^2 I_{NX}(\omega_k)
\tag{5.40}
$$

$$
+ \frac{2\pi}{N} \sum_{k=-[N/2]}^{[N/2]} 2A(\omega_k)\hat{A}(\omega_k)\left[1 - \cos\left(\hat{\Phi}(\omega_k)\right)\right] I_{NX}(\omega_k)
$$

The first sum can be interpreted as that part of the (estimated) revision error variance which is caused by differences of the amplitude functions. This is called 'amplitude matching' which characterizes the selectivity of $\hat{\Gamma}(\cdot)$. The second sum corresponds to that part of the (estimated) revision error variance which is caused by differences of the phase functions (here : departures from $\Phi(\omega) \equiv 0$). This is called 'phase matching' and it measures the time shift effect of the asymmetric filter. These considerations lead to the following *time shift condition* :

$$
\frac{2\pi}{N} \sum_{k=-[N/2]}^{[N/2]} 2A(\omega_k)\hat{A}(\omega_k)\left[1 - \cos\left(\hat{\Phi}(\omega_k)\right)\right] I_{NX}(\omega_k) < \delta
\tag{5.41}
$$

The proposed restriction affects directly that part of the revision error variance which is due to time shift effects of the asymmetric filter. Note also that (5.41) can be approximated by

$$
\frac{2\pi}{N} \sum_{k=-[N/2]}^{[N/2]} A(\omega_k)\hat{A}(\omega_k)\omega_k^2\hat{\phi}(\omega_k)^2 I_{NX}(\omega_k) < \delta
\tag{5.42}
$$

where $2\left[1 - \cos\left(\hat{\Phi}(\omega_k)\right)\right] \simeq \hat{\Phi}(\omega_k)^2 = \omega_k^2\hat{\phi}(\omega_k)^2$.

A minimization of (5.40) subject to the constraint (5.41) can be achieved alternatively by minimizing

$$\frac{2\pi}{N} \sum_{k=-[N/2]}^{[N/2]} \left\{ (A(\omega_k) - \hat{A}(\omega_k))^2 \right. \tag{5.43}$$

$$\left. +(1+\lambda)2A(\omega_k)\hat{A}(\omega_k)\left[1 - \cos\left(\hat{\Phi}(\omega_k)\right)\right] \right\} I_{NX}(\omega_k)$$

where $\lambda \geq 0$ is a Lagrange multiplier. The latter 'controls' the relative importance of time shift (phase matching) and selectivity (amplitude matching) of the asymmetric filter.

The parameter λ can be determined as follows. Define the *excess mean time shift* τ of the filter by

$$\tau := \frac{\sum_{k=-[N/2]}^{[N/2]} A(\omega_k)\hat{A}(\omega_k)2\left[1 - \cos\left(\hat{\Phi}(\omega_k)\right)\right] I_{NX}(\omega_k)}{\sum_{k=-[N/2]}^{[N/2]} A(\omega_k)\hat{A}(\omega_k)\omega_k^2 I_{NX}(\omega_k)}$$

$$\simeq \frac{\sum_{k=-[N/2]}^{[N/2]} A(\omega_k)\hat{A}(\omega_k)\hat{\phi}(\omega_k)^2\omega_k^2 I_{NX}(\omega_k)}{\sum_{k=-[N/2]}^{[N/2]} A(\omega_k)\hat{A}(\omega_k)\omega_k^2 I_{NX}(\omega_k)}$$

where the same approximation as in (5.42) is used. It is readily seen that if the (absolute value of the) time shift $|\hat{\phi}(\omega)|$ systematically exceeds k time units, then $\tau > k$. The excess mean time shift corresponds to a suitable weighting of the time shifts at ω_k. Define now

$$\lambda := \tau \tag{5.44}$$

The parameter λ gives more importance to 'time shift matching' in (5.43) if the excess mean time shift is large.

Remarks :

1. Model-based approaches cannot account for time shift restrictions because corresponding asymmetric boundary filters are not obtained explicitly (rather they are defined implicitly by (1.4) which is equivalent to (1.3)).

2. The expression (5.43) can generally no more be interpreted as an estimate of the (final) revision error variance. Therefore, if $\hat{\Gamma}_0(\cdot)$ minimizes (5.43), then an estimate of the variance (of the corresponding filter output) is obtained by inserting $\hat{\Gamma}_0(\cdot)$ into (5.40).

3. The expressions involved in (5.40) reveal the antagonism between amplitude and phase fitting in the optimum. Improving the fit of either one results in less accurate matching of the other (in such a way that the mean square error of the filter output increases). This problem corresponds to the famous uncertainty principle in physics, see for example Priestley [75] chap.7 and Grenander [42].

4. The approximation of the cosine by a second order polynomial in (5.42) makes sense because the conditional optimization constrains its argument (the phase). A shift of one time unit at the frequency $\lambda := \pi/6$ (the fundamental seasonal frequency for monthly data) corresponds to a phase $\hat{\Phi}(\pi/6) = \pi/6$ so that $\cos(\pi/6) - (1 - (\pi/6)^2/2) \simeq 0.0031$ which is negligible. For higher frequencies ($> \pi/6$) the trend filter generally damps so that the corresponding time shift restrictions can be neglected (since they are weighted by the amplitude functions).

In previous sections, the consistency of the DFA has been derived for a large class of input signals and signal extraction filters. The *efficiency* of the DFA is analyzed in the following section. The obtained theoretical results are confirmed empirically in chapter 7.

5.5 Efficiency

It is shown in proposition 5.2 and theorem 5.3 that the error terms r_N and R_N in (5.7) and (5.9) are of orders $o(1)/\sqrt{N}$ and $O(1)/\sqrt{N}$ under suitable regularity assumptions. If the $O(1)$-term is 'small' then the DFA is efficient. Therefore, the error term R_N is analyzed in this section. Moreover, a method is proposed for which $r_N = O(N^{-1/2-\alpha})$ where $\alpha > 0$ depends on regularity assumptions.

Let the assumptions of theorem 5.3 be satisfied (thus $X_t \in C_f^0$: results straightforwardly extend to integrated processes using theorem 5.5). Let $\hat{\Gamma}_{0N}(\cdot)$ denote the solution of (the left hand side of) (5.19) with corresponding output $\hat{Y}_{t0N}$. Also, let

$$r'_{0N} := E[(Y_t - \hat{Y}_{t0N})^2] - \frac{1}{N}\sum_{t=1}^{N}(Y_t - \hat{Y}_{t0N})^2$$

be the error of the arithmetic mean of the process $(Y_t - \hat{Y}_{t0N})^2$ and let

$$r_{0N} := \frac{2\pi}{N}\sum_{k=-[N/2]}^{[N/2]} w_k |\Delta\Gamma_{0N}(\omega_k)|^2 I_{NX}(\omega_k) - \frac{1}{N}\sum_{t=1}^{N}(Y_t - Y_{0Nt})^2$$

be the 'convolution error' in proposition 5.2, then

$$R_{0N} = r'_{0N} - r_{0N} \tag{5.45}$$

where R_{0N} is the interesting error term in theorem 5.3 (it is the error term induced by the DFA). It is shown in the following proposition that the first component $r'_{0N} = O(1/\sqrt{N})$ is 'small'.

Proposition 5.7. *Assume $X_t \in C_f^0$, $\Gamma(\cdot) \in C_f^0$ and ϵ_t is an iid sequence with finite fourth order moments. Assume also that the solutions $\hat{\Gamma}_{0N}(\cdot)$ of (5.19) (left hand side) define a uniformly stable sequence and that the signal Y_t is known. Then*

$$\frac{1}{N}\sum_{t=1}^{N}(Y_t - \hat{Y}_{t0N})^2$$

is an asymptotically best linear unbiased estimate of $E[(Y_t - \hat{Y}_{t0N})^2]$.

Proof. Let $\Delta Y_{t0N} := Y_t - \hat{Y}_{t0N}$ and $\Delta\Gamma_{0N}(\cdot) := \Gamma(\cdot) - \hat{\Gamma}_{0N}(\cdot)$. $\Gamma(\cdot) \in C_f^0$ and the uniform stability of the sequence $\hat{\Gamma}_{0N}(\cdot)$ imply that $\Delta\Gamma_{0N}(\cdot) \in C_f^0$ uniformly i.e. there exists an $M > 0$ independent of N such that

$$\sum_{k=-\infty}^{\infty}|\gamma_k - \hat{\gamma}_{k0N}| \leq \sum_{k=-\infty}^{\infty}|\gamma_k| + |\hat{\gamma}_{k0N}| < M$$

If $X_t \in C_f^0$ (as assumed), then proposition E.2 in the appendix implies that

$$\sum_{j=0}^{\infty}|R_{(\Delta Y_{0N})^2}(j)| < M'$$

where $R_{(\Delta Y_{0N})^2}(j)$ is the autocovariance function of the process $(\Delta Y_{t0N})^2$ and M' does not depend on N. Therefore the spectral density of $(\Delta Y_{t0N})^2$ exists and is a continuous function (because its Fourier coefficients $R_{(\Delta Y_{0N})^2}(k)$ are absolutely summable). Grenander and Rosenblatt [43], section 7.3, then show that $\overline{(\Delta Y)_{0N}^2} := \frac{1}{N}\sum_{t=1}^{N}(\Delta Y_{t0N})^2$ is an asymptotically best linear unbiased estimate of $E[(Y_t - \hat{Y}_{t0N})^2]$ which completes the proof of the proposition. □

Note that the linearity in proposition 5.7 refers to the process $z_t := (Y_t - \hat{Y}_{t0N})^2$: the arithmetic mean $\bar{z}$ is a linear estimate of its expectation. The close correspondence of the sample mean $\overline{(\Delta Y)_{0N}^2}$ and the maximum likelihood estimate of $E[(Y_t - \hat{Y}_{t0N})^2]$ can be seen by setting $z_t := \Delta Y_{t0N}^2$ and assuming that z_t is a stationary gaussian AR-process. One can show (see for example Priestley [75], p.348) that the maximum likelihood estimate of the expectation of z_t is then given by

$$\hat{\mu}_z = \frac{\bar{z}_1 + \hat{a}_1\bar{z}_2 + ... + \hat{a}_p\bar{z}_p}{\hat{a}_1 + \hat{a}_2 + ... + \hat{a}_p}$$

where $\bar{z}_{i+1} := \frac{1}{N-p}\sum_{t=p+1-i}^{N-i}z_t$ and $\hat{a}_j$ are the maximum likelihood estimates of the AR-parameters (a generalization to arbitrary stationary processes is suggested in Brockwell and Davis [10], exercise 7.2, p.236). Since $\bar{z}_i$, $i = 1, ..., p$ are 'almost' identical to $\bar{z}$ it follows that the sample mean $\bar{z}$ is 'almost' equal (up to order $O(1/N)$) to the maximum likelihood estimate of the expectation of z_t (which is the revision error variance $E[(Y_t - \hat{Y}_{t0N})^2]$).

These results show that the first error component r'_{0N} in (5.45) is 'small'. Proposition 5.2 and the proof of theorem 5.3 reveal that $r_{0N} = o(1/\sqrt{N})$ so that the DFA (5.19) 'inherits' its efficiency from $\frac{1}{N}\sum_{t=1}^{N}(\Delta Y_{t0N})^2$. In fact, the expression on the left hand side of (5.19) is a *superconsistent* estimate of the asymptotically best linear unbiased estimate $\frac{1}{N}\sum_{t=1}^{N}(\Delta Y_{t0N})^2$ (of the revision error variance).

Although the first error term r_{0N} is asymptotically negligible, 'closer' approximations of

$$\frac{1}{N}\sum_{t=1}^{N}(\Delta Y_{t0N})^2$$

are still possible. A corresponding method is proposed now.

The error term r_{0N} is induced by convolution errors $R_{N\Delta Y_{0N}X}(\omega)$. The latter result from the approximation of the unknown periodogram

$$I_{N\Delta Y_{0N}}(\omega) = \left| \sum_{k=-\infty}^{\infty} \Delta\gamma_{k0N}\exp(-ik\omega)\frac{\sqrt{2\pi}}{\sqrt{N}} \sum_{t=1-k}^{N-k} X_t\exp(-it\omega) \right|^2$$

(see (4.23)) by $|\Delta\Gamma_{0N}(\omega)|^2 I_{NX}(\omega)$. $I_{N\Delta Y_{0N}}(\omega)$ is a 'non-linear' discrete convolution (the summation limits of the inner sum depend on the index of the outer sum), which assumes knowledge of the infinite sample of X_t. $|\Delta\Gamma_{0N}(\omega)|^2 I_{NX}(\omega)$ can then be interpreted as a first order ('linearized') approximation which assumes knowledge of the available sample only. In the following, a 'non-linear' convolution is proposed which assumes knowledge of $X_1, ..., X_N$ only. The subscript '0' for filters or time series (indicating solutions of the DFA) is now dropped for notational convenience. Let M and β be such that $N = M + 2N^\beta$, where $1 > \beta > 0$, and define

$$\Xi'_{N\Delta Y}(\omega) := \sum_{k=-N^\beta}^{N^\beta} \Delta\gamma_k\exp(-ik\omega)\frac{\sqrt{2\pi}}{\sqrt{M}} \sum_{t=1+N^\beta-k}^{N-N^\beta-k} X_t\exp(-it\omega) \quad (5.46)$$

$$+ \sum_{k=-\infty}^{-N^\beta-1} \Delta\gamma_k\exp(-ik\omega)\frac{\sqrt{2\pi}}{\sqrt{M}} \sum_{t=1+2N^\beta}^{N} X_t\exp(-it\omega)$$

$$+ \sum_{k=N^\beta+1}^{\infty} \Delta\gamma_k\exp(-ik\omega)\frac{\sqrt{2\pi}}{\sqrt{M}} \sum_{t=1}^{N-2N^\beta} X_t\exp(-it\omega)$$

$$=: (\text{I}) + (\text{II}) + (\text{III})$$

This expression can be computed for the sample $(X_1, ..., X_N)$. Moreover, the convolution is 'non-linear' for $0 \le |k| \le N^\beta$ (corresponding to the first term

(I)) and is 'linear' for $k > N^\beta$ or $k < N^\beta$ (corresponding to (II) or (III)). If $\Delta\gamma_k$ decays 'sufficiently fast', then the errors arising from the 'linear' terms (II) and (III) may become negligible. The following theorem gives a precise result:

Theorem 5.8. *Let β and M be such that $N = M + 2N^\beta$, where $1 > \beta > 0$. Assume $\Gamma(\cdot) \in C_f^{\alpha+1/2}$, $X_t \in C_f^0$ and $\hat\Gamma(\cdot)$ is a stable ARMA-filter. Define*

$$D_N(\omega) := \Xi_{M\Delta Y}(\omega) - \Xi'_{N\Delta Y}(\omega) \tag{5.47}$$

where $\Xi_{M\Delta Y}(\omega)$ is the Fourier transform of the sample $\Delta Y_{1+N^\beta}, ..., \Delta Y_{M+N^\beta}$ (assuming knowledge of the infinite sample of X_t) and $\Xi'_{N\Delta Y}(\omega)$ is defined by (5.46). Then

$$E[|D_N(\omega)|^2] = O(N^{-1-2\alpha\beta}) \tag{5.48}$$

Proof.

$$
\begin{aligned}
D_N(\omega) = &\sum_{k=-\infty}^{-N^\beta-1} \Delta\gamma_k \exp(-ik\omega) \\
&\frac{\sqrt{2\pi}}{\sqrt{M}}\left(\sum_{t=1+N^\beta-k}^{N-N^\beta-k} X_t \exp(-it\omega) - \sum_{t=1+2N^\beta}^{N} X_t \exp(-it\omega) \right) \\
&+ \sum_{k=N^\beta+1}^{\infty} \Delta\gamma_k \exp(-ik\omega) \\
&\frac{\sqrt{2\pi}}{\sqrt{M}}\left(\sum_{t=1+N^\beta-k}^{N-N^\beta-k} X_t \exp(-ik\omega) - \sum_{t=1}^{N-2N^\beta} X_t \exp(-it\omega) \right) \\
= &\, D_{N1}(\omega) + D_{N2}(\omega) \tag{5.49}
\end{aligned}
$$

say. It is now shown that $E[|D_{N2}(\omega)|^2] = O(N^{-1-2\alpha\beta})$.

$$
\begin{aligned}
E[|D_{N2}(\omega)|^2] = E\Bigg[&\sum_{j=N^\beta+1}^{\infty} \sum_{k=N^\beta+1}^{\infty} \Delta\gamma_j \Delta\gamma_k \exp(-ij\omega)\exp(ik\omega) \\
&\times \frac{\sqrt{2\pi}}{\sqrt{M}}\left(\sum_{t=1+N^\beta-j}^{N-N^\beta-j} X_t \exp(-it\omega) - \sum_{t=1}^{N-2N^\beta} X_t \exp(-it\omega) \right) \\
&\times \frac{\sqrt{2\pi}}{\sqrt{M}}\left(\sum_{t=1+N^\beta-k}^{N-N^\beta-k} X_t \exp(it\omega) - \sum_{t=1}^{N-2N^\beta} X_t \exp(it\omega) \right) \Bigg] \\
\leq &\, \frac{2\pi}{M} \sum_{j=N^\beta+1}^{\infty} \sum_{k=N^\beta+1}^{\infty} |\Delta\gamma_j||\Delta\gamma_k| 2\min(j-N^\beta, k-N^\beta)
\end{aligned}
$$

$$\times \sum_{l=-\infty}^{\infty} |R(l)|$$

$$\leq 2 \sum_{l=-\infty}^{\infty} |R(l)| \frac{2\pi}{M} \frac{1}{N^{2\alpha\beta}}$$

$$\times \sum_{j=N^\beta+1}^{\infty} \sum_{k=N^\beta+1}^{\infty} |\Delta\gamma_j||j|^\alpha |\Delta\gamma_k||k|^\alpha \min(j,k)$$

$$\leq 2 \sum_{l=-\infty}^{\infty} |R(l)| \frac{2\pi}{M} \frac{1}{N^{2\alpha\beta}}$$

$$\times \sum_{j=N^\beta+1}^{\infty} \sum_{k=N^\beta+1}^{\infty} |\Delta\gamma_j||j|^{\alpha+1/2} |\Delta\gamma_k||k|^{\alpha+1/2}$$

$$= O(1)N^{-1-2\alpha\beta}$$

(where $1/M = 1/(N - 2N^\beta) = O(N^{-1})$ is used). A similar proof with obvious modifications shows that

$$E[|D_{N1}(\omega)|^2] = O(N^{-1-2\alpha\beta})$$

which completes the proof of the theorem.   □

The following corollary is the analogue of proposition 5.2 for the proposed 'non-linear' convolution.

Corollary 5.9. *Assume $X_t \in C_f^0$, $\Gamma \in C_f^{\alpha+1/2}$, $\alpha \geq 0$ and let M, β be defined as in theorem 5.8. Let*

$$\frac{2\pi}{M} \sum_{k=-[M/2]}^{[M/2]} w_k I'_{N\Delta Y}(\omega_k) = \frac{1}{M} \sum_{t=1}^{M} (\Delta Y_{t+N^\beta})^2 + r_N \qquad (5.50)$$

where $I'_{N\Delta Y}(\omega_k) := |\Xi'_{N\Delta Y}(\omega_k)|^2$ (defined by (5.46)) and $\omega_k \in \Omega_M := \left\{ k2\pi/M \mid 0 \leq |k| \leq [M/2] \right\}$. Then

$$E[|r_N|] = O(N^{-1/2-\alpha\beta})$$

Proof. • Theorem 5.8 and (4.28) show that

$$I'_{N\Delta Y}(\omega_k) = I_{N\Delta Y}(\omega_k) + O(N^{-1/2-\alpha\beta})$$

uniformly in k.

• The proof of proposition 5.2 shows that

$$\frac{2\pi}{M} \sum_{k=-[M/2]}^{[M/2]} w_k I_{N\Delta Y}(\omega_k) = \frac{1}{M} \sum_{t=1}^{M} (\Delta Y_{t+N^\beta})^2$$

combining both results completes the proof of the corollary.   □

Let $\check{\Gamma}_{0N}(\cdot)$ (with $p(N)$ parameters) denote the solution of

$$\min_{\check{\Gamma}} \frac{2\pi}{M} \sum_{k=-[M/2]}^{[M/2]} w_k I'_{N\Delta Y}(\omega_k)$$

where $I'_{N\Delta Y}(\omega_k)$ are the squared moduli of (5.46) (see corollary 5.9). Assume that $\check{\Gamma}_{0N}(\cdot)$ is a uniformly stable sequence. Then corollary 5.4 implies

$$\min_{\check{\Gamma}} \frac{2\pi}{M} \sum_{k=-[M/2]}^{[M/2]} w_k I'_{N\Delta Y}(\omega_k) \leftrightarrow \min_{\check{\Gamma}} E[(Y_t - \hat{Y}_t)^2] + R_{0N} \qquad (5.51)$$

where ARMA-filters with p parameters are optimized on both sides and where $R_{0N} = O(1)/\sqrt{N}$ (i.e. a solution of the left hand side is also a solution of the right hand side and conversely). The convolution error part r_{0N} in R_{0N} is now of order $O(N^{-1/2-\alpha\beta})$.

Note also that the obtained results straightforwardly extend to integrated input processes because theorem 5.5 and its corollary transpose the non-stationary in the (constrained) stationary case.

The obtained results suggest that the convolution error r_{0N} may be reduced at the expense of r'_{0N} in (5.45). Indeed, increasing β in corollary 5.9 implies that $r_{0N} = O(N^{-1/2-\alpha\beta})$ and $M := N - 2N^\beta$ both decrease (at least asymptotically for the former). But a smaller M implies poorer performances of $\frac{1}{M}\sum_{t=1}^{M}(\Delta Y_{t+N^\beta})^2$ (i.e. a larger r'_{0N}).

The consistency and the efficiency of the DFA have been proved for a large class of input signals and extraction filters. The asymptotic distribution of the filter parameters for the DFA is analyzed in the following section. Results are derived which can be used for inferring the filter orders Q and $q + r$ in (3.6). Moreover, hypothesis tests for the filter parameters are proposed.

5.6 Inference Under 'Conditional' Stationarity

The assumption here is that X_t is stationary or, more generally, that the conditions (5.22) are satisfied if X_t is integrated (so that $\tilde{X}_t$ in (5.20) is stationary). The latter requirement is called 'conditional stationarity' which is subject to the constraints (5.22). A hypothesis test for the conditions (5.22) is proposed in section 5.7.

In the previous section, the efficiency of the DFA was derived for the resulting estimate $\hat{Y}_t$ of the unknown signal Y_t. However, nothing was said about the estimates of the filter parameters (zeroes, poles and normalizing constant). An expression for the asymptotic distribution of the filter parameter estimates for the DFA is obtained in the first section 5.6.1 under the above 'stationarity' assumption. Applications of this result are given in the remaining two sections: section 5.6.2 analyzes the spurious decrease of the optimization criterion (from which estimates of the unknown filter orders Q and q can be derived) and section 5.6.3 proposes a test of parameter hypotheses.

5.6.1 The Asymptotic Distribution of the Parameters of the 'Linearized' DFA

It is first assumed that X_t is stationary. An extension to non-stationary integrated processes is provided in the remarks below. Consider an ARMA-difference equation in the time domain as given in (3.4):

$$\hat{Y}_t = \sum_{k=1}^{Q} a_k \hat{Y}_{t-k} + \sum_{k=-r}^{q} b_k X_{t-k} \tag{5.52}$$

Such a filter can be used for estimating Y_{N-r} but not Y_{N-r+1} because it assumes knowledge of the regressors $X_{t+r}, X_{t+r-1}, ..., X_{t-q}$. Instead of the 'traditional' AR- and MA-parameters in (5.52) the parameter set could be defined by z_k and p_k in (3.33). The latter is often preferred because useful restrictions can be more easily implemented (so for example the ZPC-constraint or unit-root constraints (5.22)).

The following theorem proposes an expression for the asymptotic distribution of filter parameter estimates for the DFA (5.19). For that purpose denote the (unknown) stable ARMA$(Q, q + r)$-filter minimizing the revision error variance (in the class of ARMA$(Q, q + r)$ filters) by $\tilde{\Gamma}_{Qq}(\cdot)$ and denote the corresponding (unknown) $(Q+q+r+1)$-dimensional vector of parameters by $\tilde{\mathbf{b}}$.

Theorem 5.10. *Assume*

- $\Gamma(\cdot) \in C_f^{5/2}$ *and* $X_t \in C_f^{1/2}$. *The white noise sequence* ϵ_t *(defining X_t) is an iid sequence satisfying* $\mathrm{E}[\epsilon_t^8] < \infty$.
- *The parameter set is given either by 'traditional' AR- and MA-parameters in (5.52) or by z_j and p_k in (3.33).*
- *The DFA solutions $\hat{\Gamma}_{Qq}(\cdot)$ of (5.19) (for estimating Y_{N-r}) define a uniformly stable sequence of ARMA$(Q, q + r)$ filters.*
- *The matrix (hessian)*

$$\mathbf{U}_{Qq} := \int_{-\pi}^{\pi} \frac{\partial^2}{\partial \mathbf{b}^2} \left(|\Gamma(\omega) - \tilde{\Gamma}_{Qq}(\omega)|^2 \right) h(\omega) d\omega \tag{5.53}$$

is strictly positive definite in a neighborhood of $\tilde{\mathbf{b}}$.

It then follows that

1. *the vector* $\sqrt{N}(\hat{\mathbf{b}} - \tilde{\mathbf{b}})$ *is asymptotically normally distributed with mean zero. More precisely*

$$\sqrt{N}(\hat{\mathbf{b}} - \tilde{\mathbf{b}}) \sim AN(0, \mathbf{U}_{\mathbf{Qq}}^{-1} \mathbf{V}_{\mathbf{Qq}} \mathbf{U}_{\mathbf{Qq}}^{-1}) \tag{5.54}$$

where AN *means asymptotically multivariate normally distributed and where* $\mathbf{U}_{Qq}$ *is defined in (5.53) and*

$$\mathbf{V}_{Qq} := 4\pi \int_{-\pi}^{\pi} \frac{\partial}{\partial \mathbf{b}} \left(|\Gamma(\omega) - \tilde{\Gamma}_{Qq}(\omega)|^2 \right) \left(\frac{\partial}{\partial \mathbf{b}} \left(|\Gamma(\omega) - \tilde{\Gamma}_{Qq}(\omega)|^2 \right) \right)'$$
$$\times h(\omega)^2 d\omega \tag{5.55}$$

and the operators $\frac{\partial^2}{\partial \mathbf{b}^2}(\cdot)$ *and* $\frac{\partial}{\partial \mathbf{b}}(\cdot)$ *are the hessian and the gradient (of their arguments) respectively and* $h(\cdot)$ *is the spectral density of* X_t;

2. *the matrices* $\mathbf{U}_{Qq}$ *and* $\mathbf{V}_{Qq}$ *can be consistently estimated by*

$$\hat{\mathbf{U}}_{Qq} := \frac{2\pi}{N} \sum_{k=-[N/2]}^{[N/2]} \frac{\partial^2}{\partial \mathbf{b}^2} |\Gamma(\omega_k) - \hat{\Gamma}_{Qq}(\omega_k)|^2 I_{NX}(\omega_k) \tag{5.56}$$

$$\hat{\mathbf{V}}_{Qq} := \frac{4\pi^2}{N} \sum_{k=-[N/2]}^{[N/2]} \frac{\partial}{\partial \mathbf{b}} \left(|\Gamma(\omega_k) - \hat{\Gamma}_{Qq}(\omega_k)|^2 \right)$$
$$\times \left(\frac{\partial}{\partial \mathbf{b}} \left(|\Gamma(\omega_k) - \hat{\Gamma}_{Qq}(\omega_k)|^2 \right) \right)' I_{NX}(\omega_k)^2 \tag{5.57}$$

More precisely

$$\mathbf{U}_{Qq} = \hat{\mathbf{U}}_{Qq} + O(1/\sqrt{N})$$

and

$$\mathbf{V}_{Qq} = \hat{\mathbf{V}}_{Qq} + O(1/\sqrt{N})$$

where the approximations are defined elementwise and in absolute mean.

Remark

- Note that $\tilde{\Gamma}(\cdot)$ and $\hat{\Gamma}(\cdot)$ have the same ARMA-structure (same AR- and MA-orders) but different parameters. One could set $\tilde{\Gamma}(\omega) := \Gamma(\tilde{\mathbf{b}}, \omega)$ and $\hat{\Gamma}(\omega) := \Gamma(\hat{\mathbf{b}}, \omega)$ where $\Gamma(\cdot, \omega)$ represents the common ARMA-structure. Therefore

$$\frac{\partial}{\partial b_i} \tilde{\Gamma}(\cdot) := \left. \frac{\partial}{\partial b_i} \Gamma(\mathbf{b}, \cdot) \right|_{\mathbf{b}=\tilde{\mathbf{b}}}$$
$$\frac{\partial}{\partial b_i} \hat{\Gamma}(\cdot) := \left. \frac{\partial}{\partial b_i} \Gamma(\mathbf{b}, \cdot) \right|_{\mathbf{b}=\hat{\mathbf{b}}}$$

and similarly for second order derivatives. The derivatives are taken either
with respect to AR- and MA-parameters or with respect to arguments and
moduli of z_k and p_k as defined in (3.33).

• The strict positive definiteness of the Hessian implies that the parameters
are uniquely identified in the vicinity of $\tilde{\mathbf{b}}$. So for example, cancelling zeroes
and poles of the ARMA-filters $\tilde{\Gamma}_{Qq}(\cdot)$ and $\hat{\Gamma}_{Qq}(\cdot)$ are not allowed.

Proof of theorem 5.10. For notational convenience the index Qq is dropped
from $\tilde{\Gamma}_{Qq}(\cdot)$ and $\hat{\Gamma}_{Qq}(\cdot)$ and from the matrices $\mathbf{U}_{Qq}$, $\mathbf{V}_{Qq}$, $\hat{\mathbf{U}}_{Qq}$ and $\hat{\mathbf{V}}_{Qq}$.
Define

$$\mathbf{P}(\tilde{\mathbf{b}}) := \frac{2\pi}{N} \sum_{k=-[N/2]}^{[N/2]} \frac{\partial}{\partial \mathbf{b}} |\Gamma(\omega_k) - \tilde{\Gamma}(\omega_k)|^2 I_{NX}(\omega_k)$$

A first order Taylor series development of $\mathbf{P}(\cdot)$ centered in $\hat{\mathbf{b}}$ then leads to

$$\mathbf{P}(\tilde{\mathbf{b}}) = \hat{\mathbf{U}}(\tilde{\mathbf{b}} - \hat{\mathbf{b}}) + \mathbf{O}((\tilde{\mathbf{b}} - \hat{\mathbf{b}})^2) \tag{5.58}$$

Since the DFA is consistent the higher order term is asymptotically negligible.
It is shown in proposition 10.8.6 in Brockwell and Davis [10] that

$$\mathbf{l}'\mathbf{P}(\tilde{\mathbf{b}}) \sim$$

$$\mathrm{AN}\left(0, \frac{4\pi}{N} \int_{-\pi}^{\pi} \left(\sum_{j=1}^{Q+q+r+1} l_j \frac{\partial}{\partial b_j} |\Gamma(\omega) - \tilde{\Gamma}(\omega)|^2 \right)^2 h(\omega)^2 d\omega \right) \tag{5.59}$$

for any arbitrary array $\mathbf{l}$ of dimension $Q + q + r + 1$ (the proof is given for
ARMA-processes whose transfer functions are in C_f^∞; however, a closer look
shows that the proof requires $C_f^{1/2}$ 'only' as assumed by theorem 5.10). Note
also the slightly different periodogram definitions which imply a different normalization of the integral in (5.59).
The Cramer-Wold device then implies

$$\mathbf{P}(\tilde{\mathbf{b}}) \sim \mathrm{AN}\left(0, \frac{4\pi}{N} \int_{-\pi}^{\pi} \frac{\partial}{\partial \mathbf{b}} |\Gamma(\omega) - \tilde{\Gamma}(\omega)|^2 \right.$$

$$\left. \times \left(\frac{\partial}{\partial \mathbf{b}} |\Gamma(\omega) - \tilde{\Gamma}(\omega)|^2 \right)' h(\omega)^2 d\omega \right) \tag{5.60}$$

The matrix $\hat{\mathbf{U}}$ converges to $\mathbf{U}$ in probability. To see this, use the development
leading to (5.64) below and the consistency of the DFA-estimate : the latter
implies that the order of the approximation in (5.63) is at least $o(1)$ in mean
square (which is sufficient for the required convergence). Since $\mathbf{U}$ is strictly
positive definite by assumption, $\hat{\mathbf{U}}^{-1}$ must converge to $\mathbf{U}^{-1}$ by proposition
7.1 in Hamilton [45]. As a result, proposition 7.3 in Hamilton [45] (example
7.5) implies that asymptotically

$$(\hat{\mathbf{b}} - \tilde{\mathbf{b}}) \sim \mathbf{U}^{-1}\mathbf{P}(\tilde{\mathbf{b}}) \tag{5.61}$$

where $\sim$ means 'distributed as'. Note that

$$(\hat{\mathbf{b}} - \tilde{\mathbf{b}}) = \mathbf{O}(1/\sqrt{N}) \tag{5.62}$$

(use (5.60) and (5.61)). Taken together, these results imply (5.54) (note that the hessian $\mathbf{U}$ is symmetric so that $\mathbf{U} = \mathbf{U}'$ and that $E[\epsilon_t^8] < \infty$ is needed because otherwise the expression for the variance (5.54) would be infinite). Consider now the estimates for the variance covariance matrix of the parameter estimates. In particular

$$\hat{\mathbf{U}} := \frac{2\pi}{N} \sum_{k=-[N/2]}^{[N/2]} \frac{\partial^2}{\partial \mathbf{b}^2} |\Gamma(\omega_k) - \hat{\Gamma}(\omega_k)|^2 I_{NX}(\omega_k)$$

$$= \frac{2\pi}{N} \sum_{k=-[N/2]}^{[N/2]} \frac{\partial^2}{\partial \mathbf{b}^2} |\Gamma(\omega_k) - \hat{\Gamma}(\omega_k)|^2 h(\omega_k) + \mathbf{O}(1/\sqrt{N})$$

$$= \frac{2\pi}{N} \sum_{k=-[N/2]}^{[N/2]} \frac{\partial^2}{\partial \mathbf{b}^2} |\Gamma(\omega_k) - \tilde{\Gamma}(\omega_k)|^2 h(\omega_k) + \mathbf{O}(1/\sqrt{N}) \tag{5.63}$$

$$= \int_{-\pi}^{\pi} \frac{\partial^2}{\partial \mathbf{b}^2} |\Gamma(\omega) - \tilde{\Gamma}(\omega)|^2 h(\omega) d\omega + \mathbf{O}(1/\sqrt{N}) \tag{5.64}$$

$$= \mathbf{U} + \mathbf{O}(1/\sqrt{N})$$

The second equality follows from (B.9) in the appendix. The third equality follows from (5.62) which implies

$$\left| \frac{\partial^2}{\partial \mathbf{b}^2} \hat{\Gamma}(\omega_k) - \frac{\partial^2}{\partial \mathbf{b}^2} \tilde{\Gamma}(\omega_k) \right| = \mathbf{O}(1/\sqrt{N})$$

uniformly in ω_k. Finally, (5.64) follows from proposition 5.11 below, using the regularity of $\tilde{\Gamma}(\omega_k)$ (which is infinitely often differentiable since it is a stable ARMA filter) and the assumptions $h(\cdot) \in C_f^{1/2}$ and $\Gamma(\cdot) \in C_f^{5/2}$ so that the second order derivatives of $\Gamma(\cdot)$ are in $C_f^{1/2}$ (note that the product of these functions must be in $C_f^{1/2}$ by proposition 4.7). Finally, consider

$$\hat{\mathbf{V}} := \frac{4\pi^2}{N} \sum_{k=-[N/2]}^{[N/2]} \frac{\partial}{\partial \mathbf{b}} \left(|\Gamma(\omega_k) - \hat{\Gamma}(\omega_k)|^2 \right) \left(\frac{\partial}{\partial \mathbf{b}} \left(|\Gamma(\omega_k) - \hat{\Gamma}(\omega_k)|^2 \right) \right)'$$

$$\times I_{NX}(\omega_k)^2$$

$$= 4\pi \frac{2\pi}{N} \sum_{k=-[N/2]}^{[N/2]} \frac{\partial}{\partial \mathbf{b}} \left(|\Gamma(\omega_k) - \hat{\Gamma}(\omega_k)|^2 \right) \left(\frac{\partial}{\partial \mathbf{b}} \left(|\Gamma(\omega_k) - \hat{\Gamma}(\omega_k)|^2 \right) \right)'$$

$$\times h(\omega_k)^2 + O(1/\sqrt{N})$$

$$= 4\pi \frac{2\pi}{N} \sum_{k=-[N/2]}^{[N/2]} \frac{\partial}{\partial \mathbf{b}} \left(|\Gamma(\omega_k) - \tilde{\Gamma}(\omega_k)|^2 \right) \left(\frac{\partial}{\partial \mathbf{b}} \left(|\Gamma(\omega_k) - \tilde{\Gamma}(\omega_k)|^2 \right) \right)'$$

$$\times h(\omega_k)^2 + O(1/\sqrt{N})$$

$$= 4\pi \int_{-\pi}^{\pi} \frac{\partial}{\partial \mathbf{b}} \left(|\Gamma(\omega) - \tilde{\Gamma}(\omega)|^2 \right) \left(\frac{\partial}{\partial \mathbf{b}} \left(|\Gamma(\omega) - \tilde{\Gamma}(\omega)|^2 \right) \right)'$$

$$\times h(\omega)^2 d\omega + O(1/\sqrt{N}) \tag{5.65}$$

The second equality follows from

- the identity

$$E[I_{NX}(\omega_k)^2] = Var(I_{NX}(\omega_k)) + E[I_{NX}(\omega_k)]^2$$
$$2h(\omega_k)^2 + O(1/\sqrt{N})$$

see (B.2) and (B.18) in the appendix;
- the approximation

$$Var\left(\frac{2\pi}{N} \sum_{k=-[N/2]}^{[N/2]} g(\omega_k) I_{NX}(\omega_k)^2 \right)$$

$$= \frac{4\pi^2}{N^2} \left\{ \sum_{k=-[N/2]}^{[N/2]} g(\omega_k)^2 Var(I_{NX}(\omega_k)^2) \right.$$

$$\left. + \sum_{k=-[N/2]}^{[N/2]} \sum_{j=-[N/2], j\neq k}^{[N/2]} \left[g(\omega_k) g(\omega_j) Cov\left(I_{NX}(\omega_k)^2, I_{NX}(\omega_j)^2 \right) \right] \right\}$$

$$= O(1/N) \tag{5.66}$$

where $g(\cdot)$ is an arbitrary bounded function. The order in (5.66) is a consequence of (B.3) and the boundedness of $g(\cdot)$. Note that

$$\frac{\partial}{\partial \mathbf{b}} \left(|\Gamma(\omega) - \tilde{\Gamma}(\omega)|^2 \right) \left(\frac{\partial}{\partial \mathbf{b}} \left(|\Gamma(\omega) - \tilde{\Gamma}(\omega)|^2 \right) \right)'$$

in (5.65) is bounded elementwise because of regularity assumptions.

The last two steps leading to (5.65) are identical to the last two steps in (5.64). This completes the proof of the theorem. $\square$

The following proposition is needed in the proof of theorem 5.10:

Proposition 5.11. *Assume* $f(\cdot) \in C_f^{1/2}$. *Then*

$$\left| \int_{-\pi}^{\pi} f(\omega) d\omega - \frac{2\pi}{N} \sum_{k=-[N/2]}^{[N/2]} f(\omega_k) \right| = O(1/\sqrt{N})$$

Proof. Let ω be fixed and $\lambda \in [\omega - \pi/N, \omega + \pi/N]$ be such that

$$|f(\lambda) - f(\omega)| = \max_{\omega' \in [\omega - \pi/N, \omega + \pi/N]} |f(\omega') - f(\omega)|$$

Then

$$|f(\lambda) - f(\omega)| = \left| \sum_{k=-\infty}^{\infty} \gamma_k \{\exp(-i\lambda) - \exp(-i\omega)\} \right|$$

$$= \left| \sum_{k=-\sqrt{N}}^{\sqrt{N}} \gamma_k(-i)(\lambda - \omega) + \sum_{|k|>\sqrt{N}} \gamma_k \{\exp(-i\lambda) - \exp(-i\omega)\} \right| + O(1/\sqrt{N})$$

$$\leq \frac{2\pi}{N} \sum_{k=-\infty}^{\infty} |\gamma_k| + \frac{2}{\sqrt{N}} \sum_{|k|>\sqrt{N}} |\gamma_k||k|^{1/2} + O(1/\sqrt{N})$$

$$= O(1/\sqrt{N})$$

uniformly in ω. Therefore

$$\left| \int_{-\pi}^{\pi} f(\omega)d\omega - \frac{2\pi}{N} \sum_{k=-[N/2]}^{[N/2]} f(\omega_k) \right|$$

$$\leq \frac{2\pi}{N} \sum_{k=-[N/2]}^{[N/2]} \max_{\omega,\lambda \in [\omega_k - \pi/N, \omega_k + \pi/N]} |f(\omega) - f(\lambda)|$$

$$= O(1/\sqrt{N})$$

as claimed. $\square$

Remarks

- It is assumed in theorem 5.10 that $\tilde{\Gamma}_{Qq}(\cdot)$ is the best filter among the class of $ARMA(Q, q + r)$ filters. However, such a filter may be optimal in the class of all filters in C_f^0. To see this, assume X_t is a stationary and invertible ARMA process. Then a 'closed-form' solution of the signal estimation problem (best filter in C_f^0) is given by

$$\tilde{\Gamma}(\omega) := \frac{\sum_{k=-r}^{\infty} \left(\sum_{j=0}^{\infty} b_j \gamma_{k-j} \right) \exp(-ik\omega)}{\sum_{j=0}^{\infty} b_j \exp(-ij\omega)} \tag{5.67}$$

see (5.6). If $\Gamma(\omega)$ is a symmetric $MA(2q + 1)$-filter, then the numerator polynomial becomes

$$\sum_{k=-r}^{\infty} \left(\sum_{j=0}^{\infty} b_j \gamma_{k-j} \right) \exp(-ik\omega)$$

$$= \sum_{k=-r}^{\infty} \left(\sum_{j=\max(0,k-q)}^{k+q} b_j \gamma_{k-j} \right) \exp(-ik\omega)$$

$$= \sum_{k=-r}^{q-1} \left(\sum_{j=0}^{k+q} b_j \gamma_{k-j} \right) \exp(-ik\omega) + \sum_{k=q}^{\infty} \left(\sum_{j=k-q}^{k+q} b_j \gamma_{k-j} \right) \exp(-ik\omega)$$

$$= \sum_{k=-r}^{q-1} \left(\sum_{j=0}^{k+q} b_j \gamma_{k-j} \right) \exp(-ik\omega) + \sum_{k=q}^{\infty} \left(\sum_{j=-\infty}^{\infty} b_j \gamma_{k-j} \right) \exp(-ik\omega)$$

The first term corresponds to a MA-filter and the second one to an ARMA-filter (since it is the convolution of ARMA and MA filters). Their sum is again an ARMA-filter, see for example Hamilton [45], chap.4. Since the denominator polynomial in (5.67) is an ARMA filter too, the quotient $\tilde{\Gamma}(\cdot)$ is again an ARMA-filter.

• Theorem 5.10 can easily be generalized to integrated processes provided the conditions (5.22) are satisfied (together with regularity assumptions for $\Gamma(\cdot)$). The key result is given in theorem 5.5 which transforms the non-stationary into the stationary case. The process X_t must then be replaced by the differenced stationary process $\tilde{X}_t$ and the optimization procedure (5.19) must be replaced by (5.36).

An expression for the distribution of the filter parameter estimates for a particular 'least-squares' approach is obtained in section C.1 in the appendix. Although the approach is based on unrealistic assumptions it is nevertheless interesting from a theoretical point of view because it provides further insights into the signal estimation problem.

5.6.2 Spurious Decrease of the Optimization Criterion

The following corollary of theorem 5.10 is needed for computing estimates of the filter orders Q and q in section 6.2. It provides an expression of the decrease of

$$E \left[\frac{2\pi}{N} \sum_{k=-[N/2]}^{[N/2]} |\Gamma(\omega_k) - \hat{\Gamma}(\omega_k)|^2 I_{NX}(\omega_k) \right] \tag{5.68}$$

(where $\hat{\Gamma}(\omega_k)$ is the DFA estimate) as overparameterization arises i.e. $Q > Q'$ and $q > q'$ where Q' and q' are the filter orders of the best unknown asymmetric filter $\tilde{\Gamma}(\cdot)$ (which is supposed to exist in section 6.2). Ideally, (5.68) should remain constant for $Q > Q'$ and $q > q'$ (which would indicate the true filter orders Q and q) but overfitting leads to a 'spurious' decrease.

Corollary 5.12. *Let the assumptions of theorem 5.10 be satisfied. Then*

$$2\pi E\left[\sum_{k=-[N/2]}^{[N/2]} |\Gamma(\omega_k) - \tilde{\Gamma}_{Qq}(\omega_k)|^2 I_{NX}(\omega_k)\right.$$

$$\left. - \sum_{k=-[N/2]}^{[N/2]} |\Gamma(\omega_k) - \hat{\Gamma}_{Qq}(\omega_k)|^2 I_{NX}(\omega_k)\right]$$

$$= \frac{1}{2}\mathrm{tr}\left(\mathbf{V}_{Qq}\mathbf{U}_{Qq}^{-1}\right) + o(1) \tag{5.69}$$

where tr$(\cdot)$ *is the trace operator (i.e. the sum of the diagonal elements of a quadratic matrix) and* $\mathbf{U}_{Qq}$ *and* $\mathbf{V}_{Qq}$ *are defined in theorem 5.10.*

Remark

- If overparameterization is attained (i.e. if $Q \geq Q'$ and $q \geq q'$) then

$$\sum_{k=-[N/2]}^{[N/2]} |\Gamma(\omega_k) - \tilde{\Gamma}_{Qq}(\omega_k)|^2 I_{NX}(\omega_k)$$

does no more depend on Q nor on q. Therefore, the right hand side of (5.69) reflects the 'spurious' decrease of (5.68) as $Q(\geq Q')$ or $q(\geq q')$ vary.

Proof of corollary 5.12. As in the proof of theorem 5.10 the subscript Qq of filters and matrices is omitted for notational convenience. Consider the Taylor series development centered in $\hat{\mathbf{b}}$

$$2\pi \sum_{k=-[N/2]}^{[N/2]} |\Gamma(\omega_k) - \tilde{\Gamma}(\omega_k)|^2 I_{NX}(\omega_k)$$

$$= 2\pi \sum_{k=-[N/2]}^{[N/2]} |\Gamma(\omega_k) - \hat{\Gamma}(\omega_k)|^2 I_{NX}(\omega_k)$$

$$+ N\frac{1}{2}\left(\hat{\mathbf{b}} - \tilde{\mathbf{b}}\right)' \mathbf{U} \left(\hat{\mathbf{b}} - \tilde{\mathbf{b}}\right) + o(1)N\left(\hat{\mathbf{b}} - \tilde{\mathbf{b}}\right)'\left(\hat{\mathbf{b}} - \tilde{\mathbf{b}}\right)$$

where the first order derivative vanishes by definition of $\hat{\Gamma}(\cdot)$ and $\hat{\mathbf{U}} = \mathbf{U} + O(1/\sqrt{N})$ has been used. Since

$$N \times Var\left(\hat{\mathbf{b}} - \tilde{\mathbf{b}}\right) = \mathbf{U}^{-1}\mathbf{V}\mathbf{U}^{-1}$$

asymptotically (see (5.54)) it follows that

$$2\pi E\left[\sum_{k=-[N/2]}^{[N/2]} |\Gamma(\omega_k) - \tilde{\Gamma}(\omega_k)|^2 I_{NX}(\omega_k)\right.$$

$$- \sum_{k=-[N/2]}^{[N/2]} |\Gamma(\omega_k) - \hat{\Gamma}(\omega_k)|^2 I_{NX}(\omega_k) \Bigg]$$

$$= \frac{N}{2} E \left[\operatorname{tr} \left(\left(\hat{\mathbf{b}} - \tilde{\mathbf{b}} \right)' \mathbf{U} \left(\hat{\mathbf{b}} - \tilde{\mathbf{b}} \right) \right) \right] + o(1)$$

$$= \frac{N}{2} \operatorname{tr} \left(\mathbf{U} E \left[\left(\hat{\mathbf{b}} - \tilde{\mathbf{b}} \right) \left(\hat{\mathbf{b}} - \tilde{\mathbf{b}} \right)' \right] \right) + o(1)$$

$$= \frac{1}{2} \operatorname{tr} \left(\mathbf{U} \mathbf{U}^{-1} \mathbf{V} \mathbf{U}^{-1} \right) + o(1)$$

$$= \frac{1}{2} \operatorname{tr} \left(\mathbf{V} \mathbf{U}^{-1} \right) + o(1)$$

as claimed. □

5.6.3 Testing for Parameter Constraints

Assume $\Gamma(\cdot)$ and X_t satisfy the assumptions of theorem 5.10. Assume also that the parameter constraints can be set up in the form $\mathbf{R}\tilde{\mathbf{b}} = \mathbf{r}$ where $\tilde{\mathbf{b}} := (a_1, ..., a_Q, b_{-r}, ..., b_q)'$ is the true parameter vector and where $\mathbf{R}$ and $\mathbf{r}$ are a $m * (Q + q + r + 1)$-matrix (with rank m) and a m-dimensional vector respectively. The so called *Wald-form* (see for example Hamilton [45], p.213) of the test of $H_0 : \mathbf{R}\tilde{\mathbf{b}} = \mathbf{r}$ against $H_1 : \mathbf{R}\tilde{\mathbf{b}} \neq \mathbf{r}$ is given by the test-statistic

$$N(\mathbf{R}\hat{\mathbf{b}} - \mathbf{r})' \left(\mathbf{R}\hat{\mathbf{U}}^{-1}\hat{\mathbf{V}}\hat{\mathbf{U}}^{-1}\mathbf{R}' \right)^{-1} (\mathbf{R}\hat{\mathbf{b}} - \mathbf{r}) \qquad (5.70)$$

where $\hat{\mathbf{U}}$ and $\hat{\mathbf{V}}$ are defined in theorem 5.10 and $\hat{\mathbf{b}}$ is the DFA-parameter estimate. The test-statistic (5.70) is asymptotically χ^2-distributed with m degrees of freedom, where m is the number of (linear independent) restrictions. Simple hypotheses like $H_0 : a_Q = 0$ or $b_q = 0$ (i.e. verification of AR- and MA-orders Q and $q + r + 1$ of the ARMA-filter) or more complex linear constraints can be tested, using the above Wald-form of the hypothesis-test.

5.7 Inference : Unit-Roots

If X_t is stationary or if the conditions (5.22) are satisfied, then theorem 5.10 can be used in order to derive the asymptotic distribution of the test-statistic. Often, however, it is not known a priori if an input process is stationary or, more generally, if the constraints (5.22) are satisfied. Therefore, a test is needed from which conclusions about the necessity of imposing restrictions of the type (5.22) can be inferred. Unfortunately, theorem 5.10 cannot be used in this particular situation. The problem as well as the relevant theory for solving it are presented here.

Two parameter sets are distinguished for non-stationary integrated input processes:

- the set of the parameters which are 'freely' estimated and
- the set of the parameters which are determined conditionally to the estimated parameters through the restrictions (5.22).

Note that the two classes of parameters are generally not uniquely defined. For an I(1)-process with a single unit-root at frequency zero, it is assumed in the following that the normalizing constant C is determined by the condition $\hat{\Gamma}(0) = \Gamma(0)$, i.e. the parameter C belongs to the second set. For the parameters in the second set, 'tests' cannot be implemented because the parameters are not estimated actually. An estimation procedure for these parameters is presented here and the asymptotic distribution of the estimates is derived. The distribution is non-standard and asymmetric. It is shown that a suitably transformed test statistic has an asymptotic Dickey-Fuller distribution, where the transformation depends on the current signal estimation problem (i.e. on $\tilde{h}(\cdot)$ and $\Gamma(\cdot)$). As a result, it becomes possible to test hypotheses of the type (5.22).

5.7.1 I(1)-Process

Suppose that X_t is I(1) with a single unit-root located at frequency zero and assume the parameters are estimated using the procedure described in corollary 5.6, i.e. the filter parameters are estimated using the corresponding constraint (5.22)

$$C := \Gamma(0)/\hat{\Gamma}(0) \qquad (5.71)$$

(see (5.29)) and the periodogram is based on the *differenced* input process $\tilde{X}_t = X_t - X_{t-1}$. Therefore, the DFA is consistent as shown in corollary 5.6. Let now all the estimated parameters be fixed except C and assume the latter parameter is estimated using (5.10): the resulting estimate $\hat{C}$ is then based on the periodogram of the *undifferenced* input signal X_t. The resulting two-stage estimation procedure may be motivated informally as follows: in the first stage, the 'nuisance' parameters z_j and p_k are consistently estimated implying that the estimation procedure of $\hat{C}$ in the second stage may be based (at least asymptotically) on knowledge of the true (nuisance) filter parameters. If all parameters (including $\hat{C}$) were estimated simultaneously, then the estimates of the nuisance parameters would be inconsistent because $I_{NX}(\omega_k)$ is a biased estimate of the pseudo spectral density, recall section 4.3. Therefore, the estimation of $\hat{C}$ would be 'biased' too which is undesirable.

The asymptotic distribution of the proposed two-stage estimate $\hat{C}$ is derived in the following theorem. For simplicity of exposition, it is assumed that $\Gamma(0) = 1$

(trend-extraction or seasonal-adjustment filters for example satisfy this assumption).

Theorem 5.13. *Assume*

- X_t *is integrated,* $\tilde{X}_t := X_t - X_{t-1} \in C_f^{1/2}$ *and* $\Gamma(0) = 1$
- $\Gamma(\cdot) \in C_f^{\delta+5/2}$, *where* $\delta > 0$
- *the sequence of estimated* $ARMA(Q, q+r)$ *filters* $\hat{\Gamma}(\cdot)$ *in the first stage of the estimation procedure (satisfying hence the first order restriction) define a uniformly stable filter sequence (as N increases)*
- *the best (unknown) asymmetric filter* $\tilde{\Gamma}(\cdot)$ *in the class of* $ARMA(Q, q+r)$-*filters is stable*
- *the normalizing constant* $\hat{C}$ *is estimated in the second stage, conditionally on the 'nuisance' parameters* z_j, p_k *(estimated in the first stage) and using the estimation procedure (5.10).*

Then asymptotically

$$N\left(\frac{\hat{C}}{C} - 1\right) \tag{5.72}$$

$$\sim \frac{A + \nu_0^2 B}{\frac{2\pi}{3}\xi_0^2 + \frac{1}{\pi}\sum_{k>0}(\nu_k^2 + \nu_k'^2)\frac{1}{k^2} - 2\frac{\nu_0}{\pi}\sum_{k>0}\nu_k\frac{1}{k^2} + \frac{\nu_0^2}{\pi}(\pi^2/6 - 1)}$$

where $\sim$ *means 'distributed as' and where*

- *the random variable in the denominator on the right hand-side of (5.72) is positive*
- *C satisfies the restriction (5.22) (i.e. (5.71))*
- *A and B are the constants:*

$$A = \int_{-\pi}^{\pi} \frac{\Gamma(\omega)\,Re\left(\tilde{\Gamma}(\omega)\right) - \left|\tilde{\Gamma}(\omega)\right|^2}{|1 - \exp(-i\omega)|^2}\frac{\tilde{h}(\omega)}{\tilde{h}(0)}d\omega$$

$$B = \int_{-\pi}^{\pi} \frac{\Gamma(\omega)\,Re\left(\tilde{\Gamma}(\omega)\right) - \left|\tilde{\Gamma}(\omega)\right|^2}{|1 - \exp(-i\omega)|^2}d\omega$$

- *the random variables* ν_k, $k = 0, 1, ...$ *are pairwise independent standard normal variables*
- *the random variable* ξ_0 *is a standard normal random variable which is not correlated with* $\nu_k, k \geq 1$ *but which is correlated with* ν_0 *and* ν_k' *according to*

$$Cov\,[\xi_0, \nu_0] = \frac{1}{2}$$

$$Cov\,[\xi_0, \nu_k'] = -\frac{1}{k2\pi}\,,\ k \geq 1$$

The constants A and B can be consistently estimated by

$$\hat{A} = \frac{2\pi}{N} \sum_{k=-[N/2]}^{[N/2]} \left[\frac{\Gamma(\omega_k) Re\left(\hat{\Gamma}(\omega_k)\right) - \left|\hat{\Gamma}(\omega_k)\right|^2}{|1 - \exp(-i\omega_k)|^2} \right] \frac{I_{N\tilde{X}}(\omega_k)}{\hat{I}_{N\tilde{X}}(0)} \quad (5.73)$$

$$\hat{B} = \frac{2\pi}{N} \sum_{k=-[N/2]}^{[N/2]} \left[\frac{\Gamma(\omega_k) Re\left(\hat{\Gamma}(\omega_k)\right) - \left|\hat{\Gamma}(\omega_k)\right|^2}{|1 - \exp(-i\omega_k)|^2} \right]$$

where $\hat{I}_{N\tilde{X}}(0)$ is a consistent estimate of $\tilde{h}(0)$ (for example a smoothed window-estimate).

Remarks

- If X_t is integrated, then the best (unknown) ARMA$(Q, q+r)$-filter $\tilde{\Gamma}(\cdot)$ satisfies (5.22), i.e. $\tilde{\Gamma}(0) = 1$.
- The assumption $\Gamma(0) = 1$ is not necessary, but simplifies exposition of results.
- The distributional identity (5.72) implies that $\hat{C}$ is a superconsistent estimate. Moreover, its asymptotic distribution is skewed because of the presence of χ^2-random variables in the expression on the right hand-side.
- The distribution of the random variable on the right hand-side of (5.72) is non-standard. It can be tabulated, using the described stochastic properties of the random variables ξ_0, ν_k $(k \geq 0)$ and ν'_j $(j \geq 1)$. A transformation of (5.72) which has the Dickey-Fuller distribution is presented in corollary 5.14 below.

Proof of theorem 5.13. Denote $\hat{\Gamma}'(\cdot) := \hat{\Gamma}(\cdot)/C$ where $\hat{\Gamma}(\cdot)$ is the filter estimate computed in the first stage (i.e. $\hat{\Gamma}(\cdot)$ satisfies the first order condition $\hat{\Gamma}(0) (= \Gamma(0)(= 1))$) and C is the corresponding normalizing constant. As a result, $\hat{\Gamma}'(\cdot)$ is independent of the normalizing constant. Assume also that $\hat{C}$ is estimated in the second stage using the periodogram of X_t (instead of $\tilde{X}_t$ as in the first stage). The periodogram of X_t can also be expressed as

$$I_{NX}(\omega_k) = \begin{cases} \dfrac{|\Xi_{N\tilde{X}}(\omega_k) - \Xi_{N\tilde{X}}(0)|^2}{|1 - \exp(-i\omega_k)|^2} & \omega_k \neq 0 \\[2ex] \dfrac{1}{2\pi N} \left(\sum_{t=1}^{N} X_t\right)^2 & \omega_0 (= 0) \end{cases}$$

see (4.9) and (4.32). Then estimation of $\hat{C}$ is based on

$$\frac{\partial}{\partial C} \frac{2\pi}{N} \sum_{k=-[N/2]}^{[N/2]} |\Gamma(\omega_k) - C\hat{\Gamma}'(\omega_k)|^2 I_{NX}(\omega_k)$$

$$= \frac{\partial}{\partial C} \frac{2\pi}{N} \sum_{k=-[N/2]}^{[N/2]} \frac{|\Gamma(\omega_k) - C\hat{\Gamma}'(\omega_k)|^2}{|1 - \exp(-i\omega_k)|^2} |\Xi_{N\tilde{X}}(\omega_k) - \Xi_{N\tilde{X}}(0)|^2$$

$$= \frac{2\pi}{N} \sum_{k=-[N/2]}^{[N/2]} \left\{ \frac{2\mathrm{Re}\left(\Gamma(\omega_k) - C\hat{\Gamma}'(\omega_k)\right)\mathrm{Re}\left(-\hat{\Gamma}'(\omega_k)\right)}{|1 - \exp(-i\omega_k)|^2} \right.$$

$$\left. + \frac{2\mathrm{Im}\left(\Gamma(\omega_k) - C\hat{\Gamma}'(\omega_k)\right)\mathrm{Im}\left(-\hat{\Gamma}'(\omega_k)\right)}{|1 - \exp(-i\omega_k)|^2} \right\} \times |\Xi_{N\tilde{X}}(\omega_k) - \Xi_{N\tilde{X}}(0)|^2$$

$$= 0$$

where, for $\omega_0 = 0$, the singularity is replaced by its limiting value, see the corresponding expression for $I_{NX}(\omega_0)$ above. Solving for $\hat{C}$ leads to:

$$\hat{C} = \frac{\dfrac{2\pi}{N} \displaystyle\sum_{k=-[N/2]}^{[N/2]} \dfrac{\Gamma(\omega_k)\mathrm{Re}\left(\hat{\Gamma}'(\omega_k)\right)}{|1 - \exp(-i\omega_k)|^2} |\Xi_{N\tilde{X}}(\omega_k) - \Xi_{N\tilde{X}}(0)|^2}{\dfrac{2\pi}{N} \displaystyle\sum_{k=-[N/2]}^{[N/2]} \dfrac{\left|\hat{\Gamma}'(\omega_k)\right|^2}{|1 - \exp(-i\omega_k)|^2} |\Xi_{N\tilde{X}}(\omega_k) - \Xi_{N\tilde{X}}(0)|^2} \qquad (5.74)$$

where $\mathrm{Re}\left(\Gamma(\cdot)\right) = \Gamma(\cdot)$ and $\mathrm{Im}\left(\Gamma(\cdot)\right) = 0$ have been used. Consider first the numerator in (5.74):

$$\frac{2\pi}{N} \sum_{k=-[N/2]}^{[N/2]} \frac{\Gamma(\omega_k)\mathrm{Re}\left(\hat{\Gamma}'(\omega_k)\right)}{|1 - \exp(-i\omega_k)|^2} |\Xi_{N\tilde{X}}(\omega_k) - \Xi_{N\tilde{X}}(0)|^2$$

$$= \frac{2\pi}{N} \sum_{k=-[N/2]}^{[N/2]} \frac{\Gamma(0)\hat{\Gamma}'(0) + \left(\Gamma(\omega_k)\mathrm{Re}\left(\hat{\Gamma}'(\omega_k)\right) - \Gamma(0)\hat{\Gamma}'(0)\right)}{|1 - \exp(-i\omega_k)|^2} \qquad (5.75)$$

$$\times |\Xi_{N\tilde{X}}(\omega_k) - \Xi_{N\tilde{X}}(0)|^2$$

$$= \frac{2\pi}{N} \sum_{k=-[N/2]}^{[N/2]} \frac{\hat{\Gamma}'(0) + \left.\dfrac{\partial^2}{\partial\omega^2}\Gamma(\omega)\mathrm{Re}\left(\hat{\Gamma}'(\omega)\right)\right|_{\omega=0} \dfrac{\omega_k^2}{2} + \mathrm{O}(\omega_k^3)}{|1 - \exp(-i\omega_k)|^2} \qquad (5.76)$$

$$\times |\Xi_{N\tilde{X}}(\omega_k) - \Xi_{N\tilde{X}}(0)|^2$$

where $\Gamma(0) = 1$ and $\left.\dfrac{\partial}{\partial\omega}\Gamma(\omega)\mathrm{Re}\left(\hat{\Gamma}'(\omega)\right)\right|_{\omega=0} = 0$ has been used (the derivative vanishes because $\Gamma(\omega)\mathrm{Re}\left(\hat{\Gamma}'(\omega)\right)$ is an even function of ω). The equivalence of (5.75) and (5.76) implies that

$$\frac{\left(\Gamma(\omega)\mathrm{Re}\left(\hat{\Gamma}'(\omega)\right) - \hat{\Gamma}'(0)\right)}{|1 - \exp(-i\omega)|^2} = \mathrm{O}(1) \qquad (5.77)$$

is a well defined bounded function on $[-\pi, \pi]$, i.e. the numerator removes the singularity of $1/|1 - \exp(-i\omega)|^2$ where use is made of the regularity assumptions with respect to $\Gamma(\cdot)$ and $\hat{\Gamma}(\cdot)$ (which are both at least twice continuously differentiable).

The denominator in (5.74) becomes:

$$
\frac{2\pi}{N} \sum_{k=-[N/2]}^{[N/2]} \frac{\left|\hat{\Gamma}'(\omega_k)\right|^2}{|1 - \exp(-i\omega_k)|^2} |\Xi_{N\tilde{X}}(\omega_k) - \Xi_{N\tilde{X}}(0)|^2
$$

$$
= \frac{2\pi}{N} \sum_{k=-[N/2]}^{[N/2]} \frac{\hat{\Gamma}'(0)^2 + \left(\left|\hat{\Gamma}'(\omega_k)\right|^2 - \hat{\Gamma}'(0)^2\right)}{|1 - \exp(-i\omega_k)|^2} |\Xi_{N\tilde{X}}(\omega_k) - \Xi_{N\tilde{X}}(0)|^2
$$

$$
= \frac{2\pi}{N} \sum_{k=-[N/2]}^{[N/2]} \frac{\hat{\Gamma}'(0)^2 + \left.\frac{\partial^2}{\partial\omega^2}|\hat{\Gamma}'(\omega)|^2\right|_{\omega=0} \frac{\omega_k^2}{2} + O(\omega_k^3)}{|1 - \exp(-i\omega_k)|^2} |\Xi_{N\tilde{X}}(\omega_k) - \Xi_{N\tilde{X}}(0)|^2
$$

where use is made of $\hat{\Gamma}'(0) \in \mathbb{R}$ and of the symmetry of $|\hat{\Gamma}'(\omega_k)|^2$ around zero (so that the first derivative vanishes). Therefore

$$
\frac{\left|\hat{\Gamma}'(\omega_k)\right|^2 - \hat{\Gamma}'(0)^2}{|1 - \exp(-i\omega_k)|^2} = O(1) \tag{5.78}
$$

is a well defined bounded function too in $[-\pi, \pi]$ (because of the assumed uniform stability). It follows that the expression for $\hat{C}$ in (5.74) becomes

$$
\hat{C} = \frac{\dfrac{2\pi}{N} \displaystyle\sum_{k=-[N/2]}^{[N/2]} \dfrac{\hat{\Gamma}'(0) + \left(\Gamma(\omega_k)\text{Re}\left(\hat{\Gamma}'(\omega_k)\right) - \hat{\Gamma}'(0)\right)}{|1 - \exp(-i\omega_k)|^2} |\Xi_{N\tilde{X}}(\omega_k) - \Xi_{N\tilde{X}}(0)|^2}{\dfrac{2\pi}{N} \displaystyle\sum_{k=-[N/2]}^{[N/2]} \dfrac{\hat{\Gamma}'(0)^2 + \left(\left|\hat{\Gamma}'(\omega_k)\right|^2 - \hat{\Gamma}'(0)^2\right)}{|1 - \exp(-i\omega_k)|^2} |\Xi_{N\tilde{X}}(\omega_k) - \Xi_{N\tilde{X}}(0)|^2}
$$

$$
= \frac{1}{\hat{\Gamma}'(0)} + \frac{\dfrac{2\pi}{N} \displaystyle\sum_{k=-[N/2]}^{[N/2]} \dfrac{\Gamma(\omega_k)\text{Re}\left(\hat{\Gamma}(\omega_k)\right) - \left|\hat{\Gamma}(\omega_k)\right|^2}{|1 - \exp(-i\omega_k)|^2} |\Xi_{N\tilde{X}}(\omega_k) - \Xi_{N\tilde{X}}(0)|^2}{\hat{\Gamma}'(0)\dfrac{2\pi}{N} \displaystyle\sum_{k=-[N/2]}^{[N/2]} \dfrac{|\Xi_{N\tilde{X}}(\omega_k) - \Xi_{N\tilde{X}}(0)|^2}{|1 - \exp(-i\omega_k)|^2}}
$$

$$
+o(1/N) \tag{5.79}
$$

where $\hat{\Gamma}(\cdot)$ is the filter estimate in the first stage of the estimation procedure, i.e. $\hat{\Gamma}(\cdot)$ satisfies the first order constraint $\hat{\Gamma}(0) = 1(= \Gamma(0))$. In order to establish (5.79), use is made of

- the identity $\dfrac{a+b}{c+d} = \dfrac{a}{c} + \dfrac{bc-ad}{c(c+d)} = \dfrac{a}{c} + \dfrac{bc-ad}{c^2} + o(1/N)$ for the expressions

$$a := \hat{\Gamma}'(0)\frac{2\pi}{N} \sum_{k=-[N/2]}^{[N/2]} \frac{1}{|1-\exp(-i\omega_k)|^2}|\Xi_{N\tilde{X}}(\omega_k) - \Xi_{N\tilde{x}}(0)|^2$$

$$= \hat{\Gamma}'(0)\frac{2\pi}{N} \sum_{k=-[N/2]}^{[N/2]} I_{NX}(\omega_k) = O(N)$$

$$b := \frac{2\pi}{N} \sum_{k=-[N/2]}^{[N/2]} \frac{\left(\Gamma(\omega_k)\mathrm{Re}\left(\hat{\Gamma}'(\omega_k)\right) - \hat{\Gamma}'(0)\right)}{|1-\exp(-i\omega_k)|^2}|\Xi_{N\tilde{X}}(\omega_k) - \Xi_{N\tilde{x}}(0)|^2$$

$$= O(1)$$

$$c := \hat{\Gamma}'(0)^2\frac{2\pi}{N} \sum_{k=-[N/2]}^{[N/2]} \frac{1}{|1-\exp(-i\omega_k)|^2}|\Xi_{N\tilde{X}}(\omega_k) - \Xi_{N\tilde{x}}(0)|^2$$

$$= \hat{\Gamma}'(0)^2\frac{2\pi}{N} \sum_{k=-[N/2]}^{[N/2]} I_{NX}(\omega_k) = O(N)$$

$$d := \frac{2\pi}{N} \sum_{k=-[N/2]}^{[N/2]} \frac{\left(\left|\hat{\Gamma}'(\omega_k)\right|^2 - \hat{\Gamma}'(0)^2\right)}{|1-\exp(-i\omega_k)|^2}|\Xi_{N\tilde{X}}(\omega_k) - \Xi_{N\tilde{x}}(0)|^2 = O(1)$$

(note that the magnitude of the orders follow from (5.77), (5.78) and (5.85) below)

- and of the identity $\dfrac{\hat{\Gamma}'(\omega_k)}{\hat{\Gamma}'(0)} = \hat{\Gamma}(\omega_k)$, i.e. $C = \dfrac{\Gamma(0)}{\hat{\Gamma}'(0)} = \dfrac{1}{\hat{\Gamma}'(0)}$ where C is the 'true' value of the normalizing constant (conditionally on the estimated parameters in the first stage).

Equation (5.79) implies that $\hat{C} - C = O(1/N)$. Moreover, the numerator in (5.79) can be approximated by

$$\frac{2\pi}{N} \sum_{k=-[N/2]}^{[N/2]} \frac{\Gamma(\omega_k)\mathrm{Re}\left(\hat{\Gamma}(\omega_k)\right) - \left|\hat{\Gamma}(\omega_k)\right|^2}{|1-\exp(-i\omega_k)|^2} \times |\Xi_{N\tilde{X}}(\omega_k) - \Xi_{N\tilde{x}}(0)|^2$$

$$= \frac{2\pi}{N} \sum_{k=-[N/2]}^{[N/2]} \frac{\Gamma(\omega_k)\mathrm{Re}\left(\tilde{\Gamma}(\omega_k)\right) - \left|\tilde{\Gamma}(\omega_k)\right|^2}{|1-\exp(-i\omega_k)|^2}$$

$$\times \left(I_{N\tilde{X}}(\omega_k) - 2\Xi_{N\tilde{x}}(0)\mathrm{Re}\left(\Xi_{N\tilde{x}}(\omega_k)\right) + I_{N\tilde{x}}(0)\right) + o(1) \qquad (5.80)$$

$$= \frac{2\pi}{N} \sum_{k=-[N/2]}^{[N/2]} \frac{\Gamma(\omega_k)\mathrm{Re}\left(\tilde{\Gamma}(\omega_k)\right) - \left|\tilde{\Gamma}(\omega_k)\right|^2}{|1 - \exp(-i\omega_k)|^2}\left(\tilde{h}(\omega_k) + I_{N\tilde{X}}(0)\right) + o(1)$$

$$= \int_{-\pi}^{\pi} \frac{\Gamma(\omega)\mathrm{Re}\left(\tilde{\Gamma}(\omega)\right) - \left|\tilde{\Gamma}(\omega)\right|^2}{|1 - \exp(-i\omega)|^2}\tilde{h}(\omega)d\omega$$

$$+I_{N\tilde{X}}(0)\int_{-\pi}^{\pi} \frac{\Gamma(\omega)\mathrm{Re}\left(\tilde{\Gamma}(\omega)\right) - \left|\tilde{\Gamma}(\omega)\right|^2}{|1 - \exp(-i\omega)|^2}d\omega + o(1) \tag{5.81}$$

where use is made of

- the consistency of $\hat{\Gamma}(\cdot)$ which allows replacing $\hat{\Gamma}(\cdot)$ by $\tilde{\Gamma}(\cdot)$ in (5.80)
- theorem B.4 in the appendix which states that the 'midterm'

$$-2\Xi_{N\tilde{X}}(0)\frac{2\pi}{N}\sum_{k=-[N/2]}^{[N/2]} \frac{\Gamma(\omega_k)\mathrm{Re}\left(\hat{\Gamma}(\omega_k)\right) - \Gamma(0)\left|\hat{\Gamma}(\omega_k)\right|^2}{|1 - \exp(-i\omega_k)|^2}\mathrm{Re}\left(\Xi_{N\tilde{X}}(\omega_k)\right)$$

  in (5.80) vanishes asymptotically since the random variables $\Xi_{N\tilde{X}}(\omega_k)$ (and therefore $\mathrm{Re}\left(\Xi_{N\tilde{X}}(\omega_k)\right)$) are 'centered' and asymptotically independent
- corollary B.3 (which allows replacing $I_{N\tilde{X}}(\cdot)$ by $\tilde{h}(\cdot)$ on the right of the second equality), noting that $\tilde{X}_t \in C_f^{1/2}$ implies $\tilde{h}(\cdot) \in C_f^{1/2}$
- proposition 5.11 (for the transition from the discrete sums to integrals), using the assumed regularity requirements for $\Gamma(\cdot)$ and $\hat{\Gamma}(\cdot)$: specifically

$$\Gamma(\omega)\mathrm{Re}\left(\hat{\Gamma}(\omega)\right) - \left|\hat{\Gamma}(\omega)\right|^2 = O(\omega_k^2)$$

because the function vanishes in 0 and its derivative vanishes too since it is an even function. It is then easily verified that the regularity requirements of theorem 5.5 are satisfied for the function

$$\Gamma(\omega)\mathrm{Re}\left(\hat{\Gamma}(\omega)\right) - \left|\hat{\Gamma}(\omega)\right|^2 \tag{5.82}$$

(in place of $\Delta\Gamma(\cdot)$), assuming $\alpha = 1/2$ and $d = 2$ (recall that $\Gamma(\cdot) \in C_f^{\delta+2+1/2}$ and $\hat{\Gamma}(\cdot)$ is uniformly stable by assumption). Therefore the same proof as that used in theorem 5.5 can be used to show that the function in (5.82) is in $C_f^{1/2}$. Noting that $\tilde{h}(\cdot) \in C_f^{1/2}$ (since $X_t \in C_f^{1/2}$ by assumption), it then follows that the integrated functions in (5.81) are in $C_f^{1/2}$. Thus, proposition 5.11 can be used.

The denominator in (5.79) can be approximated by

$$\hat{\Gamma}'(0)\frac{2\pi}{N}\sum_{k=-[N/2]}^{[N/2]}\frac{|\Xi_{N\tilde{X}}(\omega_k)-\Xi_{N\tilde{X}}(0)|^2}{|1-\exp(-i\omega_k)|^2} \tag{5.83}$$

$$=\hat{\Gamma}'(0)\frac{2\pi}{N}\left(I_{NX}(0)+2\sum_{k=1}^{[N/2]}\frac{|\Xi_{N\tilde{X}}(\omega_k)-\Xi_{N\tilde{X}}(0)|^2}{|1-\exp(-i\omega_k)|^2}\right)$$

$$=\hat{\Gamma}'(0)\frac{2\pi}{N}\left(I_{NX}(0)+2\sum_{k=1}^{\sqrt{N}}\frac{|\Xi_{N\tilde{X}}(\omega_k)-\Xi_{N\tilde{X}}(0)|^2}{\omega_k^2}\right)+\mathrm{o}(N)$$

$$=\hat{\Gamma}'(0)\frac{2\pi}{N}\left(I_{NX}(0)+2\sum_{k=1}^{\sqrt{N}}\frac{I_{N\tilde{X}}(\omega_k)}{k^2\pi^2/[N/2]^2}-2\sum_{k=1}^{\sqrt{N}}\frac{2\Xi_{N\tilde{X}}(0)\mathrm{Re}\,(\Xi_{N\tilde{X}}(\omega_k))}{k^2\pi^2/[N/2]^2}\right.$$

$$\left.+2\sum_{k=1}^{\sqrt{N}}\frac{I_{N\tilde{X}}(0)}{k^2\pi^2/[N/2]^2}\right)+\mathrm{o}(N) \tag{5.84}$$

$$=\hat{\Gamma}'(0)2\pi N\zeta_0$$

$$+\tilde{h}(0)\hat{\Gamma}'(0)\frac{N}{\pi}\left(\sum_{k=1}^{\sqrt{N}}(\nu_k^2+\nu_k'^2)\frac{1}{k^2}-2\nu_0\sum_{k=1}^{\sqrt{N}}\nu_k\frac{1}{k^2}+\nu_0^2(\pi^2/6-1)\right)+\mathrm{o}(N)$$

$$\approx N\frac{1}{C}\tilde{h}(0)$$

$$\times\left(\frac{2\pi}{3}\xi_0^2+\frac{1}{\pi}\sum_{k>0}(\nu_k^2+\nu_k'^2)\frac{1}{k^2}-2\frac{\nu_0}{\pi}\sum_{k>0}\nu_k\frac{1}{k^2}+\frac{\nu_0^2}{\pi}(\pi^2/6-1)\right) \tag{5.85}$$

where

- $C=1/\hat{\Gamma}'(0)$ satisfies the first order constraint (5.22)
- $\pi^2/6-1=\sum_{k>0}1/k^2$,
- ν_k and ν_k' are iid standard normal distributed random variables corresponding to the real and imaginary parts of the (normalized) discrete Fourier transforms

$$\Xi_{N\tilde{X}}(\omega_k)/\sqrt{\tilde{h}(0)}\ ,\ k=0,...,\sqrt{N}$$

(see the first assertion of theorem B.4 in the appendix). Note that $\tilde{X}_t\in C_f^0$ implies that $\tilde{h}(\omega)$ is a continuous function so that $\tilde{h}(\omega_k)\approx\tilde{h}(0)$, $k=0,...,\sqrt{N}$. Therefore

$$I_{N\tilde{X}}(\omega_k)\approx\tilde{h}(0)(\nu_k^2+\nu_k'^2)$$

- $N^2\zeta_0=I_{NX}(0)$, see (4.33). In particular $E[\zeta_0]=\tilde{h}(0)/3$, see (B.35),
- $\sqrt{\tilde{h}(0)}\dfrac{\xi_0}{\sqrt{3}}$ is the square root of ζ_0. In particular, ξ_0 is standard normal distributed asymptotically. The covariances of $\eta_0:=\sqrt{\tilde{h}(0)}\dfrac{\xi_0}{\sqrt{3}}$ with ν_0

and ν_k, ν'_k are described in corollary B.11 in the appendix where it is shown that η_0 is asymptotically correlated with the imaginary part of $\Xi_{N\tilde{X}}(\omega_k)$ only (corresponding to the random variable ν'_k), see the remark on p.254.

- the summations in (5.85) may be extended from $k = 1$ to infinity because the sequence $1/k^2$ is absolutely convergent,
- the o(N)-term has been neglected in (5.85).

Note that $\dfrac{2\pi}{N} \displaystyle\sum_{k=-[N/2]}^{[N/2]} \dfrac{|\Xi_{N\tilde{X}}(\omega_k) - \Xi_{N\tilde{X}}(0)|^2}{|1 - \exp(-i\omega_k)|^2}$ in (5.83) is a positive random

variable so that the random variable in (5.85) and therefore the denominator in (5.72) must be positive too, as claimed. Collecting the results obtained for the numerator and the denominator in (5.79) completes the proof of the theorem (it is not difficult to extend the proof to the case $\Gamma(0) \neq 1$). □

Consider the numerator in (5.72): $A + \nu_0^2 B$. If X_t is a pure random-walk so that $\tilde{X}_t = \epsilon_t$ is a white noise sequence, then $A = B$ and the numerator simplifies to $A(1+\nu_0^2)$. If X_t is not a random-walk, then $A \neq B$ and the random variable on the right of (5.79) depends on the signal estimation problem (i.e. on the ratio A/B). This is undesirable since tabulation of percentiles of the random variable then depends on a 'nuisance' parameter A/B which can take on any real value. A completely analogous situation arises for 'traditional' unit-root tests when allowing for serial dependence of $\tilde{X}_t$, see for example formula 17.6.6 in Hamilton [45] where a 'nuisance' parameter $(\lambda^2 - \gamma_0)/\lambda_2$ enters in the determination of the resulting random variable for the approach taken by Phillips and Perron. By analogy to the Phillips-Perron unit-root test, a term correcting for 'departures of the pure random-walk hypothesis' i.e. correcting for serial dependence of $\tilde{X}_t$ can be subtracted on both sides of (5.72):

$$ N\left(\frac{\hat{C}}{C} - 1\right) - \frac{A}{Z} \sim \frac{\nu_0^2 B}{Z} $$

where Z is the random variable in the denominator of (5.72). Dividing on both sides by B and replacing A and B by their estimates then leads to the 'corrected' test statistic

$$ \frac{N}{\hat{B}}\left(\frac{\hat{C}}{C} - 1 - \frac{\hat{D}}{\dfrac{2\pi}{N} \displaystyle\sum_{k=-[N/2]}^{[N/2]} I_{NX}(\omega_k)} \right) = \eta \qquad (5.86) $$

where

- the estimate $\hat{D}$ is defined by

$$\hat{D} := \hat{A}\hat{I}_{N\tilde{X}}(0)$$

$$= \frac{2\pi}{N} \sum_{k=-[N/2]}^{[N/2]} \frac{\Gamma(\omega_k)\mathrm{Re}\left(\hat{\Gamma}(\omega_k)\right) - \left|\hat{\Gamma}(\omega_k)\right|^2}{|1 - \exp(-i\omega_k)|^2} I_{N\tilde{X}}(\omega_k) \quad (5.87)$$

Note that $Z\tilde{h}(0) \approx \frac{2\pi}{N}\sum_{k=-[N/2]}^{[N/2]} I_{NX}(\omega_k)$ by the proof of theorem 5.13.
Multiplying numerator and denominator in A/Z by $\tilde{h}(0)$ then implies, that
$\hat{D}$ is independent of $\tilde{h}(0)$ (or of the estimate $\hat{I}_{N\tilde{X}}(0)$).

- $\hat{A}$ and $\hat{B}$ are defined in theorem 5.13
- $\hat{I}_{N\tilde{X}}(0)$ is the consistent estimate of $\tilde{h}(0)$ used in determining $\hat{A}$, see (5.73): this estimate disappears in (5.87) and therefore it disappears in the test-statistic (5.86) too
- $\hat{\Gamma}(\cdot)$ is the filter estimate obtained in the first stage of the estimation procedure (therefore $\hat{\Gamma}(0) = \Gamma(0)$)
- the random variable η is asymptotically distributed as

$$\eta \sim \frac{\nu_0^2}{\frac{2\pi}{3}\xi_0^2 + \frac{1}{\pi}\sum_{k>0}(\nu_k^2 + \nu_k'^2)\frac{1}{k^2} - 2\frac{\nu_0}{\pi}\sum_{k>0}\nu_k\frac{1}{k^2} + \frac{\nu_0^2}{\pi}(\pi^2/6 - 1)} \quad (5.88)$$

which does no more depend on 'nuisance' parameters.

Note that η corresponds to the restterm on the right hand-side of (5.79)
(after correction for serial dependence of $\tilde{X}_t$ in (5.86)). After normalization
with $N/\hat{B}$ this restterm becomes:

$$\frac{N}{\hat{B}}\left(\frac{\hat{B}I_{N\tilde{X}}(0)}{\frac{2\pi}{N}\sum_{k=-[N/2]}^{[N/2]} I_{NX}(\omega_k)} + o(1/N)\right)$$

$$= \frac{NI_{N\tilde{X}}(0)}{\frac{2\pi}{N}\sum_{k=-[N/2]}^{[N/2]} I_{NX}(\omega_k)} + o(1) \quad (5.89)$$

$$\approx \frac{NI_{N\tilde{X}}(0)}{\frac{2\pi}{N}\sum_{k=-[N/2]}^{[N/2]} I_{NX}(\omega_k)} \quad (5.90)$$

if X_t is integrated. It is tempting to replace the expression (5.86) for the test
statistic η by the simpler expression (5.90) which does involve neither $\Gamma(\cdot)$
nor $\hat{\Gamma}(\cdot)$ and which is therefore independent of the signal estimation problem.

However, one should keep in mind that the error $(o(1))$-term in (5.89) was shown to be negligible under the assumption that X_t is integrated, see (5.79). If X_t is stationary, then it is not difficult to show that this error term is of order $O(1)$ so that (5.86) and (5.90) differ ((5.90) has low power against stationary alternatives because it is of order $O(\sqrt{N})$ if $X_t \in C_f^0$ so it is clearly not interesting as a test-statistic candidate).

Tabulation of percentiles of η for given significance levels provides corresponding critical regions for the test statistic (5.86). In this context it may be interesting to compare the distribution of η to the Dickey-Fuller distribution of the random variable $N(\hat{\rho} - 1)$ where $\hat{\rho}$ is the estimated AR-coefficient for a pure random-walk process, see Hamilton [45], p.488. This is done in the following corollary.

Corollary 5.14. *Let the assumptions of the preceding theorem 5.13 be satisfied. Then the random variable*

$$\eta' := \pi\eta - \frac{N\pi\tilde{h}(0)}{\frac{2\pi}{N}\sum_{k=-[N/2]}^{[N/2]} I_{NX}(\omega_k)} \tag{5.91}$$

where η is the test statistic (5.86), has the Dickey-Fuller distribution tabulated in Table B.5 (case 1) in Hamilton [45], p.762.

Proof. Under the assumption of the preceding theorem X_t is integrated, so that (5.90) is a valid approximation (recall the above comment). Inserting (5.90) into (5.91) (and ignoring the approximation error in (5.90)) leads to

$$
\begin{aligned}
\eta' &= N\pi \frac{I_{N\tilde{X}}(0) - \tilde{h}(0)}{\frac{2\pi}{N}\sum_{k=-[N/2]}^{[N/2]} I_{NX}(\omega_k)} \\
&= \frac{1/2\left(\frac{1}{N}\left(\sum_{t=1}^{N}\tilde{X}_t\right)^2 - 2\pi\tilde{h}(0)\right)}{\frac{1}{N^2}\sum_{t=1}^{N}X_t^2} \\
&\sim \frac{2\pi\tilde{h}(0)1/2\left(W(1)^2 - 1\right)}{2\pi\tilde{h}(0)\int_0^1 W(r)^2 dr} \\
&= \frac{1/2\left(W(1)^2 - 1\right)}{\int_0^1 W(r)^2 dr} \tag{5.92}
\end{aligned}
$$

where $\sim$ means 'asymptotically distributed as' and where $W(r)$ is the standard Brownian motion process (a continuous parameter process), see Hamilton [45], proposition 17.3, identities a) and h), p.506 (noting that the parameter λ in the cited literature is simply $\sqrt{2\pi\tilde{h}(0)}$). The third equality in the above proof follows from the definition of the periodogram and from (4.13) : note that the 'weights' w_k in (4.13) are ignored since their contribution is of order $O(1/N)$ if N is even (for N odd $w_k = 1$ for all k, see (4.2)). This completes the proof of the corollary since the random variable in (5.92) has the asserted Dickey-Fuller distribution, see for example 17.4.7 in Hamilton [45].   □

The following remarks conclude the analysis for X_t being an integrated input process with a single unit-root at frequency zero.

Remarks

- Although the constraint $\hat{\Gamma}(0) = \Gamma(0)$ allows for more general non-stationarities than a single unit-root at frequency zero, the asymptotic distribution of the proposed test-statistics were derived under the hypothesis that X_t is I(1), see the first assumption of theorem 5.13. In this context, testing $H_0 : \hat{\Gamma}(0) = \Gamma(0)$ amounts to a particular unit-root test, specifically designed for the signal estimation problem. Other forms of non-stationarity (for example trend-stationarity around a linear trend function) would result in different asymptotic distributions which are not reported here.
- Since ξ_0, ν_0 and ν'_k, $k \geq 1$ in theorem 5.13 are standard normal and since ν_0 and ν'_k, $k \geq 1$ are mutually orthogonal, one deduces from the covariances (correlations) between ξ_0 and ν_0, ν'_k, $k \geq 1$:

$$\xi_0 = \frac{1}{2}\nu_0 - \sum_{k \geq 1}\frac{1}{k2\pi}\nu'_k + \delta_0$$

where δ_0 is gaussian with mean zero and variance

$$Var(\delta_0) = 1 - \frac{1}{4} - \sum_{k \geq 1}\frac{1}{k^2 4\pi^2}$$

$$= \frac{1}{4}\left(3 - \frac{1}{\pi^2}\sum_{k \geq 1}\frac{1}{k^2}\right)$$

$$= \frac{1}{4}\left(3 - \frac{\pi^2/6 - 1}{\pi^2}\right) < 1$$

Therefore, η in (5.88) can be tabulated using standard normal distributions.
- In order to use the statistic (5.86), percentiles of the distribution of η must be tabulated using the stochastic properties of the random variable described in theorem 5.13 (see the preceding remark). Note that the expression (5.86) *does not depend on* $\tilde{h}(0)$. This is an advantage because estimation of the spectral density of a process at frequency zero is a problem which affects the 'long run' behavior of the process and which cannot be satisfactorily solved for finite samples (which is precisely the crux

when testing for unit-roots). On the other hand, the distribution of the test statistic (5.91) is already tabulated (see for example table B.5, case 1 in Hamilton [45]). Unfortunately, the statistic requires a consistent estimate of $\tilde{h}(0)$. It is therefore suggested to use (5.86) instead. Note that the Phillips-Perron test(s) or the augmented Dickey-Fuller test(s) also require knowledge of $\tilde{h}(0)$, see for example Hamilton [45]p.509 and p.523.

- The distribution of the random variable η in (5.86) can be tabulated using the standard normal distribution, see the remark above. A continuous parameter process (standard Brownian motion $W(\cdot)$, see corollary 5.14) is not needed for that purpose. This simplifies the tabulation by Monte Carlo simulation, because realizations of continuous parameter processes are more difficult to generate than the expression (5.88). Although Donsker's functional central limit theorem leading to standard Brownian motion is an elegant mathematical device for computing the asymptotic distribution of unit-root tests, the distribution of the resulting random variable is more difficult to tabulate than the expression (5.88) resulting from theorem 5.13.

- If $\Gamma(\cdot)$ is a trend extraction filter then the expression $\Gamma(\omega_k)\text{Re}\left(\hat{\Gamma}(\omega_k)\right) - \left|\hat{\Gamma}(\omega_k)\right|^2$ in (5.79) becomes negative in the stop band of $\Gamma(\cdot)$. In the passband $|\hat{\Gamma}(\cdot)|$ generally exceeds $\Gamma(\cdot)$ (remember that $\hat{\Gamma}(\cdot)$ is the constrained filter satisfying $\hat{\Gamma}(0) = \Gamma(0)$). Therefore, $\hat{C}$ is downward biased if $\Gamma(\cdot)$ 'smoothes' the input signal. This can easily be seen from (5.72) since both A and B are negative and all other expressions on the right hand-side are positive (note that this statement is not necessarily true if $\Gamma(\cdot)$ does not 'smooth' the input signal).

- The preceding remark implies that the test against the interesting alternative hypothesis $H_1 : \hat{\Gamma}(0) < 1$ (which happens if X_t is stationary and $\Gamma(\cdot)$ is a 'smoothing' filter) is one-sided: large values of η in (5.86) imply a rejection of $H_0 : \hat{\Gamma}(0) = 1$.

- Consider the ratio

$$\left|\frac{A}{B}\right| = \left|\frac{\int_{-\pi}^{\pi} \dfrac{\Gamma(\omega)\text{Re}\left(\tilde{\Gamma}(\omega)\right) - \left|\tilde{\Gamma}(\omega)\right|^2}{|1 - \exp(-i\omega)|^2}\dfrac{\tilde{h}(\omega)}{\tilde{h}(0)}d\omega}{\int_{-\pi}^{\pi} \dfrac{\Gamma(\omega)\text{Re}\left(\tilde{\Gamma}(\omega)\right) - \left|\tilde{\Gamma}(\omega)\right|^2}{|1 - \exp(-i\omega)|^2}d\omega}\right|$$

This expression is 'small' if $\tilde{h}(\omega)/\tilde{h}(0)$ is 'small', i.e. if the low-frequency part of the stationary process $\tilde{X}_t$ is strong or, equivalently, if the autocorrelation function of $\tilde{X}_t$ decays slowly. Otherwise, if the low frequency part is weak, then the above ratio is 'large'. Therefore, the term correcting for serial dependence in (5.86) is 'small' for processes with pronounced low frequency content (in the sense of a slowly decaying autocorrelation function of $\tilde{X}_t$) and 'large' for processes with pronounced high frequency components. Stated otherwise: the (negative) bias of the estimate $\hat{C}$ is 'small' for processes X_t whose first differences $\tilde{X}_t$ have strong low frequency components.

5.7.2 I(2)-Process

Now consider the problem for a test of the second order constraint $\hat{\phi}(0) = 0$ which is for example useful if X_t has a second order unit-root located at frequency zero (but which allows for more general non-stationarities). Assume that all parameters are estimated simultaneously using first and second order constraints in the first stage. In the second stage, all parameters are fixed except C, Z and P where C is the normalizing constant and Z, P are real numbers defined in (5.33) or, equivalently, in (5.34). Denote by

$$\hat{\Gamma}'(\omega) := \frac{P - \exp(-i\omega)}{C(Z - \exp(-i\omega))} \hat{\Gamma}(\omega)$$

that part of the filter $\hat{\Gamma}(\cdot)$ which does not depend on C, Z or P (which cancel on the right hand-side of the above equality). In the second stage of the estimation procedure, $\hat{\Gamma}'(\cdot)$ is fixed, the first order constraint $\hat{\Gamma}(0) = \Gamma(0)$ is maintained and the second order constraint $\hat{\phi}(0) = 0$ is relaxed. Z and P are then allowed to vary independently from each other while C is uniquely determined by the condition

$$C := \frac{\Gamma(0)}{\hat{\Gamma}(0)} = \frac{1}{\frac{Z-1}{P-1}\hat{\Gamma}'(0)}$$

where $\Gamma(0) = 1$ has been assumed. Therefore, in the second stage, one has to minimize

$$\frac{2\pi}{N} \sum_{k=-[N/2]}^{[N/2]} \frac{|\Gamma(\omega_k) - \hat{\Gamma}(\omega_k)|^2}{|1 - \exp(-i\omega_k)|^2} I_{N\tilde{X}}(\omega_k)$$

$$= \frac{2\pi}{N} \sum_{k=-[N/2]}^{[N/2]} \frac{\left|\Gamma(\omega_k) - \dfrac{(Z - \exp(-i\omega_k))}{(Z-1)} \dfrac{P-1}{\hat{\Gamma}'(0)(P - \exp(-i\omega_k))} \hat{\Gamma}'(\omega_k)\right|^2}{|1 - \exp(-i\omega_k)|^2}$$

$$\times I_{N\tilde{X}}(\omega_k) \tag{5.93}$$

with respect to Z (or, alternatively, with respect to P). Note that $\hat{\Gamma}(0) = 1$ (first order restriction) so that the quotient in the above summation is well defined and continuous on $[-\pi, \pi]$ and note also that $\tilde{X}_t$ is I(1) under H_0 so that $I_{N\tilde{X}}(0)$ is of order O(N^2). Differentiating (5.93) with respect to Z and solving for Z is not difficult but leads to an expression which is 'too lengthy' to be reasonably reproduced here. Simplifying notations one can write the resulting solution $\hat{Z}$ in the following form:

$$
\hat{Z} = \frac{iP\hat{\Gamma}'(0) + (P-1)\left.\dfrac{d\hat{\Gamma}'(\omega)}{d\omega}\right|_{\omega=0}}{i\hat{\Gamma}'(0) + (P-1)\left.\dfrac{d\hat{\Gamma}'(\omega)}{d\omega}\right|_{\omega=0}}
$$

$$
+ \frac{\dfrac{2\pi}{N}\displaystyle\sum_{k=-[N/2]}^{[N/2]}\dfrac{f(\omega_k)}{|1-\exp(-i\omega_k)|^2}I_{N\Delta\tilde{X}}(\omega_k)}{g(0)\dfrac{2\pi}{N}\displaystyle\sum_{k=-[N/2]}^{[N/2]}\dfrac{1}{|1-\exp(-i\omega_k)|^2}I_{N\Delta\tilde{X}}(\omega_k)} \tag{5.94}
$$

$$
= \frac{iP\hat{\Gamma}'(0) + (P-1)\left.\dfrac{d\hat{\Gamma}'(\omega)}{d\omega}\right|_{\omega=0}}{i\hat{\Gamma}'(0) + (P-1)\left.\dfrac{d\hat{\Gamma}'(\omega)}{d\omega}\right|_{\omega=0}} + \hat{r}_N
$$

where

- the first term on the right hand-side of (5.94) corresponds to (5.34),
- $I_{N\Delta\tilde{X}}(\omega_k)$ in (5.94) is the periodogram of the stationary process $\Delta\tilde{X}_t := (1-B)^2 X_t$,
- $f(\cdot)$ and $g(\cdot)$ are 'complicated' (lengthy) expressions involving $\Gamma(\cdot)$, $\hat{\Gamma}(\cdot)$ and the spectral density of $\Delta\tilde{X}_t$
- and where the 'residual' term $\hat{r}_N$ can be shown to be of order $O(1/N)$ as in the proof of theorem 5.13 (if X_t is I(2)).

If $\hat{r}_N = 0$ then $\hat{\phi}(0) = 0$, i.e. the second order constraint (5.34) is satisfied. Otherwise,

$$
N\left(\hat{Z} - \frac{iP\hat{\Gamma}'_{CC}(0) + (P-1)\left.\dfrac{d\hat{\Gamma}'_{CC}(\omega)}{d\omega}\right|_{\omega=0}}{i\hat{\Gamma}'_{CC}(0) + (P-1)\left.\dfrac{d\hat{\Gamma}'_{CC}(\omega)}{d\omega}\right|_{\omega=0}}\right)
$$

is a 'non-degenerate' random variable whose distribution may be derived as for the case analyzed in theorem 5.13 (first order restriction), inserting the corresponding expressions for $f(\cdot)$ and $g(\cdot)$. The derivation is not difficult (it follows exactly the same line as the proof of theorem 5.13) but cumbersome and the constants corresponding to A and B in (5.72) are complicated and 'lengthy' expressions which are not reproduced here. However, the resulting test statistic has exactly the same asymptotic distribution. Evidently, the same transformation as proposed in corollary 5.14 can be used here so that the resulting transformed test statistic has the Dickey-Fuller distribution (asymptotically) which is tabulated in table B.5 (case 1) in Hamilton [45].

Remarks:

- Testing restrictions of the type (5.22) is not primarily concerned with 'unit-roots' which are a property of the DGP of the input signal X_t. Instead, performances of the asymmetric filter matter: does a particular constraint (5.22) enhance the estimation of the signal Y_t or not (wether or not the DGP is an integrated process)? Therefore, the 'spirit' of hypothesis-tests based on (5.86) or on (5.91) is not the same as for 'pure' unit-root tests (like Dickey-Fuller (ADF) or Phillips-Perron (PP) for example). Nevertheless, both approaches rely (after suitable transformations) on the same asymptotic Dickey-Fuller distribution. The differences then lie in the 'weight' given to particular properties of the input signal (as measured by the spectral density $\tilde{h}(\cdot)$ and, in particular, $\tilde{h}(0)$) and the relevant estimation problem (which, here, involves $\Gamma(\cdot)$ and $\tilde{\Gamma}(\cdot)$ via the constants A and B in (5.72)).

- The restrictions (5.22) are of interest. Since integrated processes play a major rule in modern econometrics, the term 'unit-root constraints' is reserved to (5.22) although technically the first order constraint $\Gamma(0) = \hat{\Gamma}(0)$ is a 'level' constraint and $\hat{\phi}(0) = 0$ is a 'time-shift' constraint for the asymmetric filter $\hat{\Gamma}(\cdot)$. These conditions allow for more general non-stationarities, so for example trend-stationarity around a linear (first order constraint) or a quadratic time trend (second order constraint). However, the asymptotic distribution of the test-statistics depends on the type of non-stationarity considered. In the preceding results X_t was assumed to be integrated (either I(1) or I(2)) without a trend. Asymptotic distributions for processes with deterministic (linear or quadratic) time trends can be derived analogously. They are not reported here because it is felt that the corresponding DGP's of X_t are less relevant empirically.

In the last section of this chapter, a link between the MBA and the DFA is proposed. It is shown that a slight modification of the DFA enables simpler computations if $r > 0$ in (3.6).

5.8 Links Between the DFA and the MBA

Suppose Y_{N-r} is to be estimated for $r \geq 0$. Assume for simplicity that $X_t \in C_f^0$ and that $\Gamma(\cdot) \in C_f^\alpha$ and $\alpha \geq 0$. The filter $\Gamma(\cdot)$ and the spectral density of the input signal may be arbitrary functions subject to weak regularity assumptions only. Therefore, if $r > 0$, then the corresponding asymmetric ARMA-filter $\hat{\Gamma}_r(\cdot)$ (for estimating Y_{N-r}) may require a 'large' number of parameters for an optimal approximation. The following modification proposes a simple and yet effective solution for this problem. Define

$$\hat{\Gamma}_r'(\cdot) := C_{tr}\Gamma^{tr}(\cdot) + \hat{\Gamma}_r(\cdot) \tag{5.95}$$

where $\Gamma^{tr}(\cdot) := \exp(ir\omega)\sum_{k=-r}^{N-r+1}\gamma_k\exp(-ik\omega)$ is the truncated theoretical extraction filter and $\hat{\Gamma}_r(\cdot)$ is defined in (3.6) (both filters use the whole sample for 'estimating' Y_{N-r}) and C_{tr} is a normalization. The filter $\hat{\Gamma}_r'(\cdot)$ results from an 'overlapping' of the output signals of the two (generally asymmetric) filters on the right. The ARMA-filter $\hat{\Gamma}_r(\cdot)$ may be interpreted as a correction of the output of $\Gamma^{tr}(\cdot)$. The normalizing constants C in (5.1) and C_{tr} in (5.95) 'weight' the respective outputs. As r increases, $\Gamma^{tr}(\cdot)$ becomes less asymmetric and C generally decreases. It is suggested to replace $\hat{\Gamma}_r(\cdot)$ by $\hat{\Gamma}_r'(\cdot)$ in (5.19) (or (5.36)).

If X_t is a white noise process, then $\Gamma^{tr}(\cdot)$ is optimal (because back- and/or forecasts of the process vanish, see (1.4)). More generally, assume a simple preliminary model for X_t has been identified and estimated. Then $\Gamma^{tr}(\cdot)$ can be replaced by (1.4) in (5.95). The filter $\hat{\Gamma}_r(\cdot)$ can correct for model-misspecification. The resulting design of the filter $\hat{\Gamma}_r'(\cdot)$ defines a link between the DFA and the MBA (see also Wildi [97]).

Until now, the signal estimation problem was restricted to the approximation of a *symmetric* filter $\Gamma(\cdot)$ because signal extraction filters are generally symmetric. This restriction is not necessary and may be dropped. By doing so, the filter approximation problem may be interpreted as a generalization of the forecasting problem. For that purpose, define $\Gamma(\omega) := \exp(ik\omega)$ which is now an asymmetric filter. The asymmetric filter for $r = 0$ (boundary filter) which best approximates $\Gamma(\cdot)$ (in the mean square sense) provides as output a signal $\hat{Y}_t$ which best approximates X_{t+k} (in the mean square sense) given the information set $X_1, ..., X_t$. This can be seen by noting that $\exp(ik\omega)$ (in the frequency domain) corresponds to F^k (in the time domain), where $F := B^{-1}$ is the forward operator, i.e. $FX_t = X_{t+1}$. For $t = N$, $\hat{Y}_N$ is the k-step ahead forecast of X_{N+k}. Therefore, the DFA could be used for computing forecasts of an input signal X_t as does, for example, the MBA. This direction of research is not pursued further here although time delay constraints for multi-step ahead forecasts would be worth additional investigations. Instead, interest is focused on the signal estimation problem, i.e. the approximation of symmetric filters.

In this chapter, main asymptotic results have been presented for the DFA. In the next chapter, finite sample problems and regularity issues are analyzed. Particular attention is paid to overfitting problems and uniform stability of the solutions of the DFA. It is shown that both issues are related.

6

Finite Sample Problems and Regularity

In the preceding chapter, *asymptotic* properties of the DFA were presented. An important regularity assumption, namely the uniform stability of the sequence of DFA solutions, was necessary for establishing the consistency and the efficiency of the approach. However, some care is needed since 'excessively smooth' DFA solutions may be suboptimal. In the present chapter *finite sample* problems are analyzed. Methods are proposed for solving the uniform stability problem.

In section 6.1 'overfitting' is analyzed and related to the 'regularity' of the DFA (or the MBA) solution. The distinction between 'overfitting' and 'overparameterization' is stressed. This leads to different instruments for solving finite sample problems. In section 6.2 a method for selecting Q and q (or equivalently AR- and MA-filter orders) is proposed for the DFA. As such, the method emphasizes overparameterization issues. In section 6.3 an application of the so called 'cross-validation' principle to the DFA is presented. This method can be used to assess the extent of overfitting and also to infer an 'optimal' number of parameters (of the asymmetric filter).

A drawback of both methods is that they are essentially 'descriptive'. Corrections of the estimated (filter) parameters are not proposed (in case of 'serious' overfitting). Therefore, a new approach is developed in sections 6.4 and 6.5 which aims at a 'regular' solution of the DFA (necessary for the uniform stability). It is more fundamental because overfitting is closely related to 'singularity' issues (see section 6.1). The idea is to modify the original optimization criterion such that particular aspects of overfitting become 'measurable'. As a consequence, the resulting estimates are corrected for 'undesirable' properties of the asymmetric filter. The approach is felt as a promising area for future research (in particular for 'tackling' the overfitting problem).

6.1 Regularity and Overfitting

Let $X_1, ..., X_N$ be a finite sample generated by a stationary AR(p)-process. Assume p is known and suppose the parameters of the process are estimated by least-squares. The estimates are random variables whose realizations generally deviate from the true values. In the following, this phenomenon is called *overfitting*. Often, the term 'overfitting' in the time series literature means that 'too many' parameters are estimated (which results in excessive loss of 'degrees of freedom' of the data). In this chapter, the term *overparameterization* is reserved for this notion. An attempt is made here to differentiate overfitting and overparameterization.

Here, overfitting in its most general sense means random deviations of estimates from true parameter values. It is a fundamental problem which is independent of the number of parameters being estimated. Consider the above estimation problem and assume the innovations of the AR-process are iid (recall that p is known). The AR-parameters are completely determined by the second order moments of the process (by the so called Yule-Walker equations, see for example Brockwell and Davis [10], chap.8). Unfortunately, estimates of the parameters, such as for example least-squares estimates, are not functions of moments (which are unknown) but functions of the realizations of the process which are subject to 'randomness'. The least-squares principle implies

$$\sum_{t=1}^{N} \hat{\epsilon}_t^2 \leq \sum_{t=1}^{N} \epsilon_t^2$$

where ϵ_t are the true innovations. This inequality justifies the term 'overfitting' for the proposed example : the fit produced by the estimated model seems better than that of the true model, when measured by the squared errors. More generally, assume unknown 'entities' must be estimated (to simplify, call them 'parameters'). This is often achieved by searching for the extremum (say a minimum) of a particular criterion which is a function of the unknown parameters (for example the left hand side of (5.9)). Then the minimum of this criterion is smaller than (or equal to) the realized value for the 'true' parameter values. This inequality again justifies the term 'overfitting' for the general case (recall the 'spurious decrease' of the optimization criterion for the DFA in section 5.6.2). It is a consequence of fitting unintentionally the generally unknown random component of the stochastic process. Note that the overfitting problem often vanishes asymptotically if the sample length increases faster than the number of estimated parameters. This effect is due to the well known 'law of large numbers'.

If the order p of the AR-process is unknown, then various orders p' may be tried by fitting corresponding models to the data. It is then well known that estimates from 'too large' models ($p' > p$) are 'poorer' (the estimates are subject to larger variances). This effect is described here by the term overparameterization. It is an unnecessary reduction of the 'degrees of freedom' of the data. The impact of overparameterization is to exacerbate the over-fitting effect. However, overfitting exists even without overparameterization. This distinction is useful for evaluating the effects of 'finite sample' instruments, see below.

Box [8], p.792 argues that: "since all models are wrong the scientist can not obtain a correct one by excessive elaboration ... Just as the ability to devise simple but evocative models is the signature of the great scientist so elaboration and overparameterization is often the mark of mediocrity". This comment stresses the importance of parsimonious models (see Box and Jenkins [9]) or parsimonious filter designs (recall section 3.3).

Overparameterization ("excessive elaboration") of filters or models often results in overfitting characterized by almost discontinuous or unstable transfer functions. The 'typical shape' of the amplitude functions is generally unnecessarily complicated by peaks and troughs. Overfitting and regularity ('smoothness') of the transfer function are therefore related. In the sense of Box's comment one can argue that *regularity (of the transfer function) and simplicity (of the model or of the filter) are linked*. Overfitting problems due to insufficient regularity of the DFA solution are now described.

Assume for simplicity that the input signal X_t is stationary and recall the approximation (5.16):

$$\frac{2\pi}{N} \sum_{k=-[N/2]}^{[N/2]} w_k |\Delta\Gamma(\omega_k)|^2 I_{NX}(\omega_k) \simeq \frac{2\pi}{N} \sum_{k=-[N/2]}^{[N/2]} w_k |\Delta\Gamma(\omega_k)|^2 h(\omega_k) \quad (6.1)$$

$$\simeq \frac{1}{2\pi} \int_{-\pi}^{\pi} |\Delta\Gamma(\omega)|^2 h(\omega) d\omega$$

$$= E[(Y_t - \hat{Y}_t)^2]$$

Overfitting, i.e. random errors of finite sample parameter estimates, can appear because the unknown spectral density $h(\cdot)$ is replaced by the periodogram $I_{NX}(\cdot)$. It can also appear because the continuous integral is approximated by a finite sum. In the latter case (discretization effect), differences between $\hat{\Gamma}(\cdot)$ and $\Gamma(\cdot)$ are 'measured' on the set of discrete frequencies $\omega_k \in \Omega_N$ only. This may be problematic if $\Delta\Gamma(\cdot)$ is not sufficiently regular ('smooth'). Consider the following cases:

- It was shown in theorem 3.10 that the effect of a single zero-pole-pair can be concentrated in an open interval of arbitrary width. It is therefore possible to achieve perfect fits (of the theoretical transfer function $\Gamma(\cdot)$) on Ω_N. Suppose for example that $\lambda = \omega_{k_0} \in \Omega_N$ and $\Gamma(\lambda) = 0$. Then it is possible to determine a real ZPC-filter such that

$$\hat{\Gamma}_\lambda(\lambda) = 0$$

$$|1 - \hat{\varGamma}_\lambda(\omega)| < \delta \text{ if } |\omega - \lambda| > \epsilon$$

where $\epsilon > 0$ and $\delta > 0$ are arbitrarily small real numbers. Therefore, the left hand side of (6.1) decreases because the contribution of $I_{NX}(\lambda)$ to the sum vanishes (other frequency ordinates remain almost unaffected if ϵ and δ are sufficiently small). It is not difficult to verify that a sufficiently large number of ZPC designs define an asymmetric filter which is able to 'reproduce' $\varGamma(\cdot)$ arbitrarily well on Ω_N (the left hand side of (6.1) vanishes in the limit). Evidently, extreme distortions may appear for $\omega \in [-\pi, \pi] - \Omega_N$. These distortions cannot be 'detected' by the optimization criterion (5.19) (left hand side). As a result, the corresponding output $\hat{Y}_t$ would be a poor approximation of the signal Y_t. Note that the ZPC-filter in the above example becomes nearly singular: the zero is on the unit circle and the pole is extremely close to the unit circle. The zero is closer to (or on) the unit circle than the pole because the component at λ is damped (eliminated), see figure 3.2. This is called a *non-invertibility singularity*. A finite discontinuity of the transfer function is induced in the limiting case.

- In the preceding example the (common) argument of the zero-pole-pair is in Ω_N. The overfitting problem is now examined for zero-pole-pairs whose argument λ does not lie in Ω_N. They are called *hidden* zero-pole-pairs because their 'main' effect (at λ) can be measured indirectly only on Ω_N. In fact, minimizing the left hand side of (6.1) 'controls' zeroes and poles by an implicit regularity assumption (residing in the invertibility and the stability of the minimum phase component of the QMP-ZPC filter, see definition 3.6). Consider the following example where this implicit regularity assumption is not satisfied (in the limiting case):

$$|\hat{\varGamma}_\lambda(\lambda)| = M$$
$$|1 - \hat{\varGamma}_\lambda(\omega)| < \delta \text{ if } |\omega - \lambda| > \epsilon$$

where $\epsilon > 0$ and $\delta > 0$ are arbitrarily small real numbers and $M > 1$ is arbitrarily large. It was shown in theorem 3.10 that such a filter exists. A strong component which distorts the filter output can be generated 'artificially' if M is sufficiently large. If $\lambda = \dfrac{\omega_k + \omega_{k+1}}{2}$, then this component cannot be 'detected' by (6.1) if ϵ and δ are sufficiently small. Again, the ZPC-filter is (nearly) singular. Now the pole is closer to the unit circle than the zero of the pair (because the component with frequency λ is amplified). This is called an *instability singularity*. An infinite discontinuity of the transfer function is induced in the limiting case ($M \to \infty$).

Both cases stress the *invertibility* and the *stability* of the approximating filter. Clearly, instability singularities are harmful: a single zero-pole-pair can completely distort the filter output. Non-invertibility singularities are 'less dangerous'. Moreover, such designs are necessary for removing components with sharp and narrow spectral 'spikes' (such as seasonal components for example, see chapter 7). Sections 6.4 and 6.5 propose solutions which ensure regularity of the asymmetric filter. In the first section, instability and invertibility singularities are both penalized. In the second section, potential instabilities (poles close to the unit circle) are 'tracked' only by allowing $\omega_k \in \Omega_N$ to vary 'locally'. Therefore, potentially dangerous zero-pole pairs become 'apparent'.

For the sake of completeness consider the following overparameterization problems:

- Complex conjugate zeroes and/or poles are located far away from the unit disk. Then their relative effect (damping or amplification or time shift) on different frequency components can be neglected. The ratio of the minimum distance (to the unit circle) to the maximum distance (to the unit circle) is almost equal to one. Therefore, the 'amplitude effect' is approximately constant. Moreover, the arguments of the complex conjugate pairs nearly cancel each other so that the phase is almost equal to zero. Thus the normalization C in (5.1) cancels the effect of such zeroes and/or poles.
- Zeroes of the numerator cancel poles of the denominator.

Both problems relate to the determination of the number of parameters. They eventually impair the speed of convergence of a numerical optimization algorithm (by unnecessarily increasing the dimension of the problem or by 'deflating' the gradient). However, they do not affect the statistical estimation problem. Instead, problems of numerical optimization are addressed here.

In the following section, the determination of the number of parameters of the asymmetric filter, i.e. overparameterization is addressed. An approach based on theorem 5.10 is presented.

6.2 Filter Selection Criterion

6.2.1 Overview

An estimation of Q and q or equivalently of AR- and MA-filter orders must account for two conflicting requirements. General signal extraction problems necessitate flexible asymmetric filter designs (i.e. 'large' Q or q) for matching the 'contour' of the best asymmetric boundary filter. Unfortunately, 'too flexible' designs (excessively large Q or q) also match random features specific to a given sample. Therefore, 'good' estimates $\hat{Q}$ and $\hat{q}$ should reflect a compromise between flexibility and parsimony.

The determination of the 'true' model order (in the MBA) is related to the identification of the data generating process (see for example Granger and Newbold [40], section 7.3). Criteria for solving the so called TS-identification problem (time series identification, see the previously cited literature) are available, see for example Stier [85], chap.8. Well known approaches are information criteria (see Akaike [2]) or minimum description length principles (see Rissanen [77] and [78]). It is shown in Caines [12], p.281 that both approaches are identical.

The determination of the number of parameters p for the asymmetric filter of the DFA is not directly related to the identification of the DGP. Instead, a filter is sought for which the expectation $E[(\Delta Y_t)^2]$ is minimized. The statistic proposed in this section does not rely on 'information' or 'identification' concepts because the DGP is not of immediate concern. However, it is shown in the appendix that information criteria can be considered in a sense (to be precised there) as special cases of the proposed filter selection criterion.

Before presenting the relevant concepts, a further difference between the MBA and the DFA is stressed here:

- The MBA tries to determine the *unknown* DGP.
- The DFA tries to approximate the *known* symmetric transfer function of the extraction filter.

Therefore, the solution of the DFA is inherently subject to 'control' by direct comparison with the symmetric transfer function in (5.19). Such a 'control' is not given for the MBA, because the DGP is unknown. Thus, it is to be expected that the DFA is less sensitive to overparameterization than the MBA. Chapter 7 confirms this conjecture from an empirical point of view: it is shown that overparameterized filters perform as well as correctly parameterized (model-based) maximum likelihood estimates for various simulated processes.

6.2.2 The MC-Criterion

A formal estimation procedure for Q and q in (3.6) is now proposed. Assume Y_{N-r} is to be estimated and recall (5.69):

$$
\frac{2\pi}{N} E \left[\sum_{k=-[N/2]}^{[N/2]} |\Gamma(\omega_k) - \tilde{\Gamma}_{Qq}(\omega_k)|^2 I_{NX}(\omega_k) \right.
$$

$$
\left. - \sum_{k=-[N/2]}^{[N/2]} |\Gamma(\omega_k) - \hat{\Gamma}_{Qq}(\omega_k)|^2 I_{NX}(\omega_k) \right]
$$

$$
= \frac{1}{2} \frac{\operatorname{tr}\left(\mathbf{V}_{Qq}\mathbf{U}_{Qq}^{-1}\right)}{N} + \mathrm{o}(N^{-1}) \tag{6.2}
$$

where $\mathbf{U}_{Qq}$ and $\mathbf{V}_{Qq}$ can be consistently estimated, see theorem 5.10. The index Qq indicates that ARMA$(Q, q + r)$ filters are considered. If the best filter is an ARMA$(Q', q' + r)$ then

$$\frac{2\pi}{N} \sum_{k=-[N/2]}^{[N/2]} |\Gamma(\omega_k) - \tilde{\Gamma}_{Qq}(\omega_k)|^2 I_{NX}(\omega_k)$$

does not depend on Q or q if $Q \geq Q'$ and $q \geq q'$. Therefore

$$\frac{2\pi}{N} E \left[\sum_{k=-[N/2]}^{[N/2]} |\Gamma(\omega_k) - \hat{\Gamma}_{Q'q'}(\omega_k)|^2 I_{NX}(\omega_k) \right.$$

$$\left. - \sum_{k=-[N/2]}^{[N/2]} |\Gamma(\omega_k) - \hat{\Gamma}_{Qq}(\omega_k)|^2 I_{NX}(\omega_k) \right]$$

$$= \frac{1}{2} \frac{\mathrm{tr}\left(\mathbf{V}_{Qq}\mathbf{U}_{Qq}^{-1}\right)}{N} - \frac{1}{2} \frac{\mathrm{tr}\left(\mathbf{V}_{Q'q'}\mathbf{U}_{Q'q'}^{-1}\right)}{N} + \mathrm{o}(N^{-1}) \qquad (6.3)$$

The last term describes the mean decrease of the criterion (5.19) subject to overparameterization (overfitting effect). A straightforward estimation of Q and q for the DFA (5.19) may then be based on the minimization of the general criterion

$$\frac{2\pi}{N} \sum_{k=-[N/2]}^{[N/2]} |\Gamma(\omega_k) - \hat{\Gamma}_{Qq}(\omega_k)|^2 I_{NX}(\omega_k) + f\left(\frac{1}{2} \frac{\mathrm{tr}\left(\mathbf{V}_{Qq}\mathbf{U}_{Qq}^{-1}\right)}{N} \right) \qquad (6.4)$$

as a function of Q and q, where $f(\cdot)$ is such that $f(x) > x$. Note that $\mathbf{U}_{Qq}$ and $\mathbf{V}_{Qq}$ and therefore $\mathbf{V}_{Qq}\mathbf{U}_{Qq}^{-1}$ are positive definite so that $\mathrm{tr}\left(\mathbf{V}_{Qq}\mathbf{U}_{Qq}^{-1}\right)$ is positive definite too. Thus the second term in (6.4) must be positive too and can be interpreted as a 'penalty' for overparameterization. Therefore, f must satisfy $f(x) > x$ for $x > 0$ only. This function can be defined according to information criteria (so for example $f(x) := 2x$ would correspond to AIC). In general, the matrices $\mathbf{U}_{Qq}$ and $\mathbf{V}_{Qq}$ must be estimated in (6.4). The MC-criterion used in chapter 7 is

$$MC(Q,q) := \frac{2\pi}{N} \sum_{k=-[N/2]}^{[N/2]} |\Gamma(\omega_k) - \hat{\Gamma}_{Qq}(\omega_k)|^2 I_{NX}(\omega_k)$$

$$+ 2\frac{1}{2} \frac{\mathrm{tr}\left(\hat{\mathbf{V}}_{Qq}\hat{\mathbf{U}}_{Qq}^{-1}\right)}{N - Q - q - r - 1}$$

$$= \frac{2\pi}{N} \sum_{k=-[N/2]}^{[N/2]} |\Gamma(\omega_k) - \hat{\Gamma}_{Qq}(\omega_k)|^2 I_{NX}(\omega_k)$$

$$+ \frac{\mathrm{tr}\left(\hat{\mathbf{V}}_{Qq}\hat{\mathbf{U}}_{Qq}^{-1}\right)}{N - Q - q - r - 1} \qquad (6.5)$$

where $\hat{U}_{Qq}$ and $\hat{V}_{Qq}$ are defined in (5.56) and (5.57) and $f(x) = 2\frac{N}{N-Q-q-r-1}x$ corresponds to the penalty term of AICC (see Brockwell and Davis [10], section 9.3). The filter orders Q and q are determined by minimizing (6.5) as a function of Q and q. Note that the penalty term of AICC increases more rapidly than that of AIC (it is known that the latter may lead to overparameterization for the MBA).

Remark

- The results in section C.2 in the appendix emphasize that the determination of Q and q based on the minimization of $M(Q, q)$ may be interpreted as a generalization of a particular identification approach of the DGP of X_t based on information criteria.

The method proposed in this section addresses mainly overparameterization. But 'good' estimates of Q and q are not necessarily a guarantee against overfitting. Therefore, the next section proposes a method assessing overfitting 'indirectly'.

6.3 Cross-Validation

Basically, cross-validation is the separation of the estimation procedure (or estimation phase) and the validation procedure (or validation phase) by partitioning a sample $X_1, ..., X_N$ into estimation- and validation-subsamples. The second subsample is used for assessing 'out of sample' performances of the filter (or model) optimized for the first subsample. Overfitting 'nuisances' (poor 'out of sample' performances) may be detected by this method, but the overfitting problem is not solved explicitly: the estimated parameters are not corrected for overfitting effects, which is a drawback of the method.

Cross-validation is often used for selecting a 'good' p (recall that $p = Q+q+r+1$). For that purpose, the sample is partitioned into $X_1, ..., X_{N_1}$ and $X_{N_1+1}, ..., X_N$ and it is assumed that ΔY_t is a stationary ergodic process (so that the stochastic properties do not vary from one subsample to the other). Then the number of parameters p of the asymmetric filter can be determined as follows.

- For a 'candidate' value $\hat{p}$ of p, the DFA solution $\hat{\Gamma}_{0\hat{p}}(\cdot)$ is computed on the first subsample.
- The sample variance $\frac{1}{N-N_1} \sum_{t=N_1+1}^{N} (\Delta Y_{t\hat{p}})^2$ is then computed on the remaining subsample.
- The value $\hat{p} := p_0$ for which $\frac{1}{N-N_1} \sum_{t=N_1+1}^{N} (\Delta Y_{tp_0})^2$ is minimal is then selected for estimating the DFA solution on the *whole* sample.

Although Y_t (and thus $\frac{1}{N-N_1} \sum_{t=N_1+1}^{N} (\Delta Y_{t\hat{p}})^2$) are generally unknown, it is often possible to find approximations on suitable shorter subsamples (see for example chapter 7 where this problem is analyzed in more detail).

During the estimation phase, a smaller subsample ($N_1 < N$) is used which implies poorer parameter estimates. For the DFA, an alternative separation of 'estimation' and 'validation' is possible which preserves the original sample length. This is presented now.

The idea is to perform the estimation in the frequency domain (as given by the left hand side of (5.7)) and to conduct the validation in the time domain (as given by the right hand side of (5.7)). A comparison of both expressions reveals potential instabilities of the asymmetric filter. It amounts to assess the 'convolution error' r_N. Unfortunately, the remaining error r'_N in (5.45) cannot be assessed which is the 'price' paid for using the whole sample for the estimation (instead of a subsample only). The procedure is fairly similar to 'traditional' cross-validation.

- For a 'candidate' value $\hat{p}$ of p, the DFA solution $\hat{\Gamma}_{0\hat{p}}(\cdot)$ is computed (in the frequency domain and using the whole sample).
- The sample variance $\frac{1}{N}\sum_{t=1}^{N}(\Delta Y_{t\hat{p}})^2$ is then computed (in the time domain and for the whole sample).
- The value $\hat{p} := p_0$ for which $\frac{1}{N}\sum_{t=N}^{N}(\Delta Y_{tp_0})^2$ is minimized is chosen as estimate of p.

A weakness of both approaches lies in the absence of explicit parameter corrections. Basically, this is because both methods rely on an 'outer control' (of the DFA solution) only. The next two sections propose methods including an 'inner control' by suitably modifying the original optimization criterion (as given by the left hand side of (5.19)) such that overfitting becomes 'measurable'. As a result, estimates are explicitly corrected for 'insufficient' regularity of the filter.

6.4 A Singularity-Penalty

Overfitting often results in 'too complicated' asymmetric filters which may be even singular (or 'nearly' singular), recall section 6.1. Assume for the moment that $X_t \in C_f^\beta$ and that $\Gamma \in C_f^\alpha$, where β and α are positive real numbers. From the discussion at the beginning of section 5.2, it seems 'natural' to require

$$\hat{\Gamma}_{0r}(\cdot) \in C_f^{\min(\alpha,\beta)} \qquad (6.6)$$

(where $\hat{\Gamma}_{0r}(\cdot)$ is the DFA solution for estimating Y_{N-r}) in some sense 'uniformly' in N because:

- otherwise poles of $\hat{\Gamma}_{0r}(\cdot)$ can approach the unit circle arbitrarily closely (as N increases) which may induce noticeable distortions of the output signal, see section 6.1;

- from (5.6) (and proposition 4.7) the best filter satisfies $\hat{\Gamma}_{\infty r} \in C_f^{\min(\alpha,\beta)}$, where the subscript ∞ indicates that the filter minimizing the revision error variance may involve infinitely many parameters.

For notational ease the subscript 'r' is dropped from now on but it should be clear that asymmetric filters are optimized for particular time points $t = N - r$. If the number of parameters $p(N)$ is a bounded function of N, then uniform stability (see definition 5.1) implies (6.6) for all α, β. However, if $p(N)$ may grow unboundedly, then the uniform stability requirement does no more necessarily imply (6.6) uniformly in N. The following definition generalizes uniform stability for the case of unbounded $p(N)$:

Definition 6.1. *A sequence of QMP-filters $\hat{\Gamma}_N(\cdot)$ (with $p(N)$ parameters) is called uniformly α-stable if*

$$\sum_{k=-r}^{\infty} |\hat{\gamma}_{Nk}||k|^{\alpha} < M_{\alpha} \qquad (6.7)$$

for some $M_{\alpha} > 0$ which does not depend on N.

Definitions 5.1 and 6.1 are identical if $p(N)$ is bounded.

Consider now the criterion

$$\min_{\hat{\Gamma}} \left\{ \frac{2\pi}{N} \sum_{k=-[N/2]}^{[N/2]} |\Gamma(\omega_k) - \hat{\Gamma}(\omega_k)|^2 I_{NX}(\omega_k) + \lambda \sum_{k=0}^{\infty} |\hat{\gamma}_k||k|^{\min(\alpha,\beta)} \right\} \qquad (6.8)$$

For increasing N its solutions define a uniform $\min(\alpha, \beta)$-stable sequence (required by (6.6)) provided $\lambda > 0$. The parameter λ controls the regularity of the asymmetric QMP-filter. Unfortunately, the proposed 'penalty' term has undesirable properties:

- Increasing λ 'forces' $\hat{\Gamma}(\cdot)$ towards zero (i.e. it becomes 'too smooth').
- The weight λ depends on the extraction filter $\Gamma(\cdot)$. The 'regularity' of $\Gamma(\cdot)$, as measured by $\sum_{k=0}^{\infty} |\gamma_k||k|^{\min(\alpha,\beta)}$, has an influence on the value attained by $\sum_{k=0}^{\infty} |\hat{\gamma}_k||k|^{\min(\alpha,\beta)}$ in (6.8).
- The weight λ depends on the sample $X_1, ..., X_N$. The 'scaling' of the variables and the difficulty of the approximation problem are reflected in $\frac{2\pi}{N} \sum_{k=-[N/2]}^{[N/2]} |\Gamma(\omega_k) - \hat{\Gamma}(\omega_k)|^2 I_{NX}(\omega_k)$ in (6.8).

Therefore, some kind of 'normalization' is needed. Assume that $\hat{\Gamma}(\cdot)$, the DFA solution, is an ARMA$(Q, q+r)$ filter and let $\bar{\Gamma}(\cdot)$ denote the best asymmetric ARMA$(Q, q+r)$ filter. Then

$$\ln \left(1 + \frac{2\pi}{N} \sum_{k=-[N/2]}^{[N/2]} |\Gamma(\omega_k) - \hat{\Gamma}(\omega_k)|^2 I_{NX}(\omega_k) \right)$$

$$\approx C_1 + \frac{1 + \sum_{k=-[N/2]}^{[N/2]} |\Gamma(\omega_k) - \hat{\Gamma}(\omega_k)|^2 I_{NX}(\omega_k)}{1 + \sum_{k=-[N/2]}^{[N/2]} |\Gamma(\omega_k) - \tilde{\Gamma}(\omega_k)|^2 I_{NX}(\omega_k)}$$

where C_1 is a constant that does not depend on the parameters of $\hat{\Gamma}(\cdot)$, see for example (C.22) in the appendix. Equivalently,

$$\ln\left(1 + \sum_{k=-r}^{N-r-1} |\hat{\gamma}_k - \gamma_k||k|^{\min(\alpha,\beta)}\right) \approx C_2 + \frac{1 + \sum_{k=-r}^{N-r-1} |\hat{\gamma}_k - \gamma_k||k|^{\min(\alpha,\beta)}}{1 + \sum_{k=-r}^{N-r-1} |\tilde{\gamma}_k - \gamma_k||k|^{\min(\alpha,\beta)}}$$

where C_2 does not depend on Q or on q. The logarithm can be used as a 'natural' normalization. A new criterion can then be defined by

$$\min_{\hat{\Gamma}} \left\{ \ln\left(1 + \frac{2\pi}{N} \sum_{k=-[N/2]}^{[N/2]} |\Gamma(\omega_k) - \hat{\Gamma}(\omega_k)|^2 I_{NX}(\omega_k)\right) \right.$$
$$\left. + \lambda \ln\left(1 + \sum_{k=-r}^{N-r-1} |\hat{\gamma}_k - \gamma_k||k|^{\min(\alpha,\beta)}\right) \right\} \tag{6.9}$$

Equivalently, a simple multiplicative criterion

$$\min_{\hat{\Gamma}} \left\{ \left(1 + \frac{2\pi}{N} \sum_{k=-[N/2]}^{[N/2]} |\Gamma(\omega_k) - \hat{\Gamma}(\omega_k)|^2 I_{NX}(\omega_k)\right) \right.$$
$$\left. \left(1 + \sum_{k=-r}^{N-r-1} |\hat{\gamma}_k - \gamma_k||k|^{\min(\alpha,\beta)}\right)^{\lambda} \right\} \tag{6.10}$$

can be used. The proposed optimization criteria (6.9) or (6.10) are characterized by the following properties.

- From the assumption $\Gamma(\cdot) \in C_f^{\min(\alpha,\beta)}$ and from

$$||\hat{\gamma}_k| - |\gamma_k|| \leq |\hat{\gamma}_k - \gamma_k| \leq |\hat{\gamma}_k| + |\gamma_k|$$

  it follows at once that (6.9) or (6.10) penalize filters which are not sufficiently regular if $\lambda > 0$.
- Increasing λ does no more 'force' the asymmetric filter towards zero. Moreover, as shown below, the penalty term is 'optimal' if the input signal is white noise.
- The logarithms 'normalize' both sums in (6.9). The additional '1' in the argument of the logarithms prevent the criterion (6.9) to diverge to $-\infty$ for 'overfitted' designs. Equivalently, (6.10) cannot vanish by including the additional '1'.

- Minimizing (6.9) or (6.10) corresponds to 'fuzzy' restrictions on the filter parameters. This is in contrast to 'hard' shape or exclusion restrictions of the type $|P_k| > 1 + \delta$ where δ is specified a priori. The latter restrictions may imply 'too smooth' DFA solutions, excluding thereby optimal filter solutions.

Setting $\hat{\gamma}_k := \gamma_k$ for $k = -r, ..., N - r - 1$ minimizes the penalty term in (6.9). Recall that this choice is optimal if X_t is a zero mean white noise process (because back- and/or forecasts of the process vanish in (1.4)). Therefore, increasing λ in this particular case does not impair the solution of (6.9) (on the contrary). However, in general the input signal is not a white noise process and larger λ may impair the goodness of the solution of (6.9). Therefore, a final improvement of the criterion (6.9) is proposed (a similar modification may be applied to (6.10) too):

$$
\min_{\hat{\Gamma}} \left\{ \ln \left(1 + \frac{2\pi}{N} \sum_{k=-[N/2]}^{[N/2]} |\Gamma(\omega_k) - \hat{\Gamma}(\omega_k)|^2 I_{NX}(\omega_k) \right) \right.
$$
$$
\left. + \lambda \ln \left(1 + \sum_{k=-r}^{N-r-1} |\hat{\gamma}_k - \gamma'_k| |k|^{\min(\alpha,\beta)} \right) \right\} \tag{6.11}
$$

where the coefficients γ'_k are computed using either of the following methods:

- γ'_k are derived from a DFA solution which is constrained to be regular. The regularity can be achieved by using the MC-criterion (6.5) (for estimating the filter orders Q and $q + r + 1$) and by constraining poles so that $|P_k| > 1 + \delta$ for $k = 1, ..., Q$. Experience suggests that $\delta = 0.15$ may be a 'good' choice for a variety of applications.
- γ'_k are derived from a MBA based on a simple preliminary model (for example an 'airline' model).

The role of the first sum in (6.11) is to 'fit' $\hat{\Gamma}(\cdot)$ to the sample and the role of the second sum is to penalize 'too elaborate' solutions. Therefore, when computing γ'_k using a MBA, 'best fitting' models are not a priority. Instead, a simple parsimonious model (for example an 'airline' model) is needed so that the coefficients γ'_k define a sufficiently regular 'control sequence' for $\hat{\gamma}_k$ (ensuring the uniform $\min(\alpha, \beta)$-stability of $\hat{\Gamma}(\cdot)$). Increasing λ in (6.11) strengthens the regularity of the asymmetric filter. Also, increasing λ 'pulls' the estimate towards a preliminary DFA or MBA solution which is felt better than the constant zero in (6.8) or the solution for a white noise input process in (6.9) (which is implicitly assumed by setting $\gamma'_k := \gamma_k$, for $k = -r, ..., N - r - 1$). Note that it is not intended to 'shrink' the original DFA solution towards a simple regular preliminary solution γ'_k by minimizing the criterion (6.11). 'Shrinkage' methods are well known in Bayesian estimation, see for example Litterman [62], which proposes a Bayesian approach based on mixed estimation. In (6.11), the parameter λ is typically 'small' so that the 'shrinkage effect' is small too. Moreover, $|\hat{\gamma}_k - \gamma'_k|$ is weighted by $|k|^{\min(\alpha,\beta)}$ in (6.11) which implies that regularity aspects dominate here. In fact, singularity of the transfer function has to do with slowly decaying filter coefficients, which is penalized by the weights $|k|^{\min(\alpha,\beta)}$.

A formal procedure for choosing λ and $\min(\alpha, \beta)$ is unknown up to now. It is reasonable to assume that $\lambda \to 0$ as $N \to \infty$ since otherwise the solution of (6.11) is eventually an inconsistent estimate (if γ'_k are inconsistent for example). Experience suggests that $\lambda = 1/\sqrt{N}$ and $\min(\alpha, \beta) = 1$ or 2 often provide good results for a large variety of applications. Note also that (6.11) offers a link between the DFA and the MBA if γ'_k are based on a model (a similar link was already provided in section 5.8).

As noted in section 6.1, 'instability singularities' (generated by zero-pole-pairs whose poles are closer to the unit circle than the corresponding zeroes) are potentially more 'harmful' than 'non-invertibility singularities'. Moreover, the latter may be necessary for specific tasks (like for example seasonal adjustment, see chapter 7). Unfortunately, the above penalty terms do not sufficiently differentiate both types of singularities. In the next section, an alternative modification of the optimization criterion (5.19) is proposed, which is able to realize such a differentiation. It is then possible to focus on 'instability singularities' only by tracking hidden zero-pole-pairs on the entire frequency intervall $[-\pi, \pi]$. As for the previous method, overfitting is 'tackled' directly by modifying parameter estimates accordingly.

6.5 Variable Frequency Sampling

Assume for simplicity that $X_t \in C_f^0$ is a stationary MA process, that $\Gamma(\cdot) \in C_f^0$ and that $\hat{\Gamma}(\cdot)$ is a real ZPC filter satisfying

$$|\hat{\Gamma}(\lambda)| = M \qquad (6.12)$$

$$|1 - \hat{\Gamma}(\omega)| < \delta \text{ if } |\omega - \lambda| > \epsilon$$

where $\lambda = \dfrac{\omega_k + \omega_{k+1}}{2}$ and M is a large positive number (the stationarity assumption is not required but it simplifies the exposition). Assume also $h(\omega) > 0$ for all ω, where $h(\cdot)$ is the spectral density of X_t. Then $I_{NX}(\omega_k) \neq 0$ and $I_{NX}(\omega_{k+1}) \neq 0$ with probability one (because they are real random variables with variances $h(\omega_k)^2 > 0$ and $h(\omega_{k+1})^2 > 0$ respectively, see theorem B.2). The potential instability of the ZPC-filter $\hat{\Gamma}(\cdot)$ cannot be detected by the criterion (5.19) if ϵ and δ are sufficiently small, because the frequency ordinates $\omega_k := k2\pi/N$ are *fixed*. Therefore the 'main effect' of $\hat{\Gamma}(\cdot)$ at λ is hidden. If $M > 1$, then the filter $\hat{\Gamma}(\cdot)$ amplifies components (which exist because $h(\lambda) > 0$ by assumption). Assume for example that $\Gamma(\cdot)$ satisfies

$\Gamma(\lambda) = 0$: then the estimated output $\hat{Y}_t$ can be a (very) poor estimate of Y_t (depending on the amplification M).

If ω_k were allowed to vary in (5.19) then the problem could be solved. More precisely, let λ be arbitrary and define

$$\omega_k' := \begin{cases} \omega_k, & \lambda \notin \,]\omega_k - k\pi/N, \omega_k + k\pi/N] \\ \lambda, & else \end{cases} \quad (6.13)$$

$$I_{NX}(\omega_k') := I_{NX}(\omega_k) \quad (6.14)$$

Also, define $\Omega_N' := \{\omega_k' | 0 \le |k| \le [N/2]\}$. The set Ω_N' enables to 'track' the pole of the ZPC filter $\hat{\Gamma}(\cdot)$. A new optimization criterion is defined by replacing Ω_N by Ω_N' in (5.19):

$$\min_{\hat{\Gamma}} \frac{2\pi}{N} \sum_{k=-[N/2]}^{[N/2]} |\Delta\Gamma(\omega_k')|^2 I_{NX}(\omega_k') \quad (6.15)$$

An instability singularity (an arbitrarily large M in (6.12)) would be incompatible with the minimization in (6.15) because $I_{NX}(\omega_k') := I_{NX}(\omega_k) > 0$ with probability one (as shown above).

The frequency ordinates ω_k' are variables (in fact they are random variables in (6.15)) which depend on the argument of the ZPC filter but the 'extent' of their variability is very limited as N increases. The above definition 6.13 can be straightforwardly extended to the case of multiple ZPC filters :

$$\omega_k' := \begin{cases} \omega_k & \text{if } \lambda_j \notin \,]\omega_k - k\pi/N, \omega_k + k\pi/N] \, , \; j = 1, ..., n \\ \lambda_{j_0} & \text{else} \end{cases} \quad (6.16)$$

where λ_{j_0} is defined as

$$\lambda_{j_0} := \left\{ \lambda_j \middle| \lambda_j \in \,]\omega_k - k\pi/N, \omega_k + k\pi/N] \text{ and } |1 - |P_j|| \text{ is minimal} \right\} \quad (6.17)$$

and n is the number of poles. If Ω_N' is defined as $\Omega_N' := \{\omega_k' | 0 \le |k| \le [N/2]\}$, then Ω_N' 'tracks' all poles simultaneously. Moreover, if the arguments of several poles lie in $]\omega_k - k\pi/N, \omega_k + k\pi/N]$, then Ω_N' tracks the most unstable, see (6.17).

Denote the solutions of the left hand side of (5.19) and of (6.15) by $\hat{\Gamma}_0(\cdot)$ and $\hat{\Gamma}_0'(\cdot)$ respectively, where the only differences are the sets Ω_N and Ω_N' used for the optimization (so for example $Q = Q'$ and $q = q'$ i.e. both filters are ARMA($Q, q+r$)-filters). The following proposition proves the equivalence of both solutions under regularity assumptions.

Proposition 6.2. *Let $\hat{\Gamma}_0(\cdot)$ and $\hat{\Gamma}_0'(\cdot)$ be given as above and let $n = o(N)$ be the number of poles of the filters. Then*

$$\frac{2\pi}{N} \sum_{k=-[N/2]}^{[N/2]} w_k |\Gamma(\omega_k) - \hat{\Gamma}_0(\omega_k)|^2 I_{NX}(\omega_k)$$

$$= \frac{2\pi}{N} \sum_{k=-[N/2]}^{[N/2]} w_k |\Gamma(\omega_k') - \hat{\Gamma}_0'(\omega_k')|^2 I_{NX}(\omega_k') + e_N$$

where $e_N = o(1)$ if $\Gamma(\cdot)$ and both ARMA filters are in C_f^0 uniformly in N. If $\Gamma(\cdot)$ and both ARMA filters are in C_f^1 uniformly, then $e_N = O(n/N)$.

Proof. The proof is given under the assumption that both filters are in C_f^1 uniformly in N (a similar reasoning applies if both filters are in C_f^0 uniformly). If $\hat{\Gamma}_0(\cdot) \in C_f^1$ uniformly then

$$\frac{2\pi}{N} \sum_{k=-[N/2]}^{[N/2]} w_k |\Gamma(\omega_k) - \hat{\Gamma}_0(\omega_k)|^2 I_{NX}(\omega_k)$$

$$= \frac{2\pi}{N} \sum_{k=-[N/2]}^{[N/2]} w_k |\Gamma(\omega_k') - \hat{\Gamma}_0(\omega_k')|^2 I_{NX}(\omega_k') + O(n/N)$$

because the event $\omega_k' \neq \omega_k$ occurs at most n times and because

$$\left| |\Gamma(\omega_k) - \hat{\Gamma}_0(\omega_k)| - |\Gamma(\omega_k') - \hat{\Gamma}_0(\omega_k')| \right|$$

$$\leq \left| (\Gamma(\omega_k) - \hat{\Gamma}_0(\omega_k)) - (\Gamma(\omega_k') - \hat{\Gamma}_0(\omega_k')) \right|$$

$$= \left| (\Gamma(\omega_k) - \Gamma(\omega_k')) + (\hat{\Gamma}_0(\omega_k') - \hat{\Gamma}_0(\omega_k)) \right|$$

$$\leq |\Gamma(\omega_k) - \Gamma(\omega_k')| + |\hat{\Gamma}_0(\omega_k) - \hat{\Gamma}_0(\omega_k')|$$

$$= O(1/N)$$

where the last equality follows from the regularity assumption (which implies that the filters are differentiable uniformly in N). Equivalently, assuming $\hat{\Gamma}_0'(\cdot) \in C_f^1$ uniformly implies

$$\frac{2\pi}{N} \sum_{k=-[N/2]}^{[N/2]} w_k |\Gamma(\omega_k) - \hat{\Gamma}_0'(\omega_k)|^2 I_{NX}(\omega_k)$$

$$= \frac{2\pi}{N} \sum_{k=-[N/2]}^{[N/2]} w_k |\Gamma(\omega_k') - \hat{\Gamma}_0'(\omega_k')|^2 I_{NX}(\omega_k') + O(n/N)$$

Therefore

$$\frac{2\pi}{N} \sum_{k=-[N/2]}^{[N/2]} w_k |\Gamma(\omega_k) - \hat{\Gamma}_0(\omega_k)|^2 I_{NX}(\omega_k)$$

$$= \frac{2\pi}{N} \sum_{k=-[N/2]}^{[N/2]} w_k |\Gamma(\omega_k') - \hat{\Gamma}_0(\omega_k')|^2 I_{NX}(\omega_k') + O(n/N)$$

$$\geq \frac{2\pi}{N} \sum_{k=-[N/2]}^{[N/2]} w_k |\Gamma(\omega_k') - \hat{\Gamma}_0'(\omega_k')|^2 I_{NX}(\omega_k') + O(n/N)$$

$$= \frac{2\pi}{N} \sum_{k=-[N/2]}^{[N/2]} w_k |\Gamma(\omega_k) - \hat{\Gamma}_0'(\omega_k)|^2 I_{NX}(\omega_k) + O(n/N)$$

$$\geq \frac{2\pi}{N} \sum_{k=-[N/2]}^{[N/2]} w_k |\Gamma(\omega_k) - \hat{\Gamma}_0(\omega_k)|^2 I_{NX}(\omega_k) + O(n/N)$$

where the inequalities are direct consequences of the definition of $\hat{\Gamma}_0(\cdot)$ and $\hat{\Gamma}_0'(\cdot)$. This completes the proof of the proposition. $\square$

Both solutions are (almost) identical under regularity assumptions. The filter $\hat{\Gamma}_0'(\cdot)$ is preferred because poles are 'tracked' in (6.15). Therefore, unstable designs are avoided.

An alternative to definition 6.14 is

$$I_{NX}(\omega_k') := \begin{cases} \dfrac{(\omega_k' - \omega_k)I_{NX}(\omega_{k+1}) + (\omega_{k+1} - \omega_k')I_{NX}(\omega_k)}{2\pi/N}, & \lambda > \omega_k \\ \dfrac{(\omega_k - \omega_k')I_{NX}(\omega_{k-1}) + (\omega_k' - \omega_{k-1})I_{NX}(\omega_k)}{2\pi/N}, & else \end{cases}$$

but this would lead to unnecessary additional algorithmic complexity, since not only the frequencies but also the periodogram would become a function of the filter coefficients.

The new frequency ordinates ω_k' are functions of the filter parameters. This may have incidences on the numerical optimization algorithm. Steepest-gradient or Newton-Raphson algorithms usually speed up the search. Unfortunately, (6.13) is a discontinuous function of λ (the argument of the pole). Therefore, (6.13) is replaced by a more regular (twice differentiable) function such as

$$\omega_k' := \begin{cases} \omega_k & \lambda \notin \,]\omega_k - k\pi/N - \epsilon, \omega_k + k\pi/N + \epsilon] \\ \omega_k + (\lambda - \omega_k)f(\lambda) & \lambda \in \,]\omega_k - k\pi/N - \epsilon, \omega_k - k\pi/N] \\ \lambda & \lambda \in \,]\omega_k - k\pi/N, \omega_k + k\pi/N] \\ \omega_k + (\lambda - \omega_k)g(\lambda) & \lambda \in \,]\omega_k + k\pi/N, \omega_k + k\pi/N + \epsilon] \end{cases} \qquad (6.18)$$

where ϵ is an arbitrarily small real number and $f(\lambda)$, $g(\lambda)$ generate 'smooth' (twice differentiable) transitions $\omega_k \to \lambda$ and $\lambda \to \omega_k$. Therefore, $f(\cdot)$ must satisfy:

$$f(\lambda) = \begin{cases} 0 & \lambda = \omega_k - k\pi/N - \epsilon \\ 1 & \lambda = \omega_k - k\pi/N \end{cases}$$

$$f'(\lambda) = \begin{cases} 0 & \lambda = \omega_k - k\pi/N - \epsilon \\ 0 & \lambda = \omega_k - k\pi/N \end{cases}$$

where $f'(\cdot)$ is the derivative of $f(\cdot)$ (analogous conditions must hold for $g(\cdot)$). An infinitely often differentiable solution is for example given by

$$f(\lambda) := \exp\left(1 + \frac{1}{r(\lambda)(r(\lambda) - 2)}\right) \qquad (6.19)$$

where $r(\lambda) := \dfrac{\lambda - \omega_k + k\pi/N + \epsilon}{\epsilon}$. For defining $g(\lambda)$, simply replace $r(\lambda)$ by $q(\lambda) := \dfrac{\omega_k - \lambda + k\pi/N + \epsilon}{\epsilon}$ in (6.19).

Until yet the variable frequency ordinates ω_k' 'track' a pole $P_\lambda := |P_\lambda| \exp(i\lambda)$ irrespectively of the modulus $|P_\lambda|$. This is not always necessary, especially if $|P_\lambda|$ is 'significantly' larger than 1 i.e. if the pole is sufficiently far away from the unit disk. Hence, the new frequency function ω_k'', say, should become a function of λ if and only if $|P_\lambda| < 1 + \epsilon$, where ϵ is some positive real number. Consequently, ω_k'' now becomes a function of the argument as well as of the modulus $|P_\lambda|$. A straightforward smooth (infinitely often differentiable) generalization of (6.18) is then given by

$$\omega_k'' := \begin{cases} \omega_k & |P_\lambda| > 1 + \epsilon + \delta \\ \omega_k + (\omega_k' - \omega_k)f_2(|P_\lambda|) & 1 + \epsilon < |P_\lambda| \leq 1 + \epsilon + \delta \\ \omega_k' & else \end{cases} \qquad (6.20)$$

where

$$f_2(|P_\lambda|) := \exp\left(1 + \frac{1}{r_2(|P_\lambda|)(r_2(|P_\lambda|) - 2)}\right)$$

and $r_2(|P_\lambda|) := \dfrac{1 - |P_\lambda| + \epsilon + \delta}{\delta}$. The newly defined frequency ordinates ω_k'' track poles if and only if the latter become 'nearly unstable', where the parameter ϵ defines 'near instability'. For many practical applications $\epsilon := 0.1$ may be chosen for example. The new optimization criterion is then given by replacing Ω_N by $\Omega_N'' := \{\omega_k'' || k| \leq [N/2]\}$ in (5.19).

In this chapter, finite sample methods were presented for solving the overfitting problem. They supplement the asymptotic results obtained in the preceding chapter. As a complement to the proposed theory, empirical results are presented in the last two chapters. First, the MBA and the DFA are compared for various simulated input processes. Then the performances of both methods are assessed using empirical time series. In chapter 7 both approaches are compared with respect to the mean square error criterion. In chapter 8 the methods are compared with respect to their ability to discover turning points towards the boundary of a sample.

Part II

Empirical Results

7

Empirical Comparisons : Mean Square Performance

7.1 General Framework

In the following two chapters model-based estimates (of a signal) are compared to estimates obtained by the DFA. In this chapter, attention is given to the performance as measured by the revision error variance: the smaller the variance, the better the method.

Simulated examples and a 'real-world' time series are examined. For the former, the experimental design is set up such that MBA-estimates are also maximum likelihood estimates. For the 'real-world' time series the MBA is based on TRAMO (release November 1999, see Maravall and Gomez [64]) and Census X-12-ARIMA (release version 0.2.8, see Findley et al. [32]). The DFA is based on solutions of

$$\min_{\hat{\Gamma}} \frac{2\pi}{N} \sum_{k=-[N/2]}^{[N/2]} |\Delta\Gamma(\omega_k)|^2 I_{NX}(\omega_k) \qquad (7.1)$$

(for stationary input signals, see (5.19)) or on solutions of

$$\min_{\hat{\Gamma}_C} \frac{2\pi}{N} \sum_{k=-[N/2]}^{[N/2]} |\Delta\tilde{\Gamma}(\omega_k)|^2 I_{N\tilde{X}}(\omega_k) \qquad (7.2)$$

(for integrated input processes, see (5.36)), where $\hat{\Gamma}_C$ is a constrained filter (a complete description is given below).

For notational convenience and to save space the analysis is restricted to *boundary* signal estimates only, i.e. $r = 0$ in (3.6). For $r = 0$ the estimation problem is most difficult since the approximating filters are completely asymmetric.

The methods are compared with respect to true revision error variances (for the simulated series) and with respect to estimated revision error variances (for both the simulated series and the 'real-world' time series). The following revision error variance estimates are used.

- For both approaches:
  - *sample estimates*:

$$\frac{1}{N - 2M} \sum_{t=M+1}^{N-M} (\hat{Y}_t^N - \hat{Y}_t^t)^2 \tag{7.3}$$

  where $\hat{Y}_t^t$ is the output of the asymmetric filter (which is based on $X_1, ..., X_t$, i.e. $r = 0$) and $\hat{Y}_t^N$ is the output of an 'almost' symmetric filter (which is based on the whole sample $X_1, ..., X_N$). If M is sufficiently large, then $\hat{Y}_t^N$ is a 'good' estimate of the unknown signal Y_t for $t = M + 1, ..., N - M$: a precise statement is given below.
  - *'frequency estimates'* as given by the expressions (7.1) or (7.2). Note that frequency estimates can be computed for the MBA too, since $\Delta\Gamma(\cdot)$ can be computed from knowledge of AR- and MA-parameters of the model.
- For the MBA only:
  - the expression

$$\sigma^2 \sum_{k=-\infty}^{-1} \left(\sum_{j=0}^{\infty} b_j \gamma_{k-j} \right)^2 \tag{7.4}$$

  see (2.26). In the latter case, infinite sums are always 'conveniently' truncated and unknown true parameters (σ^2 and b_j) are replaced by estimates (γ_k are known since they correspond to the symmetric extraction filter).

Seasonally adjusted time series (defined by the canonical decomposition of the airline-model, see section 2.3.2) and trends define the signals. The trend of the canonical decomposition is used. However, since this signal is based on a particular model-based approach (implemented in TRAMO/SEATS), the corresponding estimation routine is possibly favored (when compared to X-12-ARIMA for example). Therefore, another trend signal is considered here which does not 'favor' a particular approach. The transfer function of the symmetric filter is defined by

$$\Gamma(\omega) := \begin{cases} 1 & 0 \leq |\omega| \leq \pi/9 \\ \dfrac{\pi/7 - |\omega|}{\pi/7 - \pi/9} & \pi/9 \leq |\omega| \leq \pi/7 \\ 0 & \pi/7 \leq |\omega| \leq \pi \end{cases} \tag{7.5}$$

whose Fourier coefficients are

$$\gamma_k = \begin{cases} -\dfrac{1}{\pi(\pi/7 - \pi/9)} \left[\dfrac{\cos(k\pi/7) - \cos(k\pi/9)}{k^2} \right] & k \neq 0 \\ \dfrac{1}{2}\left(\dfrac{1}{7} + \dfrac{1}{9}\right) & \text{else} \end{cases} \tag{7.6}$$

This trend filter does neither 'favor' a particular MBA nor the DFA. It does not affect components with frequencies smaller than $\pi/9$ and eliminates completely components corresponding to frequencies greater than $\pi/7$ (for example seasonal components of a monthly time series). If 'smooth' signals are of interest, the above filter may be considered as 'ideal' since its output is not affected by 'high frequency' components. It can be verified (numerically) that

$$\sum_{k=1}^{30} \gamma_k^2 / \sum_{k=1}^{\infty} \gamma_k^2 > 0.997 \tag{7.7}$$

which shows that a truncated filter (of length $2 \times 30 + 1 = 61$) is very close to the 'ideal' filter (which is of infinite length). In the following, the finite approximation is normalized:

$$T_t := \sum_{k=-30}^{30} \gamma_k' X_{t-k} \tag{7.8}$$

where $\gamma_k' := \gamma_k / \sum_{k=-30}^{30} \gamma_k$ are the (normalized) Fourier coefficients of the transfer function

$$\Gamma'(\omega) := \sum_{k=-30}^{30} \gamma_k' \exp(-ik\omega) \tag{7.9}$$

Although the truncated filter does not eliminate all high frequency components, the damping is so strong the attribute 'ideal' is still justified. Note that T_t can be computed for finite samples (whose length exceed 60) and that the corresponding transfer function belongs to C_f^∞. Therefore, the regularity assumptions required by the theoretical results presented in the last chapters are satisfied. Moreover, one can set $M := 30$ in (7.3).

For the DFA, parsimonious QMP-ZPC-filter designs are used (recall section 3.3). The exact parameterization of the filters is described in the corresponding sections.

In section 7.2, different simulation experiments are analyzed. They confirm theoretical results obtained in preceding chapters and illustrate various issues related to overfitting and misspecification of integration orders. Results for a 'real-world' series are presented in section 7.3.

7.2 A Simulation Study

Airline-models are very often selected by TRAMO (and often by X-12-ARIMA) for modelling 'real-world' time series. Since these procedures are widely used for 'extracting' (estimating) signals, a corresponding simulation experiment is proposed in the first section. However, I(2)-processes (assumed by the airline-model) are not always 'well-suited' for modelling economic time series (as shown below, I(2)-processes assume 'strong' trends which are unlikely to be observed in practice). Therefore, other models (assuming I(1)- and I(0)-processes) are analyzed also in the following sections. The various experiments are designed in such a way that the MBA provides maximum likelihood estimates of the signal. The results indicate that the DFA performs as well as the maximum likelihood method if all the unit-roots are correctly accounted for by the constraints (5.22). Otherwise, misspecification is quantified empirically. Particular forms of misspecification reveal the 'robustness' of the proposed DFA. In this section, the 'test-signal' T_t is given by (7.8) which does not favor a particular approach.

7.2.1 Airline-Model

The present simulation experiment is based on the following 'design':

- Generate 100 replications of length $N = 1234$ of the process

$$(1 - B)(1 - B^{12})X_t = (1 - 0.6B)(1 - 0.5B)\epsilon_t \qquad (7.10)$$

with standard normal distributed error terms. The process is 'initialized' by setting $X_0 = .. = X_{-12} = 0$. The first 1000 sample values are discarded. The remaining sample $X_{1001}, ..., X_{1234}$ is used for the simulation experiment, which is denoted by $X_1, ..., X_{234}$. The data are generated using RATS (Regression Analysis of Time Series), version 5.1.
- Compute the boundary filters (for more details see below) of the MBA and the DFA using a subsample of length $N = 180$ (15 years) and collect 'in sample' results for $t = 112, ..., 180$ (the first 111 values are retained for avoiding initialization problems of the filters of the MBA and the DFA: this is probably excessively large but it ensures that initialization problems are not confounded with estimation issues). Compute out of sample performances for $t = 181, ..., 204$. The remaining values for $t = 205, ..., 234$ are used for implementing the symmetric (truncated) extraction filter (7.8).
- Compute the revision error variance estimates (sample variances, frequency estimates and model based estimates, see the preceding section) and compare their average value (over the 100 realizations) 'in-' and 'out of sample' with the known true revision error variance.

The boundary filters are computed as follows. For the MBA, the parameters of the model are estimated using the *true model* (no model identification) by unconditional maximum likelihood. This can be achieved by transforming the model into a state space form (using the procedure DLM -Dynamic Linear Models- of RATS for example) and initializing the Kalman-filter recursions by the first two unconditional moments (of the differenced stationary process).

Therefore, the resulting filter outputs $\hat{Y}_t$ of the MBA are maximum likelihood estimates. This is because estimated model parameters are maximum likelihood estimates and because the maximum likelihood estimate of a (well behaved) function of the parameters (such as the signal estimate) is simply the value of this function obtained for the maximum likelihood parameter estimate i.e. $f(\hat{\theta}_{ML})$ is the maximum likelihood estimate of $f(\theta)$.

For the DFA, three different filter designs are proposed. Two of them correspond to particular misspecifications of the integration order.

- The first estimate (estimate I) is the output of the solution of (7.1). By purpose, it is erroneously assumed that X_t is a stationary input signal (misspecification of order two of the true integration order).
- Estimate II is the output of the solution of (7.2). More precisely, it is assumed that

$$\tilde{X}_t = (1 - B^{12})X_t \qquad (7.11)$$

(which implies first order conditions $\hat{\Gamma}(j\pi/6) = \Gamma(j\pi/6), j = 0, ..., 6$ in (5.22)). This is misspecified too.

- Estimate III is the output of the solution of (7.2) where it is assumed that

$$\tilde{X}_t = (1 - B)(1 - B^{12})X_t$$

Therefore a *second order* condition at frequency zero (as proposed in (5.34)) together with first order conditions $\hat{\Gamma}(j\pi/6) = \Gamma(j\pi/6), j = 1, ..., 6$ in (5.22) are considered for this correctly specified design.

The corresponding filters are parameterized as follows:

- For estimate I, seven zero-pole-pairs (plus complex conjugate pairs) are used, which amounts to $7 \times 3 + 1 = 22$ parameters. Six zero-pole pairs can account for the six seasonal spectral peaks (six peaks for monthly data) and the remaining zero-pole pair can adapt for the spectral mass at frequency zero.
- For estimate II, seven zero-pole pairs are used also (plus complex conjugate pairs) but 13 degrees of freedom are lost because of the constraints $\hat{\Gamma}(j\pi/6) = \Gamma(j\pi/6)$ for $j = 0, ..., 6$ implied by (5.22). Specifically, it is assumed that $\hat{\Gamma}(0) = \Gamma(0) = 1$ and that $\hat{\Gamma}(j\pi/6) = 0$ for $j = 1, ..., 6$ (note that the latter condition is satisfied exactly by (7.5) but it is satisfied only approximately by (7.9): in the following this is neglected because the damping of (7.9) is very strong). The latter constraints require $Z_j = \exp(-ij\pi/6)$, $j = 1, ..., 6$, which determines the argument *and* the modulus of the corresponding zeroes. The first condition corresponds to a normalization so that only one degree of freedom is lost.
- For estimate III, seven zero-pole pairs are used but 14 degrees of freedom are lost (12 for the seasonal unit-roots and two for the order two constraint at frequency zero implied by (5.22)).

For the DFA, all filter designs are more or less heavily overparameterized : the experiments reveal the effect of this overparameterization on the estimates as measured 'out of sample'. In fact, the true structure (assuming two degrees of freedom only) is not assumed to be known exactly here. Therefore, a flexible filter design is required which is able to handle potentially more complex tasks. If the more general (overparameterized) filters perform well, then good results are to be expected for 'non-artificial' data too.

Table 7.1 summarizes the performances of the various approaches (the values in parentheses are empirical standard errors). The top-left $\sigma^2 = 0.132$

Table 7.1.

$\sigma^2 = 0.132$	$\hat{\sigma}^2_{is}$	$\hat{\sigma}^2_{os}$	$\hat{\sigma}^2_{ep}$	$\overline{|\sigma^2 - \hat{\sigma}^2|}$
MBA	0.136(0.0043)	0.126(0.0078)	0.121(0.012)	0.026(0.0022)
DFA III	0.132(0.0042)	0.129(0.0072)	0.118(0.012)	0.025 (0.0021)
DFA II (unadjusted)	0.182(0.0053)	0.172(0.010)	0.163(0.018)	0.045 (0.0051)
DFA II (adjusted)	0.161(0.005)	0.157(0.003)	0.145(0.011)	0.041 (0.0023)
DFA I (unadjusted)	6.732(0.457)	7.062(0.464)	6.160(0.800)	35.59 (4.42)
DFA I (adjusted)	0.288(0.0163)	0.274(0.0188)	0.259(0.045)	0.099 (0.0158)

in this table indicates the theoretical revision error variance (obtained by the optimal filter based on the true DGP). The columns '$\hat{\sigma}^2_{is}$' and '$\hat{\sigma}^2_{os}$' are sample revision error variances (7.3) 'in' and 'out of sample'. The column '$\hat{\sigma}^2_{ep}$' is the mean of $(\hat{Y}_{180} - Y_{180})^2$ over the 100 replications (it is thus an estimate of the revision error at the 'end point' $t = 180$). The column '$\overline{|\sigma^2 - \hat{\sigma}^2|}$' is defined as follows

- for the MBA and the DFA III the values correspond to the mean (over the 100 replications) of the absolute differences between the theoretical revision error variance (0.132) and the estimates (7.2) (for the DFA III) and (7.4) (for the MBA). For the DFA III the resulting error term corresponds to R_N in theorem 5.3 or, more precisely, to R_N in corollary 5.4 (the error term after minimization).

- for the misspecified DFA II and DFA I the values in the last column correspond to the mean (over the 100 replications) of the absolute differences between the sample revision error variances (7.3) and the 'frequency estimates' (7.1) (for the DFA I) or (7.2) (for the DFA II). Therefore the error term corresponds to r_N in proposition 5.2. Measuring deviations of the frequency estimates (7.1) and (7.2) from $\sigma^2 = 0.132$ would be misleading here, because the filter designs are misspecified, i.e. the corresponding (unknown) true revision error variances are larger than 0.132.

Remarks

- The estimation at the end point has been considered in a separate (third) column because the end point is a particular 'in sample' observation: parameter estimates (of the model) and periodograms cannot account for 'future' observations at the end point. Therefore, this situation reflects more precisely what happens in practice (when estimating a signal for the end point $t = N$). As can be seen, the results are not significantly different from 'in sample' results. Evidently, the variance of the estimate is larger because only one observation is available for each replication.
- A confirmation of the efficiency (or not) of the DFA can be obtained from the last column. The DFA aims at the minimization of an estimate of the revision error variance. The performance of the DFA thus depends on the performance of this estimate. The fourth column reports the latter performance.

The results obtained in table 7.1 are now briefly commented. None of the above differences between the MBA and the DFA (estimate III) are significant at a standard 5% level. Out of sample results are stable: they are even slightly (although not significantly) better than 'in sample' results. The last column for estimate III shows that the 'frequency estimate' of the revision error variance is efficient (at least as efficient as the maximum likelihood estimate of the MBA), as was shown in section 5.5. Therefore, the DFA (estimate III) makes sense since it minimizes an efficient estimate of the revision error variance. Note that both methods significantly outperform the 'misspecified' DFA designs (at a 5% level).

Both DFA II (adjusted and unadjusted) perform significantly worse than the preceding two approaches. The loss in accuracy or equivalently the increase of the revision error variance (estimates) is approximately 20% . This increase is mainly due to a non-vanishing time delay at frequency zero (which is about 0.06 time units in the mean over all realizations). The DFA II adjusted performs slightly better than the DFA II unadjusted. The periodogram of the former is based on the series

$$X_t'' := X_t - \frac{t}{12}\Big(\overline{\Delta_{12}Y} - \frac{N-1}{2}\overline{\Delta_{12}\Delta Y}\Big) - \Big(\frac{t^2}{24} + \frac{t}{2}\Big)(\overline{\Delta_{12}\Delta Y})$$

see (4.45) (adjustment of order two).

DFA I involves 22 parameters which may lead to problems for the numerical optimization algorithm. In fact, results for DFA I are not always reliable in the sense that the performance of the numerical optimization used for the above experiments depends on initial values: depending on which values are used, the optimization may 'stop' at different local minima. Alternative algorithms searching for the global minimum could be used instead (for example 'genetic' search) but they would be much more time consuming. In order to focus on the statistical problem (rather than numerical issues) the numerical optimization algorithm for DFA I is initialized by solutions obtained for DFA II or DFA III (this method is used for all simulation experiments). The latter are 'reliable' in the sense that corresponding solutions do not appear to depend on particular initial values.

The last two rows of table 7.1 show results for the DFA I which is based on the periodogram of the 'untransformed' X_t (estimate I unadjusted) and on the periodogram of

$$X_t'' := X_t - \frac{t}{12}\left(\overline{\Delta_{12}Y} - \frac{N-1}{2}\overline{\Delta_{12}\Delta Y}\right) - \left(\frac{t^2}{24} + \frac{t}{2}\right)(\overline{\Delta_{12}\Delta Y})$$

see (4.45) (estimate I adjusted). The unadjusted periodogram is subject to a 'misspecification' of integration order two which explains the poorer performances of estimate I (recall the bias problem analyzed in section 4.3.2). The periodogram of the adjusted series satisfies

$$I_{N+1X''}(\omega_k) = \frac{I_{N+1\tilde{X}}(\omega_k)}{|1 - \exp(-i\omega_k)|^4} \text{ if } \omega_k \neq j\pi/6 , \ j = 0,...,6 \quad (7.12)$$

where $\tilde{X}_t$ is the differenced stationary process, see (4.44) (note that $I_{N+1X''}(0) = 0$ has been replaced by $\frac{N+1}{2\pi}\overline{X}^2$, see the corresponding remark on p.90). The filter estimates of the 'adjusted' series perform significantly better because $I_{N+1X''}(\omega_k)$ is approximately an unbiased estimate of the pseudo spectral density of the process X_t (for $\omega_k \neq j\pi/6$, $j = 0,...,6$). Comparing (5.37) and (7.12) shows that estimate III corresponds to a constrained estimate I (adjusted case). The former is less heavily overparameterized and it accounts exactly for all unit-roots (i.e. the conditions (5.22) are satisfied). Therefore, the difference between the performances of both methods (about 50% decrease of the revision error variance) is roughly what can be gained here by imposing (5.22). Note that this result depends on the experimental design: in particular the initialization length 1000 is important here because the realizations of the I(2)-process are already strongly 'trending', see for example figure 7.2 below. For shorter initialization lengths the differences between DFA I, DFA II and DFA III become less pronounced.

Consider the following realizations of the airline model (7.10) as shown in figures 7.1 and 7.2. For both realizations initial values were set to zero i.e. $X_{-M} = ... = X_{-M-11} = 0$. The first one assumes $M = 0$ (fig.7.1) and for the second one the initialization length is $M = 1000$ (fig. 7.2). Evidently, the shape ('mean slope') of the realizations heavily depends on M : this effect is due to the integration order two of the process. The length $M = 1000$ corresponds to an effective duration of 1000 months which is approximately 80 years. If models with a double unit-root (at frequency zero) were a good approximation of the DGP of economic time series (as suggested by software packages

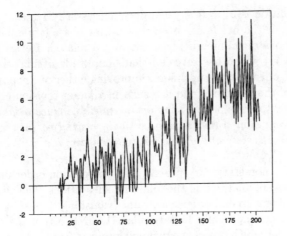

Fig. 7.1. Initialization with $M = 0$

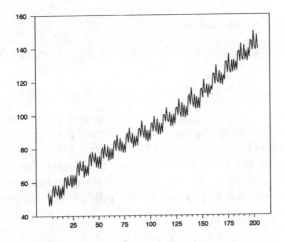

Fig. 7.2. Initialization with $M = 1000$

like TRAMO or X-12-ARIMA) then many economic time series should 'look' similarly to the realization in fig.7.2. However, this seems not to be the case. Note also that a 'preliminary' signal extraction for the second graph could be done fairly easily by fitting a straight line: in fact, 'turning-points' become very rare as the initialization length M increases.

Recall that the second order condition at frequency zero is $\hat{\phi}(0) = 0$ (the first order being $\hat{A}(0) = A(0) = 1$). It has been shown in theorem 5.5 that this is not only a sufficient but also a necessary condition. The reason is that the slope i.e. the first differences of an I(2)-process (with a double unit-root at frequency zero) grows unboundedly in absolute value. However, this 'strong' trending behavior cannot often be observed for 'real-world' time series. Therefore, the condition $\hat{\phi}(0) = 0$ is generally unnecessarily restrictive. Does this condition impair the fit? It has been shown that phase (time delay) and amplitude functions of minimum phase filters are related. Recall in particular expression (5.40) which has revealed that 'amplitude fitting' and 'phase fitting' are antagonistic in the optimum: improving either one is possible only at the expense of the other one and it results in a larger revision error variance. Therefore, it is to be expected that *airline models induce asymmetric filters satisfying a condition which is unnecessarily restrictive (at least for many 'real-world' time series) and which generally impairs the fit.*

Therefore, a non-stationary process with integration order one and a stationary process are analyzed in the following subsections. The effect of unnecessarily imposing a second order constraint (vanishing time shift at frequency zero) is quantified empirically. In particular, the first section analyzes a 'quasi-airline model' for which one of the two unit-roots at frequency zero is replaced by the stationary root $1 - 0.95B$.

7.2.2 'Quasi'-Airline Model

The general experimental 'design' remains unchanged except for the model which is now

$$(1 - 0.95B)(1 - B^{12})X_t = (1 - 0.6B)(1 - 0.5B)\epsilon_t \qquad (7.13)$$

i.e. the unit-root $1 - B$ is replaced by a stationary root $1 - 0.95B$. Parameters are estimated using the true model, so that three parameters must be estimated: the AR(1)- and the two MA-parameters (estimating airline-models would often result in non-invertible MA-terms generating forecasting difficulties). The results obtained for 100 replications are summarized in table 7.2. The various approaches DFA I to DFA III (adjusted or unadjusted) are de-

Table 7.2.

$\sigma^2 = 0.120$	$\hat{\sigma}_{is}^2$	$\hat{\sigma}_{os}^2$	$\hat{\sigma}_{ep}^2$	$\overline{\sigma^2 - \hat{\sigma}^2}$
MBA	0.123(0.0036)	0.126(0.0075)	0.128(0.012)	0.0253(0.0015)
DFA III	0.128(0.0043)	0.132(0.0085)	0.135(0.015)	0.0264 (0.0021)
DFA II (unadjusted)	0.125(0.0037)	0.128(0.0051)	0.123(0.015)	0.0242 (0.0017)
DFA II (adjusted)	0.128(0.0041)	0.128(0.0078)	0.125(0.017)	0.0252 (0.0022)
DFA I (unadjusted)	0.564(0.0463)	0.561(0.0505)	0.644(0.092)	0.358 (0.043)
DFA I (adjusted)	0.171(0.0067)	0.166(0.01)	0.172(0.018)	0.074 (0.005)

fined in the previous section. Their relative performances illustrate the effects of various filter designs (accounting for particular unit-roots) on the revision error variance. The top-left $\sigma^2 = 0.120$ is the theoretical revision error variance (for the asymmetric filter based on the true DGP). For model (7.13) the

DFA II (unadjusted) is correctly specified whereas DFA II (adjusted), DFA III (integration order two) and DFA I (stationary case) are 'misspecified'. None of the differences between the MBA and the DFA II are significant (at 'reasonable' significance levels). Comparing DFA II (unadjusted) and MBA for the last column of the above table shows that the frequency estimate (7.2) is an efficient estimate of the theoretical revision error variance (which again justifies the DFA).

The adjustment of order two for the DFA II (adjusted) is too strong since the integration order of the process is one only. The 'overadjustment' effect has been analyzed in section 4.3.2. Figure 7.3 shows a particular realization of the process (7.13) (dotted line, initialization length=1000) and its adjustment

$$X_t'' := X_t - \frac{t}{12}\Big(\overline{\Delta_{12}Y} - \frac{N-1}{2}\overline{\Delta_{12}\Delta Y}\Big) - \Big(\frac{t^2}{24} + \frac{t}{2}\Big)(\overline{\Delta_{12}\Delta Y})$$

(solid line), see (4.45). As can be seen by comparing the periodograms in fig.7.4

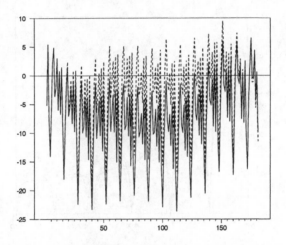

Fig. 7.3. Original (dotted) and adjusted (solid) series

the adjustment (of order two) induces spurious spectral power towards the low frequencies. Therefore, the low frequency content of the signal is overestimated and the time shift (delay) of the corresponding 'optimal' asymmetric filter (at frequency zero) is unnecessarily reduced. The DFA III (unnecessarily) constrains the time shift (delay) of the resulting filter to vanish at frequency zero.

Figures 7.5 and 7.6 compare amplitude and time shift functions of DFA II unadjusted (short marks), DFA II adjusted (long marks) and of DFA III (solid line) for a particular realization. The time shift of the (optimal) DFA II unadjusted is largest at frequency zero (about 2.8 time units) and the time shift of DFA II is larger than that of DFA III towards the low frequencies. Also, an

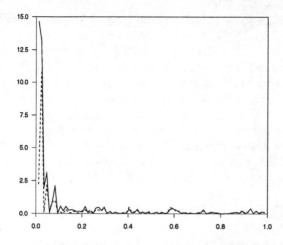

V

Fig. 7.4. Periodogram : adjusted (solid) and unadjusted (dotted)

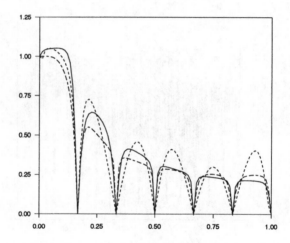

Fig. 7.5. Amplitude functions DFA II's and DFA III

examination of the amplitude function of DFA II reveals that the corresponding filter removes more power at seasonal frequencies (wider troughs). Despite these differences, the results in table 7.2 suggest that the described approaches perform quite similarly. This is because the stationary root is close to the unit-root. However, it is interesting to note in this example the impact of 'small' differences of a particular model parameter on the relative performances of the various filter designs (when compared to the preceding airline-model).

The last two rows show the performance of the DFA I estimates. DFA I unadjusted performs poorly because the stationary AR-root $1 - 0.95B$ is close to a unit-root. Therefore, the process is 'almost' I(2) which implies that the periodogram of the unadjusted series is strongly biased, see section 4.3.2. DFA

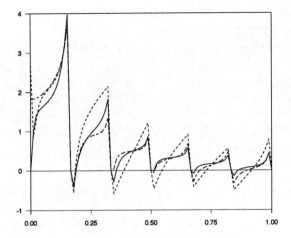

Fig. 7.6. Time shifts DFA II's and DFA III

I adjusted underestimates the spectral power at frequency zero (no unit-root is imposed at frequency zero). The loss in performance is about 30% (increase of revision error variance).

In the last two simulation experiments, the performances of the various filter designs are analyzed for particular stationary input signals. A quantification of the overadjustment effect and of the unnecessarily severe first and second order conditions (5.22) is provided for the particular examples chosen there.

7.2.3 Stationary Input Signals

The experimental design is still the same as in the preceding two sections except for the chosen input signals. The first stationary signal is generated by

$$(1 - 0.9B^{12})X_t = \epsilon_t \tag{7.14}$$

Parameters are estimated using the true model. The results obtained for 100 replications are summarized in the following table 7.3. MBA, DFA I (unadjusted) and DFA II (unadjusted) perform best. DFA III is significantly worse (at 5%) and the performances of DFA I (adjusted) and DFA II (adjusted) are in between. Imposing a second order constraint (vanishing time shift at frequency zero) results in a 25% increase of the revision error variance when compared to the best methods. Similarly, a second order adjustment as in DFA II 'adjusted' results in a 20% increase of the revision error variance. Obviously, the adjustment of order two is too strong, since the process is stationary. Figure 7.7 shows a particular realization of the process (7.14) (dotted line, initialization length=1000) and the adjusted series

Table 7.3.

$\sigma^2 = 0.0423$	$\hat{\sigma}_{is}^2$	$\hat{\sigma}_{os}^2$	$\hat{\sigma}_{ep}^2$	$\overline{\sigma^2 - \hat{\sigma}^2}$
MBA	0.040(0.0020)	0.046(0.0035)	0.043(0.0049)	0.0115 (0.0010)
DFA III	0.054(0.0022)	0.053(0.0042)	0.061(0.0071)	0.0126 (0.0011)
DFA II (unadjusted)	0.043(0.0017)	0.044(0.0031)	0.040(0.0051)	0.0111 (0.0010)
DFA II (adjusted)	0.051(0.0021)	0.047(0.0033)	0.049(0.0064)	0.0118 (0.0010)
DFA I (unadjusted)	0.041(0.0016)	0.041(0.0029)	0.047(0.0051)	0.0108 (0.0010)
DFA I (adjusted)	0.047(0.0018)	0.046(0.0032)	0.046(0.0057)	0.0118 (0.0013)

$$X_t'' := X_t - \frac{t}{12}\left(\overline{\Delta_{12}Y} - \frac{N-1}{2}\overline{\Delta_{12}\Delta Y}\right) - \left(\frac{t^2}{24} + \frac{t}{2}\right)(\overline{\Delta_{12}\Delta Y})$$

(solid line), see (4.45). As can be seen by comparing the periodograms in

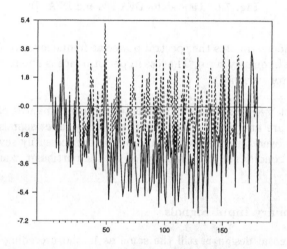

Fig. 7.7. Original (dotted) and adjusted (solid) series

fig.7.8 the adjustment (of order two) induces spurious spectral power at the lowest frequency ω_1 $(I_{NX''}(\omega_1) \simeq 14$ and $I_{NX}(\omega_1) \simeq 0.5$). Therefore, the low frequency content of the signal is overestimated and the time shift (delay) of the optimized filter at frequency zero is unnecessarily small. A comparison of the values in the last column of table 7.3 shows that 'frequency estimates' (as given by (7.1) and (7.2)) of all approaches except DFA III are 'almost' efficient (since their performances are comparable to the model-based maximum likelihood estimate).

The last experiment is based on the AR(1)-process

$$(1 - 0.6B)X_t = \epsilon_t \qquad\qquad (7.15)$$

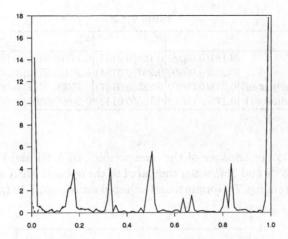

Fig. 7.8. Periodogram : adjusted (solid) and unadjusted (dotted)

Parameters are estimated using the true model, as in preceding sections. The results obtained over 100 replications are summarized in table 7.4.

Table 7.4.

$\sigma^2 = 0.182$	$\hat{\sigma}^2_{is}$	$\hat{\sigma}^2_{os}$	$\hat{\sigma}^2_{ep}$	$\overline{\sigma^2 - \hat{\sigma}^2}$
MBA	0.181(0.0088)	0.188(0.0154)	0.176(0.0226)	0.0677 (0.0059)
DFA III	0.243(0.0099)	0.257(0.0184)	0.234(0.0340)	0.0573 (0.0055)
DFA II (unadjusted)	0.218(0.0099)	0.230(0.0167)	0.253(0.0312)	0.0566 (0.0052)
DFA I (unadjusted)	0.179(0.0090)	0.195(0.0149)	0.208(0.0301)	0.0548 (0.0050)

The loss in performance of the 'misspecified' DFA III and DFA II is approximately 35% and 25% when compared to the optimal MBA and DFA I. It can be seen from figs.7.9 (original and adjusted series) and 7.10 (periodograms

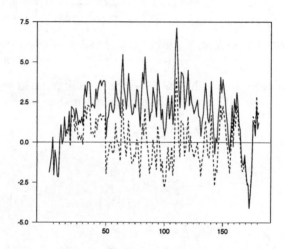

Fig. 7.9. Original (dotted) and adjusted (solid) series

of adjusted and unadjusted series) that the adjustment of order two unnecessarily induces variance or equivalently spurious spectral power (at the lowest frequency ω_1) for a particular realization of (7.15). Similarly, it is shown in figs.7.11 and 7.12 that an (unnecessary) adjustment of order one also induces spurious spectral power for the same realization. Both results indicate that differencing is unnecessary (at least for solving the signal extraction problem for the given realization).

The results obtained so far are summarized in the last section.

7.2.4 Conclusions

- If the unit-roots are correctly accounted for by the conditions (5.22), then the DFA performs as well as the maximum likelihood estimate (given by

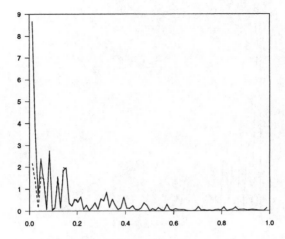

Fig. 7.10. Periodograms : original (dotted) and adjusted (solid) series

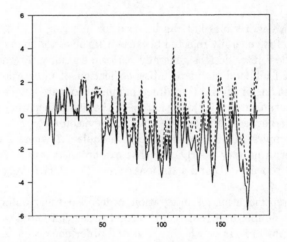

Fig. 7.11. Original (dotted) and adjusted (solid) series

the MBA). The reason for the efficiency of the DFA can be seen from the last columns of the above tables: the 'frequency estimates' (7.1) and (7.2) are efficient estimates of the revision error variance (see section 5.5). Therefore, if the numerical optimization algorithm converges to the global minimum of (7.1) or (7.2), then the DFA performs well.

• Despite a more or less pronounced overparameterization, the DFA also performs well 'out of sample'. Therefore, overfitting seems to be 'under control' for the above examples. A possible explanation for this phenomenon has been given on p.152. As a result, DFA II or DFA III designs (involving 9 and 8 parameters respectively) can often be used for 'real-world' series

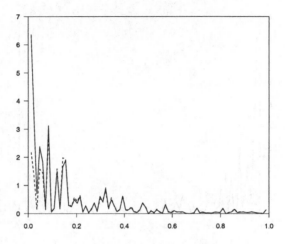

Fig. 7.12. Original (dotted) and adjusted (solid) series

too. The MC-criterion (6.5) can be used for inferring the better filter design: DFA I is generally rejected because it involves too many parameters.

• 'Misspecified' filter designs generally perform significantly worse than the maximum likelihood estimate. Misspecification of integration order one means that one or several (but different) unit-roots are ignored in the conditional optimization (7.2). In that case, the loss in accuracy generally is somewhere between 20% and 40% (of the revision error variance) for the above examples. An exception is seen in table 7.2 where DFA I 'unadjusted' performs very poorly. For that example the 'quasi' airline model has a unit-root $(1 - B)$ and a stationary root $(1 - 0.95B)$ very close to the unit circle.

For a misspecification of integration order two the results depend on whether a double unit-root, i.e. a second order constraint is ignored for an I(2) input process or whether a second order constraint is unnecessarily imposed (for example for an I(0) input process):

– In the former case, table 7.1 shows that DFA I 'unadjusted' performs markedly worse than the other methods.

– In the latter case, tables 7.3 and 7.4 show that the loss of performance of DFA III is somewhere between 30% and 40% (additional empirical evidences are given in tables 7.5, 7.6, 7.7 and 7.8 below).

• In cases of doubt (such as contradicting unit-root test results for example), one may deduce from the preceding remark that it might be preferable to account for an eventual unit-root than to ignore it. However, for finite samples the magnitude of the revision error variance depends on the length N of the sample and on the length M of the initialization phase of the process (where it is assumed that $X_{-M} = 0$ and X_1 is the first observable process value). As seen in the first example (airline model) the 'slope' of a particular realization grows unboundedly in absolute value as M increases. However, if M is small, then the second order condition $\hat{\phi}(0) = 0$ is often not stringent because the 'slope' is 'small' too. Therefore, ignoring unit-roots may be 'beneficial' for particular I(2) processes depending on N and M.

- Unit-root tests may give valuable information for imposing (or not) restrictions (5.22) for the DFA. However, conflicting evidences of different tests are often confusing for 'real-world' time series, see for example section 7.3.1. It may then be preferable to base a decision on adjusted series (and their periodograms), on the MC-criterion proposed in section 6.2 or on the test statistics (5.86) or (5.91) since these instruments are specifically designed for the DFA and the underlying signal estimation problem (see section 7.3 below for a detailed example). The reason is that model-based instruments rely on one-step ahead forecasts (for determining the DGP) whereas the proposed instruments for the DFA implicitly rely on one- and on multi-step ahead forecasts in the form required by the signal estimation problem.

- The airline-model may be misspecified for time series which are not strongly 'trending' (in the sense that their first differences are bounded for example). For such series the second order constraint $\hat{\phi}(0) = 0$ (vanishing time shift at frequency zero) is unnecessarily severe and may impair the fit of the corresponding filter output as shown in tables 7.3 and 7.4. In the next section 7.3, this statement is confirmed for a 'real-world' time series (for which different unit-root tests do not unambiguously reject the I(2)-hypothesis).

- Ignoring unit-roots (for artificially generated data) generally results in unbounded revision error variances of the resulting filter outputs for increasing sample sizes. However, the DFA is inherently 'robust' against misspecification of order one (of the integration order). As an example, consider DFA I (adjusted or unadjusted) which is optimal for stationary input signals. The proposed periodogram estimate satisfies

$$I_{NX}(0) = \frac{N}{2\pi}\overline{X}^2$$

for $\omega_0 = 0$. For an I(1)-process $\overline{X}^2$ grows linearly in N. Therefore, $I_{NX}(0)$ grows quadratically in N if X_t is an I(1)-process. As a consequence, first order constraints are satisfied for DFA I asymptotically (otherwise, if $|\hat{\Gamma}(0) - \Gamma(0)|^2 > \delta > 0$ asymptotically, then the expression (7.1) would grow unboundedly as N increases which would be a contradiction since the expression is minimized). It follows that DFA I is inherently 'robust' against I(1)-alternatives (the case of DFA II is analyzed in the remark below; robustness of DFA II against an I(2)-alternative can be seen from table 7.1). Unfortunately, second order constraints are generally not achieved for DFA I (adjusted or unadjusted) even asymptotically because the time shift is not explicitly involved in (7.1). This explains why misspecification of order two (of the integration order) may lead to poor estimates (as can be seen for DFA I in table 7.1).

- It is seen from the above tables that DFA II 'unadjusted' is particularly robust and performs well for a large class of input processes including I(0), I(1) and I(2) processes with or without stationary or non stationary seasonality. The good performance of DFA II for the I(2) process (airline model) can be explained as follows: consider the expression (5.21) for $\omega_0 = 0$ which here becomes

$$\Delta \tilde{\Gamma}(0) = \left. \frac{\frac{d}{d\omega} \Delta \Gamma(\omega)}{\frac{d}{d\omega}(1 - \exp(-i12\omega))} \right|_{\omega=0}$$

$$= \frac{-\hat{\phi}(0)}{12}$$

see for example (5.31) for the last equality and use $A(0) = 1$, $\hat{\Phi}(0) = 0$. Thus, the expression

$$\frac{2\pi}{N} |\Delta \tilde{\Gamma}(0)|^2 I_{N\tilde{X}}(0) = \frac{2\pi}{N} \left| \frac{\hat{\phi}(0)}{12} \right|^2 I_{N\tilde{X}}(0)$$

$$= \left| \frac{\hat{\phi}(0)}{12} \right|^2 \overline{\tilde{X}}^2$$

appears in (7.2) ($\overline{\tilde{X}}$ is the arithmetic mean of the I(1) process $\tilde{X}_t := X_t - X_{t-12}$). Therefore, DFA II (adjusted or unadjusted) takes the time shift at frequency zero explicitly into account. Note that $\hat{\phi}(0)$ must vanish asymptotically for DFA II, because $\overline{\tilde{X}}^2$ grows unboundedly as N increases (therefore the minimization in (7.2) implies that $\frac{2\pi}{N} |\Delta \tilde{\Gamma}(0)|^2 I_{N\tilde{X}}(0)$ must remain bounded which requires $\hat{\phi}(0) \to 0$ as $N \to \infty$). A similar analysis would reveal that the time shift of DFA II (adjusted) must vanish too asymptotically.

This concludes the analysis for simulated time series. In the next section, comparisons based on an empirical time series are presented.

7.3 'Real-World' Time Series

The (monthly) 'UK' time series (car sales from January 1985 to February 1997, $N = 146$) is shown in figure 7.13. This particular sample is chosen because the series is dominated by a strong seasonal component so that efficient filters are needed for estimating a trend or the seasonally adjusted signal. Another

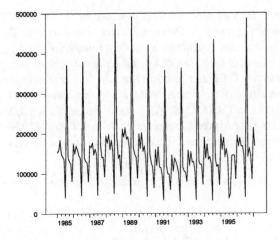

Fig. 7.13. UK-Series

reason is that the series is delivered with DEMETRA, the official seasonal adjustment 'package' of EUROSTAT (DEMETRA is a graphical interface giving access to TRAMO/SEATS and Census X-12-ARIMA, see chapter 2). Therefore, it is to be expected that the MBA as given by TRAMO or X-12-ARIMA does not perform badly for this time series.

For the DFA, the MC-statistic (6.5) selects a particular filter design, namely DFA II 'unadjusted' (see below for the corresponding realized values). This design is characterized by increased robustness against unit-root misspecification (see the simulation results in the previous section) and it is based on the solution of

$$\min_{\hat{\Gamma}_C} \frac{2\pi}{N} \sum_{k=-[N/2]}^{[N/2]} |\Delta \tilde{\Gamma}(\omega_k)|^2 I_{N\tilde{X}}(\omega_k) \qquad (7.16)$$

where $\tilde{X}_t := (1 - B^{12})X_t$ and $\hat{\Gamma}_C(\cdot)$ satisfies the first order conditions $\hat{\Gamma}_C(j\pi/6) = \Gamma(j\pi/6), j = 0, ..., 6$ in (5.22). In addition to the DFA II, a DFA III design is used to allow instructive comparisons. The latter is based on an expression similar to (7.16) (for which $\tilde{X}_t$ is replaced by $\Delta\tilde{X}_t := (1 - B)\tilde{X}_t$), with an additional second order constraint $\hat{\phi}(0) = 0$ at frequency zero (see p.107). However, the DFA III filter design is rejected by the MC-criterion in favor of DFA II, see below.

Seven zero-pole pairs (21 parameters) are used for the DFA : 13 degrees of freedom are lost for DFA II because of first order constraints at the frequencies $k\pi/6, k = 0, 1, ..., 6$ and one more degree of freedom is lost for DFA III for the second order constraint at frequency zero. The remaining degrees of freedom are sufficient to account for the width of the seasonal spectral peaks and the shape of the peak at frequency zero. Regularity of DFA-solutions is achieved by the variable frequency sampling procedure (6.20).

For the MBA, the *identification* of a 'well behaved' model becomes an important issue since the DGP is unknown (recall that corresponding issues were ignored in the simulation experiments since the true model structure was used for estimation). TRAMO/SEATS and Census X-12-ARIMA propose automatic selection procedures for choosing the 'best' model. The ARIMA models were identified and estimated by using the option 'Detailed Analysis' of DEMETRA and specifying:

- selection of the best model and maximum likelihood estimation of its parameters
- no intercept (inclusion of an intercept would result in poorer parameter estimates for the present time series)
- test for calendar effects (trading-days, Easter effect)
- inclusion of outliers (additive outliers, level shifts and transitory changes)
- test for (log) transformation.

Calendar effects were detected by TRAMO and X-12-ARIMA and the log-transform was chosen by both procedures. The input series are accordingly the *linearized* (adjusted for calendar effects and/or outliers) and *log-transformed* series because the models are identified and estimated using the corresponding transformed data sets. The transformed series are shown in figure 7.14 : a

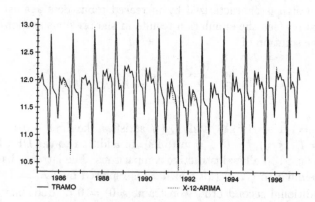

Fig. 7.14. Linearized Log-Series (TRAMO : solid, X-12-ARIMA : dotted line)

comparison with figure 7.13 shows that the original series has been adjusted for a large outlier ('missing spike') for August 1995. It can be seen from figure 7.14 that the transformations induced by TRAMO or X-12-ARIMA generate time series which are very similar. In the following, these two time series define the input signals.

In this section particular *trend estimation* and *seasonal adjustments* are analyzed for the *linearized* series. The following section analyzes the estimation of the trend defined by the filter (7.8). Model-based signals are proposed in further sections.

7.3.1 Mean-Square Approximation of the 'Ideal' Trend

It is assumed that the signal T_t is defined by the output of the (truncated) filter (7.8). This choice does not 'favor' a particular estimation method as could possibly be the case for particular model-based signals. For the series linearized by TRAMO, the model

$$(1 - B)(1 - B^{12})X_t = (1 - 0.60B)(1 - 0.27B^{12})\epsilon_t \qquad (7.17)$$

was selected and estimated (by TRAMO). For the series linearized by X-12-ARIMA, the model

$$(1 - B)(1 - B^{12})(1 + 0.57B + 0.24B^2)X_t = (1 - 0.35B^{12})\epsilon_t \quad (7.18)$$

was selected and estimated (by X-12-ARIMA). Note that the AR(2) operator of model (7.18) can be interpreted as a truncated AR(∞) representation of the MA-operator $(1 - 0.60B)$ of the airline model (7.17). The models selected and estimated by both procedures 'pass' the respective diagnostic tests: Ljung-Box and Box-Pierce for residuals and squared residuals (see for example W.Enders [29], p.87 for a description of these test statistics).

Figure 7.15 shows the periodogram of the series linearized by TRAMO. It is readily seen that the spectral peaks are of various height and width which justifies the use of individual zero-pole-pairs for each seasonal frequency. Additional and more formal evidence for choosing individual zero-pole-pairs is given by the MC-statistics (see (6.5))

$$MC(\text{DFA II}) := \frac{2\pi}{N} \sum_{k=-[N/2]}^{[N/2]} |\Gamma(\omega_k) - \hat{\Gamma}_{Qq}(\omega_k)|^2 I_{NX}(\omega_k)$$

$$+ \frac{\text{tr}\left(\hat{\mathbf{V}}_{Qq}\hat{\mathbf{U}}_{Qq}^{-1}\right)}{N - Q - q - r}$$

$$= 4.62 \times 10^{-4}$$

$$MC(\text{DFA II restricted}) = 5.02 \times 10^{-4}$$

where the zero-pole pairs of the 'DFA II restricted' are constrained to be identical for all seasonal frequencies (3 degrees of freedom left). Clearly, the less

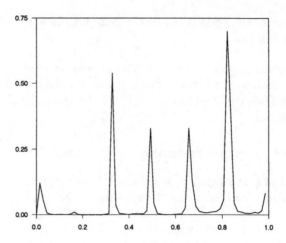

Fig. 7.15. Periodogram of linearized series

constrained DFA II is preferred by MC (similar results are obtained for the series linearized by X-12-ARIMA).

For the time series linearized by TRAMO the adjusted (dotted line) and unadjusted (solid line) time series are shown in figure 7.16. The (second order)

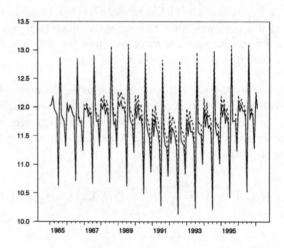

Fig. 7.16. Unadjusted (dotted) and adjusted (solid) series

adjustment is defined by

$$X''_t := X_t - \frac{t}{12}\Big(\overline{\Delta_{12}Y} - \frac{N-1}{2}\overline{\Delta_{12}\Delta Y}\Big) - \Big(\frac{t^2}{24} + \frac{t}{2}\Big)(\overline{\Delta_{12}\Delta Y})$$

see (4.45). Figure 7.17 shows the periodograms of the unadjusted (dotted)

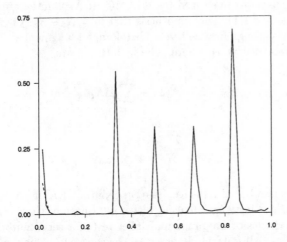

Fig. 7.17. Peridograms of unadjusted (dotted) and adjusted (solid) series

and the adjusted series (solid line). The larger spectral peak of the adjusted series at $\omega_1 = \pi/[N/2] = \pi/73$ indicates that the adjustment of order two induces spurious spectral power at ω_1. A comparison of the MC-values (see (6.5)) attained for DFA III and DFA II:

$$MC(DFA\ III) = 5.53 \times 10^{-4}$$
$$MC(DFA\ II) = 4.62 \times 10^{-4} \tag{7.19}$$

shows that the latter is to prefer, i.e. integration order one is preferred to integration of order two implied by DFA III. Finally, a test based on the conditions (5.22) leads to the following conclusions:

- The test statistic η' defined in (5.91) attains a value of -3.6 which is insignificant at the 10% significance level (the corresponding quantile of the Dickey-Fuller distribution is -5.7, see table B.5, case 1 in Hamilton [45], p.762). Therefore, the hypothesis H_0 : "the level restriction $\hat{\Gamma}(0) = \Gamma(0)$ is necessary" cannot be rejected.
- However, the second order constraint $\hat{\phi}(0) = 0$ (time-shift constraint) can be rejected since the test statistic takes on the value -17.5 which is significant at the 1% significance level (the corresponding quantile is -13.6).

These findings are in contradiction with the selected model (7.17) since the integration order two of the airline model would imply a time-shift restriction $\hat{\phi}(0) = 0$ (similar conflicting evidences are obtained for the series linearized by X-12-ARIMA). Therefore, additional 'pure' unit-root tests are computed for

$$\tilde{X}_t := X_t - X_{t-12} \qquad (7.20)$$

where X_t is the series linearized by TRAMO. If $\tilde{X}_t$ is integrated, then X_t is I(2), otherwise it is I(1). The hypothesis that $u_t = \tilde{X}_t - \tilde{X}_{t-1}$ is white noise is rejected at the 1% significance level. Therefore, an 'augmented' Dickey-Fuller (ADF) unit-root test is used here. The hypotheses are

$$H_0 : \tilde{X}_t = \tilde{X}_{t-1} + \sum_{k=1}^{p} \Delta\tilde{X}_{t-k} + u_t$$

against

$$H_1 : \tilde{X}_t = \rho\tilde{X}_{t-1} + \sum_{k=1}^{p} \Delta\tilde{X}_{t-k} + u_t$$

where p is the number of AR-lags. The procedure 'URADF' in RATS tries to determine the best lag length p, using either information criteria (AIC or BIC), Ljung-Box statistics or Lagrange multiplier tests for serial autocorrelation of the residuals u_t. All criteria choose $p = 1$ except AIC which chooses $p = 3$. For $p = 1$, the ADF t-statistic is -2.59 which is significant at the 1% level (the critical value is -2.58, see Hamilton [45], table B.6, case 1). If H_0 is tested against

$$H_1 : \tilde{X}_t = \alpha + \rho\tilde{X}_{t-1} + \sum_{k=1}^{p} \Delta\tilde{X}_{t-k} + u_t$$

then the t-statistic becomes -2.61 which is not significant at the 5% level (see Hamilton [45], table B.6, case 2). Note however that the estimate for the constant α is not significantly different from zero (this is not surprising since α is a drift term for the undifferenced series X_t which does not seem to show evidence of a linear time trend). The F-test for the composite hypothesis $\alpha = 0, \rho = 1$ is rejected at 5% . If lag-length $p = 3$ is chosen instead of $p = 1$, as suggested by AIC, then the t-statistic becomes -1.57 which is insignificant even at the 10% level.

A Phillips-Perron test of

$$H_0 : \tilde{X}_t = \tilde{X}_{t-1} + u_t$$

against

$$H_1 : \tilde{X}_t = \rho\tilde{X}_{t-1} + u_t$$

where u_t is a MA-process is implemented in the procedure 'UNITROOT' of RATS. The corresponding Z_ρ-statistics are between -3.76 (window size 1) and -3.95 (window size 4). Since the critical 10% value is -5.6 (see Hamilton [45], table B.5, case 1) H_0 cannot be rejected (this result does not change if a constant is included in the alternative hypothesis).

Note also that the estimated MA-parameters in model (7.17) do not suggest non-invertibility which favors H_0 too.

Finally, unit-roots can be inferred from the so called variance ratio test, see for example Lo and MacKinlay [63]. Briefly, the idea of the test consists in computing $\frac{\sigma_k^2}{k\sigma_1^2}$ where σ_1^2 and σ_k^2 are the variances of the one- and the k-step ahead forecasting errors of a particular process, say X_t. If X_t is a pure random-walk, then the variance ratio becomes

$$\frac{E[(X_{t+k} - X_t)^2]}{k\sigma^2} \tag{7.21}$$

where σ^2 is the variance of the noise process and X_t is the optimal forecast for X_{t+k} for all $k > 0$. Since the expectations are generally unknown in (7.21), variances are replaced by sample estimates

$$\frac{(N-1)\sum_{t=1}^{N-k}(X_{t+k} - X_t)^2}{(N-k)k\sum_{t=1}^{N-1}(X_{t+1} - X_t)^2} \tag{7.22}$$

The asymptotic distribution of the (sample) variance ratio (7.22) has been derived for X_t a pure random-walk with iid gaussian innovations (an assumption which is too restrictive for the process $\tilde{X}_t := X_t - X_{t-12}$ obtained from the car-sales series above), see for example Lo and MacKinlay [63]. Under this assumption (7.21) is equal to one and (7.22) is approximately equal to one (as functions of k) whereas for stationary processes both ratios converge to zero for increasing k, as $N \to \infty$ (because $E[(X_{t+k} - X_t)^2]$ is bounded). For general $I(1)$-processes, the ratios (7.21) and (7.22) converge to a positive number (> 0) for increasing k. This number reflects the impact of a shock on future observations of the process ('persistence') and depends on the autocorrelation structure of $X_t - X_{t-1}$. The (sample) variance ratios (7.22) for the differenced car-sales series $\tilde{X}_t$ defined by (7.20) (dotted line) and for $(1 - B)\tilde{X}_t$ (solid line) for $k = 1, ..., 100$ are plotted in fig.7.18. It can be seen from this figure that $(1 - B)\tilde{X}_t$ is stationary and that $\tilde{X}_t$ 'seems integrated' for $k < 30$ since its variance ratio has stabilized at approximately 0.2. But for $k > 30$ the statistic converges to zero. Therefore, the impact of a shock in $\tilde{X}_t$ is perceptible over a 'long' horizon although it finally seems to decline to zero which indicates stationarity of the process. *This situation is common for a large set of economic time series and it corresponds to parameter values of the DGP for which the power of unit-root tests based on one-step ahead forecasting performances is very poor.* Cochrane [18] analyzes the US-GNP-series: he argues p.898 "If fluctuations in GNP are partly temporary ... that reversal is likely to be slow, loosely structured, and not easily captured in a simple parametric model. The variance of k-differences (variance ratio) can find such loosely structured reversion whereas many other approaches cannot".

The variance ratio statistic can be used as an explorative tool (as in figure 7.18) or as a testing device. The advantage of the variance ratio test over 'traditional' unit root tests (such as the above ADF and PP procedures) is that it is based on one- and on multi-step ahead 'forecasting' performances

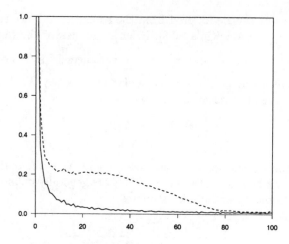

Fig. 7.18. Variance ratios of $\tilde{X}_t$ (dotted) and $(1 - B)\tilde{X}_t$ (solid line)

(of a simple random-walk model). The main disadvantage of the test is that the test result heavily depends on a particular forecasting horizon k, see for example Maddala [44], p.87. Also, the assumption of a pure random-walk are not satisfied for $\tilde{X}_t$. Therefore, an explorative approach (fig.7.18) has been preferred to a (misspecified) test result here.

The contradictory test results based on one-step ahead forecasting performances (such as ADF- and PP-tests) reflect the difficulty of the determination of the integration order for the UK-car-sales series but this is mainly an issue for the MBA. For the DFA the relevant problem is *to determine if a particular constraint of the type (5.22) is needed for improving the fit of the asymmetric filter* whether unit-roots are present in the DGP or not. For that purpose, the test statistic η' in (5.91), the MC statistic in (7.19) and the spurious spectral power induced by the second order adjustment in figure 7.17 indicate that 'integration order two' may induce an unnecessarily severe restriction for the filter of the DFA (and subsidiary a possible misspecification of the model for the MBA). Note that one- and multi-step ahead forecasting performances are simultaneously accounted for by the proposed methods so that the choice of a particular forecasting horizon k (as for the variance ratio test) is unnecessary. The term 'unit-root' is still used in the remaining of the chapter but it should be clear that *a corresponding constraint (5.22) of the filter is really meant here rather than a particular property of the DGP.*

The boundary estimates for the MBA (long marks) and the DFA II (short marks) together with the signal (7.8) (solid line) are shown in figures 7.19 (for the series linearized by TRAMO) and 7.20 (for the series linearized by X-12-ARIMA). The samples extend from December 1989 to July 1994 : 60

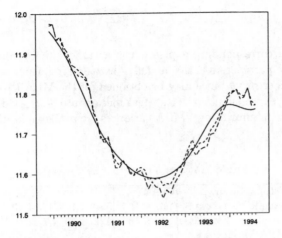

Fig. 7.19. Boundary estimates and signal (TRAMO-linearized)

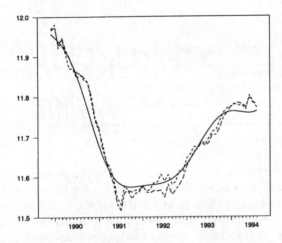

Fig. 7.20. Boundary estimates and signal : (X-12-linearized)

values were retained on the left for avoiding initialization problems and 30 values were retained on the right in order to implement (7.8).

Tables 7.5 and 7.6 compare the following revision error variance estimates:

- the *frequency estimates* (7.2),
- the *sample variances* (7.3) and
- the *MBA-variances* (7.4).

Note that the transfer function of the boundary filter for the MBA can be explicitly computed, using the relation

$$\hat{\gamma}_{t-j} := \begin{cases} \gamma_{t-j} + \sum_{k=-\infty}^{t-N-1} \gamma_k a_{t-k,j} + \sum_{k=t}^{\infty} \gamma_k a_{t-k,j} & j = 1, ..., N \\ 0 & \text{else} \end{cases}$$

see (1.5) (the corresponding expression is a rather cumbersome non-linear function of the parameters of the model). Therefore, frequency estimates (7.2) of the revision error variance may be obtained for the MBA (by inserting the corresponding expression for the transfer function into (7.2), evidently without performing the minimization). MBA-variances are available for the MBA only of course.

Table 7.5. Series linearized by TRAMO

Estimation by	DFA II	DFA III	TRAMO
Sample Variances	4.61×10^{-4}	5.91×10^{-4}	$7.64\ 10^{-4}$
Frequency Estimates	4.16×10^{-4}	5.00×10^{-4}	$7.34\ 10^{-4}$
MBA-Variances	—	—	$6.22\ 10^{-4}$

Table 7.6. Series linearized by X-12-ARIMA

Estimation by	DFA II	DFA III	X-12-ARIMA
Sample Variances	$5.21\ 10^{-4}$	$6.38\ 10^{-4}$	$6.95\ 10^{-4}$
Frequency Estimates	$4.00\ 10^{-4}$	$4.29\ 10^{-4}$	$4.60\ 10^{-4}$
MBA-Variances	—	—	$4.19\ 10^{-4}$

For both series the DFA provides more accurate estimates with respect to sample variances (approximately 30% and 60% improvement when comparing the sample variances of DFA II and MBA for the series linearized by X-12 and TRAMO respectively). Note also that the frequency estimates for the MBA are closer to the sample variance estimates than the MBA-variances as expected by the efficiency of the DFA, see section 5.5.

In order to analyze these results in more detail, it is instructive to decompose the frequency variance estimates (7.2) into an amplitude component (selectivity) and a phase component (time delay) according to

$$\frac{2\pi}{N} \sum_{k=-[N/2]}^{[N/2]} |\Delta\tilde{\Gamma}(\omega_k)|^2 I_{N\tilde{X}}(\omega_k)$$

$$:= \frac{2\pi}{N} \sum_{k=-[N/2]}^{[N/2]} \frac{|\Delta\Gamma(\omega_k)|^2}{|1 - \exp(-i12\omega_k)|^2} I_{N\tilde{X}}(\omega_k)$$

$$= \frac{2\pi}{N} \sum_{k=-[N/2]}^{[N/2]} \frac{(A(\omega_k) - \hat{A}(\omega_k))^2}{|1 - \exp(-i12\omega_k)|^2} I_{N\tilde{X}}(\omega_k) \tag{7.23}$$

$$+\frac{2\pi}{N}\sum_{k=-[N/2]}^{[N/2]}\frac{2A(\omega_k)\hat{A}(\omega_k)\left[1-\cos\left(\hat{\Phi}(\omega_k)\right)\right]}{|1-\exp(-i12\omega_k)|^2}I_{N\tilde{X}}(\omega_k) \quad (7.24)$$

The first sum (7.23) corresponds to that part of the revision error variance which is due to the (less selective) amplitude function of the boundary filter. The second sum (7.24) corresponds to that part of the revision error variance which is due to the phase (time shift) of the boundary filter (see (5.40) in section 5.4).
The results of such a decomposition are shown in tables 7.7 (for the series linearized by TRAMO) and 7.8 (for the series linearized by X-12). The columns

Table 7.7. Series linearized by TRAMO

Estimation method :	DFA II	DFA III	TRAMO
Selectivity variance	$2.45\ 10^{-4}$	$3.81\ 10^{-4}$	$3.98\ 10^{-4}$
Time delay variance	$1.71\ 10^{-4}$	$1.19\ 10^{-4}$	$3.36\ 10^{-4}$

Table 7.8. Series linearized by X-12-ARIMA

Estimation method :	DFA II	DFA III	X-12-ARIMA
Selectivity variance	$2.29\ 10^{-4}$	$3.25\ 10^{-4}$	$2.66\ 10^{-4}$
Time delay variance	$1.71\ 10^{-4}$	$1.04\ 10^{-4}$	$1.95\ 10^{-4}$

of these two tables sum up to the frequency variance estimates of tables 7.5 and 7.6 (neglecting rounding errors).
For the series linearized by TRAMO (table 7.7), DFA II outperforms the MBA with respect to both selectivity and time delay properties. DFA III outperforms both competitors with respect to time delay 'fitting' but it also provides the worst amplitude 'fitting'. The effect of the second order constraint of DFA III is best seen by considering the ratio of the selectivity variance to the time delay variance (in the above tables). This ratio increases from approximately 1.5 (for DFA II) to over 3 for DFA III . Such a 'disequilibrium' between both variance components may be indicative for a 'misspecification' (in the sense of either missing or unnecessary constraint(s)).
Amplitude and time delay functions of the boundary filters of DFA II (solid line) and of the MBA (dotted line, the amplitude is based on model (7.17) for the series linearized by TRAMO) are shown in figures 7.21 and 7.22. The amplitude function of DFA II is closer to the amplitude of the symmetric filter (7.8) (which is almost equal to (7.5)) than the amplitude function of the MBA in the neighborhood of the 'unit-roots' (more precisely : of the spectral peaks). Note that the part of the revision error which is due to the phase of

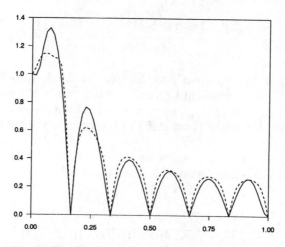

Fig. 7.21. Amplitude Functions : DFA II (solid) MBA (dotted)

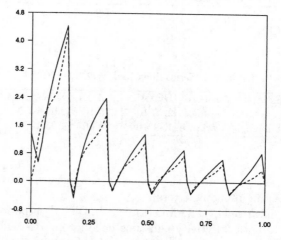

Fig. 7.22. Time shifts : DFA II (solid) MBA (dotted)

DFA II is smaller than that of the MBA because the time delay is smaller for the low frequencies (except at $\omega = 0$, but the time delay $\hat{\phi}(0)$ is less relevant provided the second order constraint is not needed which seems to be the case here).

Why does DFA II markedly outperform the MBA? The revision errors of DFA II and of the MBA are shown in figure 7.23 and the periodograms of these revision errors are shown in figure 7.24. The gain in performance of DFA II is achieved mainly towards the low frequencies which again confirms the choice of a first order constraint $\hat{\Gamma}(0) = \Gamma(0)$ 'only' at frequency zero (similar conclusions hold for the series linearized by X-12-ARIMA). All these results

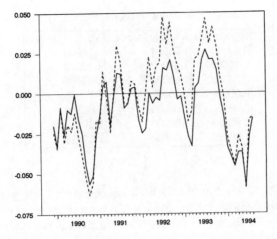

Fig. 7.23. Revision errors of DFA II (solid) and MBA (dotted)

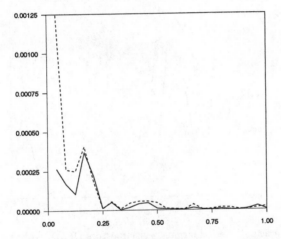

Fig. 7.24. Periodograms revision errors DFA II (solid) and MBA (dotted)

show that the I(2)-hypothesis is questionable (i.e. the integration order of the DGP seems to be less than two).

The estimated filter parameters of DFA II are listed in the following table 7.9 (note that the arguments of the zeroes and the poles are identical because of the ZPC-design). The normalizing constant is $C := \frac{1}{391.26392}$, resulting from the first order condition $\hat{\Gamma}(0) = \Gamma(0) = 1$. The moduli of the poles reflect the width of the amplitude at the different seasonal frequencies (wider spectral peaks ask for wider corresponding troughs of the amplitude function of the extraction filter which are obtained by larger moduli of the poles). Although

Table 7.9. Filter parameters for DFA II

Arguments	Moduli (Zeroes)	Moduli (Poles)
0.02202	1.08994	1.14068
0.16666	1.00000	1.23029
0.33333	1.00000	1.67798
0.50000	1.00000	1.76846
0.66666	1.00000	1.68560
0.83333	1.00000	2.20813
1.00000	1.00000	1.27615

the gain of DFA II is minor for higher frequencies, it is nevertheless instructive to reveal its behavior there. Figure 7.25 corresponds to figure 7.24 where the low frequencies (below $\pi/4$) have been omitted. It is readily seen that the

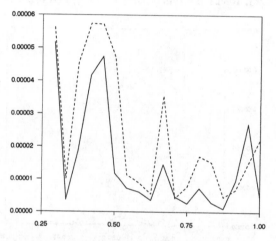

Fig. 7.25. 'Truncated' Periodograms revision errors DFA II (solid) and MBA (dotted)

DFA II outperforms the MBA almost uniformly and especially at the 'unit-root frequencies' (0.33, 0.5, 0.66, 0.83 and 1.0 in the above figure) which again motivates use of individual zero-pole-pairs.

After having performed an extensive analysis of 'in sample' properties, 'out of sample' results are now briefly compared for the MBA and the DFA II. The interesting criterion is the arithmetic mean of the squared 'out of sample' errors. For that purpose, models were selected and estimated on the subsample 85.01-92.12 ($N = 96$) which was used also for computing the periodogram. Substantially smaller subsamples lead to problems for both DFA and MBA (overfitting and misspecification). It should be specified here that some 'full sample' information is still used because the input series are the same linearized series (in order to make comparisons with 'in sample' results meaningful): adjustment for outliers and/or calendar effects is still based on the full sample but this additional information should not favor a particular approach.

The estimated (TRAMO) subsample-model is

$$(1 - B)(1 - B^{12})X_t = (1 - 0.62B)(1 - 0.29B^{12})\epsilon_t$$

Table 7.10 summarizes results for the series linearized by TRAMO. The last

Table 7.10. Out of sample results (series linearized by TRAMO)

Identification and estimation on :	Subsample	Full Sample
DFA II	8.11×10^{-4}	7.36×10^{-4}
TRAMO	9.94×10^{-4}	9.64×10^{-4}

column shows the results for the validation sample if the information of the full sample is used, i.e. model (7.17) and the full sample periodogram (these are slightly different from the results of table 7.5 because the validation samples are different). A comparison of both columns shows that the DFA II is possibly subject to slight overfitting (9 parameters are estimated for a sample of length $N = 96$). However, the gain in performance of DFA II is still over 20% (out of sample).

For X-12-ARIMA the estimated subsample-model is

$$(1 - B)(1 - B^{12})(1 + 0.49B + 0.11B^2)X_t = (1 - 0.24B^{12})\epsilon_t$$

Table 7.11 summarizes results for the series linearized by X-12-ARIMA. As

Table 7.11. Out of sample results (series linearized by X-12-ARIMA)

Identification and estimation on :	Subsample	Full Sample
DFA II	3.32×10^{-4}	3.44×10^{-4}
X-12-ARIMA	4.21×10^{-4}	4.49×10^{-4}

before, the last column shows the results for the validation sample if the information of the full sample is used (again, these are slightly different from the results of table 7.6 because the validation samples are different). A comparison of both columns shows that the DFA II is not subject to overfitting and that 'out of sample' results of both approaches even slightly outperform 'in sample' results using the full sample. The gain in performance of DFA II is over 25% (out of sample).

This concludes the analysis of the best mean square approximation of the trend (7.9). A natural question addresses the validity of these results, namely the overall better performance of the DFA, if the theoretical signal is model-based (see section 2.3.2). In fact, whereas the trend filter (7.9) does not 'favor' a particular approach, one might possibly expect that the MBA performs better for its 'own' signal. This hypothesis is analyzed from an empirical point of view in the following section.

7.3.2 Mean-Square Approximation of the 'Canonical Trend'

Let the theoretical signal be defined by the trend of the canonical decomposition ('canonical trend') for the (full sample) model (7.17) for the UK series linearized by TRAMO (as shown in fig. 7.14). X-12-ARIMA is ignored here since its implicit signal definition is not model-based. For the DFA, the selection of the filter design is based on MC which prefers DFA II

$$MC(DFA\ III) = 5.76 \times 10^{-4}$$
$$MC(DFA\ II) = 4.86 \times 10^{-4} \tag{7.25}$$

Note that these values differ from (7.19) because the MC-criterion depends on the revision error variance, i.e. on the symmetric filter which has to been approximated. The transfer function induced by model (7.17) is shown in fig. 7.26 (an analytic expression for the transfer function is cumbersome, see section

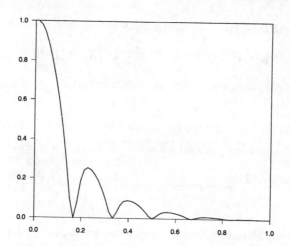

Fig. 7.26. Trend Extraction Filter

2.3.2 for a derivation). Since the filter is symmetric, its phase function vanishes. Therefore, the amplitude function in fig.7.26 is also the transfer function of the filter. Note also that the 'squared gain of trend filter' in DEMETRA is obtained by squaring the function in fig.7.26. Squaring the amplitude function can be motivated by the convolution theorem which relates spectral densities of in- and output signals (see (A.3) in the appendix). However, this transformation can distort or 'mask' important properties of the filter : figure 7.26 for example shows that the 'side lobes' of the transfer function are quite large for $\omega > \pi/6$, which means that 'subannual' high frequency components belong to the trend (see for example Stier [83] and [84] for a discussion on this topic). By squaring the amplitude function, the side lobes look much smaller which is misleading. The canonical trend (solid line) and the 'ideal' trend (7.9) are compared in figure 7.27 (i.e. the corresponding filter outputs are compared). The canonical trend cannot be computed exactly because the corresponding extraction filter is of infinite length. However, the filter coefficients decay sufficiently fast in order to obtain a good approximation.

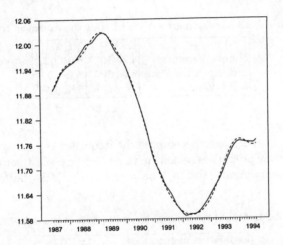

Fig. 7.27. Ideal (dotted) and Canonical (solid line) Trends

The outputs of the boundary filters for the MBA (long marks) and for the DFA II (short marks) are shown in fig.7.28 together with the canonical trend (solid line). Table 7.12 summarizes the results obtained for the revision error variance estimates. As in the preceding section, the time span for which the sample estimates are computed extends from December 1989 to July 1994. The DFA II still clearly outperforms the MBA (more than 60 percent improvement with respect to the sample variance). Also, the frequency estimate is more accurate than the MBA-variance which underestimates the mean of the squared revision errors.

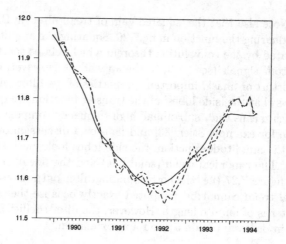

Fig. 7.28. DFA II (short marks) and MBA (long marks)

Table 7.12. Revision error Variances for the canonical trend

	DFA II	MBA
Sample Variances	$4.70 \ 10^{-4}$	$8.04 \ 10^{-4}$
Frequency Estimates	$4.34 \ 10^{-4}$	$7.19 \ 10^{-4}$
MBA-Variances	—	$5.88 \ 10^{-4}$

It is again instructive to decompose the frequency estimates into selectivity and time delay properties as done in table 7.13 (see (7.23) and (7.24) in the preceding section). Again, the DFA outperforms the MBA both with respect

Table 7.13. Amplitude (selectivity) and phase (time delay) 'fitting'

Estimation method :	DF	MBA
Selectivity	$2.07 \ 10^{-4}$	$3.76 \ 10^{-4}$
Time delay	$2.27 \ 10^{-4}$	$3.43 \ 10^{-4}$

to selectivity and time delay properties. Amplitude and time shift functions of the boundary filters (DFA II : solid line; MBA : dotted line) are shown in figs.7.29 and 7.30. For the DFA II, both functions are closer to the corresponding functions of the symmetric filter in the vicinity of the 'unit-roots' (except the time delay of the DFA II at frequency zero, but this is less important if a second order constraint is not needed which seems to be the case here).

Figure 7.31 shows the revision errors of DFA II (solid line) and MBA (dotted line). The periodograms of the revision errors are compared in figure 7.32.

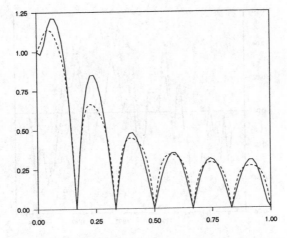

Fig. 7.29. Amplitude DFA II (solid) MBA (dotted)

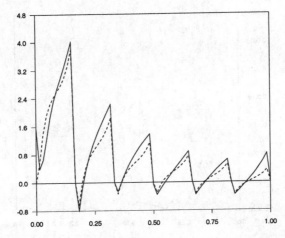

Fig. 7.30. Time Shift DFA II (solid) MBA (dotted)

One can see from these figures that the better performance of the DFA II is mainly achieved in the low frequency domain of the spectrum (which can be considered as a further evidence against the I(2)-hypothesis).

This concludes the analysis of trend signals. In the following section the DFA and the MBA are compared with respect to seasonal adjustment as performed by the canonical decomposition.

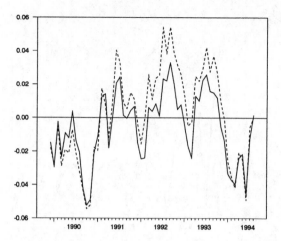

Fig. 7.31. Revision Errors DFA II (solid) MBA (dotted)

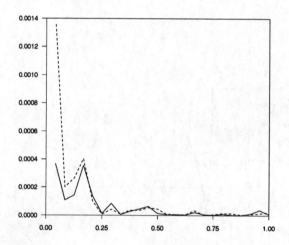

Fig. 7.32. Periodgrams DFA II (solid) MBA (dotted)

7.3.3 Mean Square Approximation of the 'Canonical Seasonal Adjustment' Filter

Let the theoretical signal be the seasonally adjusted series (as defined by the canonical decomposition of the process (7.17), see section 2.3) for the UK series linearized by TRAMO. As for the canonical trend in the preceding section, X-12-ARIMA is ignored here because its implicit signal definition is not model-based. For the DFA, the filter design DFA II is preferred by MC:

$$MC(DFA\ III) = 4.35 \times 10^{-4}$$
$$MC(DFA\ II) = 4.16 \times 10^{-4}$$

The transfer function of the canonical seasonal adjustment filter resulting from model (7.17) is shown in fig.7.33 (solid line). The squared transfer function is plotted as dotted line in the same figure. The 'squared gain of seasonal adjust-

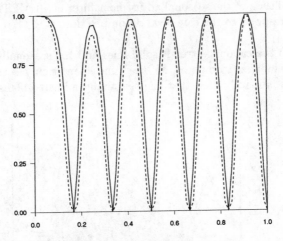

Fig. 7.33. Seasonal Adjustment Filter

ment' filter (solid line) and the 'squared gain of seasonal filter' (dotted line) as computed by DEMETRA are shown in fig.7.34. Note that the transfer func-

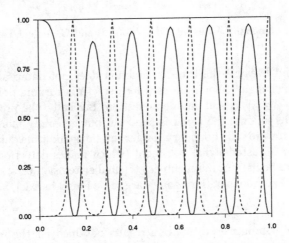

Fig. 7.34. DEMETRA-Filters: S (dotted), SA (solid)

tions of the seasonal adjustment (SA) and of the seasonal (S) filters should add to one by definition so that the square roots of the functions in figure 7.34

should add to one (note that these are the squared transfer functions). However, the (squared) S-filter vanishes between the seasonal frequencies $k\pi/6$ but the (squared) SA-filter is always substantially smaller than one. This is probably a software problem (of DEMETRA, version 2.0). In any case, the squared amplitude of the seasonal adjustment filter of DEMETRA in fig.7.34 does not correspond to the canonical decomposition.

In fig.7.35 the canonical trend (solid line) and the seasonally adjusted series (dotted line) are compared for the time span from December 1989 to July 1994. It is readily seen that the seasonally adjusted signal is 'rougher'

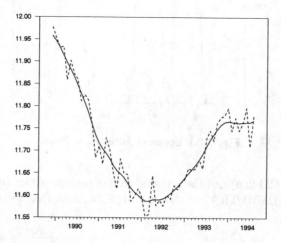

Fig. 7.35. Seasonally Adjusted signal (dotted) and Canonical Trend (solid)

than the trend because the transfer function does not damp all higher frequencies. Which signal should be used for detecting 'turning points' towards the end point $t = N$ is still an open question. Basically, the problem can be summarized as follows: the trend is 'smooth' but generally more difficult to approximate towards the boundary (larger revisions and time delays) whereas the seasonally adjusted signal is 'rough' (which makes detection of turning-points more difficult) but often subject to smaller revision errors and smaller time delays. Discussions of these topics are to be found in Edel, Schaffer, Stier [27].

Table 7.14 summarizes estimation results obtained for the revision error variance estimates. The latter are computed for the time span from December 1989 to July 1994: 60 values are retained on the left for avoiding initialization problems and 30 values are retained on the right for implementing the symmetric extraction filter. As can be seen, the DFA II outperforms the MBA by

Table 7.14. Revision error variance estimates

	DFA II	MBA
Sample Variances	$4.39\ 10^{-4}$	$6.61\ 10^{-4}$
Frequency Estimates	$3.82\ 10^{-4}$	$5.10\ 10^{-4}$
MBA-Variance	—	$5.34\ 10^{-4}$

a 30% decrease of the sample variances.

Remark

- The MA-coefficients of the seasonal adjustment filter are shown in figure 7.36. They converge very slowly to zero. In fact, if the signal is estimated for $t =$July 1994 as illustrated in figure 7.36 (30 months lie between July 94 and the end point February 1997), then non-negligible weight is still given to non-observable values beyond the end point. Therefore, in this particular situation the sample has been extended by forecasts in order to obtain sufficiently accurate outputs for the *symmetric* filter of the MBA (in all the preceding examples, forecasts were used for the asymmetric filter only). Evidently, this extension is not used for the DFA II and therefore it may possibly favor the MBA (since both asymmetric and symmetric filters rely on the same forecasts). However, this effect has not been considered here.

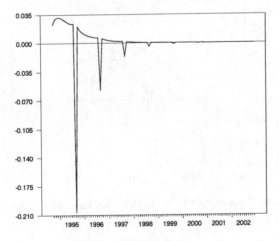

Fig. 7.36. Coefficients of SA-filter

A decomposition of the frequency estimates into selectivity and time delay components (see (7.23) and (7.24)) leads to the results in table 7.15. It is

Table 7.15. Selectivity and time delay properties of the boundary filters

Estimation method :	DFA II	MBA
Selectivity	$1.71 \ 10^{-4}$	$9.94 \ 10^{-5}$
Time shift	$2.10 \ 10^{-4}$	$4.10 \ 10^{-4}$

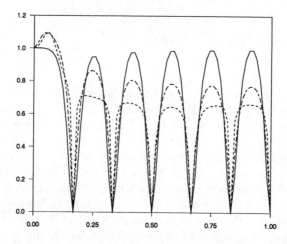

Fig. 7.37. Amplitudes : DFA II (short marks), MBA (long marks)

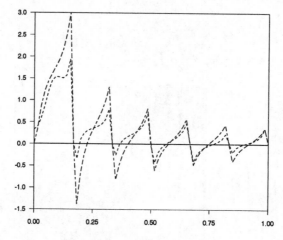

Fig. 7.38. Time shifts : DFA II (short marks), MBA (long marks)

seen that the better performance of the DFA II is due to its time shift properties. Obviously, too much 'weight' is given to the selectivity part by the MBA,
neglecting henceforth the time shift properties of the corresponding filter. The
resulting 'disequilibrium' between both components may be indicative for a

misspecification of the model (7.17). The amplitude functions of the symmetric filter (solid line), of the DFA II (short marks) and of the MBA (long marks) are shown in figure 7.37. In figure 7.38 the time shift functions of the DFA II (short marks) and the MBA (long marks) are compared.

A detailed comparison of the performances of the MBA (as given by TRAMO and X-12-ARIMA for the UK car sales series) and the DFA was conducted in this section. More precisely, the analysis focused on the mean square error criterion. In the following chapter, these methods are compared with respect to their ability to detect 'turning points' towards the boundary of a sample.

8

Empirical Comparisons : Turning Point Detection

A 'turning point' is a particular time point in a given time series. The main difficulty in defining 'turning points' formally is often due to the unprecise characterization of their particularity. In the context of economic time series Garcia-Ferrer and Bujosa-Brun [35] argue "with the exception of annual data, where turning points are easily defined, the remaining data frequencies often present many situations where precise definitions of recessions and contractions are case dependent" or "Even for seasonally adjusted quarterly data, using the NBER rule for defining a recession ... has had serious flaws in characterizing business cycle facts" and "no simple rule is sufficient to translate quarterly GNP changes into official cyclical turning points. Somehow there seems to be a need for *ad hoc* rules that work with certain types of data and also may hold for future turning points in a large number of cases".

Instead of reviewing possible definitions of turning points depending on particular contexts and/or particular time series a more formal approach is chosen here which enables straightforward comparisons of the MBA and the DFA. A turning point is defined as a 'local extremum' of a (smooth) trend component of a time series. More precisely, t_0 is a turning point for the time series X_t if $(Y_{t_0+1} - Y_{t_0})(Y_{t_0} - Y_{t_0-1}) < 0$ where Y_t is a (smooth) trend component of X_t. Examples of (smooth) trend components are the 'canonical trend' (see section 7.3.2) and the 'ideal' trend (7.8). Note that the proposed definition of a turning point generally depends on the input series X_t (which for example determines the model and thus the 'canonical' trend) or on the 'cutoff' frequency $\lambda_2 = \pi/7$ of the 'ideal' trend (7.5) (or the truncated version (7.9)).

Two different perspectives may be distinguished, namely the 'prospective' and the 'historical' perspective. For the former, 'present' and possible 'future' outcomes are of interest, whereas for the latter 'past' events are analyzed. In a historical perspective, the study of turning points (defined as extremes of a trend component) is generally easier because selective symmetric (no phase shift) trend filters can be used. However, for many applications the prospective perspective is of main interest. Therefore, asymmetric filters are needed which detect turning points 'as early as possible'.

Once turning-points are uniquely defined and the objective, namely a prospective analysis of turning points, is clarified it remains to determine a measure of the performance of the competing methods. Again, there exist many criteria which for example differ whether they account for 'true' and 'false' decisions only or whether they include also the magnitude of the error term and how 'false' and 'true' decisions are weighted. Various criteria are proposed in Edel, Schaffer and Stier [27], p.143-154. Since the aspects which they measure may be conflicting, a simple comparison is proposed here, namely a visual inspection of the time series (of the estimated trend components) produced by the competing methods.

In the following sections, the UK car sales series (linearized by TRAMO or X-12-ARIMA, see section 7.3) is considered. The presented results are based on the 'full sample' information (almost identical conclusions would hold 'out of sample', i.e. if models and periodograms were estimated for subsamples, because the revision error variances 'in' and 'out of sample' are very similar, see for example tables 7.10 and 7.11). The first section is devoted to the analysis of turning points defined by the 'ideal' trend (7.8) and the second section is devoted to a corresponding analysis for the canonical trend.

8.1 Turning Point Detection for the 'Ideal' Trend

The detection of turning points for the 'ideal' trend is based on models (7.17) (TRAMO) and (7.18) (X-12-ARIMA) for the MBA and on the filter design DFA II which is preferred by MC, see for example (7.19). For the DFA, the time series $\hat{Y}_t$ (estimated signal) is computed as follows:

- For each $t = N - r$, $r = 0, 1, ..., N - 1$, the estimate $\hat{Y}_{N-r}$ is the output of a constrained QMP-ZPC-filter (3.6) whose parameters are optimized so that the expression

$$\frac{2\pi}{N} \sum_{k=-[N/2]}^{[N/2]} |\Delta \tilde{\Gamma}_r(\omega_k)|^2 I_{N\tilde{X}}(\omega_k) \tag{8.1}$$

becomes minimal. Specifically, for DFA II

$$\Delta \tilde{\Gamma}_r(\omega_k) = \frac{\Gamma'(\omega_k) - \hat{\Gamma}'_r(\omega_k)}{1 - \exp(-i12\omega_k)}$$

$$\tilde{X}_t = (1 - B^{12})X_t$$

where $\Gamma'(\cdot)$ and $\hat{\Gamma}'_r(\cdot)$ are defined in (7.9) and (5.95) respectively (a simple truncation is used for $\Gamma^{tr}(\cdot)$ in (5.95)). For the DFA II, first order conditions (constraints) $\hat{\Gamma}'_r(j\pi/6) = \Gamma'(j\pi/6)$, $j = 0, ..., 6$ are considered. As in the preceding chapter, seven zero-pole pairs are used for each filter resulting in $7 \cdot 3 + 1 - 13 = 9$ degrees of freedom (see section 7.2.1).

- A separate optimization is needed for each $r = 0, 1, 2, ..., N - 1$ in (8.1). Note however that the differences between the resulting optimal filters are negligible for $r > 10$ (at least for the chosen trend signals). Therefore, $\hat{Y}_{N-10}, \hat{Y}_{N-11}, \hat{Y}_{N-12}...$ are all based on the same filter (optimized for estimating Y_{N-10}). For $r \leq 10$, the successive filters can be computed iteratively: the optimization procedure in the r-th step can be 'initialized' with the solution obtained in the preceding step $r - 1$. Using Newton-Raphson numerical algorithms then make computations very fast because the 'initial solutions' are already close to the optima.

- A so called 'composed' filter $\hat{\Gamma}^c(\cdot)$ may formally be defined by setting its output equal to the time series $\hat{Y}_{N-r}$ defined above.

- If N is replaced by $N' \leq N$ in the above definitions and if N' varies, then it can be observed how the composed filter $\hat{\Gamma}^c(\cdot)$ 'adapts' for new information. In fact, passing from N' to $N' + 1$ means that $\hat{Y}_{N'+1-r}$ is estimated using information up to $X_{N'+1}$ (instead of $X_{N'}$) which enhances the quality of the estimates $\hat{Y}_{N'+1-r}$ for $r \geq 1$.

An 'early' detection of turning points is often of interest because it corresponds to a particular (qualitative) forecast. However, asymmetric trend filters are often subject to substantial time delays. Therefore, the method proposed in section 5.4 is used here in order to 'control' the time delay of the asymmetric filters. The resulting constrained (smaller time shift) composed filter $\hat{\Gamma}^c(\cdot)$ can be defined in various ways. Two of them are proposed here:

- The 'end point' filter $\hat{\Gamma}_r(\cdot)$ of $\hat{\Gamma}^c(\cdot)$, where $r = 0$, is replaced by an 'end point' filter whose time delay (phase shift) is restricted. The other filters $\hat{\Gamma}_r(\cdot)$, $r \geq 1$ of $\hat{\Gamma}^c(\cdot)$ are not affected. If 'information' $X_1, ..., X_{N'}$, $N' \leq N$ is used, then the increment $\hat{Y}_{N'} - \hat{Y}_{N'-1}$ (which is generally subject to the largest time delay) tends to detect the turning point earlier.

- Another possibility is to restrict the time delay (phase shift) of the boundary *and* the subsequent filters i.e. to restrict $\hat{\Gamma}_r(\cdot)$, $r = 0, 1, ...$

Both methods are illustrated in this chapter.

8.1.1 Series Linearized by TRAMO

Assume $X_1, ..., X_N$ are available and the composed filter $\hat{\Gamma}^c(\cdot)$ is applied to $X_1, ..., X_{N'}$ with $N' \leq N$. Thus the observed filter outputs are $\hat{Y}_1, ..., \hat{Y}_{N'}$. A 'simulation' of the characteristics of the composed filter $\hat{\Gamma}(\cdot)$ can be obtained by varying $N'(\leq N)$. Figures 8.1 and 8.2 plot the outputs of composed filters for the MBA and the DFA, where N' is varying from 92.05 to 92.11. The vertical line indicates a turning point of the trend (solid line) in June 92 (92.06).

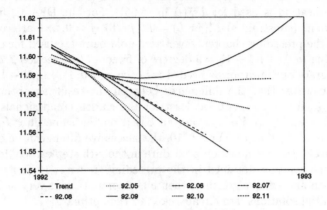

Fig. 8.1. Turning point detection : TRAMO

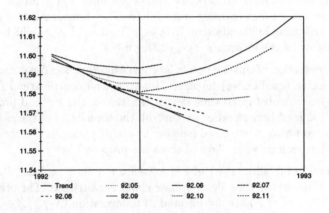

Fig. 8.2. Turning point detection : DFA II (no phase constraint)

As can be seen, DFA II (without a time delay constraint) detects the turning point one month earlier than the MBA (92.10 vs. 92.11). Moreover, in 92.11 the turning point is clearly identified by DFA II. Also, the boundary estimates of DFA II are closer to the trend than those of the MBA. The smaller revision error variance of DFA II was already observed in the preceding chapter.

Between 94.01 and 95.01 turning-points occur twice. Figs. 8.3 and 8.4 show the outputs of the composed filters of the MBA and the DFA (N' varies from 94.06 to 95.01). Here the situation is not as simple as for the preceding example. The MBA does not unambiguously 'detect' the first turning point. In fact the first increment $\hat{Y}_{N'} - \hat{Y}_{N'-1}$ is always positive (indicating a positive

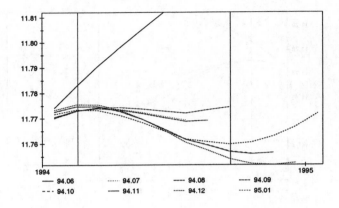

Fig. 8.3. Turning point detection : TRAMO

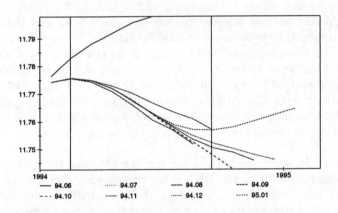

Fig. 8.4. Turning point detection : DFA II (no phase constraint)

slope) whereas successive increments become negative (indicating a negative slope). As a result, the second turning point seems to be detected very early (at least by the first increment). For the DFA, the analysis is less ambiguous since both turning points are clearly identified. But the second one does not appear before 95.01 (at this time the second increment of the MBA becomes positive also).

Up to now, the phase functions of the asymmetric boundary filters of DFA II were not restricted. In the following figure 8.5 the boundary filter ($r = 0$) has been optimized with respect to a phase constraint (see (5.43) where the Lagrangian parameter λ is defined in (5.44)). The other asymmetric filters

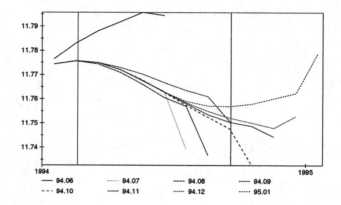

Fig. 8.5. Turning point detection : DFA II (phase constraint)

$(r > 0)$ are not affected. Comparing fig.8.5 with fig.8.4 reveals that both turning points are now detected one month earlier. As already shown in preceding chapters, a 'price' must be paid for the smaller time delay, namely a poorer (less selective) amplitude function of the new boundary filter $(r = 0)$. The resulting larger 'noise' can easily be seen in fig.8.5. Since the phase functions of subsequent filters of the composed filter $\hat{\Gamma}^c(\cdot)$ are not restricted, the difference between $\hat{Y}_{N'-1}$ (unrestricted) and $\hat{Y}_{N'}$ (restricted) is pronounced. Restricting the phase functions of the asymmetric filters for $r = 0, 1, \ldots$ results in a 'smoother' overall shape as shown in the example below.

Amplitude and phase functions of the restricted and the unrestricted end point filters $(r = 0)$ of the DFA II are compared in figs.8.6 and 8.7. As expected, the amplitude function of the conditional filter is uniformly poorer (less selective) whereas its time delay function performs uniformly better in the passband. Note also that the sample error variance (7.3) of the restricted filter is $7.38 \cdot 10^{-4}$. It is larger than that of the unconditional filter as expected, but it is still smaller than that of the MBA (TRAMO) which is $7.64 \cdot 10^{-4}$, see table 7.5.

The difference between the time shifts of the unrestricted and the restricted DFA II filters (solid line) and the difference between the time shifts of the MBA-(boundary)filter and the restricted DFA II filter are shown in figure 8.8. It is readily seen that the time shift of the conditional filter is approximately one time unit (month) smaller than that of the other competitors in the 'passband' $[0, \pi/6]$ (which corresponds to the turning points).

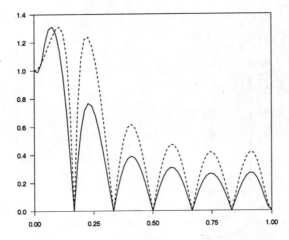

Fig. 8.6. Amplitude : restricted (dotted) and unrestricted (solid line)

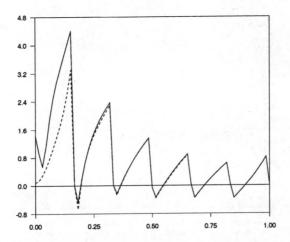

Fig. 8.7. Time shift : restricted (dotted) and unrestricted (solid line)

8.1.2 Series Linearized by X-12-ARIMA

The composed filters of the MBA and DFA II are shown in figs.8.9 and 8.10 after a trough-turning point of the trend has occurred (in October 1991, see fig.7.20). It is particularly difficult to assess the existence of the turning point because the trend is almost 'flat' in the corresponding period. However, it is seen that the MBA seems to give more evidence to a false 'down-swing' than the DFA which is 'hesitating'. In fact, the 'up-swing' is recognized one month earlier by the DFA than by the MBA. Note also the relatively smaller revision errors of the DFA.

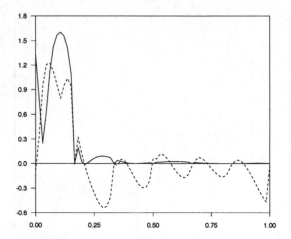

Fig. 8.8. Time shift differences: unrestr.-restr. DFA (solid); MBA-restr. DFA (dotted)

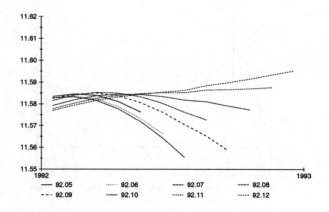

Fig. 8.9. Turning point detection : X-12

As for the series linearized by TRAMO, two turning-points occur between 94.01 and 95.01. Composed filters for the MBA and for DFA II (unrestricted phase) are shown in figs.8.11 and 8.12. The first trough-turning point is discovered two months earlier by DFA II than by the MBA. The second peak-turning point is discovered simultaneously by both approaches. The output of a composed filter whose phase functions are restricted for all asymmetric filters is shown in figure 8.13. The second turning point is detected one month earlier. Again, a 'price' must be paid as seen by the increased 'noise level' in (8.13) (when compared to fig. 8.12). Overall, the shape is smoother than in fig.8.5 because the phase functions of all filters entering $\hat{\Gamma}^c(\cdot)$ have been

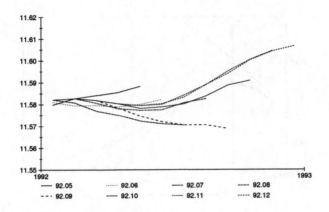

Fig. 8.10. Turning point detection : DFA II (unrestricted phase)

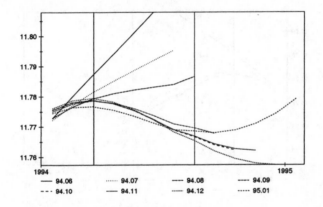

Fig. 8.11. Turning point detection : X-12

restricted.

Amplitude and phase functions of restricted and unrestricted end point filters ($r = 0$) are shown in figs.8.14 and 8.15. The amplitude function of the restricted DFA II performs poorer (especially for the 'stopband') but the conditional time delay function performs better (uniformly better in the pass-band).

In the following section empirical results based on the trend of the canonical decomposition are presented.

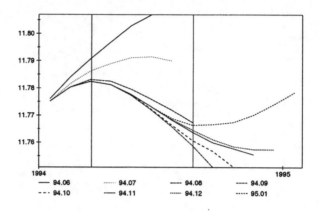

Fig. 8.12. Turning point detection : DFA II (unrestricted phase)

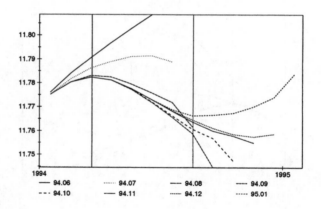

Fig. 8.13. Turning point detection : cond. DFA II

8.2 Turning Point Detection for the Canonical Trend

For the MBA, TRAMO is used only. As in the preceding chapter, X-12-ARIMA is ignored because the canonical trend is defined by the TRAMO-model (7.17). For the DFA, the filter design DFA II is preferred by MC, see (7.25). The outputs of the composed filters for the MBA and DFA II are shown in figs.8.16 and 8.17. DFA II detects the turning point in 92.10 while the MBA again leads to ambiguous evidences since the first increments have negative slope until 92.12 (where the increment is nearly flat). Note also the smaller revision errors of the DFA.

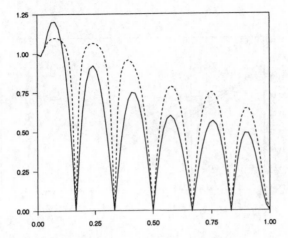

Fig. 8.14. Amplitude : restricted (dotted) and unrestricted (solid line)

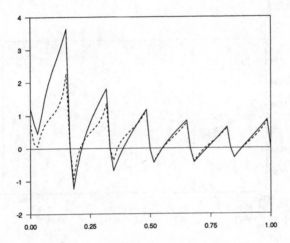

Fig. 8.15. Time delay : restricted (dotted) and unrestricted (solid line)

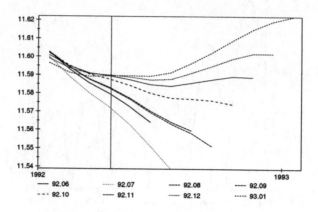

Fig. 8.16. Turning point detection : TRAMO

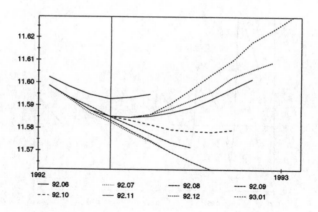

Fig. 8.17. Turning point detection : DF

These results conclude the empirical comparisons of the MBA and the DFA. A brief summary of the 'material' worked out so far is proposed in the following final chapter .

Conclusion

In the preceding chapters, an efficient signal estimation method or, stated more generally, an efficient approximation of (outputs of) symmetric filters by (outputs of) asymmetric filters was proposed for finite samples. The main difference of the DFA to the 'established' model-based approach is the direct optimization of filter parameters with respect to (an efficient estimate of) the squared filter approximation error. Therefore it is not necessary to infer an explicit model for the DGP based on available data. Although the traditional method based on the MBA is intuitively very appealing, its efficiency cannot be asserted if the DGP is unknown. The main problem is the fact that the corresponding optimization procedure - based on one-step ahead forecasting performances only - does not 'fit' the estimation problem to be solved because signal extraction requires good one- and multi-step ahead forecasting performances simultaneously. Since both objectives are generally conflicting in the presence of model misspecification (see for example Clements and Hendry [14]), a different approach is needed.

The differences between the DFA and the MBA may be illustrated on the basis of the so called 'unit-root' problem. A unit-root is a particular property of the DGP of X_t which has important implications for the estimation of a signal. In the context of the MBA, this property is 'traditionally' inferred from *short term* one-step ahead forecasting performances of a particular model despite the fact that unit roots specify particular *long run* dynamics of a time series. In the DFA, unit-roots are transposed into constraints which result in particular filter designs. In principle, these constraints allow for more general non-stationarities than 'integration' only. In particular, it is not relevant if X_t is difference stationary (I(1)-process) or trend stationary - stationary about a linear trend[1] - since the same first order constraint determines the filter design towards frequency zero for the DFA. Therefore, such constraints can

---

[1]The same reasoning would also apply for more general deterministic trends with bounded first derivative and diverging to infinity at a suitable rate.

enhance the finite sample performances of the asymmetric filter whether or not the input process is integrated. Explorative instruments (statistics based on adjusted time series) as well as formal instruments (the test statistics η and η' or the MC-criterion) can be used to indicate which filter design ought to perform better. The proposed instruments are derived directly from the signal estimation problem and implicitly account for one- and multi-step ahead forecasting performances[2]. However, these statistics cannot replace traditional unit-root tests in general because they emphasize aspects related to the long run dynamics of a time series which are specific to the (boundary) signal estimation problem. On the opposite, deducing filter constraints from traditional unit-root identification often results in inefficient filter designs. If a unit-root assumption enhances the one-step ahead forecasting performance of a particular model (for the DGP of X_t) then it does not necessarily follow that the corresponding constraint for the asymmetric filter improves the signal estimation performance (and conversely). Therefore, both methods - MBA and DFA - should rely on different statistical instruments specific to their own particular estimation problems. Both problems are related but different for finite samples and the solution of one does not necessarily solve the other optimally.

It is suggested in various places (see for example section 5.8 or chapter C in the appendix) that the signal estimation procedure of the DFA can be interpreted as a generalization of the ARIMA model-building process, for which the 'noise' term is autocorrelated[3]. A useful 'byproduct' of this generalization is the possibility of optimizing filters subject to a time delay restriction. The proposed DFA is more flexible (general) than the MBA because the filter parameters are optimized directly, so that interesting constraints (such as the time delay for example) can be 'build into' the resulting asymmetric filter.

Particular attention has been devoted to finite sample issues. First, a new parsimonious filter class, so called ZPC-filters, was introduced for which the parameters could be straightforwardly interpreted. Then, an attempt was made to distinguish overparameterization and overfitting and new instruments avoiding overparameterization (MC-criterion) or overfitting (a singularity penalty and the variable frequency sampling) were proposed. Essentially, overfitting was tackled by modifying the original optimization criterion without affecting efficiency issues of the resulting estimates. Overfitting manifests itself in an unnecessarily 'elaborate' transfer function of the asymmetric filter. If 'elaboration' is measured by the rate of decay of the MA coefficients (of the filter) then a new criterion 'penalizing' overfitting can be derived. A balance between 'fit' and 'regularity' was proposed. It was suggested that the idea of

---

[2]Although a model for the DGP is not explicitly required

[3]Note that the autocorrelated noise term is also an 'innovation' : it is orthogonal to past observations (regressors) because it is a weighted sum of *future* ϵ_t's, see formula (C.8).

penalizing excessively singular designs by including a term measuring the rate of decay of the estimated coefficients could be used for the MBA too which would open a field for future research. An alternative new method for avoiding more specifically instability of the asymmetric filter was proposed too by allowing the fixed frequency ordinates to vary in a well defined restricted manner, depending on the estimated filter parameters. Thus, potentially unstable poles could be 'tracked'.

Empirical evidences suggest that both methods - MBA and DFA - perform equally well if the MBA is based on the true DGP. However, the DFA often outperforms the MBA for real-world time series (for which model misspecification is the rule). Results similar to that obtained for the UK car sales series were obtained in Wildi/Schips[99] for a representative sample of 41 business survey indicators. For the MBA, it seems that models are often too parsimoniously parameterized[4] and that unnecessarily severe restrictions are maintained for the asymmetric filter (resulting from the I(2)-hypothesis which is often a misspecification for economic time series). In combination, these forms of misspecification can lead to severe losses in efficiency as shown in Part II and in Wildi/Schips[99]. However, diagnostic statistics based on the one-step ahead forecasting error (for example Ljung-Box or Box-Pierce statistics) are often unable to detect the relevant departures from the 'true' DGP. For the US-GNP series Cochrane [18], p.912, argues "Low-orders ARMA-models systematically overestimate the random-walk component of (US) GNP, even though they adequately represent the series by all the usual diagnostic tests".

Much effort has been and is still spent in deriving and/or modifying procedures for selecting the 'best' model for the DGP and for improving parameter estimates in the MBA. However, the criterion with respect to which the quality of empirical models is measured is (in general) the minimization of the squared one-step ahead forecasting error which is only partly in accordance with the signal estimation problem. To conclude, it is felt that the statistical 'apparatus' presented here solves the finite sample signal estimation problem more efficiently than the MBA because, unlike the latter, the optimization criterion for the DFA is derived directly from the estimation problem which has to be solved really.

---

[4]Low frequency as well as seasonal components of practical time series are generally characterized by more or less complex dynamics which cannot be suitably mapped into a two-parameter model such as for example the airline-model. Unfortunately, richer parameterized models are often unable to catch the 'salient' features of a time series and the discrepancy between the one-step ahead forecasting performance and the performance of the resulting asymmetric filter becomes more pronounced (overfitting).

A

Decompositions of Stochastic Processes

A general stochastic process can be decomposed into a weighted sum (discrete or uncountable) of orthogonal increments. Two classical decompositions are briefly presented here. Particular proofs for the DFA refer to these results. The first kind of results address (weakly) stationary processes.

A.1 Weakly Stationary Processes of Finite Variance

A weakly or wide sense stationary real stochastic process X_t of finite variance (called a stationary process in the following) is characterized by the following moment conditions :

$$E[X_t] = \mu, Cov(X_t, X_{t \pm i}) = R(i) \tag{A.1}$$

Two important decompositions of stationary processes follow.

A.1.1 Spectral Decomposition and Convolution Theorem

Theorem A.1 (Spectral Decomposition of X_t). *A stationary process X_t with mean μ can be uniquely decomposed (in the mean square sense) into a weighted continuous sum (stochastic integral)*

$$X_t = \mu + \int_{-\pi}^{\pi} \exp(it\omega) dZ(\omega) \tag{A.2}$$

where the continuous parameter process $Z(\omega)$, $\omega \in [-\pi, \pi]$ satisfies : $E[Z(\omega)] = 0$ and $Cov(Z(\omega_1) - Z(\omega_2), Z(\omega_1') - Z(\omega_2')) = 0$ whenever $[\omega_1, \omega_2] \cap [\omega_1', \omega_2'] = \emptyset$ (orthogonal increment process).

For a proof see for example Doob [25], p.480. For real processes $Z(\omega)$ is real too and the integration above may be restricted to $[0, \pi]$. More precisely, one obtains

$$X_t = \mu + \int_0^\pi \cos(t\omega)du(\omega) + \int_0^\pi \sin(t\omega)dv(\omega)$$

where $u(\cdot), v(\cdot)$ are two mutually uncorrelated real zero mean continuous parameter processes with orthogonal increments, see Doob [25], p. 482. Equation (A.2) corresponds to a spectral decomposition of the process X_t from which a spectral decomposition of the second order moments may be derived. Specifically, define the *integrated spectrum* $H(\omega)$ of X_t by

$$H(\omega) = \int_{-\pi}^\omega E[|dZ(\theta)|^2] \tag{A.3}$$

One can show that $H(\omega)$ behaves like a distribution function (see for example Doob [25], p.488) so that it may be uniquely decomposed into :

$$H(\omega) = H_1(\omega) + H_2(\omega) + H_3(\omega) \tag{A.4}$$

(Lebesgue decomposition) where $H_1(\cdot)$ is the absolutely continuous, $H_2(\cdot)$ the discrete (a step function with countably many steps) and $H_3(\cdot)$ the singular component. For univariate processes $H_3(\cdot)$ can often be neglected except for 'pathological' processes which are not considered here, see for example Whittle [95], p.25 or Priestley [75], p.226 ff. The processes corresponding to $H_1(\cdot)$ and $H_2(\cdot)$ are analyzed in section A.1.2. The next theorem relates the spectral distribution $H(\cdot)$ to the second order moments of X_t :

Theorem A.2 (Spectral Decomposition of $R(\cdot)$). *The autocovariance function $R(\cdot)$ of a weakly stationary process can be decomposed according to*

$$R(k) = \int_{-\pi}^\pi \exp(ik\omega)dH(\omega) \tag{A.5}$$

A proof can be found in Doob [25], chap. X and Priestley [75], chap.4. If $H(\omega)$ is absolutely continuous $(H(\omega) \equiv H_1(\omega))$, its 'derivative' $h(\omega) = dH(\omega)/d\omega$ is called the (non-normalized) *spectral density* of X_t. In virtue of (A.5), $h(\omega)$ is then the Fourier transform of the (discrete) autocovariance function $R(\cdot)$:

$$h(\omega) = \frac{1}{2\pi} \sum_{k=-\infty}^\infty R(k) \exp(-ik\omega) \tag{A.6}$$

It is easily verified that for a white noise process, $X_t := \epsilon_t$, the spectral density is a constant

$$h(\omega) = \frac{\sigma^2}{2\pi} \tag{A.7}$$

The terminology 'white' noise process is derived from physics by analogy to 'white' light for which the power distribution is constant too over the visible spectrum. The *normalized integrated spectrum* $F(\cdot)$ is defined by

$$F(\omega) := \frac{H(\omega)}{H(\pi)} \tag{A.8}$$

It inherits all properties of $H(\cdot)$: distribution function (more precisely, $F(\cdot)$ is a probability distribution), Lebesgue decomposition (A.4), spectral decomposition of the normalized autocovariance or the autocorrelation function (simply replace $dH(\cdot)$ by $dF(\cdot)$ and $R(\cdot)$ by $R(\cdot)/R(0)$ in (A.5)), see for example Priestley [75].

Assume the spectral density of X_t exists and the processes Y_t, X_t are related by the time invariant difference equation

$$Y_t = \sum_{k=-\infty}^{\infty} b_k X_{t-k} \tag{A.9}$$

The following important theorem relates the spectral densities of Y_t and X_t:

Theorem A.3 (Convolution Theorem). *Suppose X_t is a stationary process with spectral density $h(\omega)$ and Y_t is defined by (A.9) with (real) coefficients b_k being absolutely summable $\sum_{k=-\infty}^{\infty} |b_k| < \infty$. Then the spectral density of Y_t exists and satisfies :*

$$h_Y(\omega) = |\beta(\omega)|^2 h_X(\omega) \tag{A.10}$$

where $\beta(\cdot) := \sum_{k=-\infty}^{\infty} b_k \exp(-ik\cdot)$.

A proof of the theorem can be found in Priestley (1983) chap. 4, sec. 12. The function $\beta(\cdot)$ is called the *transfer function* of the linear time invariant transform *(filter)* : $X_t \to Y_t$ in (A.9). Spectral densities of AR-, MA- and ARMA processes are obtained from (A.7) and the above theorem by setting $X_t := \epsilon_t$ in (A.9).

The so called *Parseval relation*

$$\sum_{j=-\infty}^{\infty} b_j^2 = \frac{1}{2\pi} \int_{-\pi}^{\pi} |\beta(\omega)|^2 d\omega \tag{A.11}$$

follows from theorem A.2 (setting $k := 0$) and theorem A.3. In the following section a decomposition of a stationary process in the time domain is presented.

A.1.2 The Wold Decomposition

Denote the variance of the one-step ahead forecasting error of X_t by $\sigma(1)^2 = Var(\hat{X}_t(1))$, where $\hat{X}_t(1)$ is the best linear one-step ahead forecast of X_{t+1} given $X_t, X_{t-1}, \dots$. A process X_t is called *linear deterministic* or *singular* if

$\sigma(1)^2 = 0$. It is called *regular* if $\sigma(1)^2 > 0$. Note that the linearity assumption is important in this context. An example for a regular but nevertheless deterministic process is given for example in Priestley [75] p.760 (the 'perfect' forecast is based on a non-linear function). Wold [100] proved the following important theorem:

Theorem A.4 (Wold Decomposition). *Every stationary process X_t (of finite variance) can be uniquely decomposed into the sum of two stationary processes X_{1t}, X_{2t}*

$$X_t = X_{1t} + X_{2t} \tag{A.12}$$

where X_{1t} and X_{2t} are characterized by the following properties:

- X_{1t} *is a stationary one-sided MA(∞)-process $X_{1t} = \sum_{k=0}^{\infty} b_k \epsilon_{t-k}$ and*
- X_{2t} *is a linear deterministic process orthogonal to X_{1t}.*

If X_t is singular, then $X_{1t} \equiv 0$. If X_t is regular then X_{2t} does not necessarily vanish. In the latter case one can show that

- X_{2t} is a harmonic process

$$X_{2t} = \sum_{k=1}^{\infty} A_k \exp(i\lambda_k t + \Phi_k) \tag{A.13}$$

where λ_k and A_k are constants, the A_k being square summable $\sum_{k=1}^{\infty} A_k^2 < \infty$ and Φ_k are independent rectangularly distributed random variables in the real interval $[-\pi, \pi]$ (see for example Whittle [95], p.25 and Priestley [75], p.758) and

- the spectral distributions of X_{it} correspond to $H_i(\cdot)$ in (A.4), see Doob [25], p.572 ff.

Note that if X_t is singular ($X_t \equiv X_{2t}$) then its spectral distribution $H(\cdot)$ is not necessarily discontinuous and thus in general $H(\cdot) \neq H_2(\cdot)$ in the latter case (see for example Brockwell and Davis [10], example 5.6.1, p. 185). To analyze these differences it is useful to introduce the class of so called *general MA processes*. X_t is called a general MA process if it can be decomposed according to

$$X_t = \sum_{k=-\infty}^{\infty} b_k \epsilon_{t-k} \tag{A.14}$$

where ϵ_t is a white noise (not necessarily independent) sequence and the coefficients b_k are square summable. If ϵ_t are independent, then X_t is called a general linear process. The following two propositions relate singularity (regularity) of a process to a result in the frequency domain.

Proposition A.5. *A stationary process X_t has an absolutely continuous spectral distribution function, i.e. a well defined spectral density $h(\omega)$, if and only if it is a general MA process.*

A proof can be found in Doob [25], chap.10, sec. 8.

Proposition A.6 (Kolmogorov or Szego formula). *The variance of the one-step ahead forecasting error* $\sigma(1)^2$ *(linear forecasting function) of a general MA process* X_t *is related to the spectral density* $h(\cdot)$ *by*

$$\sigma(1)^2 = 2\pi \exp\left(\frac{1}{2\pi}\int_{-\pi}^{\pi} \ln(h(\omega))d\omega\right) \tag{A.15}$$

For a proof, see Doob [25], chap. XII and Caines [12], theorem 3.4. The following results are direct consequences from the above propositions and the Wold decomposition :

- A general MA process whose spectral density vanishes on a set with positive Lebesgue measure must be singular (linear deterministic) because for such a process (A.15) implies $\sigma(1)^2 = 0$.
- From theorem A.4 and propositions A.5 and (A.6) it follows that the two sided representation $X_t = \sum_{k=-\infty}^{\infty} b_k \epsilon_{t-k}$ of a general MA process may be transformed into a one-sided representation $\sum_{k=0}^{\infty} c_k \nu_{t-k}$ where ν_t is a white noise process if and only if $\ln(h(\omega))$ is Lebesgue integrable on $[-\pi, \pi]$.

From the above it follows that a general singular (linear deterministic) process may be represented as the sum of a singular general MA process and a harmonic process. The spectral distribution function of the former is absolutely continuous and the spectral distribution of the latter is a step function. Note also that whereas a weighted *countable* sum of harmonic processes is linearly deterministic, an *uncountable* weighted sum (as given by the stochastic integral (A.2)) may be singular or regular, depending on $\sigma(1)^2$ being greater than zero or not.

A.2 Non-Stationary Processes

For non-stationary processes (A.1) is no more true in general. A generalization of the Wold-decomposition to a non-stationary process X_t has been proposed in Cramer [20] :

$$X_t = D_t + Y_t$$

where D_t is a deterministic process and

$$Y_t = \sum_{k=0}^{\infty} b_k(t)\epsilon_{t-j} \tag{A.16}$$

is a regular process orthogonal to D_t and satisfying $\sum_{k=0}^{\infty} b_k(t)^2 < \infty$ for all t.

B

Stochastic Properties of the Periodogram

This chapter completes the results obtained in chapter 4. In the first section stochastic properties of the periodogram are analyzed which are needed in proofs for the DFA. In the second section, a generalization of the periodogram to stationary processes of infinite variance is analyzed. Although this has not been considered in the main text, it is felt that an extension of the DFA based on these results may be an interesting issue for future research.

B.1 Periodogram for Finite Variance Stationary Processes

Assume

$$X_t = \sum_{k=-\infty}^{\infty} b_k \epsilon_{t-k} \tag{B.1}$$

where ϵ_t is a white noise process and the coefficients b_k are square summable. If X_t is regular then it must admit a one-sided MA-representation, see section A.1.2. The following proposition relates smoothness properties of the spectral density of X_t to the rate of decay of the coefficients b_k.

Proposition B.1. *If $X_t \in C_f^u$ then $d^j h(\omega)/d\omega^j$ are continuous functions for all integers j satisfying $0 \le j \le [u]$, where $[u]$ is the greatest integer smaller or equal to u and $d^0 h(\omega)/d\omega^0 := h(\omega)$.*

Proof. A proof immediately follows from (4.18) and (A.6). □

In the following theorem, moments and the distribution of the periodogram are analyzed subject to various assumptions about ϵ_t. The first three assertions are 'classical' results whereas the last assertion is new and requires a complete proof. It is used in deriving the consistency of the estimate for the asymptotic variance-covariance matrix of the filter parameter estimates in theorem 5.10.

Theorem B.2.   *1. If X_t is a gaussian white noise process and $\omega_j \in \Omega_N$, then the corresponding periodogram ordinates $I_{NX}(\omega_j)$ are pairwise independent and*

$$I_{NX}(\omega_j) \sim \begin{cases} 2\sigma^2 \chi_1^2 & \omega_j = 0, \pi \\ \sigma^2 \chi_2^2 & else \end{cases}$$

where χ_1^2, χ_2^2 are chi-square random variables with one respectively two degrees of freedom.

2. Assume $X_t \in C_f^0$, ϵ_t is an iid sequence and $h(\omega) > 0$ for all ω. Then the periodogram $I_{NX}(\omega_k)$ converges in distribution to an exponentially distributed random variable with mean $h(\omega_k)$ for all $\omega_k \in \Omega_N$ satisfying $0 < \omega_k < \pi$. If $\omega_i \neq \omega_j$ then the corresponding periodogram ordinates are asymptotically independent. If $\pi \in \Omega_N$ then $I_{NX}(\pi) \sim h(\pi)\chi_1^2$, where χ_1^2 is a chi-square distributed random variable with one degree of freedom. Also $I_{NX}(0) \sim h(0)\chi_1^2$.

3. If $X_t \in C_f^{1/2}$ and ϵ_t is an iid sequence satisfying $\mathrm{E}[\epsilon_t^4] = \eta\sigma^4 < \infty$, then

$$\begin{aligned} &\mathrm{Cov}\,(I_{NX}(\omega_j), I_{NX}(\omega_k)) \\ &= \begin{cases} 2h(\omega_j)^2 + \mathrm{O}(1/\sqrt{N}) & \omega_j = \omega_k = 0 \text{ or } \pi \\ h(\omega_j)^2 + \mathrm{O}(1/\sqrt{N}) & 0 < \omega_j = \omega_k < \pi \\ \mathrm{O}(N^{-1}) & \omega_j \neq \omega_k \end{cases} \end{aligned} \qquad (B.2)$$

for $\omega_j, \omega_k \in \Omega_N$. The terms $\mathrm{O}(1/\sqrt{N})$ and $\mathrm{O}(N^{-1})$ are bounded uniformly in j and k.

4. If $X_t \in C_f^{1/2}$ and ϵ_t is an iid sequence satisfying $\mathrm{E}[\epsilon_t^8] < \infty$, then

$$\mathrm{Cov}\left(I_{NX}(\omega_j)^2, I_{NX}(\omega_k)^2\right) = \mathrm{O}(N^{-1})\ \omega_j \neq \omega_k \qquad (B.3)$$

for $\omega_j, \omega_k \in \Omega_N$. The term $\mathrm{O}(N^{-1})$ is bounded uniformly in j and k.

Proof. For proofs of the first three assertions see Priestley [75] theorem 6.1.1 and Brockwell and Davis [10] theorem 10.3.2 (for the second and the third assertion: note that equation 10.3.4 in the cited literature implies that the first extension (4.15) of the periodogram is used). A proof of the last assertion is now given. Let

$$\mathrm{E}[\epsilon_t \epsilon_{t-i} \epsilon_{t-j} \epsilon_{t-k} \epsilon_{t-l} \epsilon_{t-m} \epsilon_{t-n} \epsilon_{t-p}]$$

$$= \begin{cases} M_8 & i = j = \ldots = p = 0 \\ M_6 M_2 & i = 0, j = k = \ldots = p \\ M_5 M_3 & i = j = 0, k = l = m = n = p \\ M_4^2 & i = j = k = 0, l = m = n = p \\ M_4 M_2^2 & i = 0, j = k, l = m = n = p \\ M_3^2 M_2 & i = 0, j = k = l, m = n = p \\ M_2^4 & i = 0, j = k, l = m, n = p \\ 0 & else \end{cases} \qquad (B.4)$$

where $M_k := E[\epsilon_t^k]$ (so for example $M_2 = \sigma^2$). The less restrictive condition for a non-vanishing expectation is the last one ($i = 0, j = k, l = m, n = p$) since it involves four constraints only (whereas all others imply five or more constraints). Since

$$\mathrm{Cov}\left(I_{NX}(\omega_j)^2, I_{NX}(\omega_k)^2\right) = \frac{(2\pi)^4}{N^4}\left(\cdot\right)$$

the first six moment restrictions above all induce $O(1/N)$-terms for the covariance (because the remaining degrees of freedom are of order $O(N^3)$). Therefore, the last restriction is the only one which results in an $O(1)$-term in the expression $E[I_{NX}(\omega_k)^2 I_{NX}(\omega_j)^2]$ for the covariance. Now consider

$$E[I_{NX}(\omega_j)^2 I_{NX}(\omega_k)^2] = E\left[\frac{(2\pi)^4}{N^4}\sum_{i_1=1}^{N}\sum_{i_2=1}^{N}\cdots\sum_{i_8=1}^{N}\prod_{k=1}^{8}X_{i_k}\right] \quad (B.5)$$

$$\exp(-i\omega_j(i_1 - i_2 + i_3 - i_4))\exp(-i\omega_k(i_5 - i_6 + i_7 - i_8))\Bigg]$$

$$= M_2^4\frac{(2\pi)^4}{N^4}\sum_{i_1=1}^{N}\sum_{i_2=1}^{N}\cdots\sum_{i_8=1}^{N}\left[\sum_{P}\prod_{m=1}^{4}\left(\sum_{l=-\infty}^{\infty}b_l b_{i_{P(2m-1)}-i_{P(2m)}+l}\right)\right]$$

$$\exp(-i\omega_j(i_1 - i_2 + i_3 - i_4))\exp(-i\omega_k(i_5 - i_6 + i_7 - i_8))$$

$$+O(1/N) \quad (B.6)$$

where the terms which do not correspond to M_2^4 in (B.4) are collected in the $O(1/N)$-term and $\displaystyle\sum_{P}\prod_{m=1}^{4}\left(\sum_{l=-\infty}^{\infty}b_l b_{i_{P(2m-1)}-i_{P(2m)}+l}\right)$ is the sum over all admissible permutations P of the integer set $\{1, 2, ..., 8\}$. The set of admissible permutations is defined by all *pairwise* combinations of ϵ_t's appearing in M_2^4 in (B.4): there are $7 \times 5 \times 3 = 105$ such permutations.

It is shown in Brockwell and Davis [10], p.349, that the permutations corresponding to 'cross-products' (for which there exists an m such that $1 \leq P(2m-1) \leq 4$ and $5 \leq P(2m) \leq 8$ or for which $5 \leq P(2m-1) \leq 8$ and $1 \leq P(2m) \leq 4$) lead to terms of order $O(1/N)$ if $\omega_j \neq \omega_k$. The proof is reproduced here. Assume for simplicity that $P(2m-1) = 1$ and $P(2m) = 5$ (analogous proofs apply to all other 'cross products'). Then

$$E\left[\sum_{i_1=1}^{N}X_{i_1}\exp(-ii_1\omega_j)\sum_{i_5=1}^{N}X_{i_5}\exp(-ii_5\omega_k)\right]$$

$$= M_2\sum_{i_1=1}^{N}\sum_{I_5=1}^{N}\sum_{m=-\infty}^{\infty}b_m b_{i_5-i_1+m}\exp(-i(i_1\omega_j + i_5\omega_k))$$

$$= \sum_{s=1}^{N}\sum_{u=1}^{N}R(u-s)\exp(-i(s\omega_j + u\omega_k))$$

$$= \sum_{u=1}^{N} \sum_{s=1-u}^{N-u} R(s) \exp(-is\omega_j) \exp(-iu(\omega_j + \omega_k))$$

$$= \sum_{s=0}^{N-1} R(s) \exp(-is\omega_j) \sum_{u=1}^{N-s} \exp(-iu(\omega_j + \omega_k))$$

$$+ \sum_{s=-N+1}^{-1} R(s) \exp(-is\omega_j) \sum_{u=1-s}^{N} \exp(-iu(\omega_j + \omega_k)) \qquad (B.7)$$

where $R(s)$ is the autocovariance function of X_t. For $\omega_j \neq \omega_k$ the orthogonality relations (4.3) imply

$$\left| \sum_{u=1}^{N-s} \exp(-iu(\omega_j + \omega_k)) \right|$$

$$= \left| \sum_{u=1}^{N} \exp(-iu(\omega_j + \omega_k)) - \sum_{u=N-s+1}^{N} \exp(-iu(\omega_j + \omega_k)) \right|$$

$$= \left| 0 - \sum_{u=N-s+1}^{N} \exp(-iu(\omega_j + \omega_k)) \right|$$

$$\leq s$$

for $0 \leq s \leq N - 1$ and

$$\left| \sum_{u=1-s}^{N} \exp(-iu(\omega_j + \omega_k)) \right| \leq |s|$$

for $-N + 1 \leq s \leq -1$. Therefore, (B.7) is bounded by

$$\sum_{|s|<N} |R(s)| \, |s| \leq N^{1/2} \sum_{|s|<N} |R(s)| \, |s|^{1/2}$$

$$= O(N^{1/2})$$

which implies that

$$E\left[\sum_{i_1=1}^{N} X_{i_1} \exp(-ii_1\omega_j) \sum_{i_5=1}^{N} X_{i_5} \exp(-ii_5\omega_k) \right] = O(N^{1/2})$$

Note that this result is independent of the signs of ω_j and ω_k. Therefore,

$$E\left[\sum_{i_m=1}^{N} X_{i_m} \exp(-ii_m\omega_j) \sum_{i_n=1}^{N} X_{i_n} \exp(-ii_n\omega_k) \right] = O(N^{1/2})$$

for all 'cross products' $1 \leq i_m \leq 4$ and $5 \leq i_n \leq 8$ (or $5 \leq i_m \leq 8$ and $1 \leq i_n \leq 4$). Note also that 'cross products' must appear pairwise for the admissible permutations. Thus

$$M_2^4 \frac{(2\pi)^4}{N^4} \sum_{i_1=1}^{N} \sum_{i_2=1}^{N} \cdots \sum_{i_8=1}^{N} \left[\prod_{m=1}^{4} \left(\sum_{l=-\infty}^{\infty} b_l b_{i_{P(2m-1)} - i_{P(2m)} + l} \right) \right]$$
$$\exp(-i\omega_j(i_1 - i_2 + i_3 - i_4)) \exp(-i\omega_k(i_5 - i_6 + i_7 - i_8))$$
$$= M_2^4 \frac{(2\pi)^4}{N^4} O(N^2) O(N^{1/2}) O(N^{1/2})$$
$$= O(1/N)$$

for each permutation P enabling 'cross products' (where the two $O(N^{1/2})$-terms correspond to at least one pair of 'cross product' terms). As a result, (B.6) becomes

$$E[I_{NX}(\omega_j)^2 I_{NX}(\omega_k)^2]$$
$$= M_2^4 \frac{(2\pi)^4}{N^4} \sum_{i_1=1}^{N} \sum_{i_2=1}^{N} \cdots \sum_{i_8=1}^{N} \left[\sum_{P' \in \Pi} \prod_{m=1}^{4} \left(\sum_{l=-\infty}^{\infty} b_l b_{i_{P'(2m-1)} - i_{P'(2m)} + l} \right) \right]$$
$$\exp(-i\omega_j(i_1 - i_2 + i_3 - i_4)) \exp(-i\omega_k(i_5 - i_6 + i_7 - i_8)) + O(1/N)$$

where the permutations P' belong to Π, the set of admissible permutations which do not involve 'cross-product' terms. However, the resulting $O(1)$-expression exactly cancels with the corresponding $O(1)$-expression for

$$E[I_{NX}(\omega_j)^2] E[I_{NX}(\omega_k)^2] \tag{B.8}$$

since for the latter the set of admissible permutations is identical with Π (i.e. all admissible permutations without 'cross product' terms). The other non-vanishing term in (B.8) involves $E[\epsilon_t^4]$ and is of order $O(1/N)$ because of the constraint $i = j = k = 0$ in $E[\epsilon_t \epsilon_{t+i} \epsilon_{t+j} \epsilon_{t+k}]$ (implying only one remaining degree of freedom). The latter statement is also proved in Brockwell and Davis [10], equation 10.3.17 (note that the right hand side of 10.3.17 should be $O(N^{-1})$ instead of $O(N^{-2})$ because one degree of freedom is left in the sum 10.3.14). This completes the proof of the theorem. □

The following corollary presents a useful result needed in deriving approximations in particular proofs for the DFA.

Corollary B.3. *Let the assumptions of the preceding theorem, second or third claim, be satisfied and assume $g(\omega)$ is a bounded function. Then*

$$\frac{2\pi}{N} \sum_{k=-[N/2]}^{[N/2]} g(\omega_k) I_{NX}(\omega_k) = \frac{2\pi}{N} \sum_{k=-[N/2]}^{[N/2]} g(\omega_k) h(\omega_k) + r_N \tag{B.9}$$

where $r_N = o(1)$ (second claim) or $r_N = O(1/\sqrt{N})$ (third claim).

Proof.

$$\frac{2\pi}{N}\sum_{k=-[N/2]}^{[N/2]} g(\omega_k)I_{NX}(\omega_k) = \frac{2\pi}{N}\sum_{k=-[N/2]}^{[N/2]} g(\omega_k)\left(E[I_{NX}(\omega_k)] + \nu_k\right)$$

Consider now

$$Var\left(\frac{2\pi}{N}\sum_{k=-[N/2]}^{[N/2]} g(\omega_k)\nu_k\right) = \frac{4\pi^2}{N^2}\sum_{k=-[N/2]}^{[N/2]} g(\omega_k)^2 Var(\nu_k)$$

$$+\frac{4\pi^2}{N^2}\sum_{k=-[N/2]}^{[N/2]}\sum_{j=-[N/2],j\neq k}^{[N/2]} g(\omega_k)g(\omega_j)Cov(\nu_k,\nu_j)$$

$$\leq \|g\|_\infty^2 \frac{4\pi^2}{N^2}\left(\sum_{k=-[N/2]}^{[N/2]} Var(\nu_k) + \sum_{k=-[N/2]}^{[N/2]}\sum_{j=-[N/2],j\neq k}^{[N/2]} |Cov(\nu_k,\nu_j)|\right)$$

$$= r_N' = \begin{cases} o(1) & \text{second claim} \\ O(1/N) & \text{third claim} \end{cases}$$

where $\|g\|_\infty := \sup(|g(\omega)|)$ and the last equality follows from (B.2). Therefore

$$\frac{2\pi}{N}\sum_{k=-[N/2]}^{[N/2]} g(\omega_k)I_{NX}(\omega_k) = \frac{2\pi}{N}\sum_{k=-[N/2]}^{[N/2]} g(\omega_k)E[I_{NX}(\omega_k)] + r_N'$$

$$= \frac{2\pi}{N}\sum_{k=-[N/2]}^{[N/2]} g(\omega_k)(h(\omega_k) + r_N'') + r_N'$$

$$= \frac{2\pi}{N}\sum_{k=-[N/2]}^{[N/2]} g(\omega_k)h(\omega_k) + r_N$$

where $r_N'' = o(1)$ (second claim), see (B.17) below or $r_N'' = O(1/\sqrt{N})$ (third claim), see (B.18) below. In the last equality $r_N = O(1/\sqrt{N})$ (third claim) follows from the boundedness of $g(\cdot)$ and the uniform approximation of $E[I_{NX}(\omega_k)]$ by $h(\omega_k)$. This completes the proof of the corollary.   □

The next theorem proposes results for $\Xi_{NX}(\omega_k)$ which are usefull for deriving proofs in the case of integrated processes. Some of the assertions could not be found in the literature so that extensive proofs are provided.

Theorem B.4.   *1. Assume $X_t \in C_f^0$, ϵ_t is an iid sequence and $h(\omega) > 0$. Then real and imaginary parts of the discrete Fourier transform $\Xi_{NX}(\omega_k)$ (see (4.1)) converge in distribution to two independent gaussian random variables with mean 0 and common variance $h(\omega_k)/2$ for all $\omega_k \in \Omega_N$. If $\omega_i \neq \omega_j$ then the corresponding ordinates are asymptotically independent.*

2. If $X_t \in C_f^{1/2}$ and ϵ_t is a white noise sequence (not necessarily iid) and $\omega_j, \omega_k \in \Omega_N$, then

$$\text{Cov}\,(\Xi_{NX}(\omega_j), \Xi_{NX}(\omega_k)) = \begin{cases} h(\omega_j) + O(N^{-1/2}) & \omega_j = \omega_k \\ O(N^{-1/2}) & \omega_j \neq \pm\omega_k \end{cases} \quad \text{(B.10)}$$

where the terms $O(N^{-1/2})$ are bounded uniformly in j and k.

3. If $X_t \in C_f^{1/2}$ and ϵ_t is a white noise sequence (not necessarily iid) and $|\omega - \lambda| > 0$, then

$$|\text{Cov}\,(\Xi_{NX}(\omega), \Xi_{NX}(\lambda))| \leq \sqrt{h(\omega)h(\lambda)}\,\frac{\pi}{N|\omega - \lambda|} + O(N^{-1/2}) \text{(B.11)}$$

where the extension (4.16) is used (for $\Xi_{NX}(\omega)$).

4. • If $X_t \in C_f^0$ then

$$\lim_{N \to \infty} Var(\Xi_{NX}(\omega)) = h(\omega)$$

• If $X_t \in C_f^{1/2}$ then

$$Var(\Xi_{NX}(\omega)) = h(\omega) + O\left(\frac{1}{\sqrt{N}}\right)$$

uniformly in ω.

• If $X_t \in C_f^1$ then

$$Var(\Xi_{NX}(\omega)) = h(\omega) + O\left(\frac{\log(N)}{N}\right)$$

Proof. For X_t an iid sequence, the first assertion follows from equation 10.3.8 in Brockwell and Davis [10] (note that equation 10.3.4 in the cited literature shows that extension (4.15) is used for the discrete Fourier transform $\Xi_{NX}(\cdot)$). For MA-processes, this result together with (4.19) proves the first assertion for the general case.

In order to prove the second assertion assume first $X_t = \epsilon_t$ is a white noise process. Then

$$\text{Cov}(\Xi_{NX}(\omega), \Xi_{NX}(\lambda)) = E[\Xi_{NX}(\omega)\overline{\Xi_{NX}(\lambda)}]$$

$$= \frac{1}{2\pi N} E\left[\sum_{t=1}^{N} \epsilon_t \exp(-it\omega) \sum_{t=1}^{N} \epsilon_t \exp(it\lambda)\right]$$

$$= \frac{\sigma^2}{2\pi N} \sum_{t=1}^{N} \exp(-it(\omega - \lambda)) \quad \text{(B.12)}$$

$$= \begin{cases} 0 & \text{if } \omega = \omega_j \neq \omega_k = \lambda \\ \dfrac{\sigma^2}{2\pi} & \omega = \lambda \end{cases} \quad \text{(B.13)}$$

where the last equality follows from the orthogonality relations (4.3). For MA-processes this result together with (4.19) proves the second assertion.

In order to prove the third assertion, assume $X_t = \epsilon_t$ is a white noise process. Then

$$\frac{1}{N}\left|\sum_{t=1}^{N}\exp(-it(\omega - \lambda))\right| = \left|\frac{1 - \exp(-iN(\omega - \lambda))}{N(1 - \exp(-i(\omega - \lambda)))}\right|$$

$$\leq \frac{2}{N|1 - \exp(-i(\omega - \lambda))|}$$

$$\leq \frac{\pi}{N|\omega - \lambda|} \tag{B.14}$$

Inserting this result into (B.12) :

$$|\text{Cov}\,(\Xi_{NX}(\omega), \Xi_{NX}(\lambda))| \leq \frac{\sigma^2}{2\pi}\frac{\pi}{N|\omega - \lambda|} \tag{B.15}$$

For $X_t = \sum_{k=-\infty}^{\infty} b_k \epsilon_{t-k} \in C_f^{1/2}$ define $B(\omega) := \sum_{k=-\infty}^{\infty} b_k \exp(-it\omega)$. It follows that

$$|\text{Cov}\,(\Xi_{NX}(\omega), \Xi_{NX}(\lambda))| = \left|E\left[B(\omega)\Xi_{N\epsilon}(\omega)\overline{B(\lambda)\Xi_{N\epsilon}(\lambda)}\right]\right| + O(N^{-1/2})$$

$$= \left|B(\omega)\overline{B(\lambda)}\right||\text{Cov}\,(\Xi_{N\epsilon}(\omega), \Xi_{N\epsilon}(\lambda))| + O(N^{-1/2})$$

$$\leq \sqrt{h(\omega)h(\lambda)}\frac{\pi}{N|\omega - \lambda|} + O(N^{-1/2}) \tag{B.16}$$

where the first equality follows from (4.19) and the inequality follows from (B.15) and (A.10). The proof readily extends to the case $E[X_t] = \mu \neq 0$ with obvious modifications.

In order to prove the last assertion, note that $X_t \in C_f^0$ implies that the spectral density $h(\cdot)$ is continuous, see proposition B.1. It is then shown in Priestley [75], p. 416-418, that $\lim_{N\to\infty} Var(\Xi_{NX}(\omega)) = h(\omega)$. If $X_t \in C_f^{1/2}$, then (4.19), (A.10) and (B.13) (the case $\omega = \lambda$) imply that $Var(\Xi_{NX}(\omega)) = h(\omega) + O\left(\frac{1}{\sqrt{N}}\right)$ uniformly in ω (because the bound for the convolution error in (4.19) does not depend on ω). If $X_t \in C_f^1$ and ϵ_t is an iid sequence, then $Var(\Xi_{NX}(\omega)) = h(\omega) + O(\log(N)/N)$, see Priestley [75], equation 6.2.12. Since $Var(\Xi_{NX}(\omega))$ only depends on the first two moments of ϵ_t this result straightforwardly extends to white noise sequences (not necessarily iid random variables) which completes the proof of the theorem. $\square$

The *bias* of the periodogram is analyzed in the following corollary:

Corollary B.5. • *If $X_t \in C_f^0$ then*

$$\lim_{N\to\infty} E[I_{NX}(\omega)] = h(\omega) \tag{B.17}$$

- If $X_t \in C_f^{1/2}$ then

$$E[I_{NX}(\omega)] = h(\omega) + O\left(\frac{1}{\sqrt{N}}\right) \tag{B.18}$$

  uniformly in ω.
- If $X_t \in C_f^1$ then

$$E[I_{NX}(\omega)] = h(\omega) + O\left(\frac{\log(N)}{N}\right) \tag{B.19}$$

Proof. A proof immediately follows from the last assertion of theorem B.4 by noting that $E[\Xi_{NX}(\omega)] = 0$, i.e. $Var(\Xi_{NX}(\omega)) = E[I_{NX}(\omega)]$. $\square$

B.2 Periodogram for Infinite Variance Stationary Processes

Assume the process X_t satisfies

$$E[|X_t|^u] = \begin{cases} M_u < \infty &, u < \alpha \\ \infty &, u \geq \alpha \end{cases} \tag{B.20}$$

For $\alpha \leq 2$, X_t is a process of infinite variance. Often, a distribution $F_\alpha(\cdot)$ of the random variable X_t (satisfying (B.20)) is considered such that it is invariant (up to proper scaling and translation) under arbitrary summations of the random variables X_t. That means that

$$c + d \sum_{t=-\infty}^{\infty} b_t X_t \stackrel{d}{=} F_\alpha(\cdot)$$

where $\stackrel{d}{=}$ means equivalence in distribution and c and d depend on b_t. Such processes are called α-*stable* processes and α is called the *characteristic exponent* of the distribution $F_\alpha(\cdot)$, see for example Embrechts et al. [28], chapter 2. If $F_\alpha(\cdot)$ is symmetric, the corresponding process is called *symmetric* α-*stable* or simply sαs. One can show that $F_2(\cdot)$ is the gaussian distribution (and hence it is symmetric), see Embrechts [28], theorem 2.2.3. The results proposed below can be extended to non-symmetric and non-stable distributions but this would require more technical assumptions and more complicated notations. In the following two sections, MA-processes and suitably defined second order moments, spectral densities and periodogram estimates are proposed and analyzed.

B.2.1 Moving Average Processes of Infinite Variance

A straightforward generalization of MA-processes of finite to infinite variance is given by the following definition.

Definition B.6. *The class of so called MA_α-processes is defined by*

$$X_t = \sum_{k=-\infty}^{\infty} b_k Z_{t-k} \tag{B.21}$$

where Z_t is an iid sequence of $s\alpha s$ random variables.

A necessary and sufficient condition for the existence (stationarity) of X_t is given by

$$\sum_{k=-\infty}^{\infty} |b_k|^\alpha < \infty$$

see for example Embrechts et al. [28], p.378. Obviously, for $\alpha = 2$ the traditional stationarity assumption results. In particular, X_t is distributed according to $Z_t \left(\sum_{k=-\infty}^{\infty} |b_k|^\alpha \right)^{1/\alpha}$ (because of the stability of the distribution of Z_t, X_t is itself an $s\alpha s$ random variable).

For such a process the main theorems A.1 and A.4 are no more valid. Although a formal extension of (A.2) to the class of so called *harmonizable* processes is possible (see for example Rosinski [79] : $Z(\omega)$ in (A.2) then becomes a so called $s\alpha s$-random measure) this generalization suffers from the fact that the class of harmonizable processes does not even contain the MA_α-processes of definition B.6, see Rosinski [79]. However, decompositions are still possible for suitably *normalized* moments. The latter are introduced in the following section.

B.2.2 Autocorrelation Function, Normalized Spectral Density and (Self) Normalized Periodogram

It is assumed that the coefficients of X_t in (B.21) satisfy

$$\sum_{k=-\infty}^{\infty} |b_k|^\delta k < \infty, \text{ where}$$

$$\delta = 1 \text{ if } 1 < \alpha < 2 \tag{B.22}$$
$$\delta < \alpha \text{ if } \alpha \leq 1$$

Define the sample autocorrelation $\hat{r}(\cdot)$ by

$$\hat{r}(k) := \frac{\hat{R}(k)}{\hat{R}(0)} = \frac{\sum_{t=1}^{N-k} X_t X_{t+k}}{\sum_{t=1}^{N} X_t^2}$$

and the theoretical autocorrelation by

$$r(k) := \frac{\sum_{j=-\infty}^{\infty} b_j b_{j+k}}{\sum_{j=-\infty}^{\infty} b_j^2} \tag{B.23}$$

Theorem B.7 (Estimation of the Autocorrelation Function). *Assume that X_t is a MA_α process satisfying (B.22) and assume also that the distribution of Z_t is sαs. Then for each m*

$$\left(\frac{N}{\ln(N)}\right)^{1/\alpha} (\hat{r}(1) - r(1), ..., \hat{r}(m) - r(m)) \overset{d}{\to} (Y_1, ..., Y_m) \qquad \text{(B.24)}$$

where $Y_k := \sum_{j=1}^{\infty}\{r(k+j) + r(k-j) - 2r(j)r(k)\}\dfrac{U_j}{U_0}$ and where U_j, $j \geq 0$ are independent stable random variables.

A proof of this theorem can be found in Brockwell and Davis [10], theorem 13.3.1. As an immediate consequence

$$\hat{r}(k) = r(k) + O_P\left(\left\{\frac{N}{\ln(N)}\right\}^{-1/\alpha}\right) \qquad \text{(B.25)}$$

for $m = 1$, where the symbol $O_P(1)$ means *boundedness in probability*, see for example Brockwell/Davis [10] chap.6.

Remark

- Although second order moments do not exist if $\alpha < 2$, (B.23) is well defined and evidently corresponds to the (linear) dependency structure of the process X_t in the form of its (properly defined) autocorrelation function.

Definition B.8. *The normalized spectral density of a MA_α-process X_t is defined by*

$$f(\omega) := \frac{1}{2\pi} \sum_{k=-\infty}^{\infty} r(k)\exp(-ik\omega) = \frac{1}{2\pi} \frac{\left|\sum_{k=-\infty}^{\infty} b_k \exp(-ik\omega)\right|^2}{\sum_{k=-\infty}^{\infty} b_k^2} \qquad \text{(B.26)}$$

The normalized periodogram is defined by

$$I_{NX}(\omega) := \frac{1}{N^{2/\alpha}2\pi} \left|\sum_{t=1}^{N}(X_t - \bar{X})\exp(-it\omega)\right|^2 \qquad \text{(B.27)}$$

The self normalized periodogram is defined by

$$\hat{I}_{NX}(\omega) := \frac{1}{2\pi} \frac{\left|\sum_{t=1}^{N}(X_t - \bar{X})\exp(-it\omega)\right|^2}{\sum_{t=1}^{N}(X_t - \bar{X})^2} \qquad \text{(B.28)}$$

The last definition may be motivated by

- the fact that α is generally unknown in (B.27) and

- that $N^{-2/\alpha} \sum_{t=1}^{N} X_t^2 \overset{d}{\to} \sum_{k=-\infty}^{\infty} b_k^2 G_0$ where G_0 is a positive $\alpha/2$ stable random variable. Hence the normalization in (B.28) "stabilizes" the estimate, see for example Embrechts et al [28], p.390.

Theorem B.9 (Convergence of the (Self) Normalized Periodogram). *Assume that X_t is a MA_α process satisfying (B.22) and assume also that Z_t is sαs-distributed. Suppose $f(\omega) > 0$, $\forall \omega$. Then*

- *for arbitrary frequencies $0 < \omega_1 < ... < \omega_m < \pi$,*

$$(I_{NX}(\omega_1), ..., I_{NX}(\omega_m)) \overset{d}{\to} (f(\omega_1)V_1, ..., f(\omega_m)V_2) \qquad (B.29)$$

  where V_i are dependent sαs-random variables.
- *for an arbitrary frequency ω*

$$\hat{I}_{NX}(\omega) \overset{d}{\to} f(\omega)(1 + T(\omega)) \qquad (B.30)$$

  where $P[1 + T(\omega) > x] \le \exp(-cx)$, $x > 0$ where c is independent of the (sαs) distribution of Z_t, $E[T(\omega)] = 0$ and $Cov(T(\omega), T(\omega')) = 0$, $0 < \omega \ne \omega' < \pi$.

A proof of these results can be found in Kluppelberg and Mikosch [58] and [59]. The close relationship to the finite variance case is revealed by the second claim. Note however, that *different periodogram ordinates are no more independent*, see for example theorem 7.4.3 in Embrechts et al. [28].

The above results allow a formal extension of the direct filter approach to input processes of infinite variance. In the following section, properties of the periodogram for non-stationary integrated processes are analyzed.

B.3 The Periodogram for Integrated Processes

Theorem 4.10 has been presented in chapter 4. A complete proof is provided here.

Theorem B.10. *Let X_t and $\tilde{X}_t$ be defined by (4.30) i.e. $\tilde{X}_t \in C_f^0$, $E[\tilde{X}_t] = 0$, $Z = \exp(i\lambda), \tilde{h}(\lambda) > 0$ and let*

$$\Omega_{N+1} := \{\omega_k \,|\, \omega_k = k2\pi/(N+1), \; |k| = 0, ..., [(N+1)/2]\}$$

For $\omega \notin \Omega_{N+1}$ define the periodogram $I_{N+1X}(\omega)$ by (4.16) and use a similar extension for the discrete Fourier transform $\Xi_{N+1X}(\omega)$.

- *If $\omega_k \ne \lambda$ then*

$$I_{N+1X}(\omega_k) = \frac{\left| \Xi_{N+1\tilde{X}}(\omega_k) - \nu \right|^2}{|1 - Z\exp(-i\omega_k)|^2} \qquad (B.31)$$

where the random variable $\nu := Z^{N+1}\Xi_{N+1\tilde{x}}(\lambda)$ *is independent of* ω_k. *More precisely, suppose* $|\omega_k - \lambda| > \pi/(N+1)$. *Then*

$$I_{N+1X}(\omega_k) = \frac{\zeta_{\omega_k}}{|1 - \exp(-i(\omega_k - \lambda))|^2} \qquad (B.32)$$

where the random variable ζ_{ω_k} *satisfies*

$$\lim_{N \to \infty} E[\zeta_{\omega_k}] = \tilde{h}(\lambda) + \tilde{h}(\omega_k)$$

If ϵ_t *is an iid sequence and* $\omega \neq \omega'$, *both different from* λ, *then*

$$\lim_{N \to \infty} \text{Cov}[\zeta_\omega, \zeta_{\omega'}] = \begin{cases} 2\tilde{h}(\lambda)^2 & \lambda = \pi \\ \tilde{h}(\lambda)^2 & else \end{cases} \qquad (B.33)$$

- *If* $X_t \in C_f^{1/2}$, *then the approximation for the first moment becomes :*

$$E[\zeta_{\omega_k}]$$
$$= \begin{cases} \tilde{h}(\lambda) + \tilde{h}(\omega_k) + O(1/\sqrt{N}) & \text{if } \lambda \in \Omega_{N+1} \\ \left(\tilde{h}(\lambda) + \tilde{h}(\omega_k)\right)\left(1 + O\left(\frac{1}{N(\omega_k - \lambda)}\right)\right) + O(N^{-1/2}) & else \end{cases} \qquad (B.34)$$

- *If* $X_t \in C_f^0$ *and* $\lambda \in \Omega_{N+1}$, *then*

$$I_{N+1X}(\lambda) = (N+1)^2 \zeta_\lambda \text{ where } \lim_{N \to \infty} E[\zeta_\lambda] = \tilde{h}(\lambda)/3 \qquad (B.35)$$

Proof. Consider:

$$I_{N+1X}(\omega) =$$
$$\frac{1}{2\pi(N+1)} \left| \sum_{t=0}^{N} X_t \exp(-it\omega) \right|^2$$
$$= \frac{1}{2\pi(N+1)} \left| \sum_{t=0}^{N} \left(\sum_{j=0}^{t} Z^j \tilde{X}_{t-j} \right) \exp(-it\omega) \right|^2$$
$$= \frac{1}{2\pi(N+1)} \left| \sum_{t=0}^{N} \tilde{X}_t \left(\sum_{j=0}^{N-t} Z^j \exp\left(-i(j+t)\omega\right) \right) \right|^2$$
$$= \frac{1}{2\pi(N+1)} \left| \sum_{t=0}^{N} \tilde{X}_t \exp(-it\omega) \left(\sum_{j=0}^{N-t} Z^j \exp(-ij\omega) \right) \right|^2 \qquad (B.36)$$
$$= \frac{1}{2\pi(N+1)} \left| \sum_{t=0}^{N} \tilde{X}_t \exp(-it\omega) \frac{1 - Z^{N-t+1}\exp(-i(N-t+1)\omega)}{1 - Z\exp(-i\omega)} \right|^2$$

$$= \frac{1}{|1 - Z\exp(-i\omega)|^2} \frac{1}{2\pi(N+1)}$$

$$\left| \sum_{t=0}^{N} \tilde{X}_t \exp(-it\omega) - Z^{N+1}\exp(-i(N+1)\omega)\sum_{t=0}^{N}\tilde{X}_t Z^{-t} \right|^2$$

$$= \frac{\left|\Xi_{N+1\tilde{X}}(\omega) - Z^{N+1}\exp(-i(N+1)\omega)\Xi_{N+1\tilde{X}}(\lambda)\right|^2}{|1 - Z\exp(-i\omega)|^2} \tag{B.37}$$

If $\omega \in \Omega_{N+1}$, then $\exp(-i(N+1)\omega) \equiv 1$ which proves the first assertion. The first moment of the periodogram satisfies

$$E[I_{N+1X}(\omega_k)] = \frac{1}{|1 - Z\exp(-i\omega_k)|^2} E\left[\left|\Xi_{N+1\tilde{X}}(\omega_k) - Z^{N+1}\Xi_{N+1\tilde{X}}(\lambda)\right|^2\right]$$

$$= \frac{1}{|1 - Z\exp(-i\omega_k)|^2}\Bigg(E\left[I_{N+1\tilde{X}}(\omega_k)\right]$$

$$-2\mathrm{Re}\left(E\left[\Xi_{N+1\tilde{X}}(\omega_k)\overline{Z^{N+1}\Xi_{N+1\tilde{X}}(\lambda)}\right]\right) + E\left[I_{N+1\tilde{X}}(\lambda)\right]\Bigg)$$

$$= \frac{1}{|1 - Z\exp(-i\omega_k)|^2}\left(\tilde{h}(\lambda) + \tilde{h}(\omega_k) + R'_N + 2R_N\right)$$

where

- $\lim_{N\to\infty} R'_N = 0$ or $R'_N = O(1/\sqrt{N})$ or $R'_N = O(\ln(N)/N)$ according to (B.17) or (B.18) or (B.19), depending on whether $\tilde{X}_t \in C_f^0$ or $\tilde{X}_t \in C_f^{1/2}$ or $\tilde{X}_t \in C_f^1$.
- From (B.10) respectively (B.11) one deduces

$$|R_N| \leq \begin{cases} O(N^{-1/2}) & \lambda \in \Omega_N \\ \sqrt{\tilde{h}(\lambda)\tilde{h}(\omega_k)}\dfrac{\pi}{(N+1)|\omega_k - \lambda|} + O(N^{-1/2}) & else \end{cases}$$

In order to verify the assertion for the second order moments, let $\omega \neq \omega'$ be two arbitrary but fixed frequencies different from λ. Then

$$\lim_{N\to\infty} |1 - Z\exp(-i\omega)|^2 |1 - Z\exp(-i\omega')|^2 \mathrm{Cov}[I_{N+1X}(\omega)I_{N+1X}(\omega')]$$

$$= \lim_{N\to\infty} \mathrm{Cov}\Bigg[\bigg\{I_{N+1\tilde{X}}(\omega)$$

$$-2\mathrm{Re}\left(\Xi_{N+1\tilde{X}}(\omega)\overline{Z^{N+1}\exp(-i(N+1)\omega)\Xi_{N+1\tilde{X}}(\lambda)}\right) + I_{N+1\tilde{X}}(\lambda)\bigg\}$$

$$\bigg\{I_{N+1\tilde{X}}(\omega') - 2\mathrm{Re}\left(\Xi_{N+1\tilde{X}}(\omega')\overline{Z^{N+1}\exp(-i(N+1)\omega')\Xi_{N+1\tilde{X}}(\lambda)}\right)$$

$$+ I_{N+1\tilde{X}}(\lambda)\bigg\}\Bigg] \tag{B.38}$$

$$= \lim_{N \to \infty} \mathrm{Var}(I_{N+1\tilde{X}}(\lambda))$$

$$= \begin{cases} 2\tilde{h}(\lambda)^2 & \lambda = 0, \pi \\ \tilde{h}(\lambda)^2 & \text{else} \end{cases}$$

where in the first equality (B.37) is used and the second equality follows from the asymptotic independence of $\Xi_{N+1\tilde{X}}(\omega)$ and $\Xi_{N+1\tilde{X}}(\omega')$, see theorem B.4. In order to prove the third assertion set $\omega_k := \lambda$ which, inserted into (B.36), leads to

$$I_{N+1X}(\lambda) = \frac{1}{2\pi(N+1)} \left| \sum_{t=0}^{N} \tilde{X}_t(N+1-t)\exp(-it\lambda) \right|^2$$

$$= (N+1)^2 \frac{1}{2\pi(N+1)} \left| \sum_{t=0}^{N} \tilde{X}_t \left(1 - \frac{t}{N+1}\right) \exp(-it\lambda) \right|^2 \qquad (B.39)$$

$$= (N+1)^2 \frac{1}{2\pi(N+1)} \sum_{t=0}^{N} \sum_{u=0}^{N} \tilde{X}_t \tilde{X}_u \left(1 - \frac{t}{N+1}\right)\left(1 - \frac{u}{N+1}\right)\cos((t-u)\lambda)$$

$$= (N+1)^2 \frac{1}{2\pi} \sum_{s=-N}^{N} \left(\frac{1}{N+1} \sum_{t=0}^{N-|s|} \tilde{X}_t \tilde{X}_{t+|s|} \right.$$

$$\left(1 - \frac{t}{N+1}\right)\left(1 - \frac{t+|s|}{N+1}\right) \right) \cos(s\lambda)$$

see for example Priestley [75], p.399 for the last two equalities above. Using the approximations

$$\sum_{t=0}^{M} t = \frac{M(M+1)}{2} \simeq \frac{M^2}{2} \quad \text{and}$$

$$\sum_{t=0}^{M} t^2 = \frac{M(M+1)(M+2)}{3} - \frac{M(M+1)}{2} \simeq \frac{M^3}{3}$$

one obtains

$$\frac{1}{N+1} \sum_{t=0}^{N-|s|} \left(1 - \frac{t}{N+1}\right)\left(1 - \frac{t+|s|}{N+1}\right)$$

$$\simeq \frac{1}{N+1} \left((N-|s|) - \frac{(N-|s|)^2}{2(N+1)} - \frac{|s|(N-|s|)}{N+1} \right.$$

$$\left. - \frac{(N-|s|)^2}{2(N+1)} + \frac{(N-|s|)^3}{3(N+1)^2} + \frac{|s|(N-|s|)^2}{2(N+1)^2} \right)$$

$$= \frac{1}{3} + O\left(\frac{|s|}{N+1}\right)$$

Thus

$$E[I_{N+1X}(\lambda)] = (N+1)^2 \frac{1}{2\pi} \sum_{s=-N}^{N} \tilde{R}(s) \left(\frac{1}{3} + O\left(\frac{|s|}{N+1}\right)\right) \cos(s\lambda)$$

$$\simeq (N+1)^2 \frac{1}{2\pi} \frac{1}{3} \sum_{s=-N}^{N} \tilde{R}(s) \cos(s\lambda)$$

$$\simeq (N+1)^2 \frac{\tilde{h}(\lambda)}{3} \tag{B.40}$$

The first equality follows from $E[\tilde{X}_t] = 0$ (recall the discussion concerning (4.30)). The assumption $\tilde{X}_t \in C_f^0$ implies $\sum_{k=0}^{\infty} |\tilde{R}(k)| < \infty$, see (4.18). Therefore, the first approximation follows from Lebesgue's dominated convergence theorem and $\lim_{N\to\infty} O(|s|/N) = 0$ for all s. The second approximation again follows from the absolute summability of the autocovariance function, which completes the proof of the theorem. $\square$

Remarks

- As was seen in (B.31), the bias of the periodogram (see (B.34)) depends on the discrete Fourier transform of the differenced signal at the unit-root frequency λ. As well, (B.31) implies that different periodogram ordinates are *correlated* (through the common random variable ν), see for example (B.33). Note that a dependence structure of periodogram ordinates was already observed for stationary processes of infinite variance, see theorem B.9.
- Theorem 4.8 does not apply here, since the filter coefficients of $1/|1 - Z_\lambda \exp(-i\omega_k)|^2$ never decay (or, equivalently, the MA-coefficients of X_t never decay). It is thus the 'long memory' of the integration operator which makes periodogram ordinates biased and correlated.
- The interpretation of the random variable ν is fairly easy : for finite samples its purpose is to replace the singularity of the theoretical pseudo spectral density $h(\omega)$ at λ by

$$\lim_{\omega_k \to \lambda} I_{N+1X}(\omega_k) \simeq N^2 \frac{\tilde{h}(\lambda)}{3}$$

This reflects the finite sample information about the true integration order 1 as given by the periodogram.
- Equation (B.39) reveals that the periodogram at λ is obtained by 'tapering' the series $\tilde{X}_t$ (see for example Priestley [75], section 7.4.1 or Cooley and Tukey [19]), i.e. by replacing the original data $\tilde{X}_t$ by $\tilde{X}_t h_t$ where the sequence of constants $h_t := 1 - t/(N+1)$ is called a 'taper'. The effect of a taper essentially consists in reducing bias and increasing variance of the spectral estimate for $\tilde{h}(\lambda)$.

The following corollary proposes a result needed for 'unit-root' tests, more precisely, for testing conditions of the type (5.22) (whose importance is assessed empirically in section 7.2). For that, assume $\lambda = 0$ in theorem B.10 so that $\tilde{X}_t = X_t - X_{t-1}$ is stationary. The random variable ζ_0 defined in (B.35) (where $\lambda = 0$) can be represented as $\zeta_0 = \eta_0^2$ where

$$\eta_0 := \frac{1}{\sqrt{2\pi N}} \sum_{t=1}^{N} \tilde{X}_t (1 - t/N) \tag{B.41}$$

see (B.39). The dependency of η_0 and $\Xi_{N\tilde{X}}(\omega_k)$ is analyzed in the following corollary.

Corollary B.11. *Let the assumptions of the preceding theorem B.10 be satisfied and assume that the unit-root of the process X_t is located at frequency zero so that $X_t - X_{t-1} = \tilde{X}_t \in C_f^0$ i.e. $\lambda = 0$. Then*

$$Cov\,[\eta_0, \Xi_{N\tilde{X}}(\omega_k)] = \begin{cases} \dfrac{\tilde{h}(0)}{2} + o(1) & \omega_k = 0 \\[2mm] -\dfrac{i}{k2\pi}\left(\tilde{h}(0) + o(1)\right) & \omega_k = o(1) \neq 0 \end{cases} \tag{B.42}$$

where η_0 is defined in (B.41), i is the imaginary number and $k = [N/2]\omega_k/\pi$.

Proof. By assumption $\omega_k = o(1)$. Assume first, $\omega_k \neq 0$. A proof then follows from

$$E\left[\frac{1}{\sqrt{2\pi N}} \sum_{t=1}^{N} \tilde{X}_t (1 - t/N)\frac{1}{\sqrt{2\pi N}} \sum_{t'=1}^{N} \tilde{X}_{t'} \exp(-i\omega_k t')\right]$$

$$= \frac{1}{2\pi N} \sum_{t=1}^{N}\sum_{t'=1}^{N} \tilde{R}(t - t')(1 - t/N)\exp(-i\omega_k t')$$

$$= \frac{1}{2\pi N} \sum_{s=-(N-1)}^{N-1} \sum_{t=\max(0,s)+1}^{N+\min(0,s)} \tilde{R}(s)(1 - t/N)\exp(-i\omega_k(t - s))$$

$$= \frac{1}{2\pi N} \sum_{s=-(N-1)}^{N-1} \tilde{R}(s)\exp(i\omega_k s)$$

$$\left(\sum_{t=\max(0,s)+1}^{N+\min(0,s)} \exp(-i\omega_k t) - \frac{1}{N}\sum_{t=\max(0,s)+1}^{N+\min(0,s)} t\exp(-i\omega_k t)\right) \tag{B.43}$$

$$= -\frac{1}{2\pi N} \sum_{s=-(N-1)}^{N-1} \tilde{R}(s)\exp(i\omega_k s)$$

$$\times \frac{1}{N}\sum_{t=\max(0,s)+1}^{N+\min(0,s)} t\exp(-i\omega_k t) + o(1) \tag{B.44}$$

where the last equality follows from

- the bound

$$\left| \frac{1}{2\pi N} \sum_{t=\max(0,s)+1}^{N+\min(0,s)} \exp(-i\omega_k t) \right| = \left| \frac{1}{2\pi N} \sum_{t=1}^{|s|} \exp(-i\omega_k t) \right|$$

$$\leq \frac{|s|}{2\pi N}$$

  see the orthogonality relations (4.3)
- the absolute summability of the autocovariance sequence $\tilde{R}(s)$
- and Lebesgue's dominated convergence theorem.

If $s \geq 0$ then

$$\frac{1}{N} \sum_{t=s+1}^{N} t \exp(-i\omega_k t) =$$

$$i\frac{1}{N}\frac{\partial}{\partial \omega} \sum_{t=s+1}^{N} \exp(-i\omega_k t) \bigg|_{\omega=\omega_k} \tag{B.45}$$

$$= i\frac{1}{N}\frac{\partial}{\partial \omega} \frac{\exp(-iN\omega_k) - \exp(-is\omega_k)}{(1 - \exp(i\omega_k))} \bigg|_{\omega=\omega_k}$$

$$= i\frac{1}{N} \left(\frac{-iN\exp(-iN\omega_k) + is\exp(-is\omega_k)}{(1 - \exp(i\omega_k))} \right.$$

$$\left. + \frac{(\exp(-iN\omega_k) - \exp(-is\omega_k))i\exp(i\omega_k)}{(1 - \exp(i\omega_k))^2} \right)$$

$$= i\frac{1}{N} \left(\frac{-iN + is\exp(-is\omega_k)}{(1 - \exp(i\omega_k))} \right.$$

$$\left. + \frac{(1 - \exp(-is\omega_k))i\exp(i\omega_k)}{(1 - \exp(i\omega_k))^2} \right)$$

$$= i\frac{1}{N}\frac{-iN + is\exp(-is\omega_k) + O(s)}{(1 - \exp(i\omega_k))}$$

$$= \frac{1 + O(s/N)}{(1 - \exp(i\omega_k))} \tag{B.46}$$

If $s < 0$ then

$$\frac{1}{N} \sum_{t=1}^{N-|s|} t \exp(-i\omega_k t) = i\frac{1}{N}\frac{\partial}{\partial \omega} \sum_{t=1}^{N-|s|} \exp(-i\omega_k t) \bigg|_{\omega=\omega_k} \tag{B.47}$$

$$= i\frac{1}{N}\frac{\partial}{\partial \omega}\frac{\exp(-i(N-|s|)\omega_k) - 1}{(1 - \exp(i\omega_k))} \bigg|_{\omega=\omega_k}$$

$$= i\frac{1}{N}\left(\frac{-i(N-|s|)\exp(-i(N-|s|)\omega_k)}{(1-\exp(i\omega_k))}\right.$$
$$\left.+\frac{(\exp(-i(N-|s|)\omega_k)-1)i\exp(i\omega_k)}{(1-\exp(i\omega_k))^2}\right)$$
$$= \exp(i|s|\omega_k)i\frac{1}{N}\left(\frac{-i(N-|s|)}{(1-\exp(i\omega_k))}\right.$$
$$\left.+\frac{(1-\exp(-i|s|\omega_k))i\exp(i\omega_k)}{(1-\exp(i\omega_k))^2}\right)$$
$$= \exp(i|s|\omega_k)i\frac{1}{N}\frac{-iN+is+O(s)}{(1-\exp(i\omega_k))}$$
$$= \exp(i|s|\omega_k)\frac{1+O(s/N)}{(1-\exp(i\omega_k))} \tag{B.48}$$

Inserting (B.46) and (B.48) into (B.44) leads to

$$E\left[\frac{1}{\sqrt{2\pi N}}\sum_{t=1}^{N}\tilde{X}_t(1-t/N)\frac{1}{\sqrt{2\pi N}}\sum_{t'=1}^{N}\tilde{X}_{t'}\exp(-i\omega_k t')\right]$$

$$= -\frac{1}{2\pi N}\sum_{s=-(N-1)}^{N-1}\tilde{R}(s)\exp(is\omega_k)\frac{1}{N}\sum_{t=\max(0,s)+1}^{N+\min(0,s)}t\exp(-i\omega_k t)+\mathrm{o}(1)$$

$$= -\frac{1}{2\pi N}\sum_{s=0}^{N-1}\tilde{R}(s)\exp(is\omega_k)\frac{1+O(s/N)}{(1-\exp(i\omega_k))}$$
$$-\frac{1}{2\pi N}\sum_{s=-(N-1)}^{-1}\tilde{R}(s)\frac{1+O(s/N)}{(1-\exp(i\omega_k))}+\mathrm{o}(1)$$

$$= -\frac{1}{(1-\exp(i\omega_k))}\frac{1}{2\pi N}$$
$$\times\left(\sum_{s=0}^{N-1}\tilde{R}(s)\exp(is\omega_k)(1+O(s/N))+\sum_{s=-(N-1)}^{-1}\tilde{R}(s)(1+O(s/N))\right)$$
$$+\mathrm{o}(1)$$

$$= -\frac{1}{(1-\exp(i\omega_k))}\frac{1}{2\pi N}\left(\sum_{s=0}^{\infty}\tilde{R}(s)\exp(is\omega_k)+\sum_{s=-\infty}^{-1}\tilde{R}(s)+\mathrm{o}(1)\right)$$

$$= -\frac{1}{(1-\exp(i\omega_k))}\frac{1}{2\pi N}\left(\sum_{s=-\infty}^{\infty}\tilde{R}(s)+\mathrm{o}(1)\right)$$

$$= -\frac{1}{N(1-\exp(i\omega_k))}\left(\tilde{h}(0)+\mathrm{o}(1)\right)$$

$$= -\frac{i}{k2\pi}\left(\tilde{h}(0)+\mathrm{o}(1)\right)$$

where the fourth and fifth equalities follow from the absolute summability of the autocovariance function and Lebesgue's dominated convergence theorem (using $\omega_k = o(1)$ so that $\lim_{N\to\infty} \exp(is\omega_k) = 1$ for all s in the fifth equality). If $\omega_k = 0$ then the left hand-sides of (B.45) and (B.47) can both be approximated by $\frac{N-1}{2} + O(s)$. Note that now

$$\left| \frac{1}{2\pi N} \sum_{t=\max(0,s)+1}^{N+\min(0,s)} \exp(-i\omega_k t) \right| = N - |s|$$

in (B.43) so that the corresponding expression becomes

$$E\left[\frac{1}{\sqrt{2\pi N}} \sum_{t=1}^{N} \tilde{X}_t(1 - t/N) \frac{1}{\sqrt{2\pi N}} \sum_{t'=1}^{N} \tilde{X}_{t'} \right]$$

$$= \frac{1}{2\pi N} \sum_{s=-(N-1)}^{N-1} \tilde{R}(s) \left(\sum_{t=\max(0,s)+1}^{N+\min(0,s)} 1 - \frac{1}{N} \sum_{t=\max(0,s)+1}^{N+\min(0,s)} t \right)$$

$$= \frac{1}{2\pi N} \sum_{s=-(N-1)}^{N-1} \tilde{R}(s) \left(N - |s| - \frac{N-1}{2} \right)$$

$$= \frac{1}{2\pi} \sum_{s=-\infty}^{\infty} \tilde{R}(s)/2 + o(1)$$

$$= \frac{\tilde{h}(0)}{2} + o(1) \tag{B.49}$$

This completes the proof of the corollary.   □

Remark

- The approximation

$$Cov\left[\eta_0, \Xi_{N\tilde{X}}(\omega_k) \right] = -\frac{i}{k2\pi} \left(\tilde{h}(0) + o(1) \right)$$

for $\omega_k \neq 0$ in (B.42) implies that η_0 is correlated with the imaginary part of $\Xi_{N\tilde{X}}(\omega_k)$ only since the expression on the right hand-side is purely imaginary. Therefore, η_0 and the real part of the discrete Fourier transforms are not correlated (asymptotically and for $\omega_k = o(1)$).

C

A 'Least-Squares' Estimate

C.1 Asymptotic Distribution of the Parameters

Assume that the output $\tilde{Y}_{tr}$ of the filter minimizing

$$E[(Y_t - \hat{Y}_{tr})^2] \tag{C.1}$$

is known for $t = 1 - Q, ..., N - 1$ but that the filter parameters are unknown and are estimated by 'least-squares'. For that purpose, consider an estimate based on an ordinary least-squares regression of Y_t on $\tilde{Y}_{t-1,r}, ..., \tilde{Y}_{t-Q,r}$ and $X_{t+r}, ..., X_{t-q}$

$$Y_t = \sum_{k=1}^{Q} a_k \tilde{Y}_{t-k,r} + \sum_{k=-r}^{q} b_k X_{t-k} + \Delta Y_t \tag{C.2}$$

Note that the filter corresponding to $\tilde{Y}_{tr}$ is based on 'future' $X_{t+1}, ..., X_{t+r}$: it is thus optimal for estimating Y_{N-r} where N is the end point of the sample (for $r = 0$ the filter is completely asymmetric). In the following, the subscript r of $\tilde{Y}_{tr}$ is omitted for notational convenience. It is assumed that the signal Y_t, $t = 1, ...N$ is known too in (C.2) and that the best (unknown) asymmetric filter minimizing (C.1) is an ARMA$(Q', q' + r)$-filter say. If $X_{N+1}, ..., X_{N+r}$ are known too, then N equations are available for estimating the filter parameters in (C.2).

Remark:

- If $\tilde{Y}_t$ is known, then the filter parameters could be determined exactly since the true error terms $\Delta \tilde{Y}_t$ would be observable. However, this is not the point here: what really imports are the properties of the resulting least-squares parameter estimates or, more precisely, their asymptotic distribution since it can be shown that the latter coincides with the asymptotic distribution of the DFA parameter estimates. The above 'setup' is artificial: it is needed for showing that filter parameter estimates of the DFA are as good (asymptotically) as the least-squares estimates which assume knowledge of Y_t and $\tilde{Y}_t$.

Assume $Q \geq Q'$ and $q \geq q'$ in (C.2) and assume cancelling zeroes and poles of ARMA filters are not allowed. Let $\hat{\mathbf{b}}$ denote the least squares estimate of the unknown parameter vector $\bar{\mathbf{b}} := (a_1, ..., a_Q, b_{-r}, ..., b_q)'$ in (C.2), where $a_{Q'+1} = ... = a_Q = b_{q'+1} = ... = b_q = 0$ (because the best filter is an ARMA$(Q', q' + r)$ and zeroes cannot cancel poles). Denote by $\mathbf{Z}$ the $N * p$-matrix whose $p = Q + q + r + 1$ columns correspond to the time series of the regressors involved on the right of (C.2). Therefore, the least squares estimate is

$$\hat{\mathbf{b}} = (\mathbf{Z}'\mathbf{Z})^{-1}\mathbf{Z}'\mathbf{Y} \qquad (C.3)$$

where $\mathbf{Y}' = (Y_1, ..., Y_N)$. Consider the so called 'projection matrix'

$$\mathbf{M} := \mathbf{I} - \mathbf{Z}(\mathbf{Z}'\mathbf{Z})^{-1}\mathbf{Z}'$$

It can be shown that $\mathbf{M} = \mathbf{M}'$ and that it is idempotent with rank $N - p$, see Theil [88], p.40. Moreover

$$\Delta\mathbf{Y} = \mathbf{M}\Delta\tilde{\mathbf{Y}}$$

where $\Delta\mathbf{Y}$ is the vector of least squares 'residuals' and $\Delta\tilde{\mathbf{Y}}$ is the vector of 'true' error terms. Note that if $Q \geq Q'$ and $q \geq q'$ (as assumed), then $\Delta\tilde{Y}_t$ does not depend on Q nor on q.

Assume $\Delta\tilde{Y}_t$ is stationary (which may be achieved by suitable constraints (5.22) for example). Assume also for convenience that X_t, $\tilde{Y}_t$ are stationary too (the latter two assumptions may be relaxed) and define

$$w_{ij} :=$$
$$\begin{cases} \sum_{k=-\infty}^{\infty} R_{\Delta\tilde{Y}}(k)R_{\tilde{Y}}(i-j+k) & 1 \leq i, j \leq Q \\ \sum_{k=-\infty}^{\infty} R_{\Delta\tilde{Y}}(k)R_X(i-j+k) & Q < i, j \leq Q+q+r+1 \\ \sum_{k=-\infty}^{\infty} R_{\Delta\tilde{Y}}(k)E\left[\tilde{Y}_0 X_{k-|j-i|+r+Q+1}\right] & \text{else} \end{cases} \quad (C.4)$$

where $R_{\Delta\tilde{Y}}(\cdot)$, $R_{\tilde{Y}}(\cdot)$ and $R_X(\cdot)$ denote the autocovariance functions of $\Delta\tilde{Y}_t$, $\tilde{Y}_t$ and X_t respectively. It is not difficult to show that the $(Q+q+r+1) * (Q+q+r+1)$-matrix $\mathbf{W} := (w_{ij})$ is symmetric (a formal proof is provided in the following theorem).

The 'least-squares' estimate (C.3) is analyzed in the following theorem.

Theorem C.1. *Assume*

- $\Gamma(\cdot) \in C_f^0$ and $X_t \in C_f^0$ *is a zero mean stationary MA-process. The white noise sequence ϵ_t (of X_t) is iid and satisfies $E[\epsilon_t^8] < \infty$.*

- *The best asymmetric filter $\tilde{\Gamma}(\cdot)$ for estimating Y_{N-r} is a stable ARMA(Q', $q'+r$) filter. It is assumed that the AR- and MA-orders Q and $q+r$ used for the least squares estimate satisfy $Q \geq Q'$ and $q+r \geq q'+r$ and that cancelling zeroes and poles of ARMA filters are not allowed.*
- Y_t *and* $\tilde{Y}_t$ *are known for* $t = 1, ..., N$ *and* $t = 1-Q, ..., N-1$ *respectively.*
- $\mathbf{Q} := \lim_{N\to\infty}(\frac{1}{N}\mathbf{Z'Z})$ *is strictly positive definite (its existence as a limes in probability is shown in the proof below).*

Then

- *The asymptotic distribution of the (suitably normalized) estimated filter parameters is*

$$\sqrt{N}(\hat{\mathbf{b}} - \bar{\mathbf{b}}) \sim AN\big(0, \mathbf{Q}^{-1}\mathbf{W}\mathbf{Q}^{-1}\big) \tag{C.5}$$

where $\bar{\mathbf{b}}$ is the true parameter vector and the elements w_{ij} of the (symmetric) matrix $\mathbf{W}$ are given by (C.4) and AN means asymptotically multivariate normally distributed.

Proof. The least squares estimate satisfies

$$\hat{\mathbf{b}} = \bar{\mathbf{b}} + (\mathbf{Z'Z})^{-1}\mathbf{Z'}\Delta\tilde{\mathbf{Y}} \tag{C.6}$$

Therefore

$$\sqrt{N}(\hat{\mathbf{b}} - \bar{\mathbf{b}}) = \left(\frac{\mathbf{Z'Z}}{N}\right)^{-1}\frac{\mathbf{Z'}\Delta\tilde{\mathbf{Y}}}{\sqrt{N}} \tag{C.7}$$

A proof that the matrix $\mathbf{Q} := \lim_{N\to\infty}\frac{1}{N}\mathbf{Z'Z}$ exists in probability is for example given in Hamilton [45], p.192 and 193 (use $\tilde{Y}_t \in C_f^0$ and $X_t \in C_f^0$). Since the inversion is a continuous operator (for the strictly positive definite matrix $\mathbf{Q}$), $\mathbf{Q}^{-1} := \lim_{N\to\infty}(\frac{1}{N}\mathbf{Z'Z})^{-1}$ also exists in probability (see for example Hamilton [45], proposition 7.3).

Next, the consistency of the least-squares estimate is assessed and second order moments of the vector $\mathbf{Z'}\Delta\tilde{\mathbf{Y}}/\sqrt{N}$ are derived. Let $z_{it} := \tilde{Y}_{t-i}$ for $1 \leq i \leq Q$ and $z_{it} := X_{t+r+Q+1-i}$ for $i > Q$ be the (i,t)-element of the matrix $\mathbf{Z'}$. For $Q \geq Q'$ and $q \geq q'$

$$\mathbf{Z}\bar{\mathbf{b}} = \tilde{\mathbf{Y}}$$

(this is not true if $Q < Q'$ or $q < q'$ since then the best asymmetric filter $\tilde{\Gamma}(\cdot)$ is no more an admissible solution of the corresponding least squares estimation problem). Thus the 'true' error term satisfies $\Delta\tilde{Y}_t = Y_t - \tilde{Y}_t$. Using (2.23) and (2.24) (note that $\tilde{Y}_t$ in (2.23) corresponds to Y_t here and that $\check{Y}_t$ in (2.24) corresponds to $\tilde{Y}_t$ here), one deduces

$$\Delta\tilde{Y}_t = Y_t - \tilde{Y}_t$$

$$= \sum_{k=-\infty}^{\infty}\left(\sum_{j=0}^{\infty}b_j\gamma_{k-j}\right)\epsilon_{t-k} - \sum_{k=-r}^{\infty}\left(\sum_{j=0}^{\infty}b_j\gamma_{k-j}\right)\epsilon_{t-k}$$

$$= \sum_{k=-\infty}^{-r-1} \left(\sum_{j=0}^{\infty} b_j \gamma_{k-j} \right) \epsilon_{t-k}$$

$$= \sum_{k=1}^{\infty} g_k \epsilon_{t+r+k} \qquad (C.8)$$

Moreover

$$z_{it} := \begin{cases} \tilde{Y}_{t-i} = \sum_{k=0}^{\infty} c_k X_{t+r-i-k} = \sum_{k=0}^{\infty} d_k \epsilon_{t+r-i-k} & \text{for } 1 \le i \le Q \\[2mm] X_{t+r+Q+1-i} = \sum_{k=0}^{\infty} b_k \epsilon_{t+r+Q+1-i-k} & \text{for } i > Q \end{cases}$$

Therefore $\Delta \tilde{Y}_t$ is orthogonal to the space spanned by the regressors so that the 'least-squares' estimate is consistent. Moreover, it follows that for $t' < t$

$$E \left[z_{it} \Delta \tilde{Y}_t z_{jt'} \Delta \tilde{Y}_{t'} \right] = E \left[z_{it} z_{jt'} \sum_{k=1}^{\infty} g_k \epsilon_{t+r+k} \sum_{k=1}^{\infty} g_k \epsilon_{t'+r+k} \right]$$

$$= E \left[z_{it} z_{jt'} \sum_{k=1}^{\infty} g_k \epsilon_{t+r+k} \sum_{k=1}^{t-t'} g_k \epsilon_{t'+r+k} \right]$$

$$+ E \left[z_{it} z_{jt'} \sum_{k=1}^{\infty} g_k \epsilon_{t+r+k} \sum_{k=t-t'+1}^{\infty} g_k \epsilon_{t'+r+k} \right]$$

$$= E \left[z_{it} z_{jt'} \sum_{k=1}^{\infty} g_k \epsilon_{t+r+k} \sum_{k=t-t'+1}^{\infty} g_k \epsilon_{t'+r+k} \right]$$

$$= E \left[z_{it} z_{jt'} \right] E \left[\sum_{k=1}^{\infty} g_k \epsilon_{t+r+k} \sum_{k=t-t'+1}^{\infty} g_k \epsilon_{t'+r+k} \right]$$

$$= E \left[z_{it} z_{jt'} \right] R_{\Delta \tilde{Y}}(t - t')$$

where $R_{\Delta \tilde{Y}}(t - t')$ is the autocovariance function of $\Delta \tilde{Y}_t$. The third and the fourth equalities follow from the independence assumption of ϵ_t. Similarly, for $t = t'$ one deduces :

$$E \left[z_{it} \Delta \tilde{Y}_t z_{jt} \Delta \tilde{Y}_t \right] = E \left[z_{it} z_{jt} \right] R_{\Delta \tilde{Y}}(0)$$

and for $t < t'$:

$$E \left[z_{it} \Delta \tilde{Y}_t z_{jt'} \Delta \tilde{Y}_{t'} \right] = E \left[z_{it} z_{jt'} \right] E \left[\sum_{k=1}^{\infty} g_k \epsilon_{t'+r+k} \sum_{k=t'-t+1}^{\infty} g_k \epsilon_{t+r+k} \right]$$

$$= E \left[z_{it} z_{jt'} \right] R_{\Delta \tilde{Y}}(t - t')$$

where use is made of the stationarity of $\Delta \tilde{Y}_t$ (so that its autocovariance function is an odd function i.e. $R_{\Delta \tilde{Y}}(t - t') = R_{\Delta \tilde{Y}}(t' - t)$). Now

$$E\left[z_{it}z_{jt'}\right] =$$

$$
\begin{cases}
E\left[\tilde{Y}_{t-i}\tilde{Y}_{t'-j}\right] = R_{\tilde{Y}}(t - t' + (j - i)) & 1 \leq i, j \leq Q \\[6pt]
E\left[\tilde{Y}_{t-i}X_{t'+r+Q+1-j}\right] & 1 \leq i \leq Q, j > Q \\[6pt]
E\left[X_{t+r+Q+1-i}\tilde{Y}_{t'-j}\right] & i > Q, 1 \leq j \leq Q \\[6pt]
E\left[X_{t+r+Q+1-i}X_{t'+r+Q+1-j}\right] = R_X(t - t' + (j - i)) & i > Q, j > Q
\end{cases}
$$

For $1 \leq i, j \leq Q$, one obtains

$$
E\left[\frac{\mathbf{z}_i'\mathbf{\Delta\tilde{Y}}}{\sqrt{N}}\frac{\mathbf{z}_j'\mathbf{\Delta\tilde{Y}}}{\sqrt{N}}\right] = E\left[\frac{1}{N}\left(\sum_{t=1}^{N} z_{it}\Delta\tilde{Y}_t \sum_{t=1}^{N} z_{jt}\Delta\tilde{Y}_t\right)\right]
$$

$$
= \frac{1}{N}\sum_{k=-N+1}^{N-1}(N - |k|)R_{\Delta\tilde{Y}}(k)R_{\tilde{Y}}(j - i + k)
$$

$$
= \sum_{k=-\infty}^{\infty} R_{\Delta\tilde{Y}}(k)R_{\tilde{Y}}(j - i + k) + \mathrm{o}(1) \tag{C.9}
$$

where $k := t - t'$. The last equality follows from Lebesgue's dominated convergence theorem. In fact, $\tilde{Y}_t \in C_f^0$ and $\Delta\tilde{Y}_t \in C_f^0$ imply that $R_{\Delta\tilde{Y}}(k)$ and $R_{\tilde{Y}}(k)$ are absolutely summable (recall (4.18)) so that $R_{\Delta\tilde{Y}}(k)R_{\tilde{Y}}(j - i + k)$ is absolutely summable too as a function of k. Lebesgue's dominated convergence theorem then implies (C.9). Similar expressions are obtained for $i > Q$ or $j > Q$ by replacing $R_{\tilde{Y}}(j - i + k)$ in (C.9) by the corresponding moments of $E\left[z_{it}z_{jt'}\right]$ given above. One obtains

$$
w_{ij} :=
\begin{cases}
\sum_{k=-\infty}^{\infty} R_{\Delta\tilde{Y}}(k)R_{\tilde{Y}}(j - i + k) & 1 \leq i, j \leq Q \\[10pt]
\sum_{k=-\infty}^{\infty} R_{\Delta\tilde{Y}}(k)R_X(j - i + k) & Q < i, j \leq Q + q + r + 1 \\[10pt]
\sum_{k=-\infty}^{\infty} R_{\Delta\tilde{Y}}(k)E\left[\tilde{Y}_{k+(j-i)-r-Q-1}X_0\right] & 1 \leq i \leq Q, j > Q \\[10pt]
\sum_{k=-\infty}^{\infty} R_{\Delta\tilde{Y}}(k)E\left[X_{k+r+Q+1+(j-i)}\tilde{Y}_0\right] & i > Q, 1 \leq j \leq Q
\end{cases}
\tag{C.10}
$$

where $k = t - t'$ and the matrix $\mathbf{W}$ with elements w_{ij} is (up to a negligible error term) the variance covariance matrix of $\mathbf{Z}'\mathbf{\Delta\tilde{Y}}$. Note that the expressions for $1 \leq i \leq Q, j > Q$ can be transformed according to

$$
\sum_{k=-\infty}^{\infty} R_{\Delta\tilde{Y}}(k)E\left[\tilde{Y}_{k+(j-i)-r-Q-1}X_0\right] =
$$

$$
\sum_{k=-\infty}^{\infty} R_{\Delta\tilde{Y}}(-k)E\left[\tilde{Y}_{k+(j-i)-r-Q-1}X_0\right]
$$

$$= \sum_{k=-\infty}^{\infty} R_{\Delta \tilde{Y}}(-k) E\left[\tilde{Y}_0 X_{-k-(j-i)+r+Q+1}\right]$$

$$= \sum_{k=-\infty}^{\infty} R_{\Delta \tilde{Y}}(k) E\left[\tilde{Y}_0 X_{k-(j-i)+r+Q+1}\right]$$

which shows that the last two expressions in (C.10) are identical to

$$\sum_{k=-\infty}^{\infty} R_{\Delta \tilde{Y}}(k) E\left[\tilde{Y}_0 X_{k-|j-i|+r+Q+1}\right]$$

Also

$$\sum_{k=-\infty}^{\infty} R_{\Delta \tilde{Y}}(k) R_{\tilde{Y}}(j-i+k) = \sum_{k=-\infty}^{\infty} R_{\Delta \tilde{Y}}(-k) R_{\tilde{Y}}(i-j-k)$$

$$= \sum_{k=-\infty}^{\infty} R_{\Delta \tilde{Y}}(k) R_{\tilde{Y}}(i-j+k)$$

and

$$\sum_{k=-\infty}^{\infty} R_{\Delta \tilde{Y}}(k) R_X(j-i+k) = \sum_{k=-\infty}^{\infty} R_{\Delta \tilde{Y}}(-k) R_X(i-j-k)$$

$$= \sum_{k=-\infty}^{\infty} R_{\Delta \tilde{Y}}(k) R_X(i-j+k)$$

so that the matrix $\mathbf{W}$ is symmetric. It is now shown that $\dfrac{\mathbf{Z}'\Delta\tilde{\mathbf{Y}}}{\sqrt{N}}$ is asymptotically normally distributed. For that, consider one particular element (say the i-th) of the vector $\dfrac{\mathbf{Z}'\Delta\tilde{\mathbf{Y}}}{\sqrt{N}}$ and assume $i \le Q$. Then

$$\frac{1}{\sqrt{N}} \sum_{t=1}^{N} z_{it} \Delta \tilde{Y}_t = \frac{1}{\sqrt{N}} \sum_{t=1}^{N} \left(\sum_{k=1}^{\infty} g_k \epsilon_{t+r+k} \sum_{j=0}^{\infty} d_j \epsilon_{t+r-i-j} \right)$$

$$= \sum_{k=1}^{\infty} g_k \left(\frac{\sum_{t=1}^{N} \epsilon_{t+r+k} \sum_{j=0}^{\infty} d_j \epsilon_{t+r-i-j}}{\sqrt{N}} \right)$$

Since ϵ_t is an iid sequence, the process $\epsilon_{t+r+k} \sum_{j=0}^{\infty} d_j \epsilon_{t+r-i-j}$ defines a martingale difference sequence. Therefore

$$\frac{\sum_{t=1}^{N} \epsilon_{t+r+k} \sum_{j=0}^{\infty} d_j \epsilon_{t+r-i-j}}{\sqrt{N}}$$

is asymptotically normally distributed $N(0, \sigma^2 Var(\hat{Y}_{t-i}^2))$, see for example Hamilton [45], example 7.15, p.194 (note that $E[\hat{Y}_{t-i}^2] = E[\hat{Y}_t^2]$ by stationarity). Since $\Delta\tilde{Y}_t \in C_f^0$, its coefficients must be absolutely summable. Therefore the random variable

$$\frac{1}{\sqrt{N}} \sum_{t=1}^{N} z_{it}\Delta\tilde{Y}_t = \sum_{k=1}^{\infty} g_k \left(\frac{\sum_{t=1}^{N} \epsilon_{t+r+k} \sum_{j=0}^{\infty} d_j \epsilon_{t+r-i-j}}{\sqrt{N}} \right)$$

is well defined and must be asymptotically normally distributed too

$$\frac{1}{\sqrt{N}} \sum_{t=1}^{N} z_{it}\Delta\tilde{Y}_t \sim AN\left(0, \sum_{k=-\infty}^{\infty} R_{\Delta\tilde{Y}}(k) R_{\tilde{Y}}(k)\right)$$

see (C.9) and recall that $i \leq Q$ is assumed. An identical proof applies if $i > Q$ with the distribution

$$\frac{1}{\sqrt{N}} \sum_{t=1}^{N} z_{it}\Delta\tilde{Y}_t \sim AN\left(0, \sum_{k=-\infty}^{\infty} R_{\Delta\tilde{Y}}(k) R_X(k)\right)$$

where $R_{\Delta\tilde{Y}}(k)$ and $R_X(k)$ are the autocovariance functions of $\Delta\tilde{Y}_t$ and X_t respectively. It can be verified that

$$1\frac{\mathbf{Z}'\Delta\tilde{\mathbf{Y}}}{\sqrt{N}} \sim AN\left(0, 1'\mathbf{W}1\right)$$

where 1 is an arbitrary $Q + q + r + 1$-vector and $\mathbf{W}$ is given by (C.10). The Cramer-Wold device can then be used to infer

$$\frac{\mathbf{Z}'\Delta\tilde{\mathbf{Y}}}{\sqrt{N}} \sim AN\left(0, \mathbf{W}\right)$$

As a consequence

$$\sqrt{N}(\hat{\mathbf{b}} - \tilde{\mathbf{b}}) = \left(\frac{\mathbf{Z}'\mathbf{Z}}{N}\right)^{-1} \frac{\mathbf{Z}'\Delta\tilde{\mathbf{Y}}}{\sqrt{N}}$$
$$\sim AN\left(0, \mathbf{Q}^{-1}\mathbf{W}\mathbf{Q}^{-1}\right) \tag{C.11}$$

see example 7.5 in Hamilton [45], p.185. Note that $E[\epsilon_t^8] < \infty$ is required because otherwise the variance in (C.11) may be infinite. This completes the proof of the theorem. $\square$

The following corollary is the equivalent of corollary 5.12 for the DFA. It provides an expression of the decrease of the variance estimate of the 'least-squares' residuals $\frac{1}{N} \sum_{t=1}^{N} \Delta Y_t^2$ due to 'overparameterization' (see below).

Corollary C.2. *If the assumptions of theorem C.1 are satisfied, then*

$$E\left[\frac{1}{N}\sum_{t=1}^{N}\Delta\tilde{Y}_t^2 - \frac{1}{N}\sum_{t=1}^{N}\Delta Y_t^2\right] = \frac{\operatorname{tr}\left(\mathbf{WQ}^{-1}\right)+o(1)}{N} \qquad (C.12)$$

where $\operatorname{tr}(\cdot)$ *is the trace operator (i.e. the sum of the diagonal elements of a quadratic matrix) and* $\mathbf{W}$ *and* $\mathbf{Q}$ *are defined in theorem C.1.*

Note that $\mathbf{W}$ and $\mathbf{Q}$ depend on the number of parameters being estimated since they are $(Q+q+r+1)*(Q+q+r+1)$ matrices. As in the previous section the subscript Qq has been dropped for notational convenience. Moreover, $\frac{1}{N}\sum_{t=1}^{N}\Delta\tilde{Y}_t^2$ does not depend on Q nor on q because theorem C.1 assumes 'overparameterization' i.e. $Q \geq Q'$ and $q \geq q'$ (where Q' and q' are the filter orders of the best ARMA filter $\tilde{\Gamma}(\cdot)$). Therefore, the right hand side of (C.12) accounts for the mean decrease of the variance estimate of the residuals $\frac{1}{N}\sum_{t=1}^{N}\Delta Y_t^2$ as 'overparameterization' arises.

Proof of corollary C.2. A Taylor series development of $\frac{1}{N}\sum_{t=1}^{N}\Delta\tilde{Y}_t^2$ 'centered' at the least squares estimate $\hat{\mathbf{b}}$ provides

$$\frac{1}{N}\sum_{t=1}^{N}\Delta\tilde{Y}_t^2 = \frac{1}{N}\sum_{t=1}^{N}\Delta Y_t^2 + \operatorname{tr}\left((\tilde{\mathbf{b}}-\hat{\mathbf{b}})'\frac{\mathbf{Z}'\mathbf{Z}}{N}(\tilde{\mathbf{b}}-\hat{\mathbf{b}})\right)+o(1)$$

$$= \frac{1}{N}\sum_{t=1}^{N}\Delta Y_t^2 + \operatorname{tr}\left((\tilde{\mathbf{b}}-\hat{\mathbf{b}})'\mathbf{Q}(\tilde{\mathbf{b}}-\hat{\mathbf{b}})\right)+o(1)$$

$$= \frac{1}{N}\sum_{t=1}^{N}\Delta Y_t^2 + \operatorname{tr}\left(\mathbf{Q}(\tilde{\mathbf{b}}-\hat{\mathbf{b}})(\tilde{\mathbf{b}}-\hat{\mathbf{b}})'\right)+o(1)$$

where the first $o(1)$-term follows from the consistency and the second one additionally accounts for the convergence of $\frac{\mathbf{Z}'\mathbf{Z}}{N}$ to $\mathbf{Q}$, see theorem C.1. The third equality follows from a property of the trace operator, see for example Theil [88], problem 1.5, p.16. Therefore, neglecting the $o(1)$-term:

$$E\left[\frac{1}{N}\sum_{t=1}^{N}\Delta\tilde{Y}_t^2 - \frac{1}{N}\sum_{t=1}^{N}\Delta Y_t^2\right] \approx \operatorname{tr}\left(\mathbf{Q}E\left[(\tilde{\mathbf{b}}-\hat{\mathbf{b}})(\tilde{\mathbf{b}}-\hat{\mathbf{b}})'\right]\right)$$

$$= \frac{\operatorname{tr}\left(\mathbf{QQ}^{-1}\mathbf{WQ}^{-1}\right)}{N}$$

$$= \frac{\operatorname{tr}\left(\mathbf{WQ}^{-1}\right)}{N}$$

where the first equality follows from theorem C.1. This completes the proof of the corollary. $\square$

The above least-squares estimate requires knowledge of Y_t and $\tilde{Y}_t$. Since the DFA solves the estimation problem without these (unrealistic) assumptions, it would be interesting to compare the asymptotic distributions of the filter parameters for the 'least-squares' and for the DFA estimates. It is shown in the following corollary that both asymptotic distributions are identical. For that purpose assume the parameter set is defined by the 'traditional' AR- and MA-parameters for both approaches (so that derivatives are taken with respect to the same variables).

Corollary C.3. *If the assumptions of theorem 5.10 and of theorem C.1 are satisfied, then*

$$Q^{-1}WQ^{-1} = U^{-1}VU^{-1} \tag{C.13}$$

More precisely:

$$Q = \frac{1}{2}U \text{ and } W = \frac{1}{4}V$$

Proof. In the proof for the last assertion of theorem 4.8 it was shown that

$$\frac{1}{N}\sum_{t=1}^{N}(\Delta\tilde{Y}_t)^2 = \frac{2\pi}{N}\sum_{k=-[N/2]}^{[N/2]} w_k|\Gamma(\omega_k) - \tilde{\Gamma}(\omega_k)|^2 I_{NX}(\omega_k) + r_N \tag{C.14}$$

where $r_N = o(1/\sqrt{N})$. The proof is based on the assumptions that the filter coefficients (here of $\Gamma(\cdot) - \tilde{\Gamma}(\cdot)$) are in $C_f^{1/2}$ and that $X_t \in C_f^0$. Therefore, the same proof can be used to show that

$$\frac{\partial}{\partial b_i}r_N = o(1/\sqrt{N})$$
$$\frac{\partial^2}{\partial b_i \partial b_j}r_N = o(1/\sqrt{N}) \tag{C.15}$$

provided the corresponding first and second order *derivatives* of the filter coefficients (of $\Gamma(\cdot) - \tilde{\Gamma}(\cdot)$ in (C.14)) are in $C_f^{1/2}$, where derivatives are taken with respect to the parameters of the optimal ARMA filter $\tilde{\Gamma}(\cdot)$ (the corresponding modifications of the proof of the last assertion of theorem 4.8 are not difficult so they are not reproduced here). The latter requirement, namely that the differentiated filter is still in $C_f^{1/2}$, can be verified as follows: since $\tilde{\Gamma}(\cdot)$ is a stable ARMA filter (by assumption, see theorem C.1) it follows that $\frac{\partial}{\partial b_i}(\Gamma(\cdot) - \tilde{\Gamma}(\cdot)) = \frac{\partial}{\partial b_i}\tilde{\Gamma}(\cdot)$ and $\frac{\partial^2}{\partial b_i \partial b_j}(\Gamma(\cdot) - \tilde{\Gamma}(\cdot)) = \frac{\partial^2}{\partial b_i \partial b_j}\tilde{\Gamma}(\cdot)$ are stable ARMA filters too. Therefore, the derivatives of the corresponding filter coefficients are in $C_f^\infty \subset C_f^{1/2}$ as required.

Using (C.15), an equivalence between Q and W can be derived. Specifically, consider

$$q_{ij} = \lim_{N \to \infty} \frac{\mathbf{z}_i' \mathbf{z}_j}{N}$$

$$= \lim_{N \to \infty} \frac{1}{2} \frac{\partial}{\partial b_i} \frac{\partial}{\partial b_j} \frac{1}{N} \sum_{t=1}^{N} (\Delta \tilde{Y}_t)^2$$

$$= \lim_{N \to \infty} \frac{1}{2} \frac{\partial}{\partial b_i} \frac{\partial}{\partial b_j} \left(\frac{2\pi}{N} \sum_{k=-[N/2]}^{[N/2]} |\Gamma(\omega_k) - \tilde{\Gamma}(\omega_k)|^2 I_{NX}(\omega_k) + r_N \right)$$

$$= \lim_{N \to \infty} \frac{1}{2} \frac{\partial}{\partial b_i} \frac{\partial}{\partial b_j} \left(\frac{2\pi}{N} \sum_{k=-[N/2]}^{[N/2]} |\Gamma(\omega_k) - \tilde{\Gamma}(\omega_k)|^2 I_{NX}(\omega_k) \right)$$

$$= \lim_{N \to \infty} \frac{1}{2} \frac{2\pi}{N} \sum_{k=-[N/2]}^{[N/2]} \frac{\partial^2}{\partial b_i \partial b_j} \left(|\Gamma(\omega_k) - \tilde{\Gamma}(\omega_k)|^2 \right) h(\omega_k)$$

$$= \frac{1}{2} \int_{-\pi}^{\pi} \frac{\partial^2}{\partial b_i \partial b_j} \left(|\Gamma(\omega) - \tilde{\Gamma}(\omega)|^2 \right) h(\omega) d\omega$$

$$= \frac{1}{2} u_{ij}$$

where the fifth equality follows from corollary B.3 (in the appendix) and proposition 5.11 is used in deriving the sixth equality. As a result

$$\mathbf{Q} = \frac{1}{2} \mathbf{U}$$

Next, an equivalence between $\mathbf{W}$ and $\mathbf{V}$ is derived. Recall (5.58):

$$\mathbf{P}(\tilde{\mathbf{b}}) = \hat{\mathbf{U}}(\tilde{\mathbf{b}} - \hat{\mathbf{b}}) + \mathbf{O}((\tilde{\mathbf{b}} - \hat{\mathbf{b}})^2)$$

where $\hat{\mathbf{b}}$ is the DFA estimate and where

$$\mathbf{P}(\tilde{\mathbf{b}}) = \frac{2\pi}{N} \sum_{k=-[N/2]}^{[N/2]} \frac{\partial}{\partial \mathbf{b}} |\Gamma(\omega_k) - \tilde{\Gamma}(\omega_k)|^2 I_{NX}(\omega_k)$$

$$= \frac{\partial}{\partial \mathbf{b}} \frac{1}{N} \sum_{t=1}^{N} (\Delta \tilde{Y}_t)^2 - \frac{\partial}{\partial \mathbf{b}} r_N$$

$$= \frac{\partial}{\partial \mathbf{b}} \frac{1}{N} \sum_{t=1}^{N} (\Delta \tilde{Y}_t)^2 + \mathbf{o}(1/\sqrt{N})$$

$$= 2 \frac{1}{N} \sum_{t=1}^{N} \Delta \tilde{Y}_t \mathbf{Z}_t + \mathbf{o}(1/\sqrt{N})$$

where $\mathbf{Z}_t$ is the $Q + q + r + 1$-vector defined by

$$\mathbf{Z}_{it} = \begin{cases} \tilde{Y}_{t-i} & 1 \leq i \leq Q \\ X_{t+Q+r+1-i} & Q < i \leq Q + q + r + 1 \end{cases}$$

Comparing (5.60) and (C.10) implies that

$$\mathbf{W} = \frac{1}{4}\mathbf{V}$$

It follows that

$$\mathbf{Q}^{-1}\mathbf{W}\mathbf{Q}^{-1} = 2\mathbf{U}^{-1}\frac{1}{4}\mathbf{V}2\mathbf{U}^{-1}$$
$$= \mathbf{U}^{-1}\mathbf{V}\mathbf{U}^{-1}$$

which completes the proof of the corollary. $\square$

Remarks

- As a special case of theorem C.1 consider the 'classical' regression assumption, i.e. $\Delta \tilde{Y}_t$ is an iid sequence. Then (C.4) becomes

$$w_{ij} := \begin{cases} R_{\Delta \tilde{Y}}(0)R_{\tilde{Y}}(j-i) & 1 \leq i,j \leq Q \\ R_{\Delta \tilde{Y}}(0)R_X(j-i) & Q < i,j \leq Q+q+r+1 \\ R_{\Delta \tilde{Y}}(0)E\left[\tilde{Y}_0 X_{r+Q+1-|j-i|}\right] & \text{else} \end{cases}$$

Therefore $\mathbf{W} = R_{\Delta \tilde{Y}}(0)\mathbf{Q}$. Setting $\sigma^2_{\Delta \tilde{Y}} := R_{\Delta \tilde{Y}}(0)$ one obtains

$$\sqrt{N}(\hat{\mathbf{b}} - \tilde{\mathbf{b}}) \sim \mathbf{AN}\left(0, \sigma^2_{\Delta \tilde{Y}}\mathbf{Q}^{-1}\right)$$

and

$$\lim_{N \to \infty} E\left[N(\hat{\mathbf{b}} - \tilde{\mathbf{b}})'\mathbf{Q}(\hat{\mathbf{b}} - \tilde{\mathbf{b}})\right] = \text{tr}\left(\sigma^2_{\Delta \tilde{Y}}\mathbf{Q}\mathbf{Q}^{-1}\right)$$
$$= p\sigma^2_{\Delta \tilde{Y}} \qquad \text{(C.16)}$$

which are the well known 'classical' regression results. If the regressors where deterministic, then these results would be true for finite sample sizes too.

- Theorem C.1 requires $X_t \in C_f^0$ and $\Gamma \in C_f^0$ whereas theorem 5.10 assumes the stronger restrictions $X_t \in C_f^{1/2}$ and $\Gamma \in C_f^{1/2}$. This is because Y_t is not assumed to be known in theorem 5.10. Therefore, stronger assumptions are needed too ensure that the convolution $|\Gamma(\cdot) - \hat{\Gamma}(\cdot)|^2 I_{NX}(\cdot)$ is 'sufficiently close' to (the unknown) $I_{N\Delta Y}(\cdot)$.

- The assumption $E[\epsilon_t^8] < \infty$ is necessary for deriving a finite expression for the variance of the least-squares estimate $\hat{\mathbf{b}}$ in the proof of theorem C.1. For the more 'traditional' case of independent $\Delta \tilde{Y}_t$, which is extensively treated in the literature, it is often assumed that $E[\epsilon_t^4] < \infty$, see for example Hamilton [45], case 4, p.215. However, this is insufficient for deriving expressions for the variance-covariance matrix of the resulting estimates, because the former involves 8-th order moments.

C.2 A Generalized Information Criterion

Consider first estimation of the parameters in (3.4) (in the time domain) by an ordinary least-squares regression of Y_t on $\tilde{Y}_{t-1}, ..., \tilde{Y}_{t-Q}$ and $X_{t+r}, X_{t+r-1}, ...$ as given in (C.2) i.e.

$$Y_t = \sum_{k=1}^{Q} a_k \tilde{Y}_{t-k} + \sum_{k=-r}^{q} b_k X_{t-k} + \Delta Y_t \qquad (C.17)$$

where Y_t, $t = 1, ..., N$ and the output (of the best unknown asymmetric filter) $\tilde{Y}_t$, $t = 1 - Q, ..., N - 1$ are assumed to be known, see section C.1. It is again assumed that the best asymmetric filter $\tilde{\Gamma}(\cdot)$ is an ARMA($Q', q' + r$)-filter, where Q' and q' are unknown.

If the 'true' error terms $\Delta \tilde{Y}_t$ would define a gaussian white noise process (which they do not for the signal estimation problem), then 'traditional' information criteria could be used for estimating Q and q. A widely used information criterion is AIC (Akaike's Information Criterion):

$$AIC(Q, q) = \log(L) + \frac{2(Q + q + r + 1)}{N} \sim \log(\hat{\sigma}_p^2) + \frac{2p}{N} \qquad (C.18)$$

where L is the likelihood function and $p = Q + q + r + 1$. Also, the sign $\sim$ means 'proportional to' and $\hat{\sigma}_p^2 := 1/N \sum_{t=1}^{N} \Delta Y_t^2$ is the sample mean square error (for a filter with p parameters). Estimates of Q, q are those values which minimize $AIC(Q, q)$. The success of AIC is due to its simplicity as well as its interpretation as a 'maximum likelihood estimation of models' (which is more general than maximum likelihood estimation of parameters of a fixed model), see for example Tong [89], section 5.4.2.

Unfortunately, the 'true' error terms $\Delta \tilde{Y}_t$ are generally correlated for the signal estimation problem. Therefore $\hat{\sigma}_p^2$ is not (proportional to) the likelihood function even if the input process X_t is gaussian. Another more general approach relying on corollary C.2 is proposed here.

Let the assumptions of corollary C.2 be satisfied and consider

$$E\left[\frac{1}{N} \sum_{t=1}^{N} \Delta \tilde{Y}_t^2 - \frac{1}{N} \sum_{t=1}^{N} \Delta Y_t^2 \right] = \frac{\text{tr}\left(\mathbf{WQ}^{-1}\right) + o(1)}{N} \qquad (C.19)$$

A comparison with (C.16) shows that (C.19) is a generalization of the well known regression result

$$E\left[\Delta \tilde{\mathbf{Y}}' \Delta \tilde{\mathbf{Y}} \right] - E\left[\Delta \mathbf{Y}' \Delta \mathbf{Y} \right] = p\sigma_{\Delta \tilde{Y}}^2 \qquad (C.20)$$

if $\Delta \tilde{Y}_t$ are iid and independent of the regressors (which is not true for the signal estimation problem).

The right hand side of (C.19) describes the mean 'loss' (decrease) of the least squares estimate $\Delta\mathbf{Y}'\Delta\mathbf{Y}$ as Q and/or q increase (because $E\left[\Delta\tilde{\mathbf{Y}}'\Delta\tilde{\mathbf{Y}}\right]$ does not depend on Q nor on q if $Q > Q'$ and $q > q'$ as assumed). Estimation of Q' and q' may now be based on this result. In fact, adding a suitable penalty term (growing faster than the mean 'loss' (C.19)) to the least squares variance estimate leads to the general criterion

$$\min_{Q,q}\left(\Delta\mathbf{Y}'\Delta\mathbf{Y} + f\left(\mathrm{tr}\left(\mathbf{Q}^{-1}\mathbf{W}\right)\right)\right)$$

where it is assumed that $f(x) > x$. Equivalently, estimation of Q and q may be achieved by defining

$$\min_{Q,q}\left(\ln\left(\frac{\Delta\mathbf{Y}'\Delta\mathbf{Y}}{N}\right) + f\left(\frac{\mathrm{tr}\left(\mathbf{Q}^{-1}\mathbf{W}\right)}{NR_{\Delta\tilde{Y}}(0)}\right)\right) \qquad (\text{C.21})$$

where $f(x) > x$ again. This can be seen by the following approximation

$$\ln\left(\frac{\Delta\mathbf{Y}'\Delta\mathbf{Y}}{N}\right) \approx R_{\Delta\tilde{Y}}(0) + \frac{\Delta\mathbf{Y}'\Delta\mathbf{Y}/N - R_{\Delta\tilde{Y}}(0)}{R_{\Delta\tilde{Y}}(0)}$$

$$= K + \frac{\Delta\mathbf{Y}'\Delta\mathbf{Y}}{NR_{\Delta\tilde{Y}}(0)} \qquad (\text{C.22})$$

where the approximation follows from a first order Taylor series development 'centered' in $R_{\Delta\tilde{Y}}(0) = E\left[\Delta\tilde{\mathbf{Y}}'\Delta\tilde{\mathbf{Y}}\right]$. Note that K is constant (it does not depend on Q or on q) so that a minimization of (C.21) provides estimates for Q and q if $f(x) > x$ (i.e. if the penalty term increases faster than the 'loss' of the least squares estimate). In the situation leading to (C.20) ($\Delta\tilde{Y}_t$ are iid and independent of the regressors) (C.21) reduces to

$$\min_{Q,q}\left(\ln\left(\frac{\Delta\mathbf{Y}'\Delta\mathbf{Y}}{N}\right) + f\left(\frac{p}{N}\right)\right) \qquad (\text{C.23})$$

For $f(x) = 2x$ this is the AIC-criterion (C.18). However, this particular choice of $f(\cdot)$ is in some sense arbitrary. Penalty functions corresponding to $AICC$ or BIC or SIC can be considered as well (see for example Brockwell and Davis [10], chap.9).

The results in this section emphasize that the determination of Q and q for the 'least squares' estimate may be interpreted (by the way it is carried out) as a generalization of a particular identification approach of the DGP of X_t based on information criteria, see (C.23). The generalization is due to the fact that $\Delta\tilde{Y}_t$ is not restricted to be a white noise process. Since the expressions (6.2) and (C.19) are identical (see corollary C.3) the MC-criterion (6.5) may be interpreted as a generalized information criterion too (whose penalty function corresponds to AICC).

Note that the expression (C.21) is not of practical interest because the 'least-squares' estimate is based on unrealistic assumptions. The 'least-squares' estimate is interesting for theoretical purposes only, since an analysis of its properties produces more insights into the signal estimation problem as solved by the DFA.

D

Miscellaneous

D.1 Initialization of ARMA-Filters

Suppose $X_1, ..., X_N$ are observed and let

$$Y_t = \sum_{k=1}^{p} a_k Y_{t-k} + \sum_{j=0}^{q} b_j X_{t-j} \qquad \text{(D.1)}$$

$$= \sum_{k=-r}^{\infty} c_k X_{t-k} \qquad \text{(D.2)}$$

At $t_0 := \max(p+1, q+1)$ the determination of the filter output Y_{t_0} depends on past filter outputs $Y_{t_0-1}, Y_{t_0-2}, ..., Y_{t_0-p}$ which are generally unknown in (D.1). Equivalently, Y_{t_0} depends on $X_0, X_{-1}, X_{-2}, ...$ which are also unknown in (D.2). If the poles of the filter are not too close to the unit-circle, then the MA-coefficients in (D.2) decay sufficiently fast in order to provide good approximations simply by truncating the representation at the origin $t = 1$ of the sample. Since one is often interested in estimating the signal towards the upper boundary $t = N$ (see section 1.5), this simple procedure can often be applied. An alternative method is to replace $X_0, X_{-1}, X_{-2}, ...$ by backcasts computed from a model (for example ARIMA) of the DGP of X_t. A third way, based on a suitable initialization of $Y_{t_0-1}, Y_{t_0-2}, ..., Y_{t_0-p}$, is briefly described in this section.

Define

$$X'_t := \begin{cases} X_t & 1 \le t \le N \\ X_{2N-t} & N < t < 2N \end{cases}$$

Thus the extension X'_t is obtained by appending the time reversed sample to the original sample at $t = N$. The unknown filter outputs $Y_{t_0-1}, Y_{t_0-2}, ..., Y_{t_0-p}$ are then estimated (initialized) by the outputs $Y'_{2N-t_0+1}, Y'_{2N-t_0+2}, ..., Y'_{2N-t_0+p}$

obtained by applying the filter to X'_t. Note that longer samples may be defined in an analogous way by appending the original sample (either reversed or not, depending on the last orientation of time) to the preceding extension. In order to start the procedure one may set $Y_{t_0-i} := X_{t_0-i}$, $i = 1, ..., p$. By extending the sample this set of initial conditions is 'forgotten'.

If at least one pole is (very) close to the unit circle then the following procedure can be used to enhance the above initialization procedure:

- Set $Y_{t_0-i} := X_{t_0-i}$, $i = 1, ..., p$
- Replace the almost unstable pole P_k at time $t \geq t_0$ by

$$P'_{kt} := P_k(1 + Dc^{t-t_0}) \tag{D.3}$$

where $0 < c < 1$ and $D > 0$ (eventually adjust the normalization of the filter at unit-root frequencies)
- compute Y'_t from its ARMA representation, replacing P_k by P'_{kt}.

Since $|P'_{kt}| > P_k$, the initial conditions $Y_{t_0-i} := X_{t_0-i}$, $i = 1, ..., p$ are 'forgotten' more rapidly.

Initialization procedures relying on the above sample extensions depend on time reversibility issues: interested readers are for example refereed to section 4.4 in Tong [89] or to Lawrance [61].

E

Non-Linear Processes

A stationary linear MA-process admits a representation

$$X_t = \mu + \sum_{k=-\infty}^{\infty} b_k \epsilon_{t-k}$$

where ϵ_t are iid. For a non-linear process, ϵ_t are uncorrelated but not necessarily iid. The first two assertions of the convolution theorem 4.8 show that the independence of ϵ_t is not a necessary condition for the asymptotic rate of decay of r_{n3} (as defined in the proof of theorem 5.3). Therefore, if the process $(\Delta Y_t)^2$ is ergodic i.e. if

$$\frac{1}{N} \sum_{t=1}^{N} (\Delta Y_t)^2 = E[(\Delta Y_t)^2] + r_N$$

where r_N converges appropriately to zero, then the assertions of theorem 5.3 remain true. The next theorem establishes a formal result.

Theorem E.1. *Assume $X_t \in C_f^0$, $\Gamma \in C_f^{\alpha}$, $\alpha \geq 1/2$ and the first four moments of ϵ_t are finite and correspond to moments of an iid sequence. Then $E[\|R_N\|] = O\left(\frac{1}{\sqrt{N}}\right)$ where R_N is defined in theorem 5.3.*

Proof. It is sufficient to show that $E[\|R_N\|] = E[\|r_{N1} + r_{N2} + r_{N3}\|] = O(1/\sqrt{N})$, where r_{Ni}, $i = 1, 2, 3$ are defined in the proof of theorem 5.3. It is shown in the last assertion of theorem 4.8 that $E[\|r_{N3}\|] = o(1/\sqrt{N})$. It remains to show that $E[\|r_{N1} + r_{N2}\|] = O(1/\sqrt{N})$. Since

$$E[(\Delta Y_t)^2] - \frac{1}{N} \sum_{t=1}^{N} (\Delta Y_t)^2 = r_{N1} + r_{N2}$$

it is sufficient to prove that the process $(\Delta Y_t)^2$ is an ergodic process with a suitable rate of convergence of its arithmetic mean (stationarity of the process is established in proposition E.2 below). Consider

$$E[|r_{N1}+r_{N2}|^2] = Var\left(\frac{1}{N}\sum_{t=1}^{N}(\Delta Y_t)^2\right)$$

$$= \frac{1}{N}\sum_{j=0}^{N-1}\left(1-\frac{j}{N}\right)R_{(\Delta Y)^2}(j)$$

$$= O(1/N)$$

where $R_{(\Delta Y)^2}(j)$ is the autocovariance function of $(\Delta Y_t)^2$. The last equality follows from the inequality (E.1) below. An application of Jensen's inequality completes the proof of the theorem. □

Evidently, corollary 5.4 can be generalized to non-linear stationary input signals, because its proof bases on theorem 5.3 which has been generalized already. Therefore, the DFA (5.19) straightforwardly extends to non-linear processes. Note however that non-linear methods may perform better than linear filters.

Proposition E.2. Let $X_t, \Gamma(\cdot) \in C_f^\alpha$, $\alpha \geq 0$ and let ϵ_t be a sequence of random variables whose first four moments are identical with the moments of an iid sequence. Assume also that the requirements of theorem E.1 are satisfied. Then Y_t^2 (where Y_t is the output of $\Gamma(\cdot)$) is a stationary process whose autocovariance function satisfies

$$\sum_{k=-\infty}^{\infty}|R_{Y^2}(k)|\,|k|^\alpha < \infty \tag{E.1}$$

Proof.

$$Y_t^2 = \left(\mu_{Y^2} + \sum_{k=-\infty}^{\infty}c_k\epsilon_{t-k}\right)^2$$

$$= \mu_{Y^2}^2 + \sigma^2\sum_{k=-\infty}^{\infty}c_k^2 + 2\mu_{Y^2}\sum_{k=-\infty}^{\infty}c_k\epsilon_{t-k}$$

$$+ \sum_{k=-\infty}^{\infty}c_k\left(c_k(\epsilon_{t-k}^2-\sigma^2) + 2\epsilon_{t-k}\sum_{j>k}c_j\epsilon_{t-j}\right)$$

where c_k are the MA-coefficients of Y_t. Define

$$v_{t,k} := 2\mu_{Y^2}\epsilon_{t-k} + c_k(\epsilon_{t-k}^2-\sigma^2) + 2\epsilon_{t-k}\sum_{j>k}c_j\epsilon_{t-j}$$

$$V_{kj} := 4\mu_{Y^2}^2\sigma^2 + 2\mu_{Y^2}(c_k+c_{k+j})E[\epsilon_0^3]$$

$$+c_kc_{k+j}(E[\epsilon_0^4]-\sigma^4) + 4\sigma^4\sum_{l>k}c_lc_{l+j} \tag{E.2}$$

The above assumptions imply : $E[\nu_{t,k}] = 0$, $E[\nu_{t,k}^2] = V_{k0}$, $E[\nu_{t,k}\nu_{t,k\pm i}] = 0$ for all t, k and all $i \neq 0$. More generally, proposition E.3 below shows that

$$E[\nu_{t+i,k+j}\nu_{t,k}] = \begin{cases} 0 & i \neq j \\ V_{kj} & \text{else} \end{cases} \tag{E.3}$$

(note that these results do not depend on t). Therefore

$$Y_t^2 = E\left[Y_t^2\right] + \sum_{k=-\infty}^{\infty} c_k\nu_{t,k} \tag{E.4}$$

From the moment properties (E.3) it follows that

$$R_{Y^2}(j) = E\left[\sum_{k=-\infty}^{\infty} c_k\nu_{t+j,k} \sum_{k=-\infty}^{\infty} c_k\nu_{t,k}\right]$$

$$= \sum_{k=-\infty}^{\infty} c_{k+j}c_k V_{kj} \tag{E.5}$$

where $R_{Y^2}(j)$ is the autocovariance function of Y_t^2. Since this result does not depend on t, the process Y_t^2 is stationary. Proposition 4.7 and the assumptions of theorem E.1 imply $Y_t \in C_f^\alpha$, so that $\sum_{k=-\infty}^{\infty} |c_k||k|^\alpha < \infty$ and V_{kj} is bounded (as a function of k, j). The boundedness of V_{kj}, (E.5) and proposition 4.7 then imply

$$\sum_{k=-\infty}^{\infty} |R_{Y^2}(k)|\,|k|^\alpha < \infty$$

which completes the proof of the proposition. $\square$

Proposition E.3. *Let the assumptions of the preceding proposition be satisfied. Then*

$$E[\nu_{t+i,k+j}\nu_{t,k}] = \begin{cases} 0 & i \neq j \\ V_{kj} & \text{else} \end{cases}$$

where $\nu_{t,k}$ and V_{kj} were defined in (E.2).

Proof

It is first assumed that $i \neq j$, More precisely, $E[\nu_{t+i,k+j}\nu_{t,k}] \neq 0$ leads to a contradiction if $i \neq j$:

$$E[\nu_{t+i,k+j}\nu_{t,k}] = E\left[\left\{2\mu_{Y^2}\epsilon_{t+i-(k+j)} + c_{k+j}\left(\epsilon_{t+i-(k+j)}^2 - \sigma^2\right)\right.\right.$$

$$\left.\left. +2\epsilon_{t+i-(k+j)}\sum_{l>k+j} c_l\epsilon_{t+i-l}\right\}\right]$$

$$\left\{ 2\mu_{Y^2}\epsilon_{t-k} + c_k \left(\epsilon_{t-k}^2 - \sigma^2 \right) + 2\epsilon_{t-k} \sum_{l>k} c_l \epsilon_{t-l} \right\} \right]$$

$$= 4E \left[\left(\epsilon_{t+i-(k+j)} \sum_{l>k+j} c_l \epsilon_{t+i-l} \right) \left(\epsilon_{t-k} \sum_{l>k} c_l \epsilon_{t-l} \right) \right] \quad (E.6)$$

All fourth order moments including an isolated $\epsilon_{t'}$ vanish by the assumptions of the proposition. The following conditions must then be satisfied in order to obtain squared terms $E[\epsilon_{t'}^2 \epsilon_{t'}^2]$ in (E.6) (which is necessary for $E[\nu_{t+i,k+j}\nu_{t,k}] \neq 0$) :

$$k + j - i \geq k \quad \text{and} \quad k + j - i \leq k$$

which contradicts the initial assumption if $i \neq j$. If $i = j$ then

$$E[\nu_{t+i,k+i}\nu_{t,k}] = E \left[\left(2\mu_{Y^2}\epsilon_{t-k} + c_{k+i} \left(\epsilon_{t-k}^2 - \sigma^2 \right) + 2\epsilon_{t-k} \sum_{l>k} c_{l+i}\epsilon_{t-l} \right) \right.$$

$$\left. \left(2\mu_{Y^2}\epsilon_{t-k} + c_k \left(\epsilon_{t-k}^2 - \sigma^2 \right) + 2\epsilon_{t-k} \sum_{l>k} c_l \epsilon_{t-l} \right) \right]$$

$$= V_{ki}$$

where V_{ki} was defined in (E.2).　□

References

1. L.V. Ahlfors. *Complex Analysis.* Mc-Graw Hill, New York, 1979.
2. H. Akaike. On entropy maximization principle. *Applications of Statistics,* 1977.
3. W. Bell. *Multivariate Time Series : Smoothing and Backward Models.* PhD thesis, University of Wisconsin-Madison, 1980.
4. W. Bell. Signal extraction for nonstationary time series. *Annals of Statistics,* (12), 1984.
5. W. Bell. Comment on "estimation and seasonal adjustment of population means using data from repeated surveys". *Journal of Business and Economic Statistics,* (9):176–177, 1991.
6. S. Beveridge and C.R. Nelson. A new approach to decomposition of economic time series into permanent and transitory components with particular attention to measurement of the business cycle. *Journal of Monetary Economics,* (7):151–174, 1981.
7. L. Bobbitt and M.C. Otto. Effects of forecasts on the revisions of seasonally adjusted values using the X-11 seasonal adjusting procedure. In *Proceedings of the Business and Economic Statistics Section,* pages 449–453, 1990.
8. G.E.P. Box. Science and statistics. *J. of the Amer. Stat. Assoc.,* (71):791–99, 1979.
9. G.E.P. Box and G.M. Jenkins. *Time Series Analysis : Forecasting and Control.* Holden Day, San Francisco, 1976.
10. P.J. Brockwell and R.A. Davis. *Time Series : Theory and Methods.* Springer, New York, 1993.
11. J.P. Burman. Seasonal adjustment by signal extraction. *J. Roy. Stat. Soc. series A,* (143):321–336, 1980.
12. Peter E. Caines. *Linear Stochastic Systems.* Wiley, New York, 1988.
13. F. Canova. Detrending and turning points. *European Economic Review,* (38):614–623, 1994.
14. Michael P. Clements and David F. Hendry. *Forecasting Economic Time Series.* Cambridge University Press, Cambridge, 1998.
15. W.P. Cleveland. *Analysis and Forecasting of Seasonal Time series.* PhD thesis, University of Wisconsin-Madison, 1972.
16. W.P. Cleveland. A comment to findley et al. *Journal of Business and Economic Statistics,* 16(2), 1998.

17. W.P. Cleveland and G.C. Tiao. Decomposition of seasonal time series. *Journal of the American Statistical Association*, (71):581–587, 1976.
18. J.H. Cochrane. How big is the random-walk in gnp? *Journal of Political Economy*, 5(96):893–920, 1988.
19. J.W. Cooley and J.W. Tukey. An algorithm for the machine calculation of complex fourier series. *Math. Comp.*, (19), 1965.
20. H. Cramer. On some classes of non-stationary stochastic processes. In J. Neyman, editor, *Proceedings of the 4-th. Berkeley Symposium on Mathematical statistics and Probability*, volume 2, Contributions to Probability Theory. Berkeley : Univ. of California Press, 1961.
21. Pierce D.A. Seasonal adjustment when both deterministic and stochastic seasonality are present. In A. Zellner, editor, *Seasonal Analysis of Economic Time Series*, pages 242–273. Washington D.C. : US Department of Commerce,Bureau of the Census, 1978.
22. E.B. Dagum. *The X11-ARIMA/88 Seasonal Adjustment method. Foundations and User's Manual*. Statistics Canada, Ottawa, 1988.
23. E.B. Dagum. A new method for reducing unwanted ripples and revisions in trend-cycle estimators from x11-arima. *Survey methodology*, (22):77–83, 1996.
24. E.B. Dagum, N. Chhab, and B. Solomon. Trend-cycle estimators for current economic analysis. In *Proceedings of The Business and Economic Statistics Section, American Statistical Association*, pages 140–145. 1996.
25. J.L. Doob. *Stochastic Processes*. Wiley, New York, 1953.
26. J Dosse and C. Planas. Revisions in seasonal adjustment methods : an empirical comparison of x12-arima and seats. Downloadable from : http://forum.europa.eu.int/Public/irc/dsis/eurosam/library (documents of methodological studies), 1996.
27. K. Edel, K.-A. Schffer, and W. Stier. *Analyse Saisonaler Zeitreihen*. Physica, Heidelberg, 1997.
28. P. Embrechts, C. Klppelberg, and T. Mikosch. *Modelling Extremal Events*. Springer, Heidelberg, 1997.
29. W. Enders. *Applied Econometric Time Series*. Wiley, New York, 1995.
30. Eurostat. *Seasonal Adjustment Methods : a Comparison*. EUROSTAT, Luxembourg, 1998.
31. M. Feldstein. Inflation, tax rules and investment : Some econometric evidence. *Econometrica*, (50):825–62, 1982.
32. D. F. Findley, B.C. Monsell, W.R. Bell, M. C. Otto, and B.C. Chen. New capabilities and methods of the X-12-arima seasonal-adjustment program. *Journal of Business and Economic Statistics*, 16(2), 1998.
33. P.H. Franses. *Periodicity and Stochastic Trends in Economic Time Series*. Oxford University Press, Oxford, 1996.
34. W.A. Fuller. *Introduction to Statistical Time Series*. Wiley, New York, 1976.
35. A. Garcia-Ferrer and M. Bujosa-Brun. Forecasting oecd industrial turning points using unobserved components models with business survey data. *Intern. J. of Forecasting*, 16(2):214, 2000.
36. C. Gasquet and P. Witomski. *Fourier Analysis and Applications*. Springer, New York, 1998.
37. Box G.E.P., Hillmer S.C., and Tiao G.C. Analysis and modelling of seasonal time series. In A. Zellner, editor, *Seasonal Analysis of Economic Time Series*, pages 309–334. Washington D.C. : US Department of Commerce,Bureau of the Census, 1978.

38. E. Ghysels. A comment to "new capabilities and methods of the X-12-arima seasonal-adjustment program". *Journal of Business and Economic Statistics*, 16(2):165–167, 1998.

39. I.I. Gihman and A.V. Skorohod. *The Theory of Stochastic Processes I.* Springer, Berlin, 1980.

40. C.W.J. Granger and P. Newbold. *Forecasting Economic Time Series*. Academic Press, New York, 1977.

41. A. Gray and P. Thomson. Design of moving average trend filters using fidelity and smoothness criteria. In *Athens Conference in Applied Probability and Time Series*, volume 2, pages 205–219. Springer, New York, 1996.

42. U. Grenander. Resolvability and reliability in spectral analysis. *Jour. Roy. Stat. Soc. serie B*, (20), 1958.

43. U. Grenander and M. Rosenblatt. *Statistical Analysis of Stationary Time Series*. John Wiley, New York, 1957.

44. In-Moo Kim G.S. Maddala. *Unit Roots, Cointegration and Structural Change*. Cambridge University Press, Cambridge, 1998.

45. James Hamilton. *Time Series Analysis*. Princeton, New Jersey, 1994.

46. P.J. Harrison and C.F. Stevens. Bayesian forecasting. *Jour. Roy. Stat. Soc. series B*, (38):205–247, 1976.

47. A.C. Harvey. *Forecasting Structural Time Series Models and the Kalman Filter*. Cambridge University Press, Cambridge, 1989.

48. A.C. Harvey. Trends, cycles and autoregressions. *The Economic Journal*, (107):192–201, 1997.

49. A.C. Harvey and P.H.J. Todd. Forecasting economic time series. In S. Hylleberg, editor, *Modelling Seasonality*. Oxford University Press, 1992.

50. R. Henderson. Note on graduation by adjusted average. *Transactions of the Actuarial Society of America*, (17):43–48, 1916.

51. R. Henderson. A new method of graduation. *Transactions of the Actuarial Society of America*, (25):29–40, 1924.

52. S.C. Hillmer and G.C. Tiao. *An Arima-Model-Based Approach to Seasonal Adjustment*. Oxford University Press, Oxford, 1992.

53. S.C. Hillmer and G.C. Tiao. Arima-model-based seasonal adjustment. In S. Hylleberg, editor, *Modelling Seasonality*. Oxford University Press, 1992.

54. R. Hodrick and E. Prescott. Post-war u.s. business cycles : an empirical investigation. Technical report, Carnegie-Mellon, working paper, 1980.

55. G.J. Huot, K. Chiu, J. Higginson, and N. Gait. Analysis of revisions in the seasonal adjustment of data using X-11-arima model-based filters. *Int. Journ. of Forec.*, (2):217–229, 1986.

56. S. Hylleberg. Comment to findley et al. *Journal of Business and Economic Statistics*, 16(2), 1998.

57. M.G. Kendall and A. Stuart. *The Advanced Theory of Statistics*, volume 3. Charles Griffin, London, 1976.

58. C. Kluppelberg and T. Mikosch. Spectral estimates and stable processes. *Stoch. Proc. Appl.*, (47), 1993.

59. C. Kluppelberg and T. Mikosch. Some limit theory for the self-normalised periodogram of stable processes. *Scand. J. Statist.*, (21), 1994.

60. N. Laniel. Design criteria for the 13-term henderson end-weights, 1994.

61. A.J. Lawrance. Directionality and reversibility in time series. Technical report, Department of Statistics, Birmingham University, 1987.

62. R. Litterman. Forecasting with bayesian vector autoregressions. *Journal of Business and Economic Statistics*, 4:25–38, 1998.

63. MacKinlay A.C. Lo A.W. Stock market prices do not follow random-walks: Evidence from simple specification tests. *Review of Financial Studies*, 1:41–66, 1988.

64. A. Maravall and V. Gomez. Program seats : User instructions, 1994.

65. A. Maravall and D.A. Pierce. A prototypical seasonal adjustment model. In S. Hylleberg, editor, *Modelling Seasonality*. Oxford University Press, 1992.

66. R. Metz. *Stochastische Trends und Langfristige Wachstumsschwankungen*. Habilitationsschrift, Hochschule St. Gallen, St. Gallen, 1995.

67. T.C. Mills. *The Econometric Modelling of Financial Time Series*. Cambridge University Press, Cambridge, 1993.

68. M. Morry and N. Chhab. A comment to findley et al. *Journal of Business and Economic Statistics*, 16(2), 1998.

69. J.C. Musgrave. A set of end weights to end all end weights, 1964.

70. M. Nerlove, D. Grether, and J. Carvalho. *Analysis of Economic Time Series*. Academic Press, New York, 1979.

71. P. Newbold. Precise and efficient computation of the beveridge-nelson decomposition of economic time series. *Journal of Monetary Economics*, (26):453–457, 1990.

72. Bureau of the census. *X12-ARIMA Reference Manual*. Bureau of the Census, Washington, DC, 1998.

73. A.V. Oppenheim and R.W. Schafer. *Digital Signal Processing*. Prentice Hall, New Jersey, 1975.

74. D.A. Pierce. Data revisions with moving average seasonal adjustment procedures. *Journal of Econometrics*, (14), 1980.

75. M.B. Priestley. *Spectral Analysis and Time Series*. Academic Press, New York, 1981.

76. T. Proietti. Comparing seasonal components for structural time series models. *Intern. Jour. of Forecasting*, 16(2):247–260, 2000.

77. J. Rissanen. Modelling by shortest data description. *Automatica*, (14), 1978.

78. J. Rissanen. A universal prior for integers and estimation by minimum description length. *Annals of Statistics*, (11), 1983.

79. J. Rosinski. On the structure of stationary stable processes. *Ann. Probab.*, (23), 1995.

80. K.-A. Schaeffer. Einfhrung in die analyse saisonaler zeitreihen. In *Analyse Saisonaler Zeitreihen*. Physica Verlag, Heidelberg, 1997.

81. B. Schips and W. Stier. *The Census X11-procedure : Theory, Assessment and Alternatives*. Technical Report 156-0, Swiss Federal Statistical Office, Bern, 1995.

82. A. Schuster. On the investigation of hidden periodicities with application to a supposed 26-day period of meteorological phenomena. *Terr. Mag. Atmos. Elec.*, (3), 1898.

83. W. Stier. Zur kanonischen Zerlegung von Zeitreihen-Bemerkungen zum Verfahren SEATS. *Allgemeines Statistisches Archiv*, (80):313–331, 1996.

84. W. Stier. Nochmals zu SEATS-Eine Duplik auf Maravall/Feldmann. *Allgemeines Statistisches Archiv*, (82):183–197, 1998.

85. W. Stier. *Methoden der Zeitreihenanalyse*. Springer, Berlin-Heidelberg-New York, 2001.

86. W. Stier and M. Wildi. Signal extraction and detection of turning-points. In *ifo Studien*, pages 467–476. Duncker und Humblot, Berlin, 1998.

87. W. Stier and M. Wildi. About model-based times series procedures: Some remarks to tramo/seats and census x-12-arima. *Allgemeines Statistisches Archiv*, (86), 2002.

88. H. Theil. *Principles of Econometrics*. Wiley, New York, 1979.

89. H. Tong. *Non-Linear Time Series*. Clarendon Press, Oxford, 1995.

90. A.M. Walker. Some asymptotic results for the periodogram of a stationary time series. *J. Austr. Math. Soc.*, (5), 1965.

91. K.F. Wallis. Seasonal adjustment and revision of current data : Linear filters for the x11 method. *Journal of the Royal Stat. Soc., Ser.A*, (145):74–85, 1982.

92. K.F. Wallis. A comment to findley et al. *Journal of Business and Economic Statistics*, 16(2), 1998.

93. E.T. Whittaker. On a new methof of graduation. *Proceedings of the Edimburgh Mathematical Society*, (41):63–75, 1923.

94. E.T. Whittaker. On the theory of graduation. *Proceedings of the Royal Society of Edimburgh Mathematical Society*, (44):77–83, 1923.

95. P. Whittle. *Prediction and Regulation by Linear Least-Square Methods*. English University Press, 1963.

96. M. Wildi. Detection of compatible turning-points and signal extraction for non-stationary time series. In *Operations Research Proceedings 1997*, pages 293–299. Springer, 1997.

97. M. Wildi. Forecasting non-stationary financial data with oiir-filters and composed threshold models. In *Decision Technologies for Computational Finance*, pages 391–402. Kluwer Academic, 1998.

98. M. Wildi. Boundary signal estimation problem. In *Zeitreihenanalyse in der empirischen Wirtschaftsforschung*, pages 189–196. Lucius und Lucius, 2004.

99. M. Wildi and B. Schips. Signal extraction: A direct filter approach and clustering in the frequency domain. Technical report, Institute for Business Cycle Research, ETH-Zurich, 2004. Working Paper presented at the International Symposium on Forecasting, 2004, Sidney.

100. H. Wold. *A Study in the Analysis of Stationary Time series*. Almquist and Wicksell, 1954.

Printing and Binding: Strauss GmbH, Mörlenbach